ESSAYS

SECOND EDITION

Kathryn A. Blake

University of Georgia

Mary Louise McBee

University of Georgia

Macmillan Publishing Co., Inc.

NEW YORK

Copyright © 1981 by Macmillan Publishing Co., Inc.

Printed in the United States of America

All rights reserved. No part of this book may be reproduced or transmitted in any form or by any means, electronic or mechanical, including photocopying, recording, or any information storage and retrieval system, without permission in writing from the Publisher.

Earlier edition copyright © 1978 by Glencoe Publishing Co., Inc.

Macmillan Publishing Co., Inc.
866 Third Avenue, New York, New York 10022

Collier Macmillan Canada, Ltd.

Library of Congress Catalog Number: 79-092694

ISBN 0-02-471990-0

Printing 1 2 3 4 5 6 7 8 Year: 1 2 3 4 5 6 7 8

ACKNOWLEDGMENTS

Acknowledgment is gratefully made to the following authors, publishers, and agents who have granted permission to use selections from their publications.

The Atlantic Monthly Company, for "Three Days to See" by Helen Keller. Copyright © by The Atlantic Monthly Company, Boston, Mass. Reprinted with permission.

Robert L. Bennett, for "The New Indians and The Old Indians: Cultural Factors in the Education of the American Indians" by Robert L. Bennett, Commissioner of Indian Affairs 1966–69, Consultant on American Indians.

Broadcast Music, Inc., for "Grant and Lee: A Study in Contrasts" by Bruce Catton. Bruce Catton, "Grant and Lee: A Study in Contrasts" from THE AMERICAN STORY, ed. Earl Schenck Miers, © 1956 by Broadcast Music, Inc. Used by permission of the copyright holder.

Robert Coles, for "On the Meaning of Work" by Robert Coles. Originally appeared in *Atlantic Monthly* (October 1971). Copyright © 1971 by The Atlantic Monthly Company, Boston, Mass. Reprinted with permission.

The Chronicle of Higher Education, for "The Human Use of Language" by Lawrence L. Langer. Reprinted with permission of The Chronicle of Higher Education, January 24, 1977. Copyright © 1977 by Editorial Projects for Education, Inc. Reprinted also by permission of Lawrence L. Langer.

Delacorte Press, for "The Necessary Enemy" by Katherine Anne Porter. Excerpted from the book THE COLLECTED ESSAYS AND OCCASIONAL WRITINGS OF KATHERINE ANNE PORTER. Copyright © 1948 by Katherine Anne Porter. Originally published in Mademoiselle as "Love and Hate." Reprinted by permission of DELACORTE PRESS/ SEYMOUR LAWRENCE.

Doubleday, for "Those Crazy Ideas" by Isaac Asimov. "Those Crazy Ideas" copyright © 1959 by Mercury Press, Inc. from FACT AND FANCY by Isaac Asimov. Reprinted by permission of Doubleday & Company, Inc.

E. P. Dutton & Co., for "Shame" by Dick Gregory with Robert Lipsyte. From *Nigger: An Autobiography* by Dick Gregory with Robert Lipsyte. Copyright © 1964 by Dick Gregory Enterprises, Inc. Reprinted by permission of the publishers, E. P. Dutton & Co.

Farrar, Straus and Giroux, Inc., for "To Alfred Corn" by Flannery O'Connor. Reprinted with the permission of Farrar, Straus and Giroux, Inc. from THE HABIT OF BEING by Flannery O'Connor. Letters edited and with an Introduction by Sally Fitzgerald. Copyright © 1979 by Regina O'Connor. Introduction Copyright © 1979 by Sarah Fitzgerald; and for "The Liberated Woman" by Susan Sontag. A selection from "The Third World of Women" by Susan Sontag. Copyright © 1973 by Susan Sontag. Reprinted by permission of Farrar, Straus and Giroux, Inc.

Harcourt Brace Jovanovich, Inc., for "Shooting an Elephant" by George Orwell. From SHOOTING AN ELEPHANT AND OTHER ESSAYS by George Orwell, copyright 1950 by Sonia Brownell Orwell; renewed 1978 by Sonia Pitt-Rivers. Reprinted by permission of Harcourt Brace Jovanovich, Inc.; and for "The Death of the Moth" by Virginia Woolf. From THE DEATH OF THE MOTH AND OTHER ESSAYS by Virginia Woolf, copyright 1942 by Harcourt Brace Jovanovich, Inc.; renewed 1970 by Marjorie T. Parsons, Executrix. Reprinted by permission of the publisher.

Harper & Row, Publishers, Inc., for "The Present" by Annie Dillard. From pp. 77–79 in PILGRIM AT TINKER CREEK by Annie Dillard. Copyright © 1974 by Annie Dillard; and for "A Nation of Nations" by John F. Kennedy. From pp. 1–3 in A NATION OF IMMIGRANTS by John F. Kennedy. Copyright © 1964 by Anti-Defamation League of B'nai B'rith; and for "Anne Frank: The Triumph of Faith Over Experience" by George F. Will. From pp. 18–20 in THE PURSUIT OF HAPPINESS AND OTHER SOBERING THOUGHTS by George F. Will. Copyright © 1978 by The Washington Post Company. Reprinted by permission of Harper & Row, Publishers, Inc.

David Higham Associates Limited, for "A Hurricane" by Richard Hughes. From IN HAZARD by Richard Hughes, published by Chatto & Windus. Reprinted by permission of David Higham Associates Limited.

Houghton Mifflin Company, for excerpt from UNBOUGHT AND UNBOSSED by Shirley Chisholm. Copyright © 1970 by Shirley Chisholm. Reprinted by permission of Houghton Mifflin Company.

Alfred A. Knopf, Inc., for "Separating" by John Updike. Copyright © 1975 by John Updike from PROBLEMS AND OTHER STORIES by John Updike. Reprinted by permission of Alfred A. Knopf, Inc.

Lawrence L. Langer, for "The Human Use of Language" by Lawrence L. Langer. Copyright © 1977 by Editorial Projects for Education, Inc. Reprinted with permission of Lawrence L. Langer and The Chronicle of Higher Education, January 24, 1977.

Mainliner Magazine, for "The American Tradition of Winning" by George Plimpton. Copyright © 1976 by George Plimpton. Reprinted with permission from Mainliner Magazine, July 1976.

Harold Matson Company, Inc., for "Love Is a Fallacy" by Max Shulman. From THE MANY LOVES OF DOBIE GILLIS by Max Shulman. Copyright © 1951 by Max Shulman, copyright renewed 1979. Reprinted by permission of the Harold Matson Company, Inc.

McCall's Magazine, for "From Popping the Question to Popping the Pill" by Margaret Mead. Originally appeared in *McCall's Magazine* (April 1976). Copyright 1976 by Margaret Mead. Reprinted by permission of *McCall's Magazine* and Rhoda Metraux.

Rhoda Metraux, for "From Popping the Question to Popping the Pill" by Margaret Mead. Originally appeared in *McCall's Magazine* (April 1976). Copyright 1976 by Margaret Mead. Reprinted by permission of *McCall's Magazine* and Rhoda Metraux.

Newsweek, Inc., for "Simple Truths" by William J. Bennett. Copyright 1980, by Newsweek, Inc.; for "On Being a Possibilist" by Max Lerner. Copyright 1979, by Newsweek, Inc.; and for "Is It Time to Stop Learning?" by David Saxon, copyright 1976 by Newsweek, Inc. All rights reserved. Reprinted by permission.

The New York Times, for "Auto Suggestion" by Russell Baker; for "Why I Write" by Joan Didion; for "The Watcher at the Gates" by Gail Godwin; and for "My Furthest-Back Person—'The African'" by Alex Haley. Copyright 1979/76/77/72 by The New York Times Company. Reprinted by permission.

W. W. Norton & Company, Inc., for "The Lifeline of the Race" by John W. Gardner. Selection is reprinted from MORALE by John W. Gardner, by permission of W. W. Norton & Company, Inc. Copyright © 1978 by John W. Gardner.

Pantheon Books, for "Channelled Whelk" by Anne Morrow Lindbergh. From GIFT FROM THE SEA, by Anne Morrow Lindbergh. Copyright © 1955 by Anne Morrow Lindbergh. Reprinted by permission of Pantheon Books, a Division of Random House, Inc.

Elizabeth Marie Pope, for "What This Country Needs Is a Good Bad-Writing Course" by Elizabeth Marie Pope. Originally published in "The Mills Stream," the college newspaper of Mills College, Oakland, California. Reprinted by permission of Elizabeth Marie Pope.

Prentice-Hall, Inc., for "Four Types of Presidential Character" by James David Barber. From the book THE PRESIDENTIAL CHARACTER, 2nd Edition, by James David Barber. © 1977 by James David Barber. Published by Prentice-Hall, Inc., Englewood Cliffs, New Jersey, 07632.

QUEST/77, for "Surrender as the Noble Course" by Andrew M. Greeley. Reprinted from the March/April issue of QUEST/77 by special permission. Copyright © 1977, Ambassador International Cultural Foundation. All rights reserved.

Random House, Inc., for "Hope" by Maya Angelou. Copyright © 1969 by Maya Angelou. Reprinted from I KNOW WHY THE CAGED BIRD SINGS, by Maya Angelou, by permission of Random House, Inc.; and for "The Stockholm Address" by William Faulkner. From *The Faulkner Reader,* copyright William Faulkner. Reprinted by permission of Random House, Inc.

Paul R. Reynolds, Inc., for "My Furthest Back Person—'The African'" by Alex Haley. Copyright © 1972 by Alex Haley. Reprinted by permission of Paul R. Reynolds, Inc., 12 East 41st Street, New York, N.Y. 10017. Reprinted also by permission of The New York Times.

Saturday Review, for "A Debt to Dickens" by Pearl S. Buck, © *Saturday Review,* 1936; for "The Right to Die" by Norman Cousins, © *Saturday Review,* 1975; and for "The Lost Art of Conversation" by George S. McGhee, © *Saturday Review,* 1975. All rights reserved. Reprinted by permission of *Saturday Review*.

Charles Scribner's Sons, for "The Apple Tree" by John Galsworthy. Excerpt from "The Apple Tree" is reprinted from CARAVAN by John Galsworthy with the permission of Charles Scribner's Sons; renewal copyright 1953 Ada Galsworthy; and for "Bull Fighting, a Tragedy" by Ernest Hemingway. Reprinted from BY-LINE ERNEST HEMINGWAY by permission of Charles Scribner's Sons. Copyright © 1967 By-Line Ernest Hemingway, Inc.

Simon & Schuster, for "Acres and Pains" by S. J. Perelman. Copyright © 1943, 1944, 1947 by S. J. Perelman; and for "A Life Worth Living" by Bertrand Russell. From THE AUTOBIOGRAPHY OF BERTRAND RUSSELL by Bertrand Russell. Copyright © 1969 by George Allen and Unwin, Ltd. Reprinted by permission of SIMON & SCHUSTER, a Division of Gulf & Western Corporation.

Helen Thurber, for "The Rabbits Who Caused All the Trouble," by James Thurber. Copyright © 1940 James Thurber. Copyright © 1968 Helen Thurber. From FABLES FOR OUR TIME, published by Harper & Row. Originally printed in *The New Yorker*.

The University of Chicago Press, for "Masculinity: Real and Put On" by Harold Rosenberg. From DISCOVERING THE PRESENT: THREE DECADES OF ART, CULTURE, AND POLITICS by Harold Rosenberg. Copyright © 1973 by Harold Rosenberg. All rights reserved. Reprinted by permission of The University of Chicago Press.

Viking Penguin Inc., for "Notes on Punctuation" by Lewis Thomas. From THE MEDUSA AND THE SNAIL by Lewis Thomas. Copyright © 1979 by Lewis Thomas. Reprinted by permission of Viking Penguin Inc.

Mrs. W. L. White, for "Mary White" by William Allen White. Copyright William Allen White. Reprinted from the *Emporia Gazette,* May 15, 1921, by permission of Mrs. W. L. White.

World Publications, for "On the Far Side of Pain" by Dr. George A. Sheehan. Reprinted with permission from *Dr. Sheehan on Running,* published by *Runner's World Magazine,* Box 366, Mountain View, Calif. 94042.

CONTENTS

Preface xii

GENERAL GUIDE TO ANALYZING ESSAYS 1

I. EXPOSITION 6

DEFINITION 8

The Watcher at the Gates 9 — Gail Godwin
Of Thumbs 13 — Michel de Montaigne
The Lost Art of Conversation 15 — George C. McGhee
A Nation of Nations 20 — John F. Kennedy

CLASSIFICATION 25

From *Unbought and Unbossed* 26 — Shirley Chisholm
Those Crazy Ideas 29 — Isaac Asimov
Four Types of Presidential Character 40 — James D. Barber
A Life Worth Living 45 — Bertrand Russell

EXAMPLE 53

Love Is a Fallacy 54 — Max Shulman
The American Tradition of Winning 64 — George Plimpton
Masculinity: Real and Put On 68 — Harold Rosenberg
Acres and Pains 74 — S. J. Perelman

ANALYSIS 77

Bull Fighting 78 — Ernest Hemingway
Notes on Punctuation 85 — Lewis Thomas
A Hurricane 89 — Richard E. Hughes
Auto Suggestion 91 — Russell Baker

CAUSE AND EFFECT 95

The Human Use of Language 96 — Lawrence Langer

Hope 102 — Maya Angelou

The Necessary Enemy 106 — Katherine Anne Porter

The Rabbits Who Caused All The Trouble 112 — James Thurber

COMPARISON AND CONTRAST 114

Grant and Lee: A Study in Contrasts 116 — Bruce Catton

The Whistle 121 — Benjamin Franklin

The New Indians and the Old Indians: Cultural Factors in the Education of American Indians 124 — Robert L. Bennett

From Popping the Question to Popping the Pill 128 — Margaret Mead

II. DESCRIPTION 135

The Sparrow 137 — Ivan Turgenev

Three Days to See 139 — Helen Keller

The Present 150 — Annie Dillard

Anne Frank: The Triumph of Faith Over Experience 154 — George F. Will

On the Far Side of Pain 157 — George A. Sheehan

The Apple Tree 159 — John Galsworthy

Mary White 162 — William Allen White

III. ARGUMENT 168

The Stockholm Address 170 — William Faulkner

Is It Time to Stop Learning? 173 — David S. Saxon

A Modest Proposal 178 — Jonathan Swift

The Right to Die 187 — Norman Cousins

A Letter to Alfred 191 — Flannery O'Connor

Darwin's Conclusion on His Theory and Religion 195 — Charles Darwin

What This Country Needs Is a Good Bad-Writing Course 199 — Elizabeth Pope

The Lifeline of the Race 202 — John Gardner

IV. NARRATION 208

Shooting an Elephant 210 — George Orwell

Shame 218 — Dick Gregory

A Child's Dream of a Star 224 — Charles Dickens

Separating 228 — John Updike

My Furthest–Back Person—"The African" 239 — Alex Haley

The Death of the Moth 249 — Virginia Woolf

A Dissertation Upon Roast Pig 253 — Charles Lamb

V. ESSAYS FOR INDEPENDENT ANALYSIS 261

Simple Truths 262 — William J. Bennett

Surrender as the Noble Course 265 — Andrew M. Greeley

On the Meaning of Work 267 — Robert Coles

On Being a Possibilist 271 — Max Lerner

The Mountain of Miseries 274 — Joseph Addison

The Liberated Woman 279 — Susan Sontag

Channelled Whelk 282 — Anne Morrow Lindbergh

A Debt to Dickens 288 — Pearl S. Buck

Why I Write 292 — Joan Didion

Where I Lived, and What I Lived For 297 — Henry David Thoreau

VI. GLOSSARY 310

VII. BIBLIOGRAPHY 326

ALTERNATE THEMATIC CONTENTS

THE PHYSICAL WORLD

A Hurricane 89 — Richard E. Hughes

The Sparrow 137 — Ivan Turgenev

The Apple Tree 159 — John Galsworthy

The Death of the Moth 249 — Virginia Woolf

A Dissertation Upon Roast Pig 253 — Charles Lamb

ENDURING ISSUES

A Modest Proposal 178 — Jonathan Swift

The Right to Die 187 — Norman Cousins

A Letter to Alfred 191 — Flannery O'Connor

Darwin's Conclusion on His Theory and Religion 195 — Charles Darwin

On Being a Possibilist 271 — Max Lerner

RELATING AND RELATIONSHIPS

Love Is a Fallacy 54 — Max Shulman

The Lost Art of Conversation 15 — George C. McGhee

The Human Use of Language 96 — Lawrence Langer

The Necessary Enemy 106 — Katherine Anne Porter

A Child's Dream of a Star 224 — Charles Dickens

Separating 228 — John Updike

Surrender as the Noble Course 265 — Andrew M. Greeley

THE SELF OBSERVED

from *Unbought and Unbossed* 26 — Shirley Chisholm
A Life Worth Living 45 — Bertrand Russell
The Whistle 121 — Benjamin Franklin
Three Days to See 139 — Helen Keller
The Present 150 — Annie Dillard
Shooting an Elephant 210 — George Orwell
Shame 218 — Dick Gregory
The Liberated Woman 249 — Susan Sontag
Channelled Whelk 282 — Anne Morrow Lindbergh
Where I Lived, and What I Lived For 297 — Henry David Thoreau

ON HUMAN NATURE

Of Thumbs 13 — Michel de Montaigne
Those Crazy Ideas 29 — Isaac Asimov
Masculinity: Real and Put On 68 — Harold Rosenberg
Bull Fighting 78 — Ernest Hemingway
The Rabbits Who Caused All the Trouble 112 — James Thurber
Anne Frank: The Triumph of Faith Over Experience 154 — George F. Will
On the Far Side of Pain 157 — George A. Sheehan
Mary White 162 — William Allen White
Simple Truths 262 — William J. Bennett
The Mountains of Miseries 274 — Joseph Addison

MODERN TRENDS

Acres and Pains 74 — S. J. Perelman
Auto Suggestion 91 — Russell Baker

From Popping the Question to Popping the Pill 128 — Margaret Mead

Is It Time to Stop Learning? 173 — David S. Saxon

The Lifeline of the Race 202 — John W. Gardner

On the Meaning of Work 267 — Robert Coles

THE NATIONAL CHARACTER

A Nation of Nations 20 — John F. Kennedy

Four Types of Presidential Character 40 — James D. Barber

The American Tradition of Winning 64 — George Plimpton

Hope 102 — Maya Angelou

Grant and Lee: A Study in Contrasts 116 — Bruce Catton

The New Indians and the Old Indians: Cultural Factors in the Education of American Indians 124 — Robert L. Bennett

My Furthest–Back Person—"The African" 239 — Alex Haley

THE ART OF WRITING

The Watcher at the Gates 9 — Gail Godwin

Notes on Punctuation 85 — Lewis Thomas

The Stockholm Address 170 — William Faulkner

What This Country Needs Is a Good Bad-Writing Course 199 — Elizabeth Pope

A Debt to Dickens 288 — Pearl S. Buck

Why I Write 292 — Joan Didion

PREFACE

Essays are relatively brief nonfiction prose compositions expressing personal ideas. Their topics range from the serious to the whimsical, from the concrete to the abstract. Their structure may be highly formal or very informal.

For thousands of years, men and women have been writing what we loosely could call essays. However, about four centuries ago, Michel de Montaigne originated the essay as we know it today. Montaigne called his first works *essais*—"trials." In these works, he was not concerned with presenting complete scientific or philosophical treatises, but with communicating his own thoughts and reactions. His essays were brief, personal, and full of digressions, as he abandoned his main topic to pursue ideas as they occurred to him. Although digressions are frowned upon today, Montaigne's comment about his essays, "It is my selfe I pourtray," can be applied to many contemporary essays.

This text is designed to help you read and write essays effectively. Your opportunity as a reader is to appreciate an essay for its craftsmanship, to enjoy it, and to learn from it. Because the essay is the form of writing required in nearly all your classes, your challenge as a writer is to produce an essay that others can appreciate, enjoy, and learn from.

The Second Edition of *Essays* contains fifty-six selections. The twenty-eight essays that were most enthusiastically received in the first edition have been retained, and twenty-eight new ones have been added. Authors whose works are anthologized here for the first time include John Updike, Virginia Woolf, James Thurber, Bertrand Russell, Maya Angelou, Russell Baker, Jonathan Swift, Katherine Ann Porter, S. J. Perelman, Alex Haley, and Bruce Catton.

As in the first edition, except for those works designated for independent analysis, these essays are organized according to the four modes of discourse: *exposition,* used to explain or otherwise clarify a subject; *description,* used to relate sensory details and impressions; *argument,* used to convince the reader of the truth of a proposition; and *narration,* used to recount the unfolding of an event. The four modes are explained more fully in their respective sections of the book.

While it is true that every essay does not fit neatly into one of these four categories, they do present a convenient and widely accepted means of general organization. For those who prefer a different approach, we have included an alternate thematic table of contents.

To help you in examining and analyzing the essays presented here and in building a foundation for your own writing, we have provided six aids. (1) The text begins with a *General Guide to Analyzing Essays,* an extensive list of questions that can be used to analyze any essay—your own and those of other writers. (2) Each essay is introduced by a *Headnote* containing biographical information about the author. (3) *Questions* that ask you to consider vocabulary, content, and rhetoric follow each of the first forty-six essays. (4) *Reading and Writing Suggestions* also follow the first forty-six essays, and provide you with take-off points for writing your own essays. (5) A *Glossary* provides definitions of terms marked with an asterisk throughout the text. (6) A *Bibliography* of selections cited in the headnotes and reading and writing suggestions concludes the book.

For the valuable insights and classroom materials they shared with us, we wish to thank Nancy Edwards of Bakersfield College and Irene Jacobs of Frederick Community College. For their detailed criticisms and suggestions, we are indebted to our reviewers, David Sloane, University of New Haven; Burt Collins, Kankakee Community College; Carol Cyganowski, Roosevelt University; and Samuel Bellman, California State Polytechnic University, Pomona. For their helpful responses to our questions, we gratefully acknowledge the assistance of several instructors who used the earlier edition of *Essays,* including Elizabeth G. Westgard, Indiana State University; Steve Swanson, St. Olaf College; Joseph E. Mills, Northeastern Junior College; Sheila Juba, Lane Community College; Robert Dees, Orange Coast College; and Ed Lathy, Columbus College of Art and Design.

GENERAL GUIDE TO ANALYZING ESSAYS

A good essay is more than a random collection of ideas; it is a literary work in which the author combines form and style to express ideas as forcefully and compellingly as possible. A good essay has certain essential characteristics. Its title, introduction, thesis, supporting ideas, transitional devices, and closing are organized into a unified and coherent structure. Its style and tone are appropriate to its organization and content. The ideas proposed in the essay are supported by reliable evidence and logic. In short, a good essay conveys its meaning clearly and eloquently. Consequently, when you examine an essay, you should attend not only to *content*—the ideas the author presents and their applications to your life—but also to *rhetoric*—the way the author expresses those ideas—and to *logic*—the validity of the ideas.

We have formulated this guide to help you examine the essays you read and write. It provides questions that you can use to examine an essay's rhetoric, to evaluate its logic, and to understand, interpret, and apply its ideas. Literary terms used in this guide are defined in the Glossary, page 310.

Examining Rhetoric

Organization

1. What mode of discourse is used?
   —Argument? Logical argument? Persuasive argument?
   —Description? Objective description? Impressionistic description?
   —Narration? Dramatized narration? Generalized narration? Summarized narration?
   —Exposition? Definition? Classification? Example? Analysis? Cause and effect? Comparison and contrast?

2. Is the title general or specific? Are metaphors, alliteration, or other devices used in the title? If so, for what purpose?

   Are there subtitles? If so, what purpose do they serve?

3. Is there an introduction? Does the essay begin with a quotation? A maxim? An anecdote? A straw man? General information? Statistics? An allusion? A rhetorical question? An unusual statement? A statement about the significance of the essay's thesis?

What is the purpose of the introduction? How does it relate to the essay's thesis? How is the transition made between the introduction and the body of the essay?

4. Is the essay's thesis implied, or is it directly stated? Where is it most clearly expressed? What does this location suggest about the essay's emphasis?

   Is the thesis repeated in the course of the essay? If so, what is the purpose of this repetition?

5. Is there sufficient unity in the essay? Do all of the supporting ideas pertain to the thesis? Are enough ideas presented to support the thesis? Are too many ideas presented?

   Is there sufficient coherence? Are the ideas presented in an appropriate sequence? Is this sequence chronological, spatial, or logical? Or is some other form of organization used?

   Are ideas linked by appropriate transitional structures? Coordinating conjunctions? Subordinating conjunctions? Repetition of essential ideas? Enumeration of ideas?

   Is there foreshadowing? Flashback? If so, how is each device used?

6. How does the essay close? With a reassertion of proof? A summary of the points made in the essay? A statement of deeper meaning? A statement of the implications of the thesis?

Style and Tone

1. Is figurative language used in the essay? If so, what kinds are used? Metaphors? Personification? Similes? Idioms? Hyperbole? Alliteration? Onomatopoeia? Others?

   For what purpose are the figures of speech used? Do they contribute to the effectiveness and tone of the essay? Do they enhance or obscure the essay's meaning?

2. Does the essay contain highly technical or difficult language? Could more familiar synonyms be used with greater effectiveness?

   Does the essay use conversational or informal English as distinguished from formal English?

3. Does the essay contain many general or abstract words? Do they obscure meaning? Could specific or concrete words be substituted to express more clearly the essay's meaning?

4. Are there diction problems in the essay? Do you find examples of jargon, triteness, pretentious words, or slang? What effect do these problems have on the essay as a whole?

5. What is the tone of the essay? Humorous? Angry? Informal? Scholarly? Ironic? Matter-of-fact? Other? Does the tone coordinate well with the purpose of the essay?

6. Are the sentences in the essay long and complex? Brief and simple? Are there sentence fragments? What does the style of the sentences contribute to the essay as a whole? Does the style of the sentences detract in any way from the essay?

7. Are there any sentence problems? Do you find examples of wordiness or deadwood? Undue repetition of words, sounds, or meanings? Inappropriate cuteness? Other problems?

Evaluating Logic

Evidence

1. What are the author's qualifications? Does he or she have the education and experience necessary to write about the topic? What else has the author written? Is he or she known to have a particular bias toward the subject?

2. What magazine or book does the essay appear in? What is the reputation of that source? Can you depend on it for honesty and accuracy?

3. What is the publication date of the essay? If timeliness is important, is the material up to date? Have there been important developments in the area discussed since the essay was published? Is the issue discussed in the essay still important, or is it outdated?

4. Has the essay been cut? If so, do you think the deleted material could provide important clues as to the honesty and accuracy of the essay as a whole?

5. Are the facts accurate? Is the number of facts cited sufficient to prove the author's point?

6. Do the opinions and quotations cited come from qualified authorities?

7. Does the author use any deceptive devices to strengthen the essay's argument? Does the author use misleading statements? Loaded or slanted words? Slogans? A misleading writing style? Bandwagon

appeal? Sentimental appeal? Appeals based on misleading authority? Any other devices?

Reasoning

1. Is the major proposition (thesis) stated clearly? Is it stated in an unbiased, unslanted way? Is it arguable?
2. Are all of the relevant minor (supporting) propositions stated?
3. Are all difficult or problematical terms defined?
4. Are all counter-arguments anticipated and answered?
5. If inductive reasoning is used, are generalizations based on sufficient evidence and are hasty generalizations avoided?
6. If reasoning by analogy is used, is the analogy based on a sufficient number of characteristics shared by the things being compared? Are both weak and false analogies successfully avoided?
7. If deductive reasoning is used, has the major premise (generalization about the class) been arrived at inductively from sufficient evidence? Does the major premise ignore any significant fact? Is the fact stated in the minor premise (application to a specific member of the class) true? Does the conclusion follow logically?
8. Are there logical fallacies in the essay? Do you find examples of overgeneralization? Unsupported inferences? Assumption of proof by failure to find the opposite case? Special pleading? Avoiding the question with a non sequitur or an ad hominem attack? Begging the question? False dilemmas? False sequences? Other fallacies?

Understanding and Interpreting Ideas

1. What is the title? How can it be paraphrased? What does it suggest about the essay's thesis? The tone of the essay? The viewpoint from which the essay is written? The essay's emphasis?
2. What does the introduction tell you? Assuming that it is not aimed simply at attracting the reader's interest, what does it suggest about the essay's thesis? Its tone? Its emphasis? The author's viewpoint?
3. What is the essay's central thesis?
4. What supporting ideas are used to develop the thesis? What do the transitional structures show about relationships among ideas in the essay?

5. What ideas are presented in the closing? What do they tell you about the essay's emphasis? Its meaning? Its implications?

6. What levels of meaning lie behind the ideas given? What do the ideas suggest about what our world and our behavior are like at present? About what they should be like?

Applying Ideas

1. How do the ideas in the essay apply to your current activities and ideas?

2. Does the essay suggest any changes you might make in your life in the future?

PART ONE

EXPOSITION

Of the four modes of discourse—exposition, argument, narration, and description—exposition is used to present information most directly. The most prevalent form of nonfiction prose, expository writing comprises much of what we read in nonfiction books, in newspapers, and in magazines.

The word *exposition* comes from the Latin *exponere*, "to put forth" or "to expound," and, as this root suggests, exposition is a clear, straightforward presentation of ideas. Unlike argument, exposition does not try to persuade the reader to adopt a specific viewpoint; instead, expository writing aims for an objective approach to its subject matter. Its approach is also direct; unlike narration, it does not use a story form for developing a thesis. Exposition differs from description as well, in that it deals with ideas rather than sensory impressions of people, places, or things.

Six methods of development are most often used in expository writing. These are definition, classification, example, analysis, cause and effect, and comparison and contrast. We will examine each method in this section on exposition.

DEFINITION

Simple definition is the act of pinpointing the exact meaning of a term—making clear what the object being defined is and what it is not. One way to define a term is by means of a *formal definition*, in which the writer names the genus, or class, of the word and then lists the differentiae—that is, the characteristics that distinguish the term from the other members of its class. For example, Webster's dictionary uses formal definition when it defines soccer as "a game played on a field between two teams of eleven players each with the object to propel a round ball into the opponent's goal by kicking or by hitting it with any part of the body except the hands and arms." In this definition, soccer's genus is identified as "game," and the other items of information about soccer comprise the differentiae since they distinguish soccer from other games. Another way to define a term is to use a *synonym*. The word *bunk* may be simply defined by the synonym *nonsense*.

As an expository pattern of development, definition is more often extended than simple. Writers use *extended definition* if the term being defined is complex or controversial or if a clear understanding of it is central to the essay as a whole. An extended definition explores a term in depth, tracing its history or evolution, illustrating it with examples, or using other methods such as negation (discussing what qualities it does *not* have), to clarify its exact meaning. In some cases, entire essays may be no more than extended definitions.

In order to use definition effectively writers should observe the following guidelines. First, they should carefully consider the length of the definition, providing enough information to give the reader a clear picture of the term's meaning, but avoiding excessive or irrelevant information. A definition of soccer as "a game in which each of two teams attempts to propel an object into the opponent's goal" would not be sufficient, since this definition also applies to football, field hockey, and any number of other sports. On the other hand, it would not be necessary to describe all the rules of the game and the functions of the various team members in order to give a clear idea of what soccer is; such extraneous information would distract the reader from the matter at hand. Second, definitions should never be circular—that is, the name of the term should not be repeated in the definition. Defining "criticism" as "the art of criticizing" will hardly give the reader a clearer understanding of the term. Third, definitions should generally contain the genus of the term being described. Instead of writing "Soccer is when two teams . . .", write "Soccer is a *game* in which two teams . . . ." Once a reader knows the genus of a term, he or she is well on the way toward understanding its complete meaning.

THE WATCHER AT THE GATES

Gail Godwin

Gail Godwin (1937–) was born in Birmingham, Alabama, and received her B.A. degree from the University of North Carolina and her M.A. and Ph.D. degrees from the University of Iowa. She has worked at such varied places as the Miami Herald, *the United States Embassy in London, the University of Iowa, and the Center for Advanced Studies at the University of Illinois. Author of a number of novels, including* Dream Children *and* Glass People, *she has also contributed to such magazines as* Cosmopolitan, Esquire, Paris Review, *and* North American Review. *In this essay from* The New York Times Book Review *(January 9, 1977), Godwin explores the nature of an inner voice that plagues all creators—the voice of "The Watcher at the Gates."*

I first realized I was not the only writer who had a restraining critic who lived inside me and sapped the juice from green inspirations when I was leafing through Freud's "Interpretation of Dreams" a few years ago. Ironically, it was my "inner critic" who had sent me to Freud. I was writing a novel, and my heroine was in the middle of a dream, and then I lost faith in my own invention and rushed to "an authority" to check whether she could have such a dream. In the chapter on dream interpretation, I came upon the following passage that has helped me free myself, in some measure, from my critic and has led to many pleasant and interesting exchanges with other writers.

Freud quotes Schiller, who is writing a letter to a friend. The friend complains of his lack of creative power. Schiller replies with an allegory. He says it is not good if the intellect examines too closely the ideas pouring in at the gates. "In isolation, an idea may be quite insignificant, and venturesome in the extreme, but it may acquire importance from an idea which follows it. . . . In the case of a creative mind, it seems to me, the intellect has withdrawn its watchers from the gates, and the ideas rush in pell-mell, and only then does it review and inspect the multitude. You are ashamed or afraid of the momentary and passing madness which is found in all real creators, the longer or shorter duration of which distinguishes the thinking artist from the dreamer . . . you reject too soon and discriminate too severely."

So that's what I had: a Watcher at the Gates. I decided to get to know him better. I discussed him with other writers, who told me some of the quirks and habits of their Watchers, each of whom was as individual as his host, and all of whom seemed passionately dedicated to one goal: rejecting too soon and discriminating too severely.

It is amazing the lengths a Watcher will go to keep you from pursuing the flow of your imagination. Watchers are notorious pencil sharpeners, ribbon changers, plant waterers, home repairers and abhorrers of messy rooms or messy pages. They are compulsive looker-uppers. They are superstitious scaredy-cats. They cultivate self-important eccentricities they think are suitable for "writers." And they'd rather die (and kill your inspiration with them) than risk making a fool of themselves.

My Watcher has a wasteful penchant for 20-pound bond paper above and below the carbon of the first draft. "What's the good of writing out a whole page," he whispers begrudgingly, "if you just have to write it over again later? Get it perfect the first time!" My Watcher adores stopping in the middle of a morning's work to drive down to the library to check on the name of a flower or a World War II battle or a line of metaphysical poetry. "You can't possibly go on till you've got this right!" he admonishes. I go and get the car keys.

Other Watchers have informed their writers that:

"Whenever you get a really good sentence you should stop in the middle of it and go on tomorrow. Otherwise you might run dry."

"Don't try and continue with your book till your dental appointment is over. When you're worried about your teeth, you can't think about art."

Another Watcher makes his owner pin his finished pages to a clothesline and read them through binoculars "to see how they look from a distance." Countless other Watchers demand "bribes" for taking the day off: lethal doses of caffeine, alcoholic doses of Scotch or vodka or wine.

There are various ways to outsmart, pacify or coexist with your Watcher. Here are some I have tried, or my writer friends have tried, with success:

Look for situations when he's likely to be off-guard. Write too fast for him in an unexpected place, at an unexpected time. (Virginia Woolf captured the "diamonds in the dustheap" by writing at a "rapid haphazard gallop" in her diary.) Write when very tired. Write in purple ink on the back of a Master Charge statement. Write whatever comes into your mind while the kettle is boiling and make the steam whistle your deadline. (Deadlines are a great way to outdistance the Watcher.)

Disguise what you are writing. If your Watcher refuses to let you get on with your story or novel, write a "letter" instead, telling your "correspondent" what you are going to write in your story or next chapter. Dash off a "review" of your own unfinished opus. It will stand up like a bully to your Watcher the next time he throws obstacles in your path. If you write yourself a good one.

Get to know your Watcher. He's yours. Do a drawing of him (or her). Pin it to the wall of your study and turn it gently to the wall when necessary. Let your Watcher feel needed. Watchers are excellent critics after inspiration has been captured; they are dependable, sharp-eyed readers of things already set down. Keep your Watcher in shape and he'll have less time to keep you from shaping. If he's really ruining your whole working day sit down, as Jung did with his personal demons, and write him a letter. On a very bad day I once wrote my Watcher a letter. "Dear Watcher," I wrote, "What is it you're so afraid I'll do?" Then I held his pen for him, and he replied instantly with a candor that has kept me from truly despising him.

"Fail," he wrote back.

VOCABULARY

1. Define the following words as Godwin uses them in her essay: allegory, pell-mell, eccentricities, penchant, metaphysical, lethal, opus, candor.
2. If you are unfamiliar with any other words in this essay, check them in a dictionary and then define them in your own words.

CONTENT

1. Summarize Schiller's allegory*. What are the characteristics of a "Watcher at the Gates"?
2. What goal does the "Watcher" *seem* to be passionately dedicated to? What is the "Watcher" *really* doing?
3. Name at least three things that Godwin and other writers have done to outsmart their "Watchers at the Gates."
4. Give at least two examples of "Watchers" working for people in areas other than writing.
5. a. Name three things your own "Watcher" has done to protect you from failure.

   b. In what ways, if any, has this protection from failure also kept you from achieving what you might otherwise have achieved?

   c. What are three things you can do to outsmart your "Watcher at the Gates"?

---

* Definitions of all terms marked with an asterisk may be found in the Glossary.

RHETORIC

1. What does Godwin mean by the figurative* expression "the critic sapped the juice from green inspirations"?
2. What rhetorical device does Godwin use in her introduction*? Does it quickly engage your attention? What device does she use for closing* the essay? Does it leave you with a feeling of completion?
3. Where does Godwin get the metaphor* "Watcher at the Gates," which she uses as a title? What does this title suggest to you about Godwin's thesis*?
4. What adjectives would you use to describe this essay's tone*? Humorous? Sad? Matter-of-fact? Formal? Personal?

READING AND WRITING SUGGESTIONS

1. Write a brief essay defining the "courage and grace" that someone exhibits when he or she takes a chance and tries something really new.
2. Read accounts of the many failures experienced by a successful person—Winston Churchill, Abraham Lincoln, or Albert Einstein, for example. Use the information gathered in your reading to write a brief essay defining success and failure taking as your thesis: "Winners Are Losers and Losers Are Winners."

---

*Definitions of all terms marked with an asterisk may be found in the Glossary.

OF THUMBS

Michel de Montaigne

Michel de Montaigne (1533–1592), called the father of the essay, was born to a wealthy family in the south of France and received an excellent education. After working in the legal profession for a number of years, he retired to his château to devote himself to reflection and study. It was at this time that he developed the essay form as a means to clarify and express his reflections. In "Of Thumbs," he turns his attention to the historical significance of this important finger.

Tacitus reports that amongst certain barbarian kings, their manner was, when they would make a firm obligation, to join their right hands close to one another, and intertwist their thumbs; and when, by force of straining, the blood appeared in the ends, they lightly pricked them with some sharp instrument, and mutually sucked them.

Physicians say that the thumbs are the master fingers of the hand, and that their Latin etymology is derived from *pollere.*[1] The Greeks called them . . . another hand. And it seems that the Latins also sometimes take it in this sense for the whole hand.

> Sed nec vocibus excitata blandis,
> Molli pollice nec rogata, surgit.[2]

It was at Rome a signification of favour to depress and turn in the thumbs:

> Fautor utroque tuum laudabit pollice ludum,[3]

and of disfavour to elevate and thrust them outward:

> Converso pollice vulgi,
> quemlibet occidunt populariter,[4]

---

1. A Latin verb meaning "to be strong."
2. Neither to be excited by soft words, or by the thumb.
3. Thy patron will applaud thy sport with both thumbs.
4. The populace, with reverted thumbs, kill all that come before them.

The Romans exempted from war all such as were maimed in the thumbs, as having no more sufficient strength to hold their weapons. Augustus confiscated the estate of a Roman knight, who had maliciously cut off the thumbs of two young children he had, to excuse them from going into the armies: and, before him, the Senate, in the time of the Italic war, had condemned Caius Vatienus to perpetual imprisonment, and confiscated all his goods, for having purposely cut off the thumb of his left hand, to exempt himself from that expedition. Some one, I have forgotten who, having won a naval battle, cut off the thumbs of all his vanquished enemies, to render them incapable of fighting and of handling the oar. The Athenians also caused the thumbs of the Aeginatans to be cut off, to deprive them of the superiority in the art of navigation.

In Lacedaemon, pedagogues chastised their scholars by biting their thumbs.

VOCABULARY

1. Define the following words as Montaigne uses them in this essay: etymology, confiscated, maliciously, perpetual, vanquished, pedagogues, chastised.
2. If you are unfamiliar with any other words in this essay, check them in a dictionary and then define them in your own words.

CONTENT

1. Consider that the thumb is only one of the five fingers. What do Montaigne's comments indicate about the nature of that particular finger?
2. Why did some Romans cut off their own, their children's, or their enemies' thumbs?
3. Would people today maim themselves or their children to avoid military service? What would the punishment be? We often hear about POWs being killed, tortured, or heavily confined, yet we seldom hear of their being incapacitated for further warfare through the amputation of fingers, hands, or feet. Why do you think this is so?
4. Are thumbs as crucial today as they were in the past? Why or why not?

RHETORIC

1. What purpose do the Latin references and quotations serve in this

essay? What do they tell you about Montaigne? Does the essay bear out his comment: "It is my selfe I pourtray"?

2. Does Montaigne give an objective or subjective definition of thumbs? Would the other form of definition have been more effective?
3. How would you describe Montaigne's word choice or diction*? Abstract or concrete*? General or specific*? Spare or wordy? How do these characteristics contribute to the essay's tone*?

READING AND WRITING SUGGESTIONS

1. Use Montaigne's approach in a brief expository essay defining the nature of the nose. Call your essay "Of the Nose."
2. Read about Helen Keller or another deaf person. Use the ideas you encounter in your reading to write a brief definition essay titled "Of Hearing."

---

*Definitions of all terms marked with an asterisk may be found in the Glossary.

THE LOST ART OF CONVERSATION

George C. McGhee

George C. McGhee (1912–) received his undergraduate degree from the University of Oklahoma, and his Ph.D. from Oxford University, where he studied as a Rhodes scholar. He has also been awarded honorary doctorates from several universities. From 1941 until his retirement in 1969, McGhee served the government in a number of capacities, including assistant secretary of state for Near Eastern, South Asian and African affairs, ambassador to Turkey, consultant to the National Security Council, undersecretary of state for political affairs, and ambassador to Germany. In the following essay, which appeared in Saturday Review *in 1975, McGhee presents the characteristics of true conversation.*

What has happened to the art of conversation? By conversation I am not thinking merely of word exchanges between individuals. I am thinking of one of the highest manifestations of the use of human intelligence—the ability to transform abstractions into language; the ability to convey images from one mind to another; the ability to build a mutual edifice of ideas. In short, the ability to engage in a civilizing experience.

When the word *art* is applied to conversation, one conjures up an image of Dr. Johnson uttering words of wisdom, with a devoted Boswell taking them all down on paper. Boswell quoted Mrs. Thrale as having remarked about Johnson that his "conversation was much too strong for a person accustomed to obsequiousness and flattery; it was mustard in a young child's mouth."

But where does one find good conversation these days? Certainly not in the presence of the television set, which consumes half of the average American's non-sleeping, non-working hours. Much of the remaining free time is given to games. No matter how rewarding "bridge talk" may be, it is not conversation. Neither is chatter.

What makes good conversation? In the first place, it is essentially a mutual search for the essence of things. It is a zestful transaction, not a briefing or a lecture. Pushkin correctly identified the willingness to listen as one of the vital ingredients of any exchange. When two people are talking at the same time, the result is not conversation but a collision of decibels.

Nothing is more destructive of good talk than for one participant to hold the ball too long, like an over-zealous basketball dribbler playing to the gallery and keeping it away from everyone else. Pity the husband or wife with a garrulous mate who insists on talking long past the point where he or she has anything to say.

To be meaningful, a conversation should head in a general direction. It need not be artfully plotted to arrive at a predetermined point, but it should be gracefully kept on course—guided by many unforeseen ideas.

It has been said that if speech is silver, silence is golden. Certainly silence is preferable, under most circumstances, to inconsequential chitchat. Why is it then that so many people, when they are with others, are discomfited by the absence of human sound waves? Why are they not willing merely to sit with each other, silently enjoying the unheard but real linkages of congeniality and understanding? Why aren't people content to contemplate a lovely scene or read together in silence? "Made conversation" should not be a necessity among intimates. They know whether the weather is good or bad; both are as well or poorly informed about current events. If there is nothing to say—don't say it.

It is true that strangers meeting for the first time seem to feel uncomfortable if they do not engage in small talk to relieve their mutual awkwardness. This is the scourge of the cocktail party, but it is necessary if strangers are to size each other up. Usually, however, this is harmless. In desperation one seeks an artificial gambit. I remember one from an English girl: "Oh, I say, are you frightfully keen on cats and dogs?" Unfortunately, I wasn't.

There is a disease shared by many, particularly with new acquaintances, that leads to "dropping names" or "colleges." This is often a useful device, since a common friend or university experience can be a helpful point of departure for conversation leading to better understanding. It is, however, more often woefully abused as a means of showing off. The references are usually to the influential rather than to one's less distinguished friends: "Of course I know Ina Gottrocks. She is a very dear friend. Such a nice person [actually an awful bore]. We had lunch only yesterday [on an airplane, sitting in different class sections]." One is less inclined to refer to one's alma mater if it is Oshkosh U.

Genealogical topics should also be avoided. The danger of boring one's conversation partner and of becoming self-serving is far too great. In the first place, others don't really care about your ancestors. They know, as you should, that everyone has quite a variety ranging all the way from bums to princes. If one goes back eight generations, one has 256 forebears. How easy to pick out the one who glitters most as your claim to fame. Even the one who gave you your name is still only one in 256.

Cocktail-party necessities aside, however, some elementary rules for conversation are well worth our consideration. In the first place, certain subjects should be taboo in any general conversation. Kitchen topics—the best cleansers, recipes, and troubles with servants—should certainly be limited to interested women. Straight man-talk, such as business, golf, and hunting exploits, may be permissible in board or locker rooms but should be taboo in general discussion, along with bus schedules and all other dull or specialized things. One does not mention precise figures descriptive of one's wealth or income—not even an artful "The deal netted me something in six figures." The first digit was probably 1.

People even forget, I'm afraid, that their illnesses and operations should be outlawed as conversational topics. Only if some relative asks you on a need-to-know basis, or a doctor is interested from a professional standpoint, should you ever volunteer anything about your ailments. Everyone understands this; yet it never seems to apply to you. Remember, even if it's the most dramatic operation ever performed, it is not something to be offered gratuitously to friends at conversation time. They really don't want to hear about it.

There is also the conversationalist who must under every circumstance be right—who always has to win the game. There are those of us who want to moralize. There is the intruder into emotional subjects like religion or personalities, the malicious gossip. All should be inadmissible by any rules of good conversation. Vulgar words, even the four-letter words, can sometimes be effective—as in the English use of *bloody*. More often, however, they are in bad taste—particularly when they conjure up a revolting image at mealtime. Shouldn't there be some law against sonic pollution?

An intriguing conversational gambit was disclosed by H. Allen Smith, which could, if you got by with it, amaze your dinner partners. In preparation he boned up on traditional Chinese uses of funereal jade in the body orifices. It is best to choose a subject that would appear alien to your normal interests. A lawyer, after consulting the art histories, might break into the Pre-Raphaelite painters. A hostess at a country weekend might try: "Yes, the country is lovely here. The lower Catoctin greensand, Upper Jurassic, you know, underlies much of the Austin chalk of the valley." Stephen Potter's books on gamesmanship and one-upmanship are of course treasurehouses of this sort of off-putting play.

If conversation need not always be purposeful, it must at least be for pleasure. It should be congenial to good society—to better knowing one's conversation partner. Above all, it should be joyful and amiable, for as Addison put it: "Good nature is more agreeable in conversation than wit, and gives a certain air to the countenance which is more amiable than beauty." I do not object to enforced conversation—say, by the hostess who interrupts an after-dinner group with, "Come, we must all hear John tell us about his trip to Africa." I am less tolerant, however, of those who would arbitrarily stop a good conversation which has exciting possibilities with a flat "Come, now, let's stop all this serious talk." A good conversation is a fragile thing that must be nurtured carefully.

And, finally, I want to encourage the pixie of the conversation who can add zest and interest. Our talk too often reflects the dull things we do all day. Conversation does not always have to be in earnest. Provocation, whimsy, laughter, mockery, and flirtation all have their place in the art of good conversation, of which it has been said, "Be prompt without being stubborn, refute without argument, clothe weighty matters in a motley garb."

VOCABULARY

1. Define the following words as McGhee uses them in this essay: manifestation, abstraction, edifice, obsequiousness, garrulous, inconsequential, gambit, genealogical, gratuitously, orifices, countenance.
2. If you are unfamiliar with any other words in this essay, check them in a dictionary and then define them in your own words.

CONTENT

1. According to McGhee, what are four characteristics of true conversation?
2. McGhee also defines true conversation by negation* or exclusion* (showing what something is *not*). What are four characteristics that do not mark true conversation?
3. Is true conversation the same for all people? Why or why not?
   a. Suppose someone were really interested in kitchen topics and absolutely indifferent to artistic and political topics. What would true conversation consist of for that person?
   b. Does McGhee's essay show us as much about his interests as it does about the nature of conversation? Explain.
4. a. Name at least two topics that you think are conducive to true conversation and at least two topics that you think are destructive to such conversation.
   b. Describe a situation you personally witnessed in which "everybody talked and nobody listened."

RHETORIC

1. Is McGhee's title* accurate in the sense that conversation, as he defines it, has disappeared? Explain.
2. Explain the meaning of the following figures of speech*:
   a. "It was mustard in a young child's mouth."
   b. "If speech is silver, silence is golden."
   c. "A collision of decibels."
   d. Holding the (conversational) ball too long, "like an over-zealous basketball dribbler playing to the gallery and keeping it away from everyone else."
   e. "It [conversation] need not be artfully plotted to arrive at a predetermined point, but it should be gracefully kept on course—guided by many unforeseen ideas."

---

*Definitions of all terms marked with an asterisk may be found in the Glossary.

3. Is McGhee's definition of conversation simple or extended (see page 16)?
4. McGhee uses several rhetorical questions* in his essay. What purpose do these questions serve?

READING AND WRITING SUGGESTIONS

1. Write a brief essay presenting your own definition of true conversation. Use negation* as a technique along with positive assertions.
2. Read T. S. Eliot's play *The Cocktail Party* and write an essay discussing whether the characters in the play truly participated in conversation. Use McGhee's definition of conversation as the basis for your discussion.

---

* Definition of all terms marked with an asterisk may be found in the Glossary.

A NATION OF NATIONS

John F. Kennedy

John F. Kennedy (1917–1963), thirty-fifth president of the United States, was educated at Harvard and the London School of Economics. He served in the United States Navy during World War II, in the House of Representatives (1946–1952), and in the Senate (1952–1960). He served as president from 1960 until his assassination in November 1963. Kennedy was widely celebrated for his intellectual depth and brilliant wit. His book Profiles in Courage *was awarded a Pulitzer Prize in 1956, as well as the Notable Book Award of The American Library Association. In "A Nation of Nations" from* A Nation of Immigrants *(1964), Kennedy defines the essence of our society as a unified nation of immigrants.*

On May 11, 1831, Alexis de Tocqueville, a young French aristocrat, disembarked in the bustling harbor of New York City. He had crossed the ocean to try to understand the implications for European civilization of the new experiment in democracy on the far side of the Atlantic. In the next nine months, Tocqueville and his friend Gustave de Beaumont traveled the length and breadth of the eastern half of the continent—from Boston to Green Bay and from New Orleans to Quebec—in search of the essence of American life.

Tocqueville was fascinated by what he saw. He marveled at the energy of the people who were building the new nation. He admired many of the new political institutions and ideals. And he was impressed most of all by the spirit of equality that pervaded the life and customs of the people. Though he had reservations about some of the expressions of this spirit, he could discern its workings in every aspect of American society—in politics, business, personal relations, culture, thought. This commitment to equality was in striking contrast to the class-ridden society of Europe. Yet Tocqueville believed "the democratic revolution" to be irresistible.

"Balanced between the past and the future," as he wrote of himself, "with no natural instinctive attraction toward either, I could without effort quietly contemplate each side of the question." On his return to France, Tocqueville delivered his dispassionate and penetrating judgment of the American experiment in his great work *Democracy in America.* No one, before or since, has written about the United States with such insight. And, in discussing the successive waves of immigration from England, France, Spain and other European countries, Tocqueville identified a central factor in the American democratic faith:

> All these European colonies contained the elements, if not the development, of a complete democracy. Two causes led to this result. It may be said that on leaving the mother country the emigrants had, in general, no notion of superiority one over another. The happy and powerful do not go into exile, and there are no surer guarantees of equality among men than poverty and misfortune.

To show the power of the equalitarian spirit in America, Tocqueville added: "It happened, however, on several occasions, that persons of rank were driven to America by political and religious quarrels. Laws were made to establish a gradation of ranks; but it was soon found that the soil of America was opposed to a territorial aristocracy."

What Alexis de Tocqueville saw in America was a society of immigrants, each of whom had begun life anew, on an equal footing. This was the secret of America: a nation of people with the fresh memory of old traditions who dared to explore new frontiers, people eager to build lives for themselves in a spacious society that did not restrict their freedom of choice and action.

Since 1607, when the first English settlers reached the New World, over 42 million people have migrated to the United States. This represents the largest migration of people in all recorded history. It is two and a half times the total number of people now living in Arizona, Arkansas, Colorado, Delaware, Idaho, Kansas, Maine, Montana, Nevada, New Hampshire, New Mexico, North Dakota, Oregon, Rhode Island, South Dakota, Utah, Vermont and Wyoming.

Another way of indicating the importance of immigration to America is to point out that every American who ever lived, with the exception of one group, was either an immigrant himself or a descendant of immigrants.

The exception? Will Rogers, part Cherokee Indian, said that his ancestors were at the dock to meet the *Mayflower*. And some anthropologists believe that the Indians themselves were immigrants from another continent who displaced the original Americans—the aborigines.

In just over 350 years, a nation of nearly 200 million people has grown up, populated almost entirely by persons who either came from other lands or whose forefathers came from other lands. As President Franklin D. Roosevelt reminded a convention of the Daughters of the American Revolution, "Remember, remember always, that all of us, and you and I especially, are descended from immigrants and revolutionists."

Any great social movement leaves its mark, and the massive migration of peoples to the New World was no exception to this rule. The interaction of disparate cultures, the vehemence of the ideals that led the immigrants here, the opportunity offered by a new life, all gave America a flavor and a character that make it as unmistakable and as remarkable to people today as it was to Alexis de Tocqueville in the early part of the nineteenth century. The contribution of immigrants can be seen in every aspect of our national life. We see it in religion, in politics, in business, in the arts, in education, even in athletics and in entertainment. There is no part of our nation that has not been touched by our immigrant background. Everywhere immigrants have enriched and strengthened the fabric of American life. As Walt Whitman said,

> These States are the amplest poem,
> Here is not merely a nation but
> a teeming Nation of nations.

To know America, then, it is necessary to understand this peculiarly American social revolution. It is necessary to know why over 42 million people gave up their settled lives to start anew in a strange land. We must know how they met the new land and how it met them, and, most important, we must know what these things mean for our present and for our future.

VOCABULARY

1. Define the following words as Kennedy uses them: equalitarian, disparate, vehemence.
2. If you are unfamiliar with any other words in this essay, check them in a dictionary and then define them in your own words.

CONTENT

1. What was Tocqueville's purpose in coming to America? Why did he believe himself to be unbiased?
2. Explain Tocqueville's statement that "the happy and powerful do not go into exile, and there are no surer guarantees of equality among men than poverty and misfortune." Cite examples to illustrate your answer.
3. In what two ways does Kennedy dramatize the importance of immigration to America?
4. Respond to Kennedy's challenge in his closing paragraph. How did the immigrants meet the new land and how did it meet them? What do these thing mean for the present and the future?

RHETORIC

1. What was your first reaction to Kennedy's title*, "A Nation of Nations"? Does it accurately reflect his thesis*? Explain.
2. Kennedy uses several quotations in this short selection. What effect do they have on his overall tone*?
3. Kennedy opens one of his paragraphs with a sentence fragment. Why do you think students are told never to use sentence fragments when many published authors use them?

READING AND WRITING SUGGESTIONS

1. Write a brief essay defining the system of checks and balances in our federal government and show how it insures that we can retain unity in diversity.
2. Read brief biographies or encyclopedia articles about two famous

---

* Definitions of all terms marked with an asterisk may be found in the Glossary.

immigrants, such as Anne Hutchinson, John Audubon, John Jacob Astor, or Werner Von Braun. Then write an essay detailing their contributions to the United States.

3. The title of this selection comes from Walt Whitman's Preface to *Leaves of Grass*. Read this Preface, and write a short essay on Whitman's view of the United States.

CLASSIFICATION

Classification is the method of development concerned with sorting members of a large group into categories on the basis of a specific criterion or principle. Suppose, for example, that you wanted to divide presidents of the United States (a large group) into two categories: great presidents and less-than-great presidents. In order to do this, you would have to develop a sorting principle or criterion—for example, great presidents are those who have led the nation successfully through a crisis. All the presidents who met this criterion could then be classified as great, and those who did not meet this criterion would be classified as less than great.

Used correctly, classification organizes facts, ideas, and experiences in a useful way by applying a system to the unsystematic. But there are three requirements whch must be met if a classification is to have any value.

First, the sorting principle of classification must apply in a meaningful way to the writer's purpose in classifyng the members of the group. To take an extreme example, if you were classifying all American presidents as great and less than great, it would not be meaningful to use the amount of money each president had made in private life as the principle of classification. This would reveal something about the presidents' business acumen, but it would not say much about their relative ability as leaders.

Second, the categories used in classification should, taken together, exhaust the subject. If you used the categories lawyers and plantation owners, for example, to classify the presidents of the United States in terms of occupation, you would be overlooking those presidents who were businessmen, generals, and members of other occupations, and your classification would not be complete.

Third, the categories used in classification should not overlap. You would not want to divide the presidents into the categories of scholars, bachelors, and married men, since all of the presidents who could be categorized as scholars would *also* be categorized either as bachelors or as married men. These overlapping categories would destroy the meaning and usefulness of the classification.

from <u>UNBOUGHT AND UNBOSSED</u>

Shirley Chisholm

Shirley Chisholm (1924–) is a member of Congress from New York's Twelfth Congressional District. She has had a great deal of positive influence in Congress, in the black liberation movement, and in the women's liberation movement. She ran unsuccessfully for the 1972 Democratic presidential nomination. In this selection from her book Unbought and Unbossed *(1970), Chisholm decries the tendency to classify people in terms of stereotypes and meaningless categories. She also weighs her two major "handicaps"—being black and being female.*

There are 435 members of the House of Representatives and 417 are white males. Ten of the others are women and nine are black. I belong to both of these minorities, which makes it add up right. That makes me a celebrity, a kind of side show attraction. I was the first American citizen to be elected to Congress in spite of the double drawbacks of being female and having skin darkened by melanin.

When you put it that way, it sounds like a foolish reason for fame. In a just and free society it would be foolish. That I am a national figure because I was the first person in 192 years to be at once a congressman, black, and a woman proves, I would think, that our society is not yet either just or free.

Sometimes the media make me feel like a monkey in a cage. As soon as I was elected, the newspapers and networks started to besiege me. The first question was almost always, "How does it feel?" Naturally, it feels good. I am proud and honored that the people of my district believed in me enough to choose me to represent them. My Twelfth Congressional District of Brooklyn is mostly composed of poor neighborhoods with all the problems of poverty in an aggravated form: slum housing, high unemployment, too few medical services, high crime rate, neglected schools—the whole list. About 69 percent of my people are black and Puerto Rican. The rest are Jewish, Polish, Ukrainian, and Italian. Speaking for them at this moment in history is a great responsibility because they have been unrepresented and ignored for so long and their needs are so many and so urgent.

But I hope if I am remembered it will finally be for what I have done, not for what I happen to be. And I hope that my having made it, the hard way, can be some kind of inspiration, particularly to women. The number of women in politics has never been large, but now it is getting even smaller.

Women are a majority of the population, but they are treated like a minority group. The prejudice against them is so widespread that, paradoxically, most persons do not yet realize it exists. Indeed, most women do not realize it. They even accept being paid less for doing the same work as a man. They are as quick as any male to condemn a woman who ventures outside the limits of the role men have assigned to females: that of toy and drudge.

Of my two "handicaps," being female put many more obstacles in my path than being black. Sometimes I have trouble, myself, believing that I made it this far against the odds. No one, not even my father, whose hopes for me were extravagant, would ever have dared to predict it.

VOCABULARY

1. Define the following words as Chisholm uses them in her essay: melanin, besiege, paradoxically.
2. Chisholm uses *toy* and *drudge* to describe the roles of women. What do these terms mean? Do they accurately describe the role of women in today's society? Explain your answer.

CONTENT

1. Of what three groups has Chisholm been classified as a member? What does Chisholm want to be remembered for?
2. It is possible to classify people into a great number of categories: black/white, hardworking/lazy, male/female, intelligent/not intelligent, and so on.
    a. What criteria would be useful in helping to determine the members of the House of Representatives who are valuable and those who are not valuable? What criteria would you use to classify good and poor teachers?
    b. Chisholm states, "That I am a national figure because I was the first person in 192 years to be at once a congressman, black, and a woman proves, I would think, that our society is not yet either

just or free." What do people's responses to the kind of classification Chisholm is referring to have to do with our having a just and free society?

3. Chisholm can be classified as a black person, a female, a member of Congress, national figure, a contributor to her constituents' welfare, and so on.
   a. Name at least six groups in which you could be classified.
   b. Are you particularly admired or valued for your membership in any of these groups? Do you feel particularly proud of your membership in any of these groups? Explain your answer.

RHETORIC

1. In her title*, *Unbought and Unbossed,* Chisholm uses a negative prefix, parallel structure*, and alliteration*. Would the title "An Independent Congressperson" have been as compelling? Why or why not?
2. How would you describe Chisholm's tone* in this essay? How is this tone achieved?

READING AND WRITING SUGGESTIONS

1. Chisholm maintains that she has achieved national prominence because of the juxtaposition of three groups into which she is classified—that is, because she is simultaneously a woman, black, and a member of Congress. Write a brief expository essay in which you explore how people might react to a person who belongs to two categories which are seldom juxtaposed—for example, a blind physician.
2. Read a book such as Laura Z. Hobson's *Gentlemen's Agreement* that describes what happens when people respond negatively to a person on the basis of his or her social class, race, religion, or nationality instead of responding to the person's character and accomplishments. Write a brief essay in which you discuss the results of such negative reactions to irrelevant classifications.

* Definitions of all terms marked with an asterisk may be found in the Glossary.

THOSE CRAZY IDEAS

Isaac Asimov

Isaac Asimov (1920–), a native Russian, was brought to the United States when he was three and became an American citizen at the age of eight. He earned his B.S., M.A., and Ph.D. degrees at Columbia University. Until recently he was a member of the biochemistry faculty at the Boston University School of Medicine. One of our most prolific contemporary writers, Asimov is the author of over two hundred books—six under his pseudonym, Paul French. He wrote his first book, Pebble in the Sky, *in 1950, and since then he has written on a variety of subjects, including science, human physiology, and outer space. In this essay from* Fact and Fancy *(1962), Asimov presents some interesting ideas about characteristics which help us classify someone as a creative person.*

Time and time again I have been asked (and I'm sure others who have, in their time, written science fiction have been asked too): Where do you get your crazy ideas?

Over the years, my answers have sunk from flattered confusion to a shrug and a feeble smile. Actually, I don't really know, and the lack of knowledge doesn't really worry me, either, as long as the ideas keep coming.

But then some time ago, a consultant firm in Boston, engaged in a sophisticated space-age project for the government, got in touch with me.

What they needed, it seemed, to bring their project to a successful conclusion were novel suggestions, startling new principles, conceptual breakthroughs. To put it into the nutshell of a well-turned phrase, they needed "crazy ideas."

Unfortunately, they didn't know how to go about getting crazy ideas, but some among them had read my science fiction, so they looked me up in the phone book and called me to ask (in essence), "Dr. Asimov, where do you get your crazy ideas?"

Alas, I still didn't know, but as speculation is my profession, I am perfectly willing to think about the matter and share my thoughts with you.

The question before the house, then, is: How does one go about creating or inventing or dreaming up or stumbling over a new and revolutionary scientific principle?

For instance—to take a deliberately chosen example—how did Darwin come to think of evolution?

To begin with, in 1831, when Charles Darwin was twenty-two, he joined the crew of a ship called the *Beagle*. This ship was making a five-year voyage about the world to explore various coast lines and to increase man's geographical knowledge. Darwin went along as ship's naturalist, to study the forms of life in far-off places.

This he did extensively and well, and upon the return of the *Beagle* Darwin wrote a book about his experiences (published in 1840) which made him famous. In the course of this voyage, numerous observations led him to the conclusion that species of living creatures changed and developed slowly with time; that new species descended from old. This, in itself was not a new idea. Ancient Greeks had had glimmerings of evolutionary notions. Many scientists before Darwin, including Darwin's own grandfather, had theories of evolution.

The trouble, however, was that no scientist could evolve an explanation for the *why* of evolution. A French naturalist, Jean Baptiste de Lamarck, had suggested in the early 1800s that it came about by a kind of conscious effort or inner drive. A tree-grazing animal, attempting to reach leaves, stretched its neck over the years and transmitted a longer neck to its descendants. The process was repeated with each generation until a giraffe in full glory was formed.

The only trouble was that acquired characteristics are not inherited and this was easily proved. The Lamarckian explanation did not carry conviction.

Charles Darwin, however, had nothing better to suggest after several years of thinking about the problem.

But in 1798, eleven years before Darwin's birth, an English clergyman named Thomas Robert Malthus had written a book entitled *An Essay on the Principle of Population*. In this book Malthus suggested that the human population always increased faster than the food supply and that the population had to be cut down by either starvation, disease, or war; that these evils were therefore unavoidable.

In 1838 Darwin, still puzzling over the problem of the development of species, read Malthus's book. It is hackneyed to say "in a flash" but that, apparently, is how it happened. In a flash, it was clear to Darwin. Not only human beings increased faster than the food supply; all species of living things did. In every case, the surplus population had to be cut down by starvation, by predators, or by disease. Now no two members of any species are exactly alike; each has slight individual variations from the norm. Accepting this fact, which part of the population was cut down?

Why—and this was Darwin's breakthrough—those members of the species who were less efficient in the race for food, less adept at fighting off or escaping from predators, less equipped to resist disease, went down.

The survivors, generation after generation, were better adapted, on the average, to their environment. The slow changes toward a better fit with the environment accumulated until a new (and more adapted) species had replaced the old. Darwin thus postulated the reason for evolution as being the action of *natural selection*. In fact, the full title of his book is *On the Origin of Species by Means of Natural Selection, or the Preservation of Favoured Races in the Struggle for Life*. We just call it *The Origin of Species* and miss the full flavor of what it was he did.

It was in 1838 that Darwin received this flash and in 1844 that he began writing his book, but he worked on for fourteen years gathering evidence to back up his thesis. He was a methodical perfectionist and no amount of evidence seemed to satisfy him. He always wanted more. His friends read his preliminary manuscripts and urged him to publish. In particular, Charles Lyell (whose book *Principles of Geology,* published in 1830–1833, first convinced scientists of the great age of the earth and thus first showed there was *time* for the slow progress of evolution to take place) warned Darwin that someone would beat him to the punch.

While Darwin was working, another and younger English naturalist, Alfred Russel Wallace, was traveling in distant lands. He too found copious evidence to show that evolution took place and he too wanted to find a reason. He did not know that Darwin had already solved the problem.

He spent three years puzzling, and then in 1858, he too came across Malthus's book and read it. I am embarrassed to have to become hackneyed again, but in a flash he saw the answer. Unlike Darwin, however, he did not settle down to fourteen years of gathering and arranging evidence.

Instead, he grabbed pen and paper and at once wrote up his theory. He finished this in two days.

Naturally, he didn't want to rush into print without having his notions checked by competent colleagues, so he decided to send it to some well-known naturalist. To whom? Why, to Charles Darwin. To whom else?

I have often tried to picture Darwin's feeling as he read Wallace's essay which, he afterward stated, expressed matters in almost his own words. He wrote to Lyell that he had been forestalled "with a vengeance."

Darwin might easily have retained full credit. He was well-known and there were many witnesses to the fact that he had been working on his project for a decade and a half. Darwin, however, was a man of the highest integrity. He made no attempt to suppress Wallace. On the contrary, he passed on the essay to others and arranged to have it published along with a similar essay of his own. The year after, Darwin published his book.

Now the reason I chose this case was that here we have two men making one of the greatest discoveries in the history of science independently and simultaneously and under precisely the same stimulus. Does that mean *anyone* could have worked out the theory of natural selection if they had but made a sea voyage and combined that with reading Malthus?

Well, let's see. Here's where the speculation starts.

To begin with, both Darwin and Wallace were thoroughly grounded in natural history. Each had accumulated a vast collection of facts in the field in which they were to make their breakthrough. Surely this is significant.

Now every man in his lifetime collects facts, individual pieces of data, items of information. Let's call these "bits" (as they do, I think, in information theory). The "bits" can be of all varieties: personal memories, girls' phone numbers, baseball players' batting averages, yesterday's weather, the atomic weights of the chemical elements.

Naturally, different men gather different numbers of different varieties of "bits." A person who has collected a larger number than usual of those varieties that are held to be particularly difficult to obtain—say, those involving the sciences and the liberal arts—is considered "educated."

There are two broad ways in which the "bits" can be accumulated. The more common way, nowadays, is to find people who already possess many "bits" and have them transfer those "bits" to your mind in good order and in predigested fashion. Our schools specialize in this transfer of "bits" and those of us who take advantage of them receive a "formal education."

The less common way is to collect "bits" with a minimum of live help. They can be obtained from books or out of personal experience. In that case you are "self-educated." (It often happens that "self-educated" is confused with "uneducated." This is an error to be avoided.)

In actual practice, scientific breakthroughs have been initiated by those who were formally educated, as for instance by Nicolaus Copernicus, and by those who were self-educated, as for instance by Michael Faraday.

To be sure, the structure of science has grown more complex over the years and the absorption of the necessary number of "bits" has become more and more difficult without the guidance of someone who has already absorbed them. The self-educated genius is therefore becoming rarer, though he has still not vanished.

However, without drawing any distinction according to the manner in which "bits" have been accumulated, let's set up the first criterion for scientific creativity:

1) The creative person must possess as many "bits" of information as possible; i.e. he must be educated.

Of course, the accumulation of "bits" is not enough in itself. We have probably all met people who are intensely educated, but who manage to be abysmally stupid, nevertheless. They have the "bits," but the "bits" just lie there.

But what is there one can do with "bits"?

Well, one can combine them into groups of two or more. Everyone does that; it is the principle of the string on the finger. You tell yourself to remember *a* (to buy bread) when you observe *b* (the string). You enforce a combination that will not let you forget *a* because *b* is so noticeable.

That, of course, is a conscious and artificial combination of "bits." It is my feeling that every mind is, more or less unconsciously, continually making all sorts of combinations and permutations of "bits," probably at random.

Some minds do this with greater facility than others; some minds have greater capacity for dredging the combinations out of the unconscious and becoming consciously aware of them. This results in "new ideas," in "novel outlooks."

The ability to combine "bits" with facility and to grow consciously aware of the new combinations is, I would like to suggest, the measure of what we call "intelligence." In this view, it is quite possible to be educated and yet not intelligent.

Obviously, the creative scientist must not only have his "bits" on hand but he must be able to combine them readily and more or less consciously. Darwin not only observed data, he also made deductions—clever and far-reaching deductions—from what he observed. That is, he combined the "bits" in interesting ways and drew important conclusions.

So the second criterion of creativity is:

2) The creative person must be able to combine "bits" with facility and recognize the combinations he has formed; i.e. he must be intelligent.

Even forming and recognizing new combinations is insufficient in itself. Some combinations are important and some are trivial. How do you tell which are which? There is no question but that a person who cannot tell them apart must labor under a terrible disadvantage. As he plods after each possible new idea, he loses time and his life passes uselessly.

There is also no question but that there are people who somehow have the gift of seeing the consequences "in a flash" as Darwin and Wallace did; of feeling what the end must be without consciously going through every step of the reasoning. This, I suggest, is the measure of what we call "intuition."

Intuition plays more of a role in some branches of scientific knowledge than others. Mathematics, for example, is a deductive science in which, once certain basic principles are learned, a large number of items of information become "obvious" as merely consequences of those principles. Most of us, to be sure, lack the intuitive powers to see the "obvious."

To the truly intuitive mind, however, the combination of the few necessary "bits" is at once extraordinarily rich in consequences. Without too much trouble they see them all, including some that have not been seen by their predecessors.[1]

It is perhaps for this reason that mathematics and mathematical physics has seen repeated cases of first-rank breakthroughs by youngsters. Evariste Galois evolved group theory at twenty-one. Isaac Newton worked out calculus at twenty-three. Albert Einstein presented the theory of relativity at twenty-six, and so on.

In those branches of science which are more inductive and require larger numbers of "bits" to begin with, the average age of the scientists at the time of the breakthrough is greater. Darwin was twenty-nine at the time of his flash, Wallace was thirty-five.

But in any science, however inductive, intuition is necessary for creativity. So:

3) The creative person must be able to see, with as little delay as possible, the consequences of the new combinations of "bits" which he has formed; i.e. he must be intuitive.

But now let's look at this business of combining "bits" in a little more detail. "Bits" are at varying distances from each other. The more closely related two "bits" are, the more apt one is to be reminded of one by the other and to make the combination. Consequently, a new idea that arises from such a combination is made quickly. It is a "natural consequence" of an older idea, a "corollary." It "obviously follows."

The combination of less related "bits" results in a more startling idea; if for no other reason than it takes longer for such a combination to be made, so that the new idea is therefore less "obvious." For a scientific breakthrough of the first rank, there must be a combination of "bits" so widely spaced that the random chance of the combination being made is small indeed. (Otherwise, it will be made quickly and be considered but a corollary of some previous idea which will then be considered the "breakthrough.")

But then, it can easily happen that two "bits" sufficiently widely spaced to make a breakthrough by their combination are not present in the same mind. Neither Darwin nor Wallace, for all their education, intelligence, and intuition, possessed the key "bits" necessary to work out the theory of evolution by natural selection. Those "bits" were lying in Malthus's book, and both Darwin and Wallace had to find them there.

---

1. The Swiss mathematician, Leonhard Euler, said that to the true mathematician, it is at once obvious that $e^{\pi i} = -1$.

To do this, however, they had to read, understand, and appreciate the book. In short, they had to be ready to incorporate other people's "bits" and treat them with all the ease with which they treated their own.

It would hamper creativity, in other words, to emphasize intensity of education at the expense of broadness. It is bad enough to limit the nature of the "bits" to the point where the necessary two would not be in the same mind. It would be fatal to mold a mind to the point where it was incapable of accepting "foreign bits."

I think we ought to revise the first criterion of creativity, then, to read:

1) The creative person must possess as many "bits" as possible, falling into as wide a variety of types as possible; i.e. he must be broadly educated.

As the total amount of "bits" to be accumulated increases with the advance of science, it is becoming more and more difficult to gather enough "bits" in a wide enough area. Therefore, the practice of "brain-busting" is coming into popularity; the notion of collecting thinkers into groups and hoping that they will cross-fertilize one another into startling new breakthroughs.

Under what circumstances could this conceivably work? (After all, anything that will stimulate creativity is of first importance to humanity.)

Well, to begin with, a group of people will have more "bits" on hand than any member of the group singly since each man is likely to have some "bits" the others do not possess.

However, the increase in "bits" is not in direct proportion to the number of men, because there is bound to be considerable overlapping. As the group increases, the smaller and smaller addition of completely new "bits" introduced by each additional member is quickly outweighed by the added tensions involved in greater numbers; the longer wait to speak, the greater likelihood of being interrupted, and so on. It is my (intuitive) guess that five is as large a number as one can stand in such a conference.

Now of the three criteria mentioned so far, I feel (intuitively) that intuition is the least common. It is more likely that none of the group will be intuitive than that none will be intelligent or none educated. If no individual in the group is intuitive, the group as a whole will not be intuitive. You cannot add non-intuition and form intuition.

If one of the group is intuitive, he is almost certain to be intelligent and educated as well, or he would not have been asked to join the group in the first place. In short, for a brain-busting group to be creative, it must be quite small and it must possess at least one creative individual. But in that case, does that one individual need the group? Well, I'll get back to that later.

Why did Darwin work fourteen years gathering evidence for a theory he himself must have been convinced was correct from the beginning?

Why did Wallace send his manuscript to Darwin first instead of offering it for publication at once?

To me it seems that they must have realized that any new idea is met by resistance from the general population who, after all, are not creative. The more radical the new idea, the greater the dislike and distrust it arouses. The dislike and distrust aroused by a first-class breakthrough are so great that the author must be prepared for unpleasant consequences (sometimes for expulsion from the respect of the scientific community; sometimes, in some societies, for death).

Darwin was trying to gather enough evidence to protect himself by convincing others through a sheer flood of reasoning. Wallace wanted to have Darwin on his side before proceeding.

It takes courage to announce the results of your creativity. The greater the creativity, the greater the necessary courage in much more than direct proportion. After all, consider that the more profound the breakthrough, the more solidified the previous opinions; the more "against reason" the new discovery seems; the more against cherished authority.

Usually a man who possesses enough courage to be a scientific genius seems odd. After all, a man who has sufficient courage or irreverence to fly in the face of reason or authority *must* be odd, if you define "odd" as "being not like most people." And if he is courageous and irreverent in such a colossally big thing, he will certainly be courageous and irreverent in many small things so that being odd in one way, he is apt to be odd in others. In short, he will seem to the noncreative, conforming people about him to be a "crackpot."

So we have the fourth criterion:

4) The creative person must possess courage (and to the general public may, in consequence, seem a crackpot).

As it happens, it is the crackpottery that is most often most noticeable about the creative individual. The eccentric and absent-minded professor is a stock character in fiction; and the phrase "mad scientist" is amost a cliche´.

(And be it noted that I am never asked where I get my interesting or effective or clever or fascinating ideas. I am invariably asked where I get my *crazy* ideas.)

Of course, it does not follow that because the creative individual is usually a crackpot, that any crackpot is automatically an unrecognized genius. The chances are low indeed, and failure to recognize that the proposition cannot be so reversed is the cause of a great deal of trouble.

Then, since I believe that combinations of "bits" take place quite at random in the unconscious mind, it follows that it is quite possible that a person may possess all four of the criteria I have mentioned in superabundance and yet may never happen to make the necessary combination.

After all, suppose Darwin had never read Malthus. Would he ever have thought of natural selection? What made him pick up the copy? What if someone had come in at the crucial time and interrupted him?

So there is a fifth criterion which I am at a loss to phrase in any other way than this:

5) A creative person must be lucky.

To summarize:

A creative person must be 1) broadly educated, 2) intelligent, 3) intuitive, 4) courageous, and 5) lucky.

How, then, does one go about encouraging scientific creativity? For now, more than ever before in man's history, we must; and the need will grow constantly in the future.

Only, it seems to me, by increasing the incidence of the various criteria among the general population.

Of the five criteria, number 5 (luck) is out of our hands. We can only hope; although we must also remember Louis Pasteur's famous statement that "Luck favors the prepared mind." Presumably, if we have enough of the four other criteria, we shall find enough of number five as well.

Criterion 1 (broad education) is in the hands of our school system. Many educators are working hard to find ways of increasing the quality of education among the public. They should be encouraged to continue doing so.

Criterion 2 (intelligence) and 3 (intuition) are inborn and their incidence cannot be increased in the ordinary way. However, they can be more efficiently recognized and utilized. I would like to see methods devised for spotting the intelligent and intuitive (particularly the latter) early in life and treating them with special care. This, too, educators are concerned with.

To me, though, it seems that it is criterion 4 (courage) that receives the least concern, and it is just the one we may most easily be able to handle. Perhaps it is difficult to make a person more courageous than he is, but that is not necessary. It would be equally effective to make it sufficient to be less courageous; to adopt an attitude that creativity is a permissible activity.

Does this mean changing society or changing human nature? I don't think so. I think there are ways of achieving the end that do not involve massive change of anything, and it is here that brain-busting has its greatest chance of significance.

Suppose we have a group of five that includes one creative individual. Let's ask again what that individual can receive from the non-creative four.

The answer to me, seems to be just this: Permission!

They must permit him to create. They must tell him to go ahead and be a crackpot.

How is this permission to be granted? Can four essentially non-creative people find it within themselves to grant such permission? Can the one creative person find it within himself to accept it?

I don't know. Here, it seems to me, is where we need experimentation and perhaps a kind of creative breakthrough about creativity. Once we learn enough about the whole matter, who knows—I may even find out where I get those crazy ideas.

VOCABULARY

1. Define the following words as Asimov uses them in this essay: conceptual, hackneyed, predators, postulated, copious, abysmally, permutation, corollary, irreverence.
2. Give at least three definitions of *crazy* and indicate which you think is closest to Asimov's meaning in this essay.

CONTENT

1. Why does Asimov call creativity "crazy ideas"? Are such "crazy ideas" really crazy? Explain.
2. Asimov speaks of the importance of collecting "bits." What does he mean by "bits" and what does he say is even more important than collecting "bits"?
3. How does Asimov distinguish among "formal education," "self-education," and "intelligence"?
4. Asimov quotes Louis Pasteur's statement that "luck favors the prepared mind." Do you agree? Why or why not?
5. What does Asimov mean by "brain-busting"? Have you ever done any "brain-busting"? How does it feel?
6. Review Godwin's comments about "The Watcher at the Gates" (page 9). Would Asimov agree or disagree? Summarize his comments which support your answer.
7. Asimov discusses criteria for classifying someone as creative. Summarize these criteria and use them to classify three of your acquaintances as creative or noncreative.
8. In Asimov's opinion, what are ways we can encourage creativity? Which way does he consider most important? Do you agree?

RHETORIC

1. Does Asimov's title* suggest that a serious essay is going to follow? Why do you think that Asimov chose this title*?

2. Three requirements must be met if classification is to have any value. Review these in the introduction to this section. Does Asimov meet these requirements? Explain your answer.

3. What is Asimov's thesis*? Does he state it or imply it?

4. Refer to the glossary for a discussion of the conclusion* of an essay. How well does Asimov's summary meet the criteria listed?

5. Asimov uses rhetorical questions* frequently. Locate them and describe how they contribute to the essay's organization.

READING AND WRITING SUGGESTIONS

1. Asimov discusses courage as an essential ingredient for the creative thinker. Write an essay describing groups of people who must display courage in reaching their goals. The courage might be in facing danger or in enduring criticism. Reread the introduction to this section before you begin and observe the principles of classification. Remember you are dividing those people who display courage from those who do not.

2. Isaac Asimov is an outstanding example of a creative person. Read *In Memory Yet Green: The Autobiography of Isaac Asimov*. Write an essay classifying experiences that might have led Asimov to his creative life. You might consider such things as his schools, his parents, his friends, and his hobbies.

---

* Definitions of all terms marked with an asterisk may be found in the Glossary.

FOUR TYPES OF PRESIDENTIAL CHARACTER

James D. Barber

James D. Barber (1930–) is professor of political science at Duke University. He earned his bachelor's and master's degrees at the University of Chicago and his doctorate at Yale. Barber has written widely. This essay is from his book Presidential Character: Predicting Performance in the White House *(1972). Barber's intention is to identify some clear criteria for choosing presidents, that is, for classifying candidates into those who will be good presidents and those who will not.*

The first baseline in defining Presidential types is *activity-passivity*. How much energy does the man invest in his Presidency? Lyndon Johnson went at his day like a human cyclone, coming to rest long after the sun went down. Calvin Coolidge often slept eleven hours a night and still needed a nap in the middle of the day. In between the Presidents array themselves on the high or low side of the activity line.

The second baseline is *positive-negative affect* toward one's activity—that is, how he feels about what he does. Relatively speaking, does he seem to experience his political life as happy or sad, enjoyable or discouraging, positive or negative in its main effect. The feeling I am after here is not grim satisfaction in a job well done, not some philosophical conclusion. The idea is this: Is he someone who, on the surfaces we can see, gives forth the feeling that he has *fun* in political life? Franklin Roosevelt's Secretary of War, Henry L. Stimson wrote that the Roosevelts "not only understood the *use* of power, they knew the *enjoyment* of power, too. . . . Whether a man is burdened by power or enjoys power; whether he is trapped by responsibility or made free by it; whether he is moved by other people and outer forces or moves them—that is the essence of leadership."

The positive-negative baseline, then, is a general symptom of the fit between the man and his experience, a kind of register of *felt* satisfaction.

Why might we expect these two simple dimensions to outline the main character types? Because they stand for two central features of anyone's orientation toward life. In nearly every study of personality, some form of the active-passive contrast is critical; the general tendency to act or be acted upon is evident in such concepts as dominance-submission, extraversion-introversion, aggression-timidity, attack-defense, fight-flight, engagement-withdrawal, approach-avoidance. In everyday life we sense quickly the general energy output of the people we deal with. Similarly we catch on fairly quickly to the affect dimension—whether the person seems to be optimistic or pessimistic, hopeful or skeptical, happy or sad. The two baselines are clear and they are also independent of one another: all of us know people who are very active but seem discouraged, others who are quite passive but seem happy, and so forth. The activity baseline refers to what one does, the affect baseline to how one feels about what he does.

Both are crude clues to character. They are leads into four basic character patterns long familiar in psychological research. In summary form, these are the main configurations:

Active-positive: There is a congruence, a consistency, between much activity and the enjoyment of it, indicating relatively high self-esteem and relative success in relating to the environment. The man shows an orientation toward productiveness as a value and an ability to use his styles flexibly, adaptively, suiting the dance to the music. He sees himself as developing over time toward relatively well defined personal goals—growing toward his image of himself as he might yet be. There is an emphasis on rational mastery, on using the brain to move the feet. This may get him into trouble; he may fail to take account of the irrational in politics. Not everyone he deals with sees things his way and he may find it hard to understand why.

Active-negative: The contradiction here is between relatively intense effort and relatively low emotional reward for that effort. The activity has a compulsive quality, as if the man were trying to make up for something or to escape from anxiety into hard work. He seems ambitious, striving upward, power-seeking. His stance toward the environment is aggressive and he has a persistent problem in managing his aggressive feelings. His self-image is vague and discontinuous. Life is a hard struggle to achieve and hold power, hampered by the condemnations of a perfectionistic conscience. Active-negative types pour energy into the political system, but it is an energy distorted from within.

Passive-positive: This is the receptive, compliant, other-directed character whose life is a search for affection as a reward for being agreeable and cooperative rather than personally assertive. The contradiction is between low self-esteem (on grounds of being unlovable, unattractive) and a superficial optimism. A hopeful attitude helps dispel doubt and elicits encouragement from others. Passive-positive types help soften the harsh edges of politics. But their dependence and the fragility of their hopes and enjoyments make disappointment in politics likely.

Passive-negative: The factors are consistent—but how are we to account for the man's *political* role-taking? Why is someone who does little in politics and enjoys it less there at all? The answer lies in the passive-negative's character-rooted orientation toward doing dutiful service; this compensates for low self-esteem based on a sense of uselessness. Passive-negative types are in politics because they think they ought to be. They may be well adapted to certain nonpolitical roles, but they lack the experience and flexibility to perform effectively as political leaders. Their tendency is to withdraw, to escape from the conflict and uncertainty of politics by emphasizing vague principles (especially prohibitions) and procedural arrangements. They become guardians of the right and proper way, above the sordid politicking of lesser men.

Active-positive Presidents want most to achieve results. Active-negatives aim to get and keep power. Passive-positives are after love. Passive-negatives emphasize their civic virtue. The relation of activity to enjoyment in a President thus tends to outline a cluster of characteristics, to set apart the adapted from the compulsive, compliant, and withdrawn types.

The first four Presidents of the United States, conveniently, ran through this gamut of character types. (Remember, we are talking about tendencies, broad directions; no individual man exactly fits a category.) George Washington—clearly the most important President in the pantheon—established the fundamental legitimacy of an American government at a time when this was a matter in considerable question. Washington's dignity, judiciousness, his aloof air of reserve and dedication to duty fit the passive-negative or withdrawing type best. Washington did not seek innovation, he sought stability. He longed to retire to Mount Vernon, but fortunately was persuaded to stay on through a second term, in which, by rising above the political conflict between Hamilton and Jefferson and inspiring confidence in his own integrity, he gave the nation time to develop the organized means for peaceful change.

John Adams followed, a dour New England Puritan, much given to work and worry, an impatient and irascible man—an active-negative President, a compulsive type. Adams was far more partisan than Washington; the survival of the system through his Presidency demonstrated that the nation could tolerate, for a time, domination by one of its nascent political parties. As President, an angry Adams brought the United States to the brink of war with France, and presided over the new nation's first experiment in political repression: the Alien and Sedition Acts, forbidding, among other things, unlawful combinations "with intent to oppose any measure or measures of the government of the United States," or "any false, scandalous, and malicious writing or writings against the United States, or the President of the United States, with intent to defame . . . or to bring them or either of them, into contempt or disrepute."

Then came Jefferson. He too had his troubles and failures—in the design of national defense, for example. As for his Presidential character (only one element in success or failure), Jefferson was clearly active-positive. A child of the Enlightenment, he applied his reason to organizing connections with Congress aimed at strengthening the more popular forces. A man of catholic interests and delightful humor, Jefferson combined a clear and open vision of what the country could be with a profound political sense, expressed in his famous phrase, "Every difference of opinion is not a difference of principle."

The fourth President was James Madison, "Little Jemmy," the constitutional philosopher thrown into the White House at a time of great international turmoil. Madison comes closest to the passive-positive, or compliant, type; he suffered from irresolution, tried to compromise his way out, and gave in too readily to the "warhawks" urging combat with Britain. The nation drifted into war, and Madison wound up ineptly commanding his collection of amateur generals in the streets of Washington. General Jackson's victory at New Orleans saved the Madison administration's historical reputation; but he left the Presidency with the United States close to bankruptcy and secession.

These four Presidents—like all Presidents—were persons trying to cope with the roles they had won by using the equipment they had built over a lifetime. The President is not some shapeless organism in a flood of novelties, but a man with a memory in a system with a history. Like all of us, he draws on his past to shape his future. The pathetic hope that the White House will turn a Caligula into a Marcus Aurelius is as naive as the fear that ultimate power inevitably corrupts. The problem is to understand—and to state understandably—what in the personal past foreshadows the Presidential future.

VOCABULARY

1. Define the following words as Barber uses them in his essay: affect (*n*), compulsive, pantheon, dour, irascible, nascent.
2. If you are unfamiliar with any other words in this essay, check them in a dictionary and define them in your own words.

CONTENT

1. Barber presents two baselines to outline types of presidential character.
    a. Explain these baselines.
    b. Why does Barber feel these baselines are sufficient? Do you agree? Why or why not?
2. Briefly define the four types of presidential character Barber presents.
3. Review Asimov's comments about creativity (pages 32–37). How well do you think Barber's baselines and character types predict creativity? Give a rationale for your answer.
4. Classify yourself in terms of Barber's baselines and character types.
    a. On the basis of your classification, what prediction can you make about your ultimate success in the field you are presently working in or working toward?
    b. On the basis of your prediction, do you need to change your behavior in any way? If so, how?

RHETORIC

1. Barber uses a technique called *defining in context* to give a simple definition of *congruence*. What synonym does he use? How is this technique an aid to the reader?
2. Chisholm (*Unbought and Unbossed,* page 26), Asimov ("Those Crazy Ideas," page 29), and Barber use similar diction*, tone*, and style* in their essays.
    a. Why do you think these authors write in a similar way?
    b. Do you think someone with a background in the humanities or the fine arts would write differently? Explain your answer.
3. For what purposes does Barber use the first four United States presidents as examples? Is it necessary that his classification system apply to other presidents as well? Explain.
4. Barber uses only masculine pronouns in this selection.
    a. What is your reaction to this practice?

---

* Definitions of all terms marked with an asterisk may be found in the Glossary.

b. Barber's essay was published in 1972. Do you think that an editor would allow only masculine pronouns today? Why?

READING AND WRITING SUGGESTIONS

1. Barber's baselines and categories are useful in predicting success in areas other than the presidency. Choose a person you know who is fully engaged in some activity. Write an essay classifying that person according to Barber's baselines and categories.
2. Read a biography or autobiography of a president or other leader, for example, *The Rise of Theodore Roosevelt* by Edmund Morris, *The White House Years* by Henry Kissinger, or *American Caesar: Douglas MacArthur (1880–1964)* by William Manchester. Write a brief essay classifying that person's character according to Barber's baselines and categories.

A LIFE WORTH LIVING

Bertrand Russell

Bertrand Russell (1872–1970), renowned British philosopher, was born in Monmouthshire, England, the son of Lord John and Lady Katherine Russell. He graduated with honors from Trinity College, Cambridge University. He returned to Cambridge in 1894 as a fellow and lecturer and stayed there until 1916 when he was dismissed for his opposition to World War I and sentenced to four and a half months in prison. Russell was one of the most productive writers and thinkers of his time. He became an advocate for disarmament following World War II and was again arrested for antigovernment activity. He also was openly antagonistic to American policy in Vietnam. Russell held lectureships at a number of colleges and universities including Harvard, the University of Chicago, the University of California, and City College of New York. His interests were many and were reflected in his writing. Among his best known works are Education and the Social Order, History of Western Philosophy, The Principles of Mathematics, *and* My Philosophical Development.

Russell won the Nobel Prize for Literature in 1950. The selections below are from his autobiography published in 1967–69. The poem was written to Edith Finch, his fourth and last wife, whom he married in 1952.

To Edith

Through the long years
I sought peace.
I found ecstasy, I found anguish,
I found madness,
I found loneliness.
I found the solitary pain
that gnaws the heart,
But peace I did not find.

Now, old & near my end,
I have known you,
And, knowing you,
I have found both ecstasy & peace.
I know rest.
After so many lonely years.
I know what life & love may be.
Now, if I sleep,
I shall sleep fulfilled.

Prologue: What I Have Lived For

Three passions, simple but overwhelmingly strong, have governed my life: the longing for love, the search for knowledge, and unbearable pity for the suffering of mankind. These passions, like great winds, have blown me hither and thither, in a wayward course, over a deep ocean of anguish, reaching to the very verge of despair.

I have sought love, first, because it brings ecstasy—ecstasy so great that I would often have sacrificed all the rest of life for a few hours of this joy. I have sought it, next, because it relieves loneliness—that terrible loneliness in which one shivering consciousness looks over the rim of the world into the cold unfathomable lifeless abyss. I have sought it, finally, because in the union of love I have seen, in a mystic miniature, the prefiguring vision of the heaven that saints and poets have imagined. This is what I sought, and though it might seem too good for human life, this is what—at last—I have found.

With equal passion I have sought knowledge. I have wished to understand the hearts of men. I have wished to know why the stars shine. And I have tried to apprehend the Pythagorean power by which number holds sway above the flux. A little of this, but not much, I have achieved.

Love and knowledge, so far as they were possible, led upward toward the heavens. But always pity brought me back to earth. Echoes of cries of pain reverberate in my heart. Children in famine, victims tortured by oppressors, helpless old people a hated burden to their sons, and the whole world of loneliness, poverty, and pain make a mockery of what human life should be. I long to alleviate the evil, but I cannot, and I too suffer.

This has been my life. I have found it worth living, and would gladly live it again if the chance were offered me.

Epilogue: Reflections

The serious part of my life ever since boyhood has been devoted to two different objects, which for a long time remained separate and have only in recent years united into a single whole. I wanted, on the one hand, to find out whether anything could be known; and, on the other hand, to do whatever might be possible toward creating a happier world. Up to the age of thirty-eight I gave most of my energies to the first of these tasks. I was troubled by scepticism and unwillingly forced to the conclusion that most of what passes for knowledge is open to reasonable doubt. I wanted certainty in the kind of way in which people want religious faith. I thought that certainty is more likely to be found in mathematics than elsewhere. But I discovered that many mathematical demonstrations, which my teachers expected me to accept, were full of fallacies, and that, if certainty were indeed discoverable in mathematics, it would be in a new kind of mathematics, with more solid foundations than those that had hitherto been thought secure. But as the work proceeded, I was continually reminded of the fable about the elephant and the tortoise. Having constructed an elephant upon which the mathematical world could rest, I found the elephant tottering, and proceeded to construct a tortoise to keep the elephant from falling. But the tortoise was no more secure than the elephant, and after some twenty years of very arduous toil, I came to the conclusion that there was nothing more that *I* could do in the way of making mathematical knowledge indubitable. Then came the First World War, and my thoughts became concentrated on human misery and folly. Neither misery nor folly seems to me any part of the inevitable lot of man. And I am convinced that intelligence, patience, and eloquence can, sooner or later, lead the human race out of its self-imposed tortures provided it does not exterminate itself meanwhile.

On the basis of this belief, I have had always a certain degree of optimism, although, as I have grown older, the optimism has grown more sober and the happy issue more distant. But I remain completely incapable of agreeing with those who accept fatalistically the view that man is born to trouble. The causes of unhappiness in the past and in the present are not difficult to ascertain. There have been poverty, pestilence, and famine, which were due to man's inadequate mastery of nature. There have been wars, oppressions, and tortures which have been due to men's hostility to their fellow-men. And there have been morbid miseries fostered by gloomy creeds, which have led men into profound inner discords that made all outward prosperity of no avail. All these are unnecessary. In the regard to all of them, means are known by which they can be overcome. In the modern world, if communities are unhappy it is often because they have ignorances, habits, beliefs, and passions, which are dearer to them than happiness or even life. I find many men in our dangerous age who seem to be in love with misery and death, and who grow angry when hopes are suggested to them. They think hope is irrational and that, in sitting down to lazy despair, they are merely facing facts. I cannot agree with these men. To preserve hope in our world makes calls upon our intelligence and our energy. In those who despair it is frequently the energy that is lacking.

The last half of my life has been lived in one of those painful epochs of human history during which the world is getting worse, and past victories which had seemed to be definitive have turned out to be only temporary. When I was young, Victorian optimism was taken for granted. It was thought that freedom and prosperity would spread gradually throughout the world by an orderly process, and it was hoped that cruelty, tyranny, and injustice would continually diminish. Hardly anyone was haunted by the fear of great wars. Hardly anyone thought of the nineteenth century as a brief interlude between past and future barbarism. For those who grew up in that atmosphere, adjustment to the world of the present has been difficult. It has been difficult not only emotionally but intellectually. Ideas that had been thought adequate have proved inadequate. In some directions valuable freedoms have proved very hard to preserve. In other directions, specially as regards relations between nations, freedoms formerly valued have proved potent sources of disaster. New thoughts, new hopes, new freedoms, and new restrictions upon freedom are needed if the world is to emerge from its present perilous state.

I cannot pretend that what I have done in regard to social and political problems has had any great importance. It is comparatively easy to have an immense effect by means of a dogmatic and precise gospel, such as that of Communism. But for my part I cannot believe that what mankind needs is anything either precise or dogmatic. Nor can I believe with any whole-heartedness in any partial doctrine which deals only with some part or aspect of human life. There are those who hold that everything depends upon institutions, and that good institutions will inevitably bring the millennium. And, on the other hand, there are those who believe that what is needed is a change of heart, and that, in comparison, institutions are of little account. I cannot accept either view. Institutions mould character, and character transforms institutions. Reforms in both must march hand in hand. And if individuals are to retain that measure of initiative and flexibility which they ought to have, they must not be all forced into one rigid mould; or to change the metaphor, all drilled into one army. Diversity is essential in spite of the fact that it precludes universal acceptance of a single gospel. But to preach such a doctrine is difficult, especially in arduous times. And perhaps it cannot be effective until some bitter lessons have been learned by tragic experience.

My work is near its end, and the time has come when I can survey it as a whole. How far have I succeeded, and how far have I failed? From an early age I thought of myself as dedicated to great and arduous tasks. Nearly three-quarters of a century ago, walking alone in the Tiergarten through melting snow under the coldly glittering March sun, I determined to write two series of books: one abstract, growing gradually more concrete; the other concrete, growing gradually more abstract. They were to be crowned by a synthesis, combining pure theory with a practical social philosophy. Except for the final synthesis, which still eludes me, I have written these books. They have been acclaimed and praised, and the thoughts of many men and women have been affected by them. To this extent I have succeeded.

But as against this must be set two kinds of failure, one outward, one inward.

To begin with the outward failure: the Tiergarten has become a desert; the Brandenburger Tor, through which I entered it on that March morning, has become the boundary of two hostile empires, glaring at each other across a barrier, and grimly preparing the ruin of mankind. Communists, Fascists, and Nazis have successively challenged all that I thought good, and in defeating them much of what their opponents have sought to preserve is being lost. Freedom has come to be thought weakness, and tolerance has been compelled to wear the garb of treachery. Old ideals are judged irrelevant, and no doctrine free from harshness commands respect.

The inner failure, though of little moment to the world, has made my mental life a perpetual battle. I set out with a more or less religious belief in a Platonic eternal world, in which mathematics shone with a beauty like that of the last Cantos of the *Paradiso*. I came to the conclusion that the eternal world is trivial, and that mathematics is only the art of saying the same thing in different words. I set out with a belief that love, free and courageous, could conquer the world without fighting. I came to support a bitter and terrible war. In these respects there was failure.

But beneath all this load of failure I am still conscious of something that I feel to be victory. I may have conceived theoretical truth wrongly, but I was not wrong in thinking that there is such a thing, and that it deserves our allegiance. I may have thought the road to a world of free and happy human beings shorter than it is proving to be, but I was not wrong in thinking that such a world is possible, and that it is worth while to live with a view to bringing it nearer. I have lived in the pursuit of a vision, both personal and social. Personal: to care for what is noble, for what is beautiful, for what is gentle; to allow moments of insight to give wisdom at more mundane times. Social: to see in imagination the society that is to be created, where individuals grow freely, and where hate and greed and envy die because there is nothing to nourish them. These things I believe, and the world, for all its horrors, has left me unshaken.

VOCABULARY

1. Define the following words as Russell uses them in this selection: unfathomable, abyss, mystic, prefiguring, skepticism, indubitable, dogmatic.
2. If you are unfamiliar with any other words in this selection, check them in a dictionary and define them in your own words.

CONTENT

1. Russell concluded that "mathematics is only the art of saying the same thing in different words." Many people agree with him. What does this conclusion suggest to you about the nature of language?

2. Three motives governed Russell's life. Describe in detail what these passions were, why he sought them, and what he accomplished or did not accomplish in terms of them.
3. Accomplishments are objective facts about performance. Success and failure are values one ascribes to accomplishments in relation to aspirations (hopes, intentions). In Russell's judgment, what were his successes? his failures?
4. George Orwell once said that every life, viewed from within, is a series of defeats.
   a. Are Russell's comments consistent with Orwell's insight?
   b. Do you think mankind will ever reach perfect love, complete knowledge, and perfect social justice?
   c. Did Russell set himself up for failure by his reach exceeding his grasp, to paraphrase Browning[1]?
5. Russell was finally concerned with weighing, "How far have I succeeded and how far have I failed?"
   a. This sentence shows that he sees success as a matter of degree, not as an either/or decision. Do you agree? Explain your answer.
   b. Considering his accomplishents, do you agree with Russell's value judgments about how far he succeeded and failed? Why?
6. Do you think there is some external standard we can use to judge how successful or unsuccessful someone's accomplishments are? Or must we consider them against that person's motives or expectations for himself/herself?

RHETORIC

1. The poem reproduced here opens Russell's autobiography. What function does it serve? What does it help you see about the content and tone* of Russell's life?
2. In classification, one identifies categories for grouping specific entities.
   a. In his prologue, what categories does Russell identify?

---

[1] "Man's reach must exceed his grasp or what's a heaven for?"

* Definitions of all terms marked with an asterisk may be found in the Glossary.

b. Are these categories sufficient to classify a life? In other words, are they general enough to apply to everyone's life?

3. Russell uses a great deal of figurative language* starting with "these passions like great winds . . . ." Identify and interpret at least four of these figures of speech. What do they contribute to your grasp of the ideas and feelings he is seeking to present?

4. Describe Russell's diction* and style*. Are they what you would expect from a great thinker? Explain your answer.

5. Is there a difference in tone* between Russell's prologue and epilogue? Does this tone* result from his rhetoric, his message, or both?

READING AND WRITING SUGGESTIONS

1. Write a brief essay classifying as a success or failure your own life or the life of someone you know well. Take as your thesis, "Nobody bats a thousand."

2. Read a biography of Robert Frost, for example, Daniel Smythe's *Robert Frost Speaks* or Lawrence Thompson and R. H. Winnick's *Robert Frost: The Later Years, 1938–1963*. Consider his poetic accomplishments. Also consider his personal relations, for example, the accounts about how his wife was so bitter toward him that she would not allow him near her when she was dying. Write an essay in which you classify Robert Frost as a success or failure.

---

* Definitions of all terms marked with an asterisk may be found in the Glossary.

EXAMPLE

One of the most powerful ways to make an abstraction meaningful to a reader is to illustrate it by means of an example. The right to a trial by jury may seem a dry abstraction to some, but a few concrete examples of events that took place during the Spanish Inquisition or of the brutal lynchings that occurred in the early American West make this right seem much more vital and necessary.

There are four requirements that must be met if the examples used in an essay are to be effective. First—and most basically—an example should be a true illustration of the proposition or subject it is supporting. In a discussion of the mating behavior of fish, an example describing the mating behavior of a particular species of frog will only cause the reader confusion.

Second, examples should represent a fair cross section of the subject under discussion. If the only people named as examples in an essay on great scientists are Marie Curie, Louis Pasteur, and Andre Ampere, the reader might get the false impression that all great scientists are French.

Third, a suitable number of examples should be provided, depending on the nature of the subject under discussion. Simple or familiar subjects require only a few examples. Difficult, complex, or unfamiliar subjects require more examples.

Finally, examples should be appropriate to the nature of the essay and audience. A highly technical essay requires technical examples, whereas an essay intended for a general audience calls for examples that the average reader can easily understand. Examples will also be far more effective if they are interesting to the reader; an example that captures a reader's imagination can have great impact on the reader's response to the essay as a whole.

LOVE IS A FALLACY

Max Shulman

Max Shulman (1919–), American humorist, was born in St. Paul, Minnesota. While attending the University of Minnesota, he served as editor of the campus humor magazine and columnist for the university newspaper. The year after he graduated, Shulman's first book, Barefoot Boy with Cheek, *was published. He has written several other books, including* Sleep Till Noon *and* Rally Round the Flag, Boys; *a Broadway comedy,* The Tender Trap; *and the television series,* The Adventures of Dobie Gillis. *The following selection from* The Many Loves of Dobie Gillis *(1951) is a good example of Shulman's lampoon of college life and logic.*

Cool was I, and logical. Keen, calculating, perspicacious, acute, and astute—I was all of these. My brain was as powerful as a dynamo, as precise as a chemist's scale, as penetrating as a scalpel. And—think of it!—I was only eighteen.

It is not often that one so young has such a giant intellect. Take, for example, Petey Burch, my roommate at the University of Minnesota. Same age, same background, but dumb as an ox. A nice enough fellow, you understand, but nothing upstairs. Emotional type. Unstable. Impressionable. Worst of all, a faddist. Fads, I submit, are the very negation of reason. To be swept up in every new craze that comes along, to surrender yourself to idiocy just because everybody else is doing it—this, to me, is the acme of mindlessness. Not, however, to Petey.

One afternoon I found Petey lying on his bed with an expression of such distress on his face that I immediately diagnosed appendicitis. "Don't move," I said. "Don't take a laxative. I'll get a doctor."

"Raccoon," he mumbled thickly.

"Raccoon?" I asked, pausing in my flight.

"I want a raccoon coat," he wailed.

I perceived that his trouble was not physical, but mental. "Why do you want a raccoon coat?"

"I should have known it," he cried, pounding his temples. "I should have known they'd come back when the Charleston came back. Like a fool I spent all my money on textbooks, and now I can't get a raccoon coat."

"Can you mean," I asked incredulously, "that people are actually wearing raccoon coats again?"

"All the Big Men on Campus are wearing them. Where've you been?"

"In the library," I said, naming a place that, as it happens, is not frequently inhabited by Big Men on Campus.

He leaped from the bed and paced the room. "I've got to have a raccoon coat," he said passionately. "I've got to!"

"Petey, why? Look at it rationally. Raccoon coats are unsanitary. They shed. They smell bad. They weigh too much. They're unsightly. They—"

"You don't understand," he interrupted impatiently. "It's the thing to do. Don't you want to be in the swim?"

"No," I said truthfully.

"Well, I do," he declared. "I'd give anything for a raccoon coat. Anything!"

My brain, that precision instrument, slipped into high gear. "Anything?" I asked, looking at him narrowly.

"Anything," he affirmed in ringing tones.

I stroked my chin thoughtfully. It so happened that I knew where to get my hands on a raccoon coat. My father had had one in his undergraduate days; it lay now in a trunk in the attic back home. It also happened that Petey had something I wanted. He didn't *have* it exactly, but at least he had first rights to it. I refer to his girl, Polly Espy.

I had long coveted Polly Espy. Let me emphasize that my desire for this young woman was not emotional in nature. She was, to be sure, a girl who excited the emotions, but I was not one to let my heart rule my head. I wanted Polly for a shrewdly calculated, entirely cerebral reason.

I was a freshman in law school. In a few years I would be out in practice. I was well aware of the importance of the right kind of wife in furthering a lawyer's career. The successful lawyers I had observed were, almost without exception, married to beautiful, gracious, intelligent women. With one omission, Polly fitted these specifications perfectly.

Beautiful she was. She was not yet of pin-up proportions, but I felt sure that time would supply the lack. She already had the makings.

Gracious she was. By gracious, I mean full of graces. She had an erectness of carriage, an ease of bearing, a poise that clearly indicated the best of breeding. At table, her manners were exquisite. I had seen her at the Kozy Kampus Korner eating the specialty of the house—a sandwich that contained scraps of pot roast, gravy, chopped nuts, and a dipper of sauerkraut—without even getting her fingers moist.

Intelligent she was not. In fact, she veered in the opposite direction. But I believed that under my guidance she would smarten up. At any rate, it was worth a try. It is, after all, easier to make a beautiful dumb girl smart than to make an ugly smart girl beautiful.

"Petey," I said, "are you in love with Polly Espy?"

"I think she's a keen kid," he replied, "but I don't know if you'd call it love. Why?"

"Do you," I asked, "have any kind of formal arrangement with her? I mean are you going steady or anything like that?"

"No. We see each other quite a bit, but we both have other dates. Why?"

"Is there," I asked, "any other man for whom she has a particular fondness?"

"Not that I know of. Why?"

I nodded with satisfaction. "In other words, if you were out of the picture, the field would be open. Is that right?"

"I guess so. What are you getting at?"

"Nothing, nothing," I said innocently, and took my suitcase out of the closet.

"Where are you going?" asked Petey.

"Home for the weekend." I threw a few things into the bag.

"Listen," he said, clutching my arm eagerly, "while you're home, you couldn't get some money from your old man, could you, and lend it to me so I can buy a raccoon coat?"

"I may do better than that," I said with a mysterious wink.

"Look," I said to Petey when I got back Monday morning. I threw open the suitcase and revealed the huge, hairy, gamy object that my father had worn in his Stutz Bearcat in 1925.

"Holy Toledo!" said Petey reverently. He plunged his hands into the raccoon coat and then his face. "Holy Toledo!" he repeated fifteen or twenty times.

"Would you like it?" I asked.

"Oh, yes!" he cried, clutching the greasy pelt to him. Then a canny look came into his eyes. "What do you want for it?"

"Your girl," I said, mincing no words.

"Polly?" he asked in a horrified whisper.

"That's right."

He flung the coat from him. "Never," he said stoutly.

I shrugged. "Okay. If you don't want to be in the swim, I guess it's your business."

I sat down in a chair and pretended to read a book, but out of the corner of my eye I kept watching Petey. He was a torn man. First he looked at the coat with the expression of a waif at a bakery window. Then he turned away and set his jaw resolutely. Then he looked back at the coat, with even more longing in his face. Then he turned away, but with not so much resolution this time. Back and forth his head swiveled—desire waxing, resolution waning. Finally he didn't turn away at all; he just stood and stared with mad lust at the coat.

"It isn't as though I were in love with Polly," he said thickly. "Or going steady or anything like that."

"That's right," I murmured.

"What's Polly to me, or me to Polly?"

"Not a thing," said I.

"It's just been a casual kick—just a few laughs, that's all."

"Try on the coat," said I.

He complied. The coat bunched high over his ears and dropped all the way down to his shoetops. He looked like a mound of dead raccoons. "Fits fine," he said happily.

I rose from my chair. "Is it a deal?" I asked, extending my hand.

He swallowed. "It's a deal," he said, and shook my hand.

My first date with Polly took place the next evening. This was in the nature of a survey; I wanted to find out just how much work I had to do to get her mind up to the standard I required. First I took her to dinner. "Gee, that was a delish dinner," she said as we left the restaurant. Then I took her to a movie. "Gee, that was a marvy movie," she said as we left the theatre. And then I took her home. "Gee, I had a sensaysh time," she said as she bade me good night.

I went back to my room with a heavy heart. I had gravely underestimated the size of my task. This girl's lack of information was terrifying. Nor would it be enough merely to supply her with information. First she had to be taught to ***think***. This loomed as a project of no small dimensions, and at first I was tempted to give her back to Petey. But then I got to thinking about her abundant physical charms and about the way she entered a room and the way she handled a knife and fork, and I decided to make an effort.

I went about it, as in all things, systematically. I gave her a course in logic. It happened that I, as a law student, was taking a course in logic myself, so I had all the facts at my fingertips. "Polly," I said to her when I picked her up for our next date, "tonight we are going over to the Knoll and talk."

"Oo, terrif," she replied. One thing I will say for this girl: you would go far to find another so agreeable.

We went to the Knoll, the campus trysting place, and we sat down under an old oak, and she looked at me expectantly. "What are we going to talk about?" she asked.

"Logic."

She thought this over for a minute and decided she liked it. "Magnif," she said.

"Logic," I said, clearing my throat, "is the science of thinking. Before we can think correctly, we must first learn to recognize the common fallacies of logic. These we will take up tonight."

"Wow-dow!" she cried, clapping her hands delightedly.

I winced, but went bravely on. "First let us examine the fallacy called *Dicto Simpliciter*."

"By all means," she urged, batting her lashes eagerly.

"*Dicto Simpliciter* means an argument based on an unqualified generalization. For example: Exercise is good. Therefore everybody should exercise."

"I agree," said Polly earnestly. "I mean exercise is wonderful. I mean it builds the body and everything."

"Polly," I said gently, "the argument is a fallacy. *Exercise is good* is an unqualified generalization. For instance, if you have heart disease, exercise is bad, not good. Many people are ordered by their doctors *not* to exercise. You must *qualify* the generalization. You must say exercise is *usually* good, or exercise is good *for most people*. Otherwise you have committed a *Dicto Simpliciter*. Do you see?"

"No," she confessed. "But this is marvy. Do more! Do more!"

"It will be better if you stop tugging at my sleeve," I told her, and when she desisted, I continued. "Next we take up a fallacy called Hasty Generalization. Listen carefully: You can't speak French. I can't speak French. Petey Burch can't speak French. I must therefore conclude that nobody at the University of Minnesota can speak French."

"Really?" inquired Polly, amazed. "*Nobody?*"

I hid my exasperation. "Polly, it's a fallacy. The generalization is reached too hastily. There are too few instances to support such a conclusion."

"Know any more fallacies?" she asked breathlessly. "This is more fun than dancing even."

I fought off a wave of despair. I was getting nowhere with this girl, absolutely nowhere. Still, I am nothing if not persistent. I continued. "Next comes *Post Hoc*. Listen to this: Let's not take Bill on our picnic. Every time we take him out with us, it rains."

"I know somebody just like that," she exclaimed. "A girl back home—Eula Becker, her name is. It never fails. Every time we take her on a picnic—"

"Polly," I said sharply, "it's a fallacy. Eula Becker doesn't *cause* the rain. She has no connection with the rain. You are guilt of *Post Hoc* if you blame Eula Becker."

"I'll never do it again," she promised contritely. "Are you mad at me?"

I sighed deeply. "No, Polly, I'm not mad."

"Then tell me some more fallacies."

"All right. Let's go on to Contradictory Premises."

"Yes, let's," she chirped, blinking her eyes happily.

Frowning, I plunged ahead. "Here's an example of Contradictory Premises: If God can do anything, can He make a stone so heavy that He won't be able to lift it?"

"Of course," she replied promptly.

"But if he can do anything, He can lift the stone," I pointed out.

"Yeah," she said thoughtfully. "Well, then I guess He can't make the stone."

"But He can do anything," I reminded her.

She scratched her pretty, empty head. "I'm all confused," she admitted.

"Of course you are. Because when the premises of an argument contradict each other, there can be no argument. If there is an irresistible force, there can be no immovable object. If there is an immovable object, there can be no irresistible force. Get it?"

"Tell me some more of this keen stuff," she said eagerly.

I consulted my watch. "I think we'd better call it a night. I'll take you home now, and you go over all the things you've learned. We'll have another session tomorrow night."

I deposited her at the girls' dormitory, she assured me that she had had a perfectly terrif evening, and I went glumly to my room. Petey lay snoring in his bed, the raccoon coat huddled like a great hairy beast at his feet. For a moment I considered waking him and telling him that he could have his girl back. It seemed clear that my project was doomed to failure. The girl simply had a logic-proof head.

But then I reconsidered. I had wasted one evening; I might as well waste another. Who knew? Maybe somewhere in the extinct crater of her mind, a few embers still smoldered. Maybe somehow I could fan them into flame. Admittedly it was not a prospect fraught with hope, but I decided to give it one more try.

Seated under the oak the next evening, I said, "Our first fallacy tonight is called *Ad Misericordiam*."

She quivered with delight.

"Listen closely," I said. "A man applies for a job. When the boss asks him what his qualifications are, he replies that he has a wife and six children at home, the wife is a helpless cripple, the children have nothing to eat, no clothes to wear, no shoes on their feet, there are no beds in the house, no coal in the cellar, and winter is coming."

A tear rolled down each of Polly's pink cheeks. "Oh, this is awful, awful," she sobbed.

"Yes, it's awful," I agreed, "but it's no argument. The man never answered the boss's question about his qualifications. Instead he appealed to the boss's sympathy. He committed the fallacy of *Ad Misericordiam*. Do you understand?"

"Have you got a handkerchief?" she blubbered.

I handed her a handkerchief and tried to keep from screaming while she wiped her eyes. "Next," I said in a carefully controlled tone, "we shall discuss False Analogy. Here's an example: Students should be allowed to look at their textbooks during examinations. After all, surgeons have X rays to guide them during an operation, lawyers have briefs to guide them during a trial, carpenters have blueprints to guide them when they are constructing a house. Why, then, shouldn't students be allowed to look at their textbooks during an examination?"

"There now," she said enthusiastically, "is the most marvy idea I've heard in years."

"Polly," I said testily, "the argument is all wrong. Doctors, lawyers, and carpenters aren't taking a test to see how much they have learned, but the students are. The situations are altogether different, and you can't draw an analogy between them."

"I still think it's a good idea," said Polly.

"Nuts," I muttered. Doggedly I pressed on. "Next we'll try Hypothesis Contrary to Fact."

"Sounds yummy," was Polly's reaction.

"Listen: If Madame Curie had not happened to leave a photographic plate on a drawer with a chunk of pitchblende, the world today would not know about radium."

"True, true," said Polly, nodding her head. "Did you see the movie? Oh, it just knocked me out. That Walter Pidgeon is so dreamy. I mean he fractures me."

"If you can forget Mr. Pidgeon for a moment," I said coldly, "I would like to point out that the statement is a fallacy. Maybe Madame Curie would have discovered radium at some later date. Maybe somebody else would have discovered it. Maybe any number of things would have happened. You can't start with a hypothesis that is not true and then draw any supportable conclusions from it."

"They ought to put Walter Pidgeon in more pictures," said Polly. "I hardly ever see him anymore."

One more chance, I decided. But just one more. There is a limit to what flesh and blood can bear. "The next fallacy is called Poisoning the Well."

"How cute!" she gurgled.

"Two men are having a debate. The first one gets up and says, 'My opponent is a notorious liar. You can't believe a word that he is going to say.' Now, Polly, think. Think hard. What is wrong?"

I watched her closely as she knit her creamy brow in concentration. Suddenly a glimmer of intelligence—the first I had seen—came into her eyes. "It's not fair," she said with indignation. "It's not a bit fair. What chance has the second man got if the first man calls him a liar before he even begins talking?"

"Right!" I cried exultantly. "One hundred per cent right. It's not fair. The first man had *poisoned the well* before anybody could drink from it. He had hamstrung his opponent before he could even start. Polly, I'm proud of you."

"Pshaw," she murmured, blushing with pleasure.

"You see, my dear, these things aren't so hard. All you have to do is concentrate. Think—examine—evaluate. Come now, let's review everything we have learned."

"Fire away," she said with an airy wave of her hand.

Heartened by the knowledge that Polly was not altogether a cretin, I began a long patient review of all I had told her. Over and over again I cited instances, pointed out flaws, kept hammering away without letup. It was like digging a tunnel. At first everything was work, sweat, and darkness. I had no idea when I would reach the light, or even *if* I would. But I persisted. I pounded and clawed and scraped, and finally I was rewarded. I saw a chink of light. And then the chink got bigger and the sun came pouring in and all was bright.

Five grueling nights this took, but it was worth it. I had made a logician out of Polly; I had taught her to think. My job was done. She was worthy of me at last. She was a fit wife for me, a proper hostess for my many mansions, a suitable mother for my well-heeled children.

It must not be thought that I was not without love for this girl. Quite the contrary. Just as Pygmalion loved the perfect woman he had fashioned, so I loved mine. I determined to acquaint her with my feelings at our very next meeting. The time had come to change our relationship from academic to romantic.

"Polly," I said when next we sat beneath our oak, "tonight we will not discuss fallacies."

"Aw, gee," she said, disappointed.

"My dear," I said, favoring her with a smile, "we have now spent five evenings together. We have got along splendidly. It is clear that we are well matched."

"Hasty Generalization," said Polly brightly.

"I beg your pardon," said I.

"Hasty Generalization," she repeated. "How can you say that we are well matched on the basis of only five dates?"

I chuckled with amusement. The dear child had learned her lessons well.

"My dear," I said, patting her hand in a tolerant manner, "five dates is plenty. After all, you don't have to eat a whole cake to know that it's good."

"False Analogy," said Polly promptly. "I'm not a cake. I'm a girl."

I chucked with somewhat less amusement. The dear child had learned her lessons perhaps too well. I decided to change tactics. Obviously the best approach was a simple, strong, direct declaration of love. I paused for a moment while my massive brain chose the proper words. Then I began:

"Polly, I love you. You are the whole world to me, and the moon and the stars and the constellations of outer space. Please, my darling, say that you will go steady with me, for if you will not, life will be meaningless. I will languish. I will refuse my meals. I will wander the face of the earth, a shambling, hollow-eyed hulk."

There, I thought, folding my arms, that ought to do it.

"*Ad Misericordiam*," said Polly.

I ground my teeth. I was not Pygmalion; I was Frankenstein, and my monster had me by the throat. Frantically I fought back the tide of panic surging through me. At all costs, I had to keep cool.

"Well, Polly," I said, forcing a smile, "you certainly have learned your fallacies."

"You're darn right," she said with a vigorous nod.

"And who taught them to you, Polly?"

"You did."

"That's right. So you do owe me something, don't you, my dear? If I hadn't come along, you never would have learned about fallacies."

"Hypothesis Contrary to Fact," she said instantly.

I dashed perspiration from my brow. "Polly," I croaked, "you mustn't take all these things so literally. I mean this is just classroom stuff. You know that the things you learn in school don't have anything to do with life.

"*Dicto Simpliciter*," she said, wagging her finger at me playfully.

That did it. I leaped to my feet, bellowing like a bull. "Will you or will you not go steady with me?"

"I will not," she replied.

"Why not?" I demanded.

"Because this afternoon I promised Petey Burch that I would go steady with him."

I reeled back, overcome by the infamy of it. After he promised, after he made a deal, after he shook my hand! "The rat!" I shrieked, kicking up great chunks of turf. "You can't go with him, Polly. He's a liar. He's a cheat. He's a rat."

"Poisoning the Well," said Polly, "and stop shouting. I think shouting must be a fallacy, too."

With an immense effort of will, I modulated my voice. "All right," I said, "You're a logician. Let's look at this thing logically. How could you choose Petey Burch over me? Look at me—a brilliant student, a tremendous intellectual, a man with an assured future. Look at Petey—a knothead, a jitterbug, a guy who'll never know where his next meal is coming from. Can you give me one logical reason why you should go steady with Petey Burch?"

"I certainly can," declared Polly. "He's got a raccoon coat."

VOCABULARY

1. Define the following words as Shulman uses them in this selection: perspicacious, astute, gamy, tryst, cretin, premises, infamy.
2. If you are unfamiliar with any other words in this selection, check them in a dictionary and define them in your own words.
3. Although the point of this essay is timeless, what slang* words date its dialogue?

CONTENT

1. Shulman once advised would-be writers to "marry money." How is this same tone apparent in his essay?
2. The narrator defines eight logical fallacies. Then he gives examples from his viewpoint and from Polly's. Give an example of your own for each of the fallacies.
3. Have you ever volunteered to help someone who really did not want your help? What were the results?
4. Why did Petey want a raccoon coat so badly? Is some type of clothing or some brand name a symbol of status on your campus? Why?

RHETORIC

1. What do you think Shulman is trying to accomplish by his repetition in the two opening paragraphs?
2. Polly's diction* conjures up a vivid picture of her. Describe her, supporting your answer with examples.

---

* Definitions of all terms marked with an asterisk may be found in the Glossary.

3. Who were Pygmalion and Frankenstein? What is the effect of contrasting these two characters?
4. What techniques does Shulman use to make this a humorous essay?

READING AND WRITING SUGGESTIONS

1. Taking as your thesis "Officious people often get their comeuppance," write an essay citing examples to support the thesis.
2. Read the legend of *Pygmalion,* or its more modern version, *My Fair Lady*. In an essay discuss how the desire to create an ideal human being frequently ends in frustrated disappointment. Use examples.

THE AMERICAN TRADITION OF WINNING

George A. Plimpton

George A. Plimpton (1927–) was born in New York City and educated at Harvard and King's College, Cambridge. While an undergraduate he was editor of The Lampoon, *Harvard's humor magazine. Plimpton has held a number of positions, most of them centered around his two primary interests—writing and sports. His works include* Out of My League, Paper Lion, *and* One For the Record: The Inside Story of Hank Aaron's Chase for the Home-Run Record. *He has also authored, with William Kronick, a number of television scripts. The distinguishing feature of Plimpton's writing is that he bases it on first-hand experience of what it feels like to be a participant. He fought in a bullfight; stayed in the ring three rounds with Archie Moore, the then light heavyweight champion; lost a tennis match to Pancho Gonzales; pitched to eight players in a post-season all-star game at Yankee Stadium; and played in an exhibition football game with the Detroit Lions. The following essay shows some of his insights about winning.*

Involvement with sports, as participant or observer in the stands, is supposed to provide a healthy uplift . . . largely by identification with winning. Chief Justice Warren once offered a pertinent observation: "At the breakfast table," he said, "I always open the newspaper to the sports page first. The sports page records people's accomplishments. The front page has nothing but man's failures."

I have never been comfortable with that comment—since in fact the sports page lists far more failures, losers, and also-rans than any other page in a newspaper short of the stock market listings on a Black Friday.

The reason for this is obvious enough: for every winner there is a loser; in the case of tournaments, with rafts of contestants entered, only one winner can emerge. Since there are so many losers, sport has not been a release at the breakfast table, but a type of daily agony. The fan looks at the paper in the morning and he probably starts off his day (unless he possesses the magnanimity of a Chief Justice) by feeling punk. Imagine being a Washington Capitals hockey fan. At this writing the team has lost 26 straight games!

The problem, of course, is that these things are taken very seriously. It was not always so. Back in the 1870s, in the infancy of football, President White of Cornell once rather testily denied the request of an undergraduate football squad to travel to the Midwest to play a Michigan team. "I will not permit 30 men to travel 400 miles," he said, "merely to agitate a bag of wind." One can scarcely imagine what the good president would have said, and the height to which his eyebrows would have arched, had his undergraduate student body turned up with the team and requested to travel out there simply to *watch* a bag of wind being agitated.

Since then a near-symbiotic relationship has developed between the player and the fan in the stands watching him—that phrase, "I just die with the Chiefs (or the Rams, or the Mets, or whatever)" . . . the fan's forefinger raised to denote that his team (and he) are Number One, the "we did it, we did it," and the self-satisfied smiles on the faces of people coming down the stadium ramps after their teams have won. We seem to require the personal assurance of an idol's triumph in the highly dramatic situation that sports provides—and a loser too, someone to jeer at and feel superior to . . . the substitute scapegoat for the tyrant down the hall who has the key to the executive washroom.

All of this is probably natural enough, and understandable—but then the fan in his intensity for a win begins to take on the same desperate excesses that sometimes the athlete must indulge in to play at his best. His team loses and he crumples up the sports page and throws it at the family cat. In the stands the fan becomes as competitive as a man striving for a championship.

Unfortunately, the champion is so often driven by a set of impulses and persuasions that are not necessarily desirable or attractive. Billie Jean King, who drove herself to championships with 40/200 vision, a bad set of knees and a famous tendency to eat too much ice cream, has said that many topflight tennis players have never become true winners because they are *afraid* to be . . . to accept the ugliness of those responsibilities—not only the grim determination to become the champion, but also the enmity and jealousy that comes with attaining the top. Her close pal Rosemary Casals called off their friendship ostensibly because she could not accept the idea of being friendly with someone whose position she coveted.

Sad and interesting—friendships disbanded, everything put aside to win. But then surely it is the athlete's prerogative to do so: the choice is personal; reputation, livelihood, the future, and so forth are obvious determinants.

It is difficult, however, to understand how such intensity applies to a *fan* (unless he has bet his wife and that family cat on the outcome of a game). Yet the honest emphasis on supporting a winner has become an obsession to such a point (witness the Soviet hockey series in which the visitors' anthem was booed, obscenities in Russian held aloft on signs, objects thrown and generally a type of bellicosity in the air that awed witnesses felt was almost palpable) that editorial writers surveying the national character, get fidgety and begin worrying once again about the win-at-all-cost grip that seizes American fans and so often makes them louts.

VOCABULARY

1. Define the following words as Plimpton uses them in this essay: magnanimity, symbiotic, enmity, prerogative, bellicosity, palpable.
2. If you are unfamiliar with any other words in this essay, check them in a dictionary and define them in your own words.

CONTENT

1. Suppose at a Super Bowl game, you laughed and loudly commented about people's getting so excited and spending so much time and money "simply to watch a bag of wind being agitated." How do you think the fans would react?
2. Plimpton describes three approaches of fans of football games and similar contests. What are they?

3. Which of these approaches to sports do you take? Cite examples in your answer.
4. What does a person taking each approach win and what does he or she lose?
5. Vince Lombardi is reported to have said, "Show me a *good* loser and I'll show you a loser." Do you think that developing the ability to deal with losing (failure) destroys a person's "competitive edge"? Why or why not?
6. Would Plimpton agree with Lombardi's statement? Do you? Explain.

RHETORIC

1. Is this essay's title* specific? Does it foretell that you will be reading about sports? Do you think Plimpton intended it to refer to other areas as well? Explain.
2. Plimpton uses many examples in this essay. Are most of them positive or are most negative? Do you think he slanted* his presentation? If so, how?
3. Plimpton uses both colloquialisms* and abstract words*; find two examples of each. What is the effect of combining these two types of diction* in the same essay?
4. How does the essay open? How does it close? Do these rhetorical devices contribute to your understanding of Plimpton's thesis*?

READING AND WRITING SUGGESTIONS

1. Choose one of the following statements as a thesis: (a) "Show me a *good* loser and I'll show you a loser." (b) "It's more important to develop the grace and style to deal with failure than to win." Then write a brief essay citing examples to support the thesis you chose.
2. Read a book like Dan Jenkins' *Semi-Tough*. Write an essay citing examples to develop this thesis: "Satisfying fans so they will continue to buy the tickets often abuses and brutalizes players."

---

* Definitions of all terms marked with an asterisk may be found in the Glossary.

MASCULINITY: REAL AND PUT ON

Harold Rosenberg

Harold Rosenberg (1906–1978), American author, educator, and art critic, was born in New York City. He held a number of positions during his career including national art editor of the American Guild Series, professor of art at the University of Chicago, lecturer at the University of California and at Princeton University, and art critic of The New Yorker *magazine. Rosenberg is best known for his books on art criticism. He was also a contributor to literary and art periodicals and popular magazines including* Partisan Review, The New Yorker *and* Esquire. *The selection below is from his book,* Discovering the Present: Three Decades in Art, Culture, and Politics, *published in 1973.*

Societies of the past have admired different personifications of the manly virtues: the warrior, the patriarch, the sage; the lover, the seducer; Zeus the Thunderer, Jehovah the Lawgiver.

In America, masculinity is associated primarily with the outdoors, and with such outdoor trades as cattledriving, railroading, whaling, and trucking. The outdoor type is presumed to possess masculine character traits: toughness, resourcefulness, love of being alone, fraternity with animals, and attractiveness to women and the urge to abandon them. To the man of the open spaces is also attributed the ultimate mark of manliness, the readiness to die.

From the outdoors America derives the boots, lumber jackets and shirts, sailor's caps, pipes, and guns that are its paraphernalia of masculinity. Oddly enough, in the United States, military and police uniforms do not confer masculinity, as they do among Cossacks and Hussars. One can as readily imagine women in our army uniform as men. To prove that he was all man, General Patton had to augment his battle costume with a pearl-handled revolver. (It is true, however, that he wrote poetry and may have felt the need to overcome this handicap.)

As to hair, masculinity is ambivalent. Long hair belongs to the style of frontier scouts and trappers, the most male of men. Yet "longhairs" is the name applied to intellectuals, a breed always suspected of sexual inauthenticity. Beards used to be a material evidence of maleness; today they are as frequently an appurtenance of masquerade.

In the last century the outdoors represented genuine hazards. It took self-reliance, identifiable with masculinity (though the pioneer mother had it, too), to venture very far from the farm or town.

Today there are still risky occupations—piloting spaceships, handling nuclear substances—but these trades have become increasingly technical and depersonalized. As for the rugged outdoors, it is used chiefly for sports; and a vacation at a ranch or ski lodge, or shooting lions in Kenya, is about as hazardous as a trip to the Riviera.

The outdoors, representing once-hostile nature, has been transformed into a stage set. Masculinity in the American sense has thus lost its locale and, perhaps, its reason for being. On the neonlighted lonesome prairie, masculinity is a matter of certain traditional costume details: the cowboy hat, jeans, and guitar. It has become clear that the traditional traits of the man's man (and the ladies' man) can be put on, too. One *plays* manliness, with or without dark goggles.

Big-game hunters, mountain climbers, horsemen, and other representative male types are actors in a charade of nostalgia. Old masculine pursuits, like baseball or wrestling, when carried on at night under the glare of fluorescent tubes, come to resemble spectacles on television and wind up in the living room. In the epoch of the picture window, outdoors and indoors have lost their separateness.

In modern mass societies the uniforms of all kinds of cults compete with one another. Masculinity is one of these cults, and to create an impression the practitioner of maleness must stand out in a crowd. Persons with other interests are not disposed to make an issue of their sex. Only psychiatrists and sociologists complain that boys and girls today look alike and are often mistaken for each other. Even tough adolescents, like members of big-city gangs, don't mind if their girls wear the same shirts and jeans as the men. All are more concerned with identifying themselves as outsiders than as males and females.

Masculinity today is a myth that has turned into a comedy. A ten-gallon hat still seems to bestow upon its wearer the old male attributes of taciturnity, resourcefulness, courage, and love of solitude. At the same time, the virility of the cowboy and the truck driver, like that of the iceman of yesterday, is a joke that everyone sees through.

A person uncertain of his sexual identity dresses up in boots, bandanna, and riding breeches not so much to fool the public as to parade his ambiguity. Those who have gone over the line may advertise their desires for male company by wearing a beard in addition to sheepskins. Women can be masculine too, of course, in the degree necessary to make them irresistible to feminine men.

Hemingway, who constantly kept the issue of masculinity alive in his writings, flaunted both the look of the outdoor man and his presumed character qualities of daring, self-detachment, contempt for the overcivilized, and eagerness to court death.

Hemingway's he-man performance was, among other things, a means of combatting the American stereotype of the writer as a sissy. In the United States, the artist and man of ideas have always lived under the threat of having their masculinity impugned. Richard Hofstadter, in his *Anti-Intellectualism in American Life,* lists a dozen instances in which the "stigma of effeminacy" was branded upon intellectuals by political bullies, ranging from Tammany Hall leaders in the nineteenth century, who attacked reformers as "political hermaphrodites," to Communist Party hacks in the 1930s, who denounced independent writers as "scented whores." Evidently, it has always been possible to convince the common man that his intellectual superiors fall short of him in manliness.

To the overhanging charge of being contaminated by a ladylike occupation, Hemingway responded by injecting the romance of masculinity into the making of literature. At least as far as he was concerned, the sexual legitimacy of the male writer was to be put beyond question. Besides lining up with traditional outdoor types, such as bullfighters and deep-sea fishermen, Hemingway's strategy included identification with the new activist male image of the Depression decade: the leather-jacketed revolutionist allied with the peasant and factory worker. One might say that each of his novels originated in a new choice of male makeup.

Unfortunately, demonstrating his own manhood was not enough for Hemingway. He found it necessary to challenge the masculinity of other writers. Like Theodore Roosevelt earlier in the century, he became an instance of the intellectual who slanders intellectuals generally, in the hope of putting himself right with the regular guys. During the Spanish Civil War he forgot himself to the extent of sneering publicly at Leon Trotsky for remaining at his typewriter in Mexico, implying that the former chief of the Red Army lacked the manliness to go to Spain and fight. He, himself, of course, went to Spain to write. In *For Whom the Bell Tolls* he identified himself with the dynamiter Jordan who also shook the earth by his love feats in a sleeping bag.

Thirty years ago not all of Hemingway's contemporaries were convinced that he had established his masculinity through displaying an appetite for violence, sex, and death. In *no thanks*, E. E. Cummings translated Hemingway's romance of maleness back into the daydreams of boyhood. . . .

The post-Hemingway he-man has labored under the handicap of a masculinity that is generally recognized to be a masquerade. The adventurer living dangerously has disintegrated into the tongue-in-cheek élan of James Bond. Neither at work nor at home is maleness any longer endowed with glamour or privilege. The cosmonaut is less a birdman than a specialist minding his signals and dials. The father who has entered into a diapering partnership with his wife has nothing in common with the patriarch. To the public of Norman Mailer (more male?) the outdoor rig (Mailer in sea captain's cap on the jacket of *Advertisements for Myself*) and chronicles of supersex are suspect, both psychologically and as playing to the gallery. It is no secret that a Bogartean toughness with women may represent the opposite of male self-confidence.

The mass media exploit the ambiguity of the male role and the sexual sophistication that goes with the increasing awareness of it. In male comedy teams, one of the partners almost invariably plays the "wife," confident that the audience will know when to smirk. Analysts of mass culture speak of the decline of the American male and of the "masculinity crisis" as topics capable of arousing libidinous responses. The public is given the image of luscious females starving in vain for the attention of men, and of men who, egged on and deprived by frigid seductresses, end by falling into each other's arms.

Masculinity-building is urged, a theme which the media are not slow to adapt for their own purposes. Masculinity is the alfalfa peddled in Marlboro Country. It is the essence of worn leather laced with campfire smoke that provides the aroma of the man of distinction. It also comes in powder form, none genuine without the Shaggy Dog on the wrapping.

To those who resent the fact that their pretension to masculinity is not taken seriously, one means is available for gaining respect: violence. The victim of rape is not inclined to question the virility of her assailant.

The relation between masculinity that has been put into doubt and violence reveals itself most clearly in the recent history of the Civil Rights movement. The black has derived from white America the lesson that physical force is the mark of manhood. White society is "the Man," whose insignia of power are the club, the whip, the bloodhounds. The presence of the Man impeaches the masculinity of the young black and demands that he prove himself. He becomes full grown when he resolves to fight the Man. To confront the Man, the black militant has resurrected the figure of the radical activist of the thirties, the model of Hemingway's he-man, honor-bound to risk his life in physical combat.

An article in *The New York Times Magazine* on the Black Panthers is illustrated by photographs of its two leaders. Both wear the traditional leather jackets and berets of the Left fighters of thirty years ago—these could be photographs of two Lincoln Brigade volunteers. A statement by one of the Panthers touches the philosophical essence of the romantic conception of masculinity: to be a man one must dare to die. "The ghetto black," said Bobby Seale, "isn't afraid to stand up to the cops, because he already lives with violence. He expects to die any day."

In our culture all human attributes tend to be over-defined and become a basis of self-consciousness. The behavioral sciences collaborate with the mass media in making a man anxious about his sex status; both then provide him with models of aggressiveness by which to correct his deficiencies. Yet the present uneasiness about masculinity, coupled with theatrical devices for attaining it, may be more harmful than any actual curtailment of manliness discovered by researchers and editorialists. The real damage may lie in the remedy rather than the ailment, since the desire to have one's masculinity acknowledged may lead, as we have seen, to absurd postures and acts of force. It is hard to believe that Americans would be worse off by becoming more gentle. Nor that mildness in manners and social relations would make them less manly. In the real world nothing is altogether what it is. True maleness is never without its vein of femininity. The Greeks understood this and made it the theme of their tales of sexual metamorphosis, the remarkable account of Hercules, of all men, taking on temporarily the character of a woman and wearing women's clothes. Total masculinity is an ideal of the frustrated, not a fact of biology. With the cult of masculinity put aside, maleness might have a better chance to develop in the United States.

VOCABULARY

1. Define the following words as Rosenberg uses them in this essay: personifications, paraphernalia, augment, appurtenance, taciturnity, élan, libidinous.
2. If you are unfamiliar with any other words in this essay, check them in a dictionary and define them in your own words.

CONTENT

1. How does Rosenberg define masculinity? maleness?
2. According to Rosenberg, overconcern with developing masculinity interferes with developing maleness. Do you agree? Why or why not?
3. Rosenberg maintains that "Persons with other interests are not disposed to make an issue of their sex." Would he agree with Shakespeare's "Methinks he doth protest too much"? Or the more colloquial, "If you've got it you don't have to flaunt it"? Explain.
4. Do you agree that violence is one means some people use for gaining respect when "their pretension to masculinity is not taken seriously"? What other means might people use?

5. Rosenberg devotes a lot of space to Hemingway. What examples does he give of Hemingway's attempts to prove his manhood? What does he think Hemingway's reasons or motives were?

6. Rosenberg gives various examples of how the pressures toward machismo force the American male to act. Review Plimpton's "The American Tradition of Winning" (page 64). Would Plimpton agree with Rosenberg's examples? What other examples might Plimpton suggest?

RHETORIC

1. What is Rosenberg's thesis*?

2. Rosenberg uses many examples but they fall roughly into six types. The first consists of historical examples. Identify the other five types.

3. Do all of Rosenberg's examples support his thesis*? Do you think that Rosenberg slants* or overstates his case? Defend your answer.

4. Give some examples from your own experience that are contrary to Rosenberg's generalization.

5. Rosenberg coins a number of metaphors* like "Masculinity is the alfalfa peddled in Marlboro Country."

   a. Interpret this statement. Find at least three other metaphors* or similes* and interpret them.

   b. In your opinion, what does such figurative language* contribute to the information and attitude Rosenberg seeks to transmit?

6. An *ad hominem* attack* is a method of assailing a person's character rather than his or her ideas. Could Rosenberg be accused of using this method in regard to Hemingway? Defend your answer.

7. Rosenberg uses a paradox* in his last paragraph. Identify this paradox* and explain what it means.

READING AND WRITING SUGGESTIONS

1. Consider this generalization: "For any characteristic, worrying too much about the outward signs gets in the way of the real thing." Apply this generalization to one of these topics or a similar one:

---

*Definitions of all terms marked with an asterisk may be found in the Glossary.

Femininity—Real and Put On; Patriotism—Real and Put On; Religion—Real and Put On. Write an essay supporting your generalization with specific examples.

2. Read an essay or book of social criticism like Mirra Komarovsky's *Dilemmas of Masculinity: A Study of College Youth* or Natalie Gittleson's *Dominus: A Woman Looks at Men's Lives.* Write an essay on the thesis "Peer group pressure causes us to do many things: some true to our inner nature and some untrue." Use examples of behavior you observe in yourself and in your friends.

ACRES AND PAINS

S. J. Perelman

S. J. Perelman (1904–1979), the widely read humorist, was born in Brooklyn and educated at Brown University. Perelman published articles in such magazines as the Saturday Evening Post, The New Yorker, *and* Holiday. *He won the New York Film Critics Award and the Academy of Motion Picture Arts and Sciences Award for the best screenplay of 1956 for* Around the World in Eighty Days. *Among his best-known books are* Acres and Pains, The Swiss Family Perelman, *and* Vinegar Puss. *In this essay from* The Most of S. J. Perelman *(1958), Perelman satirizes some romantic fantasies about country living.*

There is nothing like a farm, a mountain lodge or a seashore bungalow to bring out the latent mechanic in a man. Once the deed is filed and he stands alone at last with his utilities, he is Cortez on a peak in Darien. Of course, if your name is Cortez and you live on a peak in Darien, Connecticut, your problem is simple. You call in a plumber from Danbury and forget about it. I couldn't; when I returned to the soil, I had a ten-cent screwdriver and the mechanical skill of a turtle. Today, thanks to unremitting study, I can change a fuse so deftly that it plunges the entire county into darkness. The neighbors call me "the boy Steinmetz" and things like that (the other things are shorter). The power company has offered me as high as fifteen thousand dollars a year to stay out of my own cellar.

The other night, for example, I had invited some guests to dinner at Hysteria Hall and we were grouped around the groaning board (the board was groaning because one end was supported by a chair until I could replace the missing leg). Halfway through the meal, a strident clanking began under our very feet, as though somebody were striking the furnace with a length of chain. I raised my voice to drown it out, but I could see my audience was wool-gathering. At first I suspected my wife, who will resort to the most shameless devices to spoil an anecdote. Then I realized she was flinching in concert with the company. The noise redoubled. "Sounds like chains, doesn't it?" I stammered desperately. "You know, this house was a station on the Underground Railway, and there's an old legend—"

I was interrupted by a bubbling effect, as of water seeping through a dining-room floor, and looked down to find an inch or two of moisture lapping at my oxfords. Before I could explain that we had chosen a low, marshy situation to remind us of the English lake country, my wife rose through a jet of live steam like the devil in *Faust* and placed a monkey wrench beside my plate. I pretended it was part of the meal, a pantomime which threw my guests into gales of silence, and slunk off into the cellar.

As one who flunked trigonometry four times, it took me only a moment to detect the source of the trouble. That little square business on the electric pump—I forget just what they call it—had worked off. This in turn disengaged the stopcock or the bushing (it was a bit too dark to tell which) in such a way that the hot water was feeding into the coal bin instead of the storage tank, or flange. The whole thing was clearly the work of a master criminal, perhaps Professor Moriarty himself, who had further anticipated my movements and laid a carpet sweeper athwart the stairs. I sidestepped neatly, but my head encountered a low rafter and I sustained a bruise roughly the size of a robin's egg; I speak of this with certainty as there chanced to be a robin's egg lying on a nearby shelf. Luckily, I am as tough as nails, and picking myself up at the bottom of the steps, I set to work. By exerting a slight leverage, I succeeded in prying off the gasket, or outer jacket of the pump, exactly as you would a baked potato. (I describe this simply so that even the layman can understand.) This gave me room to poke around the innards with a sharp stick. I cleaned the pump thoroughly, laid all the different wheels and cams on a board where the plumber could find them and, as a final precaution, opened the windows to allow the water to drain off down the slope.

On the way upstairs, I found my passage blocked by a jug of peach brandy, and after some difficulty managed to squeeze past it. Either it was stuffy in the basement or I had given too freely of my strength, for when I rejoined the party, I felt dizzy. My wife said later it wasn't so much the bric-a-brac I smashed as the language I used. It cost me a quart of Bellodgia and a star sapphire to square the rap, to say nothing of a new electric pump. However, the old one was nearly played out. Anybody could have seen it with half an eye—and I had that, Jack.

VOCABULARY

1. Define the following words as Perelman uses them in his essay: latent, unremitting, wool-gathering, flange, athwart.
2. If you are unfamiliar with any other words in this essay, check them in a dictionary and then define them in your own words.

CONTENT

1. What generalization about country living does Perelman make in his essay?
2. How might you compare Perelman's treatment of the narrator in his essay with Shulman's treatment of his narrator in "Love Is a Fallacy" (page 54)?
3. What obstacle does the narrator encounter on his way up the stairs from the cellar and how does he deal with this obstacle?

RHETORIC

1. What does Perelman's title* suggest about his essay's content and style*?
2. What techniques does Perelman use to elicit humor? Were you amused by the essay? Explain.
3. Explain Perelman's references to Cortez and Steinmetz. (Check the biographical notes in your dictionary if you need help.)

READING AND WRITING SUGGESTIONS

1. Read several selections from Erma Bombeck's *The Grass Is Always Greener Over the Septic Tank.* Write an essay using examples to show what you see as the joys or problems of suburban living.
2. Propose a generalization about city living. Using Perelman's approach, write an essay using examples to support your generalization.

---

*Definitions of all terms marked with an asterisk may be found in the Glossary.

ANALYSIS

Analysis is a means of examining a subject by breaking it down into parts and studying the relationships among those parts. One of the most efficient ways of examining the nature of the United States government, for example, is to divide it into its three main branches—the executive, the judicial, and the legislative—and to examine the functions of each branch, exploring the system of checks and balances that defines the relationships among the branches.

Process analysis is a special form of analysis that shows how to perform an action, how something works, or how something happens by presenting the process in sequential steps. Consider, for example, a technical manual that shows how to repair a complex piece of machinery. The manual shows technicians how to dismantle each section of the machine in order to reach the faulty part, how to make the repair correctly, and how to reassemble the machine. The important elements here—as in all process analysis used for technical purposes—are that the steps be presented in the correct order and that each necessary step be included and precisely described so that the process can be clearly understood and accurately performed.

Writers of essays sometimes adhere strictly to sequence in the same way that writers of technical manuals do. But remember that essays are, by definition, personal reflections on a subject. If their purpose requires it, therefore, essay writers sometimes use process analysis in a way that is less dry and rigid, presenting only the broad outline of the sequence they are describing.

BULL FIGHTING

Ernest Hemingway

Ernest Hemingway (1899–1961) began writing as a newspaper reporter shortly after his graduation from high school. His life was full of action and adventure. He enjoyed big game hunting and sport fishing and participated in three wars—World War I, the Spanish Civil War, and World War II. This aspect of his life is reflected in the subject matter of many of his works and in the emphasis on physical bravery that pervades his writing. His many books include For Whom the Bell Tolls, The Sun Also Rises, A Moveable Feast, *and* The Old Man and the Sea. *In the following essay, Hemingway presents the sequence of events that comprises a classic bull fight.*

The bull ring or Plaza de Toros was a big, tawny brick amphitheatre standing at the end of a street in an open field. The yellow and red Spanish flag was floating over it. Carriages were driving up and people getting out of buses. There was a great crowd of beggars around the entrance. Men were selling water out of big terra cotta water bottles. Kids sold fans, canes, roasted salted almonds in paper spills, fruit and slabs of ice cream. The crowd was gay and cheerful but all intent on pushing toward the entrance. Mounted civil guards with patent leather cocked hats and carbines slung over their backs sat their horses like statues, and the crowd flowed through.

Inside they all stood around in the bull ring, talking and looking up in the grandstand at the girls in the boxes. Some of the men had field glasses in order to look better. We found our seats and the crowd began to leave the ring and get into the rows of concrete seats. The ring was circular—that sounds foolish, but a boxing ring is square—with a sand floor. Around it was a red board fence—just high enough for a man to be able to vault over it. Between the board fence, which is called the barrera, and the first row of seats ran a narrow alley way. Then came the seats which were just like a football stadium except that around the top ran a double circle of boxes.

Every seat in the amphitheatre was full. The arena was cleared. Then on the far side of the arena out of the crowd, four heralds in medieval costume stood up and blew a blast on their trumpets. The band crashed out, and from the entrance on the far side of the ring four horsemen in black velvet with ruffs around their necks rode out into the white glare of the arena. The people on the sunny side were baking in the heat and fanning themselves. The whole sol side was a flicker of fans.

Behind the four horsemen came the procession of the bull fighters. They had been all formed in ranks in the entrance way ready to march out, and as the music started they came. In the front rank walked the three espadas or toreros, who would have charge of the killing of the six bulls of the afternoon.

They came walking out in heavily brocaded yellow and black costumes, the familiar "toreador" suit, heavy with gold embroidery, cape, jacket, shirt and collar, knee breeches, pink stockings, and low pumps. Always at bull fights afterwards the incongruity of those pink stockings used to strike me. Just behind the three principals—and after your first bull fight you do not look at their costumes but their faces—marched the teams or cuadrillas. They are dressed in the same way but not as gorgeously as the matadors.

Back of the teams ride the picadors. Big, heavy, brown-faced men in wide flat hats, carrying lances like long window poles. They are astride horses that make Spark Plug look as trim and sleek as a King's Plate winner. Back of the pics come the gaily harnessed mule teams and the red-shirted monos or bull ring servants.

The bull fighters march in across the sand to the president's box. They march with easy professional stride, swinging along, not in the least theatrical except for their clothes. They all have the easy grace and slight slouch of the professional athlete. From their faces they might be major league ball players. They salute the president's box and then spread out along the barrera, exchanging their heavy brocaded capes for the fighting capes that have been laid along the red fence by the attendants.

We leaned forward over the barrera. Just below us the three matadors of the afternoon were leaning against the fence talking. One lighted a cigaret. He was a short, clear-skinned gypsy, Gitanillo, in a wonderful gold brocaded jacket, his short pigtail sticking out under his black cocked hat.

"He's not very fancy," a young man in a straw hat, with obviously American shoes, who sat on my left, said.

"But he sure knows bulls, that boy. He's a great killer."

"You're an American, aren't you?" asked Mike.

"Sure," the boy grinned. "But I know this gang. That's Gitanillo. You want to watch him. The kid with the chubby face is Chicuelo. They say he doesn't really like bull fighting, but the town's crazy about him. The man next to him is Villalta. He's the great one."

I had noticed Villalta. He was straight as a lance and walked like a young wolf. He was talking and smiling at a friend who leaned over the barrera. Upon his tanned cheekbone was a big patch of gauze held on with adhesive tape.

"He got gored last week at Malaga," said the American.

The American, whom later we were to learn to know and love as the Gin Bottle King, because of a great feat of arms performed at an early hour of the morning with a container of Mr. Gordon's celebrated product as his sole weapon in one of the four most dangerous situations I have ever seen, said: "The show's going to begin."

Out in the arena the picadors had galloped their decrepit horses around the ring, sitting straight and stiff in their rocking chair saddles. Now all but three had ridden out of the ring. These three were huddled against the red painted fence of the barrera. Their horses backed against the fence, one eye bandaged, their lances at rest.

In rode two of the marshals in the velvet jackets and white ruffs. They galloped up to the president's box, swerved and saluted, doffing their hats and bowing low. From the box an object came hurtling down. One of the marshals caught it in his plumed hat.

"The key to the bull pen," said the Gin Bottle King.

The two horsemen whirled and rode across the arena. One of them tossed the key to a man in torero costume, they both saluted with a wave of their plumed hats, and had gone from the ring. The big gate was shut and bolted. There was no more entrance. The ring was complete.

The crowd had been shouting and yelling. Now it was dead silent. The man with the key stepped toward an iron barred, low, red door and unlocked the great sliding bar. He lifted it and stepped back. The door swung open. The man hid behind it. Inside it was dark.

Then, ducking his head as he came up out of the dark pen, a bull came into the arena. He came out all in a rush, big, black and white, weighing over a ton and moving with a soft gallop. Just as he came out the sun seemed to dazzle him for an instant. He stood as though he were frozen, his great crest of muscle up, firmly planted, his eyes looking around, his horns pointed forward, black and white and sharp as porcupine quills. Then he charged. And as he charged I suddenly saw what bull fighting is all about.

For the bull was absolutely unbelievable. He seemed like some great prehistoric animal, absolutely deadly and absolutely vicious. And he was silent. He charged silently and with a soft galloping rush. When he turned he turned on his four feet like a cat. When he charged the first thing that caught his eye was a picador on one of the wretched horses. The picador dug his spurs into the horse and they galloped away. The bull came on in his rush, refused to be shaken off, and in full gallop crashed into the animal from the side, ignored the horse, drove one of his horns high into the thigh of the picador, and tore him, saddle and all, off the horse's back.

The bull went on without pausing to worry the picador lying on the ground. The next picador was sitting on his horse braced to receive the shock of the charge, his lance ready. The bull hit him sideways on, and horse and rider went high up in the air in a kicking mass and fell across the bull's back. As they came down the bull charged into them. The dough-faced kid, Chicuelo, vaulted over the fence, ran toward the bull and flopped his cape into the bull's face. The bull charged the cape and Chicuelo dodged backwards and had the bull clear in the arena.

Without an instant's hesitation the bull charged Chicuelo. The kid stood his ground, simply swung back on his heels and floated his cape like a ballet dancer's skirt into the bull's face as he passed.

"Olé!"—pronounced Oh-Lay!—roared the crowd.

The bull whirled and charged again. Without moving Chicuelo repeated the performance. His legs rigid, just withdrawing his body from the rush of the bull's horns and floating the cape out with that beautiful swing.

Again the crowd roared. The Kid did this seven times. Each time the bull missed him by inches. Each time he gave the bull a free shot at him. Each time the crowd roared. Then he flopped the cape once at the bull at the finish of a pass, swung it around behind him and walked away from the bull to the barrera.

"He's the boy with the cape all right," said the Gin Bottle King. "That swing he did with the cape's called a Veronica."

The chubby faced Kid who did not like bull fighting and had just done the seven wonderful Veronicas was standing against the fence just below us. His face glistened with sweat in the sun but was almost expressionless. His eyes were looking out across the arena where the bull was standing making up his mind to charge a picador. He was studying the bull because a few minutes later it would be his duty to kill him, and once he went out with his thin, red-hilted sword and his piece of red cloth to kill the bull in the final set it would be him or the bull. There are no drawn battles in bull fighting.

I am not going to describe the rest of that afternoon in detail. It was the first bull fight I ever saw, but it was not the best. The best was in the little town of Pamplona high up in the hills of Navarre, and came weeks later. Up in Pamplona, where they have held six days of bull fighting each year since 1126 A.D., and where the bulls race through the streets of the town each morning at six o'clock with half the town running ahead of them. Pamplona, where every man and boy in town is an amateur bull fighter and where there is an amateur fight each morning that is attended by 20,000 people in which the amateur fighters are all unarmed and there is a casualty list at least equal to a Dublin election. But Pamplona, with the best bull fight and the wild tale of the amateur fights, comes in the second chapter.

I am not going to apologize for bull fighting. It is a survival of the days of the Roman Coliseum. But it does need some explanation. Bull fighting is not a sport. It was never supposed to be. It is a tragedy. A very great tragedy. The tragedy is the death of the bull. It is played in three definite acts.

The Gin Bottle King—who, by the way, does not drink gin—told us a lot of this that first night as we sat in the upstairs room of the little restaurant that made a specialty of roast young suckling pig, roasted on an oak plank and served with a mushroom tortilla and vino rojo. The rest we learned later at the bull fighters' pensione in the Via San Jeronimo, where one of the bull fighters had eyes exactly like a rattlesnake.

Much of it we learned in the sixteen fights we saw in different parts of Spain from San Sebastian to Granada.

At any rate bull fighting is not a sport. It is a tragedy, and it symbolizes the struggle between man and the beasts. There are usually six bulls to a fight. A fight is called a corrida de toros. Fighting bulls are bred like race horses, some of the oldest breeding establishments being several hundred years old. A good bull is worth about $2,000. They are bred for speed, strength and viciousness. In other words a good fighting bull is an absolutely incorrigible bad bull.

Bull fighting is an exceedingly dangerous occupation. In sixteen fights I saw there were only two in which there was no one badly hurt. On the other hand it is very remunerative. A popular espada gets $5,000 for his afternoon's work. An unpopular espada though may not get $500. Both run the same risks. It is a good deal like Grand Opera for the really great matadors except they run the chance of being killed every time they cannot hit high C.

No one at any time in the fight can approach the bull at any time except directly from the front. That is where the danger comes. There are also all sorts of complicated passes that must be done with the cape, each requiring as much technique as a champion billiard player. And underneath it all is the necessity for playing the old tragedy in the absolutely custom bound, law-laid-down way. It must all be done gracefully, seemingly effortlessly and always with dignity. The worst criticism the Spaniards ever make of a bull fighter is that his work is "vulgar."

The three absolute acts of the tragedy are first the entry of the bull when the picadors receive the shock of his attacks and attempt to protect their horses with their lances. Then the horses go out and the second act is the planting of the banderillos. This is one of the most interesting and difficult parts but among the easiest for a new bull fight fan to appreciate in technique. The banderillos are three-foot, gaily colored darts with a small fish hook prong in the end. The man who is going to plant them walks out into the arena alone with the bull. He lifts the banderillos at arm's length and points them toward the bull. Then he calls "Toro! Toro!" The bull charges and the banderillero rises to his toes, bends in a curve forward and just as the bull is about to hit him drops the darts into the bull's hump just back of his horns.

They must go in evenly, one on each side. They must not be shoved, or thrown or stuck in from the side. This is the first time the bull has been completely baffled, there is the prick of the darts that he cannot escape and there are no horses for him to charge into. But he charges the man again and again and each time he gets a pair of the long banderillos that hang from his hump by their tiny barbs and flop like porcupine quills.

Last is the death of the bull, which is in the hands of the matador who has had charge of the bull since his first attack. Each matador has two bulls in the afternoon. The death of the bull is most formal and can only be brought about in one way, directly from the front by the matador who must receive the bull in full charge and kill him with a sword thrust between the shoulders just back of the neck and between the horns. Before killing the bull he must first do a series of passes with the muleta, a piece of red cloth he carries about the size of a large napkin. With the muleta the torero must show his complete mastery of the bull, must make the bull miss him again and again by inches, before he is allowed to kill him. It is in this phase that most of the fatal accidents occur.

The word "toreador" is obsolete Spanish and is never used. The torero is usually called an espada or swordsman. He must be proficient in all three acts of the fight. In the first he uses the cape and does veronicas and protects the picadors by taking the bull out and away from them when they are spilled to the ground. In the second act he plants the banderillos. In the third act he masters the bull with the muleta and kills him.

Few toreros excel in all three departments. Some, like young Chicuelo, are unapproachable in their cape work. Others like the late Joselito are wonderful banderilleros. Only a few are great killers. Most of the greatest killers are gypsies.

VOCABULARY

1. Define the following words as Hemingway uses them in his essay: tawny, terra cotta, sol, incongruity, pensione, incorrigible, remunerative, proficient.
2. If you are unfamiliar with any other words in this essay, check them in a dictionary and define them in your own words.

CONTENT

1. Consider Hemingway's description of the setting for the bull fight.
   a. How consistent is this setting with his later description of the bull fight as a tragedy?

b. Does this setting remind you of a similar event in the United States? Explain.

2. In what way(s) is bull fighting a tragedy? In Hemingway's view, what does bull fighting symbolize?
3. According to Hemingway, how is bull fighting similar to grand opera?
4. What does Hemingway mean in this comment about Chicuelo: "They say he doesn't really like bull fighting but the town's crazy about him"? Why would the town's enthusiasm convince Chicuelo to remain in the bull ring?
5. Compare Plimpton's comments in "The American Tradition of Winning" (page 64) about the relationship between the fans and the players with the relationship depicted by Hemingway in this essay.
6. Can you find any examples in this essay to support Rosenberg's comments (see "Masculinity: Real and Put On," page 68) about Hemingway's preoccupation with masculinity? If so, what are they?

RHETORIC

1. What purpose does Hemingway's introduction* serve? How does it contribute to the essay's tone*?
2. How do Hemingway's metaphors* ("The whole sol side was a flicker of fans") and similes* ("he turned on his four feet like a cat") contribute to the essay's effectiveness?
3. List the very different adjectives that a torero, a meat packer, and a Sunday hiker would use to describe a "good" bull. What does your answer tell you about the importance of point of view*?
4. Describe Hemingway's writing style.
5. Hemingway essentially describes the bull fight twice—once concretely*, once abstractly*. What effect does this have on your understanding of bull fighting?

READING AND WRITING SUGGESTIONS

1. Using Hemingway's essay as a model, write a process analysis of a football game, boxing match, or other activity with which you are familiar.

---

*Definitions of all terms marked with an asterisk may be found in the Glossary.

2. Read "The Blood Lust" in Eldridge Cleaver's *Soul on Ice*. Then write a brief essay whose thesis is "The enjoyment of a blood sport does (or does not) indicate a blood lust."

NOTES ON PUNCTUATION

Lewis Thomas

Lewis Thomas (1913–) was born in New York and attended Princeton University and Harvard Medical School. He has held appointments at a number of medical schools and hospitals. Following several years at Yale University Medical School, Dr. Thomas assumed his present position as president of the Sloan-Kettering Cancer Center in New York City. He is the author of The Lives of a Cell, *a collection of essays which won the 1974 National Book Award. The essay below is taken from Dr. Thomas's latest book of essays,* The Medusa and the Snail, *published in 1979.*

There are no precise rules about punctuation (Fowler lays out some general advice (as best he can under the complex circumstances of English prose (he points out, for example, that we possess only four stops (the comma, the semicolon, the colon and the period (the question mark and exclamation point are not, strictly speaking, stops; they are indicators of tone (oddly enough, the Greeks employed the semicolon for their question mark (it produces a strange sensation to read a Greek sentence which is a straightforward question: Why weepest thou; (instead of Why weepest thou? (and, of course, there are parentheses (which are surely a kind of punctuation making this whole matter much more complicated by having to count up the left-handed parentheses in order to be sure of closing with the right number (but if the parentheses were left out, with nothing to work with but the stops, we would have considerably more flexibility in the deploying of layers of meaning than if we tried to separate all the clauses by physical barriers (and in the latter case, while we might have more precision and exactitude for our meaning, we would lose the essential flavor of language, which is its wonderful ambiguity))))))))))))).

The commas are the most useful and usable of all the stops. It is highly important to put them in place as you go along. If you try to come back after doing a paragraph and stick them in the various spots that tempt you you will discover that they tend to swarm like minnows into all sorts of crevices whose existence you hadn't realized and before you know it the whole long sentence becomes immobilized and lashed up squirming in commas. Better to use them sparingly, and with affection, precisely when the need for each one arises, nicely, by itself.

I have grown fond of semicolons in recent years. The semicolon tells you that there is still some question about the preceding full sentence; something needs to be added; it reminds you sometimes of the Greek usage. It is almost always a greater pleasure to come across a semicolon than a period. The period tells you that that is that; if you didn't get all the meaning you wanted or expected, anyway you got all the writer intended to parcel out and now you have to move along. But with a semicolon there you get a pleasant little feeling of expectancy; there is more to come; read on; it will get clearer.

Colons are a lot less attractive, for several reasons: firstly, they give you the feeling of being rather ordered around, or at least having your nose pointed in a direction you might not be inclined to take if left to yourself, and secondly, you suspect you're in for one of those sentences that will be labeling the points to be made: firstly, secondly and so forth, with the implication that you haven't sense enough to keep track of a sequence of notions without having them numbered. Also, many writers use this system loosely and incompletely, starting out with number one and number two as though counting off on their fingers but then going on and on without the succession of labels you've been led to expect, leaving you floundering about searching for the ninethly or seventeenthly that ought to be there but isn't.

Exclamation points are the most irritating of all. Look! they say, look at what I just said! How amazing is my thought! It is like being forced to watch someone else's small child jumping up and down crazily in the center of the living room shouting to attract attention. If a sentence really has something of importance to say, something quite remarkable, it doesn't need a mark to point it out. And if it is really, after all, a banal sentence needing more zing, the exclamation point simply emphasizes its banality!

Quotation marks should be used honestly and sparingly, when there is a genuine quotation at hand, and it is necessary to be very rigorous about the words enclosed by the marks. If something is to be quoted, the *exact* words must be used. If part of it must be left out because of space limitations, it is good manners to insert three dots to indicate the omission, but it is unethical to do this if it means connecting two thoughts which the original author did not intend to have tied together. Above all, quotation marks should not be used for ideas that you'd like to disown, things in the air so to speak. Nor should they be put in place around clichés; if you want to use a cliché you must take full responsibility for it yourself and not try to fob it off on anon., or on society. The most objectionable misuse of quotation marks, but one which illustrates the dangers of misuse in ordinary prose, is seen in advertising, especially in advertisements for small restaurants, for example "just around the corner," or "a good place to eat." No single, identifiable, citable person ever really said, for the record, "just around the corner," much less "a good place to eat," least likely of all for restaurants of the type that use this type of prose.

The dash is a handy device, informal and essentially playful, telling you that you're about to take off on a different tack but still in some way connected with the present course—only you have to remember that the dash is there, and either put a second dash at the end of the notion to let the reader know that he's back on course, or else end the sentence, as here, with a period.

The greatest danger in punctuation is for poetry. Here it is necessary to be as economical and parsimonious with commas and periods as with the words themselves, and any marks that seem to carry their own subtle meanings, like dashes and little rows of periods, even semicolons and question marks, should be left out altogether rather than inserted to clog up the thing with ambiguity. A single exclamation point in a poem, no matter what else the poem has to say, is enough to destroy the whole work.

The things I like best in T. S. Eliot's poetry, especially in the *Four Quartets,* are the semicolons. You cannot hear them, but they are there, laying out the connections between the images and the ideas. Sometimes you get a glimpse of a semicolon coming, a few lines farther on, and it is like climbing a steep path through woods and seeing a wooden bench just at a bend in the road ahead, a place where you can expect to sit for a moment, catching your breath.

Commas can't do this sort of thing; they can only tell you how the different parts of a complicated thought are to be fitted together, but you can't sit, not even take a breath, just because of a comma,

VOCABULARY

1. Define the following words as Thomas uses them in his essay: deploying, rigorous, fob, parsimonious.
2. Based on Thomas's remarks on punctuation, what do you think his attitude would be toward Elizabeth Pope's ironic comment, "Never use a short exact word when you can use a long vague word instead"? Explain your answer.

CONTENT

1. Thomas begins his essay with the assertion that "there are no precise rules about punctuation."
   a. Does this assertion conflict with what you have been taught? If so, how?
   b. What does this statement indicate to you about Thomas's approach to his subject?
2. According to Thomas, what is the importance of punctuation?
3. Have Thomas's remarks on punctuation affected your own attitude toward the subject? Explain.
4. Cite an advertising slogan which bears out Thomas's observations on the misuse of quotation marks in advertising.

RHETORIC

1. What device does Thomas use to support his generalizations on punctuation? How effective do you feel this device is?
2. Is Thomas's humorous tone* suited to a subject such as punctuation? Why or why not?
3. Cite three or four instances in which Thomas's use of punctuation is particularly effective.
4. What comments do you think Thomas might have to make on Shulman's use of punctuation in the first two paragraphs of "Love Is a Fallacy" (page 54)?

READING AND WRITING SUGGESTIONS

1. Rewrite the first paragraph of Thomas's essay, inserting your own punctuation for greater clarity.
2. Write a descriptive paragraph on a subject of your choice. Following Thomas's informal remarks on the various types of punctuation marks, incorporate an example of each in your paragraph.
3. Read T. S. Eliot's *Four Quartets*. Write a brief essay discussing Eliot's use of semicolons.

---

*Definitions of all terms marked with an asterisk may be found in the Glossary.

A HURRICANE

Richard Hughes

Richard Hughes, Welsh novelist, poet, and dramatist, while an undergraduate at Oxford University, once spent his last penny for a trip to the United States. He visited this country several times and wrote the last chapters of A High Wind in Jamaica *on one of these visits. Hughes' vivid analysis of a hurricane in the following essay, from* In Hazard *(1938), gives us a clear picture of how atmospheric forces combine to form these major storms.*

The thing to remember about the atmosphere is its size. A little air is so thin, so fluid; in small amounts it can slip about so rapidly, that the conditions which give rise to a hurricane cannot be reproduced on a small scale. In trying to explain a hurricane, therefore, one must describe the large thing itself, not a model of it. For it is only when one thinks of the hugeness of a parcel of air on the world, the big distance it may have to shift to equalize some atmospheric difference, that one can realize how slow and immobile, regarded on a *large* scale, the air is.

It happens like this. The air above a warm patch of sea, somewhere near the Canaries, is warmed: so it will tend to be pushed up and replaced by the colder, weightier air around. In a warm room it would rise in a continuous gentle stream, and be replaced by a gentle draught under the door—no excitement. But on a large scale it cannot: that is what is different. It rises in a single lump, as if it were encased in a gigantic balloon—being actually encased in its own comparative sluggishness. Cold air rushes in underneath not as a gentle draught but as a great wind, owing to the bodily lifting of so great a bulk of air.

Air moving in from all around towards a central point: and in the middle, air rising: that is the beginning. Then two things happen. The turning of the earth starts the system turning: not fast at first, but in a gentle spiral. And the warm air which has risen, saturated with moisture from the surface of the sea, cools. Cooling, high up there, its moisture spouts out of it in rain. Now, when the water in air condenses, it releases the energy that held it there, just as truly as the explosion of petrol releases energy. Millions of horse-power up there loose. As in a petrol-motor, that energy is translated into motion: up rises the boundless balloon still higher, faster spins the vortex.

Thus the spin of the Earth is only the turn of the crank-handle which starts it: the hurricane itself is a vast motor, revolved by the energy generated by the condensation of water from the rising air.

And then consider this. Anything spinning fast enough tends to fly away from the centre—or at any rate, like a planet round the sun, reaches a state of balance where it cannot fly inwards. The wind soon spins round the centre of a hurricane so fast it can no longer fly into that centre, however vacuous it is. Mere motion has formed a hollow pipe, as impervious as if it were made of something solid.

That is why it is often calm at the centre of a hurricane: the wind actually cannot get in.

So this extraordinary engine, fifty miles or more wide, built of speed-hardened air, its vast power generated by the sun and by the shedding of rain, spins westward across the floor of the Atlantic, often for weeks together, its power mounting as it goes. It is only when its bottom at last touches dry land (or very cold air) that the throttle is closed; no more moist air can be sucked in, and ın a few days, or weeks at most, it spreads and dies.

VOCABULARY

You probably know the meaning of all the words in this essay. Climatology, like most sciences, has some highly technical terms. Why do you suppose Hughes does not use technical language?

CONTENT

1. Summarize the steps in the development of a hurricane.
2. Do you think that an understanding of how something potentially destructive works lessens or increases our fear of it? Explain your answer.

RHETORIC

1. What kind of introduction* does Hughes use? What is the effect of this introduction on your understanding of how a hurricane develops?
2. What is the tone* of this essay? Is it suited to the essay's message?

---

* Definitions of all terms marked with an asterisk may be found in the Glossary.

3. What one metaphor* does Hughes use in his essay? How does this metaphor affect your understanding of hurricanes? Why do you think Hughes does not use more metaphors?

READING AND WRITING SUGGESTIONS

1. Use the information Hughes presents about a hurricane to develop an analogy* for how a group of people can become a destructive mob. Write an essay presenting this analogy.
2. Read an encyclopedia article about tornados or blizzards and write a process analysis describing their development.

---

*Definitions of all terms marked with an asterisk may be found in the Glossary.

AUTO SUGGESTION

Russell Baker

Russell Baker (1925–), the celebrated contemporary humorist, has been a newspaper columnist for The New York Times *for many years. He is a native of Loudoun County, Virginia, and was educated at Johns Hopkins University. Baker is a contributor to such periodicals as* Saturday Evening Post, Sports Illustrated, Life, Look, *and* McCall's. *Among his best known works are* An American in Washington, No Cause for Panic, Baker's Dozen, All Things Considered, *and* Poor Russell's Almanac. *In "Auto Suggestion," first published in* The New York Times *on April 1, 1979, Baker shares his techniques for not buying a new car.*

Many persons have written asking the secret of my technique for not buying a new car. Aware that it could destroy the American economy and reduce the sheiks of OPEC to prowling the streets with pleas for baksheesh, I divulge it here with the greatest reluctance.

In extenuation, let me explain that my power to resist buying a new car does not derive from a resentment of new cars. In fact, I bought a new car 10 years ago and would buy another at any moment if the right new car came along.

When seized by new-car passion, however, I do not deal with it as most people do. To conquer the lust and escape without a new car, you must have a program. The first step is to face the philosophical question: Is a new car really going to give you less trouble than your old car?

In most cases the notion that a new car will free its owner of auto headache will not hold water. Common experience shows that all cars, old or new, are trouble. The belief that a change of vintage will relieve the headache is a mental exercise in willful self-deception.

A new car simply presents a new set of troubles, which may be more disturbing than the beloved, familiar old troubles the old car presented. With your old car, strange troubles do not take you by surprise, but a new car's troubles are invariably terrifying for being strange and unexpected.

Before entering the new-car bazaar, I always remind myself that I am about to acquire an entirely new set of troubles and that it is going to take me months, maybe years, to learn to live happily with them.

Step Two is to place a sensible limit on the amount you will pay for a new car. As a guide to value, I use the price my parents paid for the house in which I grew up. To own a car that costs more than a house is vulgar and reflects an alarming disproportion in one's sense of values. Wheels may be splendid but they should not be valued more highly than four bedrooms, dining room, bath and cellar.

The price of my parents' house, purchased in 1940, was $5,900. This becomes my limit, effectively ruling out the kind of new car you have to drive to get a business appointment in Los Angeles, as well as most other new cars on the market today.

After setting a price limit, the next step is to study the car's capacity to perform its duties. For this purpose I always go to the car dealer's place with two large children, a wife, a grandmother, two cats, six suitcases, an ice chest and a large club suitable for subduing quarrelsome children on the turnpike.

Loading all the paraphernalia and people into the car under study, I then ask myself whether I could drive 400 miles in this environment without suffering mental breakdown.

Since most cars within the $5,900 price limit nowadays are scarcely commodious enough to transport two persons and a strand of spaghetti, I am now approaching very close to the goal I despise, which is to avoid buying a new car.

Suppose, however, that you pack everything inside—children, wife, cats, club and grandmother—and it seems just barely possible that you might cover 400 miles despite the knees from the back seat grinding into your kidneys. Now is the time to take out your checkoff list.

Can you slide in behind the wheel without denting the skull against the door frame? Will you be able to do it at night when you have had a drink and aren't thinking about it?

If the car passes this test, which is unlikely unless you're getting an incredible deal on a pickup truck—and cats and grandmothers, remember, don't much like riding in the open beds of pickup trucks, especially when it rains—if the car passes this test, you must give it the cascading rainwater test.

For this purpose I take a garden hose to the car lot, spray the top of the car heavily and then, upon opening the door try to slide in without being drenched in a cascade of water pouring into the driver's seat. If the car soaks you with hose water, imagine what it will do with a heavy dose of rain.

If the car passes this examination, the final test is to slip a fingernail under the plastic sheathing on the dashboard and see if the entire piece peels away easily. If it does not, I buy the new car immediately. The last time I had to do so was in 1969.

VOCABULARY

You are probably familiar with most of the words in Baker's article. Do you think Baker intentionally uses simple vocabulary? Why or why not?

CONTENT

1. Briefly list the five steps in Baker's program for escaping without a new car.
2. What steps would you change or add in your own program for not buying a new car?
3. What aspects of the auto industry and the economy is Baker satirizing?

RHETORIC

1. In his title Baker uses a *double entendre*, an expression that may be interpreted in two ways. What are the two meanings of *auto suggestion*?
2. What makes Baker's essay a successful newspaper column?
3. Compare Baker's humorous tone* with Perelman's ("Acres and Pains," page 74) and Shulman's ("Love Is a Fallacy," page 64).

---

*Definitions of all terms marked with an asterisk may be found in the Glossary.

READING AND WRITING SUGGESTIONS

1. Read a current essay or article on the economy. Then write an essay discussing the ways in which you are personally prepared to deal with the economy.

2. Think of some object that you would like to develop the strength to resist buying. Write a humorous essay explaining the steps you would take to achieve your goal.

CAUSE AND EFFECT

Cause-and-effect analysis can move in one of two directions: it can either involve the examination of events or circumstances which led to a particular situation, or be concerned with the results that follow from a particular cause. In the first type of analysis, the *effect* is known, and it is the causes leading up to that effect which are being examined. Questions about such topics as why the sky is blue, why Hitler was able to gain power in Germany, and even why a person chose a particular career all lend themselves to this kind of analysis. The second type of analysis is the reverse of the first type; here the *cause* is known, and it is the effects stemming from that cause that are being sought. Questions that would invite this type of analysis include: What was the effect of World War I on the British poetry of the period? What effect will the dwindling supply of natural fuels have on the American way of life?

It is essential that writers who use cause-and-effect analysis differentiate between real and apparent causes; the fact that one event precedes another does not necessarily mean that the first event was a cause of the second. A classic example of this type of confusion is illustrated by the case of the man who drank scotch with water and got drunk. He then drank bourbon with water and again got drunk. Finally, he experimented with rye and water and again found himself totally intoxicated. At this point, he concluded that water made him drunk.

When using cause-and-effect analysis, writers must also make a distinction between necessary and sufficient conditions. For example, a student must study for a given amount of time if he or she is to pass a test. This is a *necessary* condition, but it is not *sufficient* to ensure that the student will pass. The student must also study the right material, absorb a sufficient amount of it, and successfully convey an understanding of the material while taking the test.

In many cases, writers must also make a distinction between immediate and ultimate causes and effects. *Immediate* causes and effects are most often recent, specific, and objective. *Ultimate* causes and effects are usually more remote and general, and form the basis for immediate causes and effects. For example, the immediate causes of a student's getting an A in a course may be her answering all test questions correctly, participating in class discussions effectively, and writing excellent papers. The ultimate causes, however, may be her good study habits, her willingness to work hard, and her openness to new ideas—all developed during her earlier years and all contributing to good grades in more than one course.

Finally, writers must always keep in mind that few complex situations have a single cause. It is essential that the writer search out all the causes of a specific event, even those that are not readily apparent.

THE HUMAN USE OF LANGUAGE

Lawrence Langer

Lawrence Langer (1929–), a professor of English at Simmons College, received his undergraduate degree at City College of New York and his M.A. and Ph.D. degrees at Harvard University. He is the author of The Holocaust and the Literary Imagination. *In this essay from* The Chronicle of Higher Education, *January 24, 1977, Langer shows how the misuse of language causes more difficulties in the already difficult task of communicating.*

A friend of mine recently turned in a paper to a course on behavior modification. She had tried to express in simple English some of her reservations about this increasingly popular approach to education. She received it back with the comment: "Please rewrite this in behavioral terms."

It is little wonder that human beings have so much trouble saying what they feel, when they are told that there is a specialized vocabulary for saying what they think. The language of simplicity and spontaneity is forced to retreat behind the barricades of an official prose developed by a few experts who believe that jargon is the most precise means of communication. The results would be comic, if they were not so poisonous; unfortunately, there is an attitude toward the use of language that is impervious to human need and drives some people back into silence when they realize the folly of risking human words on insensitive ears.

The comedy is easy to come by. Glancing through my friend's textbook on behavior modification, I happened on a chapter beginning with the following challenging statement: "Many of the problems encountered by teachers in the daily management of their classes could be resolved if. . . ." Although I was a little wary of the phrase "daily management," I was encouraged to plunge ahead, because as an educator I have always been interested in ideas for improving learning. So I plunged. The entire sentence reads: "Many of the problems encountered by teachers in the daily management of their classes could be resolved if the emission of desirable student behaviors was increased."

Emission? At first I thought it was a misprint for "omission," but the omission of desirable student behaviors (note the plural) hardly seemed an appropriate goal for educators. Then I considered the possibility of metaphor, both erotic and automotive, but these didn't seem to fit, either. A footnote clarified the matter: " 'Emission' is a technical term used in behavioral analysis. The verb, 'to emit,' is used specifically with a certain category of behavior called 'operant behavior.' Operant behaviors are modified by their consequences. Operant behaviors correspond closely to the behavior colloquially referred to as voluntary." Voluntary? Is jargon then an attack on freedom of the will?

Of course, this kind of abuse of the language goes on all the time—within the academic world, one regrets to say, as well as outside it. Why couldn't the author of this text simply say that we need to motivate students to learn willingly? The more I read such non-human prose, and try to avoid writing it myself, the more I am convinced that we must be in touch with ourselves before we can use words to touch others.

Using language meaningfully requires risk; the sentence I have just quoted takes no risks at all. Much of the discourse that poses as communication in our society is really a decoy to divert our audience (and often ourselves) from that shadowy plateau where our real life hovers on the precipice of expression. How many people, for example, have the courage to walk up to someone they like and actually *say* to them: "I'm very fond of you, you know"?

Such honesty reflects the use of language as revelation, and that sort of revelation, brimming with human possibilities, is risky precisely because it invites judgment and rebuff. Perhaps this is one reason why, especially in academe, we are confronted daily with so much neutral prose: Our students are not yet in touch with themselves; not especially encouraged by us, their instructors, to move in that direction; they are encouraged indeed to expect judgment and hence perhaps rebuff, too, in our evaluation of them. Thus they instinctively retreat behind the anonymity of abstract diction and technical jargon to protect themselves against us—but also, as I have suggested, against themselves.

This problem was crystallized for me recently by an encounter only peripherally related to the issue. As part of my current research, I have been interviewing children of concentration-camp survivors. One girl I have been meeting with says that her mother does not like to talk about the experience, *except with other survivors*. Risk is diminished when we know in advance that our audience shares with us a sympathy for our theme. The nakedness of pain *and* the nakedness of love require gentle responses. So this survivor is reticent, except with fellow victims.

But one day a situation arose which tempted her to the human use of language although she could not be sure, in advance, of the reception her words would receive. We all recognize it. This particular woman, at the age of 40, decided to return to school to get a college degree. Her first assignment in freshman composition was to write a paper on something that was of great importance to her personally. The challenge was immense; the risk was even greater. For the first time in 20 years, she resolved to confront a silence in her life that she obviously needed to rouse to speech.

She was 14 when the Germans invaded Poland. When the roundup of the Jews began a year later, some Christian friends sent their young daughter to "call for her" one day, so that they might hide her. A half hour later, the friends went themselves to pick up her parents, but during that interval, a truck had arrived, loaded aboard the Jewish mother and father—and the daughter never saw them or heard from them again. Their fate we can imagine. The girl herself was eventually arrested, survived several camps, and after the war came to America. She married, had children of her own, and except for occasional reminiscences with fellow survivors, managed to live adequately without diving into her buried personal past. Until one day her instructor in English composition touched a well-insulated nerve, and it began to throb with a painful impulse to express. I present verbatim the result of that impulse, a paper called "People I Have Forgotten":

> Can you forget your own Father and Mother? If so—how or why?
>
> I thought I did. To mention their names, for me is a great emotional struggle. The brutal force of this reality shakes my whole body and mind, wrecking me into ugly splinters; each crying to be mended anew. So the silence I maintain about their memory is only physical and valid as such but not true. I could never forget my parents, nor do I want to do it. True, I seldom talk about them with my husband or my children. How they looked, who they were, why they perished during the war. The love and sacrifices they have made for me during their lifetime, never get told.
>
> The cultural heritage to which each generation is entitled to have access to seems to be nonexistant [sic], since I dare not talk about anything relating to my past, my parents.
>
> This awful, awesome power of not-remembering, this heart-breaking sensation of the conspiracy of silence is my dilemma.
>
> Often, I have tried to break through my imprisoning wall of irrational silence, but failed: now I hope to be able to do it.
>
> Until now, I was not able to face up to the loss of my parents, much less talk about them. The smallest reminder of them would set off a chain reaction of results that I could anticipate but never direct. The destructive force of sadness, horror, fright would then become my master. And it was this subconscious knowledge that kept me paralyzed with silence, not a conscious desire to forget my parents.
>
> My silent wall, my locked shell existed only of real necessity; I needed time.

> I needed time to forget the tragic loss of my loved ones, time to heal my emotional wound so that there shall come a time when I can again remember the people I have forgotten.

The essay is not a confrontation, only a prelude, yet it reveals qualities which are necessary for the human use of language: In trying to reach her audience, the author must touch the deepest part of herself. She risks self-exposure—when we see the instructor's comment, we will realize how great was her risk—and she is prepared for judgment and perhaps even rebuff, although I doubt whether she was prepared for the form they took. This kind of prose, for all its hesitant phraseology, throws down a gauntlet to the reader, a challenge asking him to understand that life is pain as well as plenty, chaos as well as form. Its imagery of locked shells and imprisoning walls hints at a silent world of horror and sadness far less enchanting than the more familiar landscape of love where most of us dwell. Language is a two-edged tool, to pierce the wall which hides that world, or build high abstract barriers to protect us from its threats.

The instructor who graded the paper I have just read preferred walls to honest words. At the bottom of the last page she scrawled a large "D-minus," emphatically surrounded by a circle. Her only comment was: "Your theme is not clear—you should have developed your 1st paragraph. You talk around your subject." At this moment, two realms collide: a universe of unarticulated feeling seeking expression (and the courage and encouragement to express) and a nature made so immune to feeling by heaven-knows-what that she hides behind the tired, tired language of the professional theme-corrector.

Suddenly we realize that reading as well as writing requires risks, and that the metaphor of insulation, so central to the efforts of the Polish woman survivor to re-establish contact with her past, is a metaphor governing the response of readers, too. Some writing, like "the emission of desirable student behaviors," thickens the insulation that already separates the reader from the words that throw darts at his armor of indifference. But even when language unashamedly reveals the feeling that is hidden behind the words, it must contend with a different kind of barrier, the one behind which our instructor lies concealed, unwilling or unable to hear a human voice and then return a human echo of her own.

Ironically, the victor in this melancholy failure at communication is the villain of the piece, behavior modification. For the Polish survivor wrote her next theme on an innocuous topic, received a satisfactory grade, and never returned to the subject of her parents. The instructor, who had encountered a problem in the daily management of her class in the form of an essay which she could not respond to in a human way, altered the attitude of her student by responding in a non-human way, thus resolving her problem by increasing the emission of desirable student behavior. The student now knows how vital it is to develop her first paragraph, and how futile it is to reveal her first grief.

Even more, she has learned the danger of talking around her subject: She not only refuses to talk ***around*** it now, she refuses to talk ***about*** it. Thus the human use of language leads back to silence—where perhaps it should have remained in the first place.

VOCABULARY

1. Define the following words as Langer uses them in his essay: barricades, impervious, wary, emission, anonymity, reticent, innocuous.
2. If you are unfamiliar with any other words in this essay, check them in a dictionary and then define them in your own words.

CONTENT

1. Why was the writing of the composition "People I Have Forgotten" a significant experience for its author?
2. What effect did the instructor's response have on the writer? What might have happened if the instructor had praised the essay?
3. In your opinion, what elements should an instructor take into consideration when evaluating a composition in which a student has chosen a personal theme?
4. The main idea of behavior modification is to control (that is, cause) effects by using rewards and punishment to encourage people to act in a certain way. Are you in favor of using praise and reproof to cause what you consider desirable effects? Why or why not?
5. Langer says that "the victor in this melancholy failure at communication is the villain of the piece, behavior modification." Can a neutral tool (behavior modification) be a villain, or is the villain the person who misuses such a tool (the instructor)?
6. How does Langer believe language affects our ability to express our true feelings?

RHETORIC

1. What does the essay's title* tell you about the thesis* of Langer's work?

2. What two examples does Langer use to illustrate his thesis* and how does he make the transition between them?

3. What is the meaning of the sentence, "Many of the problems . . . could be resolved if the emission of desirable student behaviors was increased"? Why does Langer find it objectionable?

4. Cite three instances in which Langer uses figurative language* and explain how each contributes to the meaning of the idea expressed.

READING AND WRITING SUGGESTIONS

1. Write a brief cause-and-effect essay showing how someone's failure to understand kept you from taking a chance and sharing something you felt deeply about. Describe the effect this failure in understanding had on you.

2. Read an article or a book about language usage, such as Edwin Newman's *Strictly Speaking: Will America Be the Death of English?* Write a brief cause-and-effect essay about words that interfere with communication among people.

---

*Definitions of all terms marked with an asterisk may be found in the Glossary.

HOPE

Maya Angelou

Maya Angelou (1928–), author, poet, playwright, and professional stage and screen performer, was born in Missouri and attended public schools in Arkansas and California. She has served as a lecturer and writer-in-residence at a number of universities, including the University of California at Los Angeles, University of Kansas, and Wake Forest University. At the request of Martin Luther King, Angelou became the Northern Coordinator for the Southern Christian Leadership Conference. Her autobiography, I Know Why the Caged Bird Sings, *was nominated for the National Book Award and was a Book of the Month Club selection. Other books by Angelou are* Gather Together in My Name *and* Singin' and Swingin' and Gettin' Merry Like Christmas. *She was named Woman of the Year in Communications by* Ladies Home Journal *in 1976. She holds honorary degrees from Smith College, Mills College, and Lawrence University. The following selection from Angelou's autobiography relates an incident in her childhood that engendered pride and hope at a time when black people were struggling to overcome the deprivations of the past.*

The last inch of space was filled, yet people continued to wedge themselves along the walls of the Store. Uncle Willie had turned the radio up to its last notch so that youngsters on the porch wouldn't miss a word. Women sat on kitchen chairs, dining-room chairs, stools and upturned wooden boxes. Small children and babies perched in every lap available and men leaned on the shelves or on each other.

The apprehensive mood was shot through with shafts of gaiety, as a black sky is streaked with lightning.

"I ain't worried 'bout this fight. Joe's gonna whip that cracker like it's open season."

"He gone whip him till that white boy call him Momma."

At last the talking was finished and the string-along songs about razor blades were over and the fight began.

"A quick jab to the head." In the Store the crowd grunted. "A left to the head and a right and another left." One of the listeners cackled like a hen and was quieted.

"They're in a clench, Louis is trying to fight his way out."

Some bitter comedian on the porch said, "That white man don't mind hugging that niggah now, I betcha."

"The referee is moving in to break them up, but Louis finally pushed the contender away and it's an uppercut to the chin. The contender is hanging on, now he's backing away. Louis catches him with a short left to the jaw."

A tide of murmuring assent poured out the doors and into the yard.

"Another left and another left. Louis is saving that mighty right . . ." The mutter in the Store had grown into a baby roar and it was pierced by the clang of a bell and the announcer's "That's the bell for round three, ladies and gentlemen."

As I pushed my way into the Store I wondered if the announcer gave any thought to the fact that he was addressing as "ladies and gentlemen" all the Negroes around the world who sat sweating and praying, glued to their "master's voice."

There were only a few calls for R. C. Colas, Dr. Peppers, and Hire's root beer. The real festivities would begin after the fight. Then even the old Christian ladies who taught their children and tried themselves to practice turning the other cheek would buy soft drinks, and if the Brown Bomber's victory was a particularly bloody one they would order peanut patties and Baby Ruths also.

Bailey and I lay the coins on top of the cash register. Uncle Willie didn't allow us to ring up sales during a fight. It was too noisy and might shake up the atmosphere. When the gong rang for the next round we pushed through the near-sacred quiet to the herd of children outside.

"He's got Louis against the ropes and now it's a left to the body and a right to the ribs. Another right to the body, it looks like it was low . . . Yes, ladies and gentlemen, the referee is signaling but the contender keeps raining the blows on Louis. It's another to the body, and it looks like Louis is going down."

My race groaned. It was our people falling. It was another lynching, yet another Black man hanging on a tree. One more woman ambushed and raped. A Black boy whipped and maimed. It was hounds on the trail of a man running through slimy swamps. It was a white woman slapping her maid for being forgetful.

The men in the Store stood away from the walls and at attention. Women greedily clutched the babes on their laps while on the porch the shufflings and smiles, flirtings and pinching of a few minutes before were gone. This might be the end of the world. If Joe lost we were back in slavery and beyond help. It would all be true, the accusations that we were lower types of human beings. Only a little higher than the apes. True that we were stupid and ugly and lazy and dirty and, unlucky and worst of all, that God

Himself hated us and ordained us to be hewers of wood and drawers of water, forever and ever, world without end.

We didn't breathe. We didn't hope. We waited.

"He's off the ropes, ladies and gentlemen. He's moving towards the center of the ring." There was no time to be relieved. The worst might still happen.

"And now it looks like Joe is mad. He's caught Carnera with a left hook to the head and a right to the head. It's a left jab to the body and another left to the head. There's a left cross and a right to the head. The contender's right eye is bleeding and he can't seem to keep his block up. Louis is penetrating every block. The referee is moving in, but Louis sends a left to the body and it's the uppercut to the chin and the contender is dropping. He's on the canvas, ladies and gentlemen."

Babies slid to the floor as women stood up and men leaned toward the radio.

"Here's the referee. He's counting. One, two, three, four five, six, seven . . . Is the contender trying to get up again?"

All the men in the store shouted, "NO."

"—eight, nine, ten." There were a few sounds from the audience, but they seemed to be holding themselves in against tremendous pressure.

"The fight is all over, ladies and gentlemen. Let's get the microphone over to the referee . . . Here he is. He's got the Brown Bomber's hand, he's holding it up . . . Here he is . . ."

Then the voice, husky and familiar, came to wash over us—"The winnah, and still heavyweight champeen of the world . . . Joe Louis."

Champion of the world. A Black boy. Some Black mother's son. He was the strongest man in the world. People drank Coca-Colas like ambrosia and ate candy bars like Christmas. Some of the men went behind the Store and poured white lightning in their soft-drink bottles, and a few of the bigger boys followed them. Those who were not chased away came back blowing their breath in front of themselves like proud smokers.

It would take an hour or more before the people would leave the Store and head for home. Those who lived too far had made arrangements to stay in town. It wouldn't do for a Black man and his family to be caught on a lonely country road on a night when Joe Louis had proved that we were the strongest people in the world.

VOCABULARY

1. Define the following words as Angelou uses them in her essay: apprehensive, perched, assent, hewers, ambrosia.
2. Slang can be described as a kind of "social dialect," the speech used

among members of a kind of in-group. Find examples in this selection. List some slang from your social in-group.

CONTENT

1. What is meant by the phrase, "their 'master's voice' "? How would you describe the state of relations between blacks and whites as depicted in Angelou's essay?
2. What does Joe Louis's victory or defeat symbolize in this essay?
3. What is the mood of the crowd before the fight? What effect does Louis's winning have? If he had lost, what effect might it have had?
4. Name some current personalities who are considered a source of hope and pride to their people.

RHETORIC

1. What is the thesis* of this essay? Is it stated or implied?
2. List as many examples of figurative language* as you can find in this essay. How does Angelou's use of figurative language contribute to your understanding of the message she is trying to convey?
3. Does the development of this essay move from cause to effect or from effect to cause? Explain.
4. What type of closing* device does Angelou use in her final paragraph?
5. Find examples of sentence fragments. What is their effect?

READING AND WRITING SUGGESTIONS

1. Are there problems between political, ethnic, or religious groups on your campus or in your community? Write a cause-and-effect essay discussing the situation and its possible solutions.
2. Write a cause-and-effect essay about a person you know who you think is headed for trouble.
3. Read *The Jim Thorpe Story* by Gene Schoor, and write a cause-and-effect essay showing how events or circumstances led to Thorpe's being a source of pride to his people.

---

*Definitions of all terms marked with an asterisk may be found in the Glossary.

THE NECESSARY ENEMY

Katherine Anne Porter

Katherine Anne Porter (1890–), Texas-born writer, lecturer, and teacher, has spoken at more than two hundred universities and colleges in the United States and Europe. She has served as a writer in residence at many institutions, including Stanford University, University of Michigan, University of Virginia, and Washington and Lee University where she was the first woman faculty member in the school's history. Porter has won many prestigious literary awards, including the O. Henry Memorial Award, the Emerson-Thoreau Bronze Medal for Literature of the American Academy of Arts and Sciences, the Pulitzer Prize, and the National Book Award, the last two awards in 1966 for The Collected Works of Katherine Anne Porter. *Two of her books,* Flowering Judas *and* Ship of Fools, *were Book of the Month Club selections and the latter was filmed by Columbia Pictures in 1965. Porter, like her distant cousin, William Sidney Porter (O. Henry), was interested in portraying the psychology of human relationships, in discovering and understanding human motives and feelings. The following selection from* The Collected Essays and Occasional Writings of Katherine Anne Porter *(1970) is an example of this interest.*

She is a frank, charming, fresh-hearted young woman who married for love. She and her husband are one of those gay, good-looking young pairs who ornament this modern scene rather more in profusion perhaps than ever before in our history. They are handsome, with a talent for finding their way in their world, they work at things that interest them, their tastes agree and their hopes. They intend in all good faith to spend their lives together, to have children and do well by them and each other—to be happy, in fact, which for them is the whole point of their marriage. And all in stride, keeping their wits about them. Nothing romantic, mind you; their feet are on the ground.

Unless they were this sort of person, there would not be much point to what I wish to say; for they would seem to be an example of the high-spirited, right-minded young whom the critics are always invoking to come forth and do their duty and practice all those sterling old-fashioned virtues which in every generation seem to be falling into disrepair. As for virtues, these young people are more or less on their own, like most of their kind; they get very little moral or other aid from their society; but after three years of marriage this very contemporary young woman finds herself facing the oldest and ugliest dilemma of marriage.

She is dismayed, horrified, full of guilt and forebodings because she is finding out little by little that she is capable of hating her husband, whom she loves faithfully. She can hate him at times as fiercely and mysteriously, indeed in terribly much the same way, as often she hated her parents, her brothers and sisters, whom she loves, when she was a child. Even then it had seemed to her a kind of black treacherousness in her, her private wickedness that, just the same, gave her her only private life. That was one thing her parents never knew about her, never seemed to suspect. For it was never given a name. They did and said hateful things to her and to each other as if by right, as if in them it was a kind of virtue. But when they said to her, "Control your feelings," it was never when she was amiable and obedient, only in the black times of her hate. So it was her secret, a shameful one. When they punished her, sometimes for the strangest reasons, it was, they said, only because they loved her—it was for her good. She did not believe this, but she thought herself guilty of something worse than ever they had punished her for. None of this really frightened her: the real fright came when she discovered that at times her father and mother hated each other; this was like standing on the doorsill of a familiar room and seeing in a lightning flash that the floor was gone, you were on the edge of a bottomless pit. Sometimes she felt that both of them hated her, but that passed, it was simply not a thing to be thought of, much less believed. She thought she had outgrown all this, but here it was again, an element in her own nature she could not control, or feared she could not. She would have to hide from her husband, if she could, the same spot in her feelings she had hidden from her parents, and for the same no doubt disreputable, selfish reason: she wants to keep his love.

Above all, she wants him to be absolutely confident that she loves him, for that is the real truth, no matter how unreasonable it sounds, and no matter how her own feelings betray them both at times. She depends recklessly on his love; yet while she is hating him, he might very well be hating her as much or even more, and it would serve her right. But she does not want to be served right, she wants to be loved and forgiven—that is, to be sure he would forgive her anything, if he had any notion of what she had done. But best of all she would like not to have anything in her love that should ask for forgiveness. She doesn't mean about their quarrels—they are not so bad. Her feelings are out of proportion, perhaps. She knows it is perfectly natural for people to disagree, have fits of temper, fight it out; they learn quite a lot about each other that way, and not all of it disappointing either. When it passes, her hatred seems quite unreal. It always did.

Love. We are early taught to say it. I love you. We are trained to the thought of it as if there were nothing else, or nothing else worth having without it, or nothing worth having which it could not bring with it. Love is taught, always by precept, sometimes by example. Then hate, which no one meant to teach us, comes of itself. It is true that if we say I love you, it may be received with doubt, for there are times when it is hard to believe. Say I hate you, and the one spoken to believes it instantly, once for all.

Say I love you a thousand times to that person afterward and mean it every time, and still it does not change the fact that once we said I hate you, and meant that too. It leaves a mark on that surface love had worn so smooth with its eternal caresses. Love must be learned, and learned again and again; there is no end to it. Hate needs no instruction, but waits only to be provoked . . . hate, the unspoken word, the unacknowledged presence in the house, that faint smell of brimstone among the roses, that invisible tongue-tripper, that unkempt finger in every pie, that sudden oh-so-curiously *chilling* look—could it be boredom?—on your dear one's features, making them quite ugly. Be careful: love, perfect love, is in danger.

If it is not perfect, it is not love, and if it is not love, it is bound to be hate sooner or later. This is perhaps a not too exaggerated statement of the extreme position of Romantic Love, more especially in America, where we are all brought up on it, whether we know it or not. Romantic Love is changeless, faithful, passionate, and its sole end is to render the two lovers happy. It has no obstacles save those provided by the hazards of fate (that is to say, society), and such sufferings as the lovers may cause each other are only another word for delight: exciting jealousies, thrilling uncertainties, the ritual dance of courtship within the charmed closed circle of their secret alliance; all *real* troubles come from without, they face them unitedly in perfect confidence. Marriage is not the end but only the beginning of true happiness, cloudless, changeless to the end. That the candidates for this blissful condition have never seen an example of it, nor ever knew anyone who had, makes no difference. That is the ideal and they will achieve it.

How did Romantic Love manage to get into marriage at last, where it was most certainly never intended to be? At its highest it was tragic: the love of Héloïse and Abélard. At its most graceful, it was the homage of the trouvère for his lady. In its most popular form, the adulterous strayings of solidly married couples who meant to stray for their own good reasons, but at the same time do nothing to upset the property settlements or the line of legitimacy; at its most trivial, the pretty trifling of shepherd and shepherdess.

This was generally condemned by church and state and a word of fear to honest wives whose mortal enemy it was. Love within the sober, sacred realities of marriage was a matter of personal luck, but in any case, private feelings were strictly a private affair having, at least in theory, no bearing whatever on the fixed practice of the rules of an institution never intended as a recreation ground for either sex. If the couple discharged their religious and social obligations, furnished forth a copious progeny, kept their troubles to themselves, maintained public civility and died under the same roof, even if not always on speaking terms, it was rightly regarded as a successful marriage. Apparently this testing ground was too severe for all but the stoutest spirits; it too was based on an ideal, as impossible in its way as the ideal Romantic Love. One good thing to be said for it is that society took responsibility for the conditions of marriage, and the sufferers within its bonds could always blame the system, not themselves. But Romantic Love crept into the marriage bed, very stealthily, by centuries, bringing its absurd notions about love as eternal springtime and marriage as a personal adventure meant to provide personal happiness. To a Western romantic such as I, though my views have been much modified by painful experience, it still seems to be a charming work of the human imagination, and it is a pity its central notion has been taken too literally and has hardened into a convention as cramping and enslaving as the older one. The refusal to acknowledge the evils in ourselves which therefore are implicit in any human situation is as extreme and unworkable a proposition as the doctrine of total depravity; but somewhere between them, or maybe beyond them, there does exist a possibility for reconciliation between our desires for impossible satisfactions and the simple unalterable fact that we also desire to be unhappy and that we create our own sufferings; and out of these sufferings we salvage our fragments of happiness.

Our young woman who has been taught that an important part of her human nature is not real because it makes trouble and interferes with her peace of mind and shakes her self-love, has been very badly taught; but she has arrived at a most important stage of her re-education. She is afraid her marriage is going to fail because she has not love enough to face its difficulties; and this because at times she feels a painful hostility toward her husband, and cannot admit its reality because such an admission would damage in her own eyes her view of what love should be, an absurd view, based on her vanity of power. Her hatred is as real as her love is real, but her hatred has the advantage at present because it works on a blind instinctual level, it is lawless; and her love is subjected to a code of ideal conditions, impossible by their very nature of fulfillment, which prevents its free growth and deprives it of its right to recognize its human limitations and come to grips with them. Hatred is natural in a sense that love, as she conceives it, a young person brought up in the tradition of Romantic

Love, is not natural at all. Yet it did not come by hazard, it is the very imperfect expression of the need of the human imagination to create beauty and harmony out of chaos, no matter how mistaken its notion of these things may be, nor how clumsy its methods. It has conjured love out of the air, and seeks to preserve it by incantations; when she spoke a vow to love and honor her husband until death, she did a very reckless thing, for it is not possible by an act of the will to fulfill such an engagement. But it was the necessary act of faith performed in defense of a mode of feeling, the statement of honorable intention to practice as well as she is able the noble, acquired faculty of love, that very mysterious overtone to sex which is the best thing in it. Her hatred is part of it, the necessary enemy and ally.

VOCABULARY

1. Define these words as Porter uses them in her essay: sterling, forebodings, precept, copious, progeny, depravity, incantations.
2. If you are unfamiliar with any other words in this essay, check them in a dictionary and then define them in your own words.

CONTENT

1. What is "the oldest and ugliest dilemma of marriage"?
2. What does Porter see as the cause of hatred in marriage and other close relationships?
3. In earlier times, romantic love was not considered a necessary ingredient of marriage.
   a. What *were* the preconditions and ingredients for marriage?
   b. How was romantic love portrayed: In its tragic form? In its graceful form? In its popular form? In its trivial form?
   c. How did romantic love become associated with marriage?
   d. Do you consider romantic love a necessary condition for a successful marriage? Explain.
4. Compare Porter's attitude towards romantic love with that of Bertrand Russell's in "A Life Worth Living" (page 45).
5. If, as Porter maintains, our desires for the impossible cause our unhappiness, and most people want to be happy, what would Porter suggest we do to cause this desired effect?

RHETORIC

1. Note Porter's use of a woman's point of view* in her essay. Would discussing the topic from the husband's, children's, or parents' viewpoint have been as meaningful? Defend your answer.
2. Does Porter adequately define her title* in the essay? What does she mean by "The Necessary Enemy"?
3. List the metaphors* Porter uses for hate, and generate for each a corresponding metaphor for love.
4. Simplify Porter's stated thesis* by paraphrasing it.
5. At one point toward the end of the essay Porter moves from the third person to the first person. What is the effect of this change in viewpoint?

READING AND WRITING SUGGESTIONS

1. Write a cause-and-effect essay, taking as your thesis* the paradox* "Without love there would be no hate."
2. Read a study of love such as James Gould Cozzens' *By Love Possessed* or Eric Fromm's *The Art of Loving*. Choose one of the types/levels of love and show how it affects people's happiness and well-being.

---

*Definitions of all terms marked with an asterisk may be found in the Glossary.

THE RABBITS WHO CAUSED ALL THE TROUBLE

James Thurber

James Thurber (1894–1961), blending whimsy and satire, established himself as a leading American humorist and writer. For many years he was a staff writer for The New Yorker, *which published a large number of his cartoons, short stories, and essays. Many of these essays and short stories were collected in volumes. Among the best known are* A Thurber Carnival, Is Sex Necessary? *and* Fables for Our Time, *from which this 1940 selection is taken. Like most effective humorists, Thurber used simple situations of humor to convey serious observations. In this fable Thurber comments on our foibles and on our inhumanity to one another.*

Within the memory of the youngest child there was a family of rabbits who lived near a pack of wolves. The wolves announced that they did not like the way the rabbits were living. (The wolves were crazy about the way they themselves were living, because it was the only way to live.) One night several wolves were killed in an earthquake and this was blamed on the rabbits, for it is well known that rabbits pound on the ground with their hind legs and cause earthquakes. On another night one of the wolves was killed by a bolt of lightning and this was also blamed on the rabbits, for it is well known that lettuce-eaters cause lightning. The wolves threatened to civilize the rabbits if they didn't behave, and the rabbits decided to run away to a desert island. But the other animals, who lived at a great distance, shamed them, saying, "You must stay where you are and be brave. This is no world for escapists. If the wolves attack you, we will come to your aid, in all probability." So the rabbits continued to live near the wolves and one day there was a terrible flood which drowned a great many wolves. This was blamed on the rabbits, for it is well known that carrot-nibblers with long ears cause floods. The wolves descended on the rabbits, for their own good, and imprisoned them in a dark cave, for their own protection.

When nothing was heard about the rabbits for some weeks, the other animals demanded to know what had happened to them. The wolves replied that the rabbits had been eaten and since they had been eaten the affair was a purely internal matter. But the other animals warned that they might possibly unite against the wolves unless some reason was given for the destruction of the rabbits. So the wolves gave them one. "They were trying to escape," said the wolves, "and, as you know, this is no world for escapists."

Moral: Run, don't walk, to the nearest desert island.

VOCABULARY

Fables* generally contain simple vocabulary. Based on your reading of Thurber's fable, what is the effect of this simplified vocabulary?

CONTENT

1. Describe the attitude of the wolves toward the rabbits.
2. What fatal mistake do the rabbits make?
3. What human characteristics is Thurber satirizing in this fable?
4. What deeper level of meaning* is implied in the moral Thurber offers at the end of this selection?

RHETORIC

1. How does Thurber use anthropomorphism* in this selection?
2. How does the fable* form help Thurber make his point more effectively?
3. What logical fallacy* do the wolves use in giving the causes they do?

READING AND WRITING SUGGESTIONS

1. Read four or five other selections from Thurber's *Fables for Our Time*. Then write an essay comparing any three of these in terms of morals given and how effective you personally found them to be.
2. Using Thurber's fables as a model, choose some human foible to satirize and write a fable of your own.

---

*Definitions of all terms marked with an asterisk may be found in the Glossary.

COMPARISON AND CONTRAST

Comparisons show how two or more things are similar; *contrasts,* the reverse of comparisons, show how things are different. Comparison and contrast has three main uses. First, it can be used to explain the nature of a thing more fully. For example, it is easier to comprehend what the term "female" means when it is compared and contrasted with the term "male." The second purpose is determining the superiority of one thing over another. In deciding whether to buy a Ford Pinto or a Ford LTD, for example, it would be advisable to compare and contrast the two cars in terms of such features as cost, gas mileage, durability, and safety in order to decide which car would best suit your needs. Third, it is sometimes possible to use comparison and contrast to suggest the causes of a condition or an event. If you wanted to discover why children were being born with a certain birth defect, you would probably begin your search by comparing and contrasting the backgrounds of such children's parents—examining their family histories, finding out what medication the mothers took during pregnancy, etc. You would, of course, be looking for a common element in the backgrounds of the parents, because this might be a cause of the birth defect.

Comparison-and-contrast essays may be organized in two ways: subject by subject or point by point. If you were using the subject-by-subject pattern, you would first give all the information about one of the subjects of the essay and then all the information about the next subject. For example, you would discuss all the pros and cons of the Ford Pinto and then present all the corresponding information about the LTD. In a point-by-point essay, you would deal consecutively with each point of comparison, showing how the subjects of the essay compared and contrasted in each area. If you were discussing the relative merits of the two cars, you would first compare and contrast their cost, and then discuss how they compared in gas mileage, and so on.

There are five special requirements for using comparison and contrast effectively. First, the subjects being weighed against each other must relate in a meaningful way to the purpose of the essay. If you were attempting to determine which of the two cars was the better buy, it would be useless to compare a Pinto and a bicycle. But this *would* be a useful comparison if you were weighing the virtues and drawbacks of different *forms of transportation*.

Second, the points of comparison and contrast also should bear a direct relationship to the purpose of the essay. If you were considering which of three cars was most economical, you would want to use original cost, maintenance costs, and probable resale value as points of comparison and contrast—not the beauty or comfort of the cars.

Third, when using comparison and contrast to determine the cause of a condition or event, you should try to ascertain whether the similarities between the things being compared are logically related to the cause. If, for example, you were comparing the backgrounds of parents of children with birth defects and you discovered that all the parents had eaten hamburgers at one time or another, you should not automatically assume that this similarity meant that the hamburgers were the cause of the problem.

Fourth, all conclusions arrived at through comparison and contrast must be accurately qualified. If Pintos are as comfortable as LTDs—but only for persons under six feet tall—you should clearly note this qualification.

Fifth, subjects should be compared and contrasted on all relevant points. If your point is to show that car X is more economical than car Y, it would be unfair to quote only car X's lower purchase price, omitting the fact that the maintenance costs for car X are higher than those for car Y.

Analogy is a special type of comparison that explains a difficult or inaccessible thing by comparing it with a simpler, more familiar thing. For example, the role of the president of the United States has often been compared with the role of a ship's captain. Needless to say, the two roles are not identical, but it is easier to visualize the more complex, abstract role of the president when we imagine him at the helm, steering the ship of state through the rough seas of national crisis. However, it is essential that analogies not be carried too far; the fact that two things are similar in some ways does not mean that they are similar in all respects. The passengers on the ship of state, for example, cannot be unloaded in a foreign port like the passengers on a sailing vessel.

GRANT AND LEE: A STUDY IN CONTRASTS

Bruce Catton

Bruce Catton (1899–1978) spent most of his life as a journalist and civil servant. At the age of fifty, he began writing about the Civil War, a topic that had been a lifelong interest. A Stillness at Appomattox, *the last in his series on the war, won the National Book Award and the Pulitzer Prize. All of his writing on the Civil War was acclaimed for its historical accuracy and vivid description. In the following selection from* The American Story *(1956), Catton compares and contrasts the two men who led the armies of the North and the South.*

When Ulysses S. Grant and Robert E. Lee met in the parlor of a modest house at Appomattox Court House, Virginia, on April 9, 1865, to work out the terms for the surrender of Lee's Army of Northern Virginia, a great chapter in American life came to a close, and a great new chapter began.

These men were bringing the Civil War to its virtual finish. To be sure, other armies had yet to surrender, and for a few days the fugitive Confederate government would struggle desperately and vainly, trying to find some way to go on living now that its chief support was gone. But in effect it was all over when Grant and Lee signed the papers. And the little room where they wrote out the terms was the scene of one of the poignant, dramatic contrasts in American history.

They were two strong men, these oddly different generals, and they represented the strengths of two conflicting currents that, through them, had come into final collision.

Back of Robert E. Lee was the notion that the old aristocratic concept might somehow survive and be dominant in American life.

Lee was tidewater Virginia, and in his background were family, culture, and tradition . . . the age of chivalry transplanted to a New World which was making its own legends and its own myths. He embodied a way of life that had come down through the age of knighthood and the English country squire. America was a land that was beginning all over again, dedicated to nothing much more complicated than the rather hazy belief that all men had equal rights and should have an equal chance in the world. In such a land Lee stood for the feeling that it was somehow of advantage to human society to have a pronounced inequality in the social structure. There should be a leisure class, backed by ownership of land; in turn, society itself should be keyed to the land as the chief source of wealth and influence. It would bring forth (according to this ideal) a class of men with a strong sense of obligation to the community; men who lived not to gain advantage for themselves, but to meet the solemn obligations which had been laid on them by the very fact that they were privileged. From them the country would get its leadership; to them it could look for the higher values—of thought, of conduct, of personal deportment—to give it strength and virtue.

Lee embodied the noblest elements of this aristocratic ideal. Through him, the landed nobility justified itself. For four years, the Southern states had fought a desperate war to uphold the ideals for which Lee stood. In the end, it almost seemed as if the Confederacy fought for Lee; as if he himself was the Confederacy . . . the best thing that the way of life for which the Confederacy stood could ever have to offer. He had passed into legend before Appomattox. Thousands of tired, underfed, poorly clothed Confederate soldiers, long past the simple enthusiasm of the early days of the struggle, somehow considered Lee the symbol of everything for which they had been willing to die. But they could not quite put this feeling into words. If the Lost Cause, sanctified by so much heroism and so many deaths, had a living justification, its justification was General Lee.

Grant, the son of a tanner on the Western frontier, was everything Lee was not. He had come up the hard way and embodied nothing in particular except the eternal toughness and sinewy fiber of the men who grew up beyond the mountains. He was one of a body of men who owed reverence and obeisance to no one, who were self-reliant to a fault, who cared hardly anything for the past but who had a sharp eye for the future.

These frontier men were the precise opposites of the tidewater aristocrats. Back of them, in the great surge that had taken people over the Alleghenies and into the opening Western country, there was a deep, implicit dissatisfaction with a past that had settled into grooves. They stood for democracy, not from any reasoned conclusion about the proper ordering for human society, but simply because they had grown up in the middle of democracy and knew how it worked. Their society might have privileges, but they would be privileges each man had won for himself. Forms and patterns meant nothing. No man was born to anything, except perhaps to a chance to show how far he could rise. Life was competition.

Yet along with this feeling had come a deep sense of belonging to a national community. The Westerner who developed a farm, opened a shop, or set up in business as a trader, could hope to prosper only as his own community prospered—and his community ran from the Atlantic to the Pacific and from Canada down to Mexico. If the land was settled, with towns and highways and accessible markets, he could better himself. He saw his fate in terms of the nation's own destiny. As its horizons expanded, so did his. He had, in other words, an acute dollars-and-cents stake in the continued growth and development of his country.

And that, perhaps, is where the contrast between Grant and Lee becomes most striking. The Virginia aristocrat, inevitably, saw himself in relation to his own region. He lived in a static society which could endure almost anything except change. Instinctively, his first loyalty would go to the locality in which that society existed. He would fight to the limit of endurance to defend it, because in defending it he was defending everything that gave his own life its deepest meaning.

The Westerner, on the other hand, would fight with an equal tenacity for the broader concept of society. He fought so because everything he lived by was tied to growth, expansion, and a constantly widening horizon. What he lived by would survive or fall with the nation itself. He could not possibly stand by unmoved in the face of an attempt to destroy the Union. He would combat it with everything he had, because he could only see it as an effort to cut the ground out from under his feet.

So Grant and Lee were in complete contrast, representing two diametrically opposed elements in American life. Grant was the modern man emerging; beyond him, ready to come on the stage, was the great age of steel and machinery, of crowded cities and a restless, burgeoning vitality. Lee might have ridden down from the old age of chivalry, lance in hand, silken banner fluttering over his head. Each man was the perfect champion of his cause, drawing both his strengths and his weaknesses from the people he led.

Yet it was not all contrast, after all. Different as they were—in background, in personality, in underlying aspiration—these two great soldiers had much in common. Under everything else, they were marvelous fighters. Furthermore, their fighting qualities were really very much alike.

Each man had, to begin with, the great virtue of utter tenacity and fidelity. Grant fought his way down the Mississippi Valley in spite of acute personal discouragement and profound military handicaps. Lee hung on in the trenches at Petersburg after hope itself had died. In each man there was an indomitable quality . . . the born fighter's refusal to give up as long as he can still remain on his feet and lift his two fists.

Daring and resourcefulness they had, too; the ability to think faster and move faster than the enemy. These were the qualities which gave Lee the dazzling campaigns of Second Manassas and Chancellorsville and won Vicksburg for Grant.

Lastly, and perhaps greatest of all, there was the ability, at the end, to turn quickly from war to peace once the fighting was over. Out of the way these two men behaved at Appomattox came the possibility of a peace of reconciliation. It was a possibility not wholly realized, in the years to come, but which did, in the end, help the two sections to become one nation again . . . after a war whose bitterness might have seemed to make such a reunion wholly impossible. No part of either man's life became him more than the part he played in their brief meeting in the McLean house at Appomattox. Their behavior there put all succeeding generations of Americans in their debt. Two great Americans, Grant and Lee—very different, yet under everything very much alike. Their encounter at Appomattox was one of the great moments of American history.

VOCABULARY

1. Define the following words as Catton uses them in this selection: virtual, poignant, obeisance, implicit, burgeoning, tenacity, indomitable.
2. If you are unfamiliar with any other words in this selection, check them in a dictionary and then define them in your own words.
3. Explain why Catton uses the word *poignant* in the second paragraph to describe Grant and Lee's signing of the surrender.

CONTENT

1. List the similarities and differences which Catton cites between Grant and Lee. What quality that Grant and Lee shared does Catton regard as the greatest? Explain.
2. In addition to Catton's interest in the two generals as individuals, he also views them as representatives of larger forces in American life.
   a. What were these larger forces?
   b. Do you agree with Catton's suggestion that the collision of these larger forces was a basic cause of the Civil War? Defend your answer.
3. List some countries of the world which have recently been torn by struggles similar to the American Civil War. Note ways the conflict is similar to, and ways it is different from, our Civil War.
4. In discussing Lee in the fifth paragraph, Catton describes the concept of *noblesse oblige*—a French expression meaning nobility obligates. Do

you see any evidence of this concept in the United States today? What are the advantages and disadvantages of such a concept?

RHETORIC

1. How does Catton organize his comparison and contrast? How else could he have done it?
2. What are some of the metaphors* Catton uses in this essay? What is the effect of this figurative language*?
3. How does Catton's technique of concluding the essay by presenting the similarities between Grant and Lee alter the essay's tone*?

READING AND WRITING SUGGESTIONS

1. If you could be transported back in history for just one day and had your choice of spending that day with either Grant or Lee, whom would you choose? Read a biography of this person, and then write an essay describing your day with him.
2. Catton characterizes Lee as a "tidewater aristocrat" and Grant as a "frontier man." Take two well-known individuals on the American scene, or two people of your acquaintance, who typify the aristocrat and the frontier type and write an essay comparing and contrasting them.

---

*Definitions of all terms marked with an asterisk may be found in the Glossary.

THE WHISTLE

Benjamin Franklin

Benjamin Franklin (1706–1790), one of the most distinguished figures in American history, was a man of numerous and varied talents. Among many other accomplishments, he founded America's first circulating library, studied lightning, electricity, earthquakes, and the Gulf Stream, and gained fame as an inventor and writer. He also had a distinguished political career, becoming one of the signers of the Declaration of Independence. Poor Richard's Almanac *is his best-known work. In "The Whistle," he uses a childhood experience as an analogy to comment on the relative value of the things people desire and seek in life.*

When I was a child, at seven years old, my friends on a holiday filled my pockets with coppers. I went directly to a shop where they sold toys for children; and, being charmed with the sound of a whistle, that I met by the way in the hands of another boy, I voluntarily offered him all my money for one. I then came home, and went whistling all over the house, much pleased with my whistle, but disturbing all the family. My brothers and sisters and cousins, understanding the bargain I had made, told me I had given four times as much for it as it was worth. This put me in mind what good things I might have bought with the rest of the money; and they laughed at me so much for my folly that I cried with vexation; and the reflection gave me more chagrin than the whistle gave me pleasure.

This, however, was afterwards of use to me, the impression continuing on my mind, so that often, when I was tempted to buy some unnecessary thing, I said to myself, "Don't give too much for the whistle"; and so I saved my money.

As I grew up, came into the world, and observed the actions of men, I thought I met with many, very many, who gave too much for the whistle.

When I saw any one too ambitious of court favor, sacrificing his time in attendance on levees[1], his repose, his liberty, his virtue, and perhaps his friends, to attain it, I have said to myself, "This man gave too much for his whistle."

---

[1]Receptions.

If I knew a miser, who gave up every kind of comfortable living, all the pleasure of doing good to others, all the esteem of his fellow-citizens, and the joys of benevolent friendship, for the sake of accumulating wealth; "Poor man," says I, "you do indeed pay too much for your whistle."

When I meet a man of pleasure, sacrificing every laudable improvement of the mind, or of his fortune, to mere corporeal sensations; "Mistaken man," says I, "you are providing pain for yourself instead of pleasure; you give too much for your whistle."

If I see one fond of fine clothes, fine furniture, fine equipages, all above his fortune, for which he contracts debts, and ends his career in prison; "Alas," says I, "he has paid, dear, very dear, for his whistle."

When I see a beautiful, sweet-tempered girl, married to an ill-natured brute of a husband; "What a pity it is," says I, "that she has paid so much for a whistle."

In short, I conceived that great part of the miseries of mankind were brought upon them by the false estimates they had made of the value of things, and by their giving too much for their whistles.

VOCABULARY

1. Define the following words as Franklin uses them in his essay: vexation, chagrin, repose, laudable, corporeal.
2. Identify those words which date Franklin's essay.
3. *Gullible, innocent, inexperienced,* and *dumb* are all terms that might be used to describe someone who "paid too much for a whistle." Identify the two terms that are euphemisms* for the two other terms.

CONTENT

1. What reaction did Franklin have to his family's laughter?
2. In what way did Franklin benefit from this childhood experience?
3. In your opinion, is the worth of something absolute or does it depend on what the buyer values? If the people Franklin describes valued the things they bartered for, did they really "pay too much for their whistles"?
4. Bertrand Russell in "A Life Worth Living" (page 45) suggests, like Franklin, that we can learn wisdom from pain.
   a. Do you agree with them and with Shakespeare that "sweet are the uses of adversity"?

b. Do you think we might become quite as wise if we lived a trouble-free, mistake-free existence? Defend your answer.

RHETORIC

1. What phrase signals Franklin's thesis* statement, and how does its location affect your grasp of the essay's message?
2. What idea does Franklin portray with his analogy* of the whistle, and to what other situations does he apply this idea?
3. How would you describe Franklin's style*? How does his style* influence your understanding of the ideas he seeks to convey?
4. a. What is Franklin's tone* in this essay? Does his tone* influence your enjoyment of the essay?

   b. What do Franklin's style and tone, as well as the title* of his work, *Poor Richard's Almanac,* suggest about the kind of man he was?

READING AND WRITING SUGGESTIONS

1. Write a brief essay using an analogy* to tell about a time when you paid more than something was worth. Describe whether the experience had positive or negative effects on your subsequent behavior.
2. Read two articles from different magazines or newspapers on the same current event. Write a comparison and contrast essay discussing the similarities and differences between the two articles and tell which you felt was more effective. In addition to the articles' content, consider their point of view*, tone*, and style* in your paper.

---

* Definitions of all terms marked with an asterisk may be found in the Glossary.

THE NEW INDIANS AND THE OLD INDIANS: CULTURAL FACTORS IN THE EDUCATION OF AMERICAN INDIANS

Robert L. Bennett

Robert L. Bennett (1912–) was born on the Oneida Indian Reservation in Wisconsin. Beginning his career as a junior clerk, he held a number of positions in the Bureau of Indian Affairs and, in 1966, was appointed Commissioner of Indian Affairs by President Lyndon B. Johnson. In 1969 Bennett presented the following ideas about Indian education in an address at Dartmouth College on the occasion of its two hundredth anniversary.

Although Indians are a very small minority in this country—the Indian population is well under a million—there is considerable new political action taking place among the Indian communities. For more than a hundred years, Indians had remained the stolid and silent prototypes of what the white man alleged they were. But, today, Indian young people have moved in upon the fronts of community action. The Indian warrior today is fighting his great battle on the social level. He has abandoned the arrow and the musket for books and public platforms.

The transition from obscurity to a conspicuous role in contemporary political affairs has not been an easy one for the new generation of Indian youth. It has been accompanied by some confusion as to goals, some hostility to the dominant society, and a great deal of defensiveness in the way Indians see themselves. These are traits that characterize many of the social activists in this country today; but, in the Indian, they are often more acute because the culture gap between Indians and other Americans is wide and deep.

There are fundamental differences, however, between Indian social action and some of the current social movements by other groups. Indian youth are motivated by the desire to *stabilize* their communities, not disrupt them; to make them more economically viable rather than more dependent upon government largesse. They are turning to the government for increasing help, but are rejecting the paternalism that was the core of the special Indian relationship for so many decades.

"We are building, not burning," is the way one youthful Indian leader puts it. It is, indeed, true. From Florida to Alaska, there is evidence that building is going on in Indian communities. Not merely construction of facilities, like homes, and schools, and water and power lines, and roads. Community spirit is building up, too. . . .

Indians understand the tremendous importance to themselves of quality education and equality of educational opportunity. The various tribes invest about $20 million annually in college scholarships; and during the past three years that I have served as Commissioner of Indian Affairs, the Bureau of Indian Affairs contributed another $10 million for higher education aid.

Even so, only about twenty percent of the Indian college age population continues schooling beyond high school, whereas the national rate exceeds forty percent. There are serious blocks to their success in school and college—financial need being one, but the culture gap being an even greater obstacle. . . .

Even while adopting the outward aspects of modern American life, Indians today, as a whole, are probably less fully attuned to the non-Indian lifeway than many of them were in the early part of the last century. Some of the eastern tribes in those days assumed with ease and great success such European culture add-ons as systematic farming and formal schooling.

Back in the days when Oklahoma was Indian territory, Indian groups operated schools and colleges that later formed the core of the state's public school system. This kind of *leadership* in education on the part of the Indians has been absent for many, many years, except in individual instances. It is only now beginning to reappear, currently in the form of Indian demands for control of elementary and secondary schools serving their children. The new interest in education is prompted by a sense of frustration with the average school program that ignores the Indian cultural backgrounds.

Indians today feel threatened by the pressures now forcing total assimilation, because they fear the loss of their self-identity. Being *Indian* and being aware of it sustained them during years of oppression. They challenge the motives of those who would make them less Indian. They seek from education the ability to be both Americans *and* Indians. An either/or choice is intolerable to them. Because Indian history and Indian contributions to the building of this Nation are an integral part of our national history, Indians ask that these facts be fully acknowledged within the framework of our educational programs. . . .

The Indian's determination to retain his identity has contributed to a social phenomenon in modern America—the revival of tribalism. To be sure, today's tribalism has little in common with primitive tribalism, other than to retain remnants of the religious orientation of the Indian society. Today's tribal structures are usually modeled upon American governmental forms, and the objectives and services of tribal governments are, broadly speaking, comparable to those of county governments. The new tribalism is multi-ethnic in character, as is the Indian culture itself. Indian lifeways have been modified by the Spanish horse and Spanish weaving and by the industrious, acquisitive English *mores*. They have also been modified by the trade and agricultural schools of the nineteenth and early twentieth centuries, and by commercialized farming and motorized deep-sea fishing; by World War II and the enlistment of thousands of young Indian men; by air transportation and rocketry. Native Alaskans man the defense early-warning system on the Arctic, Navajos and others assemble intricate electronic devices for space exploration, and the tribes are turning to computers to help keep account of their natural resources.

But the new Indian doesn't always feel comfortable in his new role. The tenor of Indian thinking is well expressed by a student who recently graduated from the federal Institute of American Indian Arts in Santa Fe. He composed a brief piece of poetry that is memorable to me not only because it demonstrates literary artistry but also because of its revealing undertone of bravado. It goes like this:

> We shall learn all these devices the white man has.
> We shall handle his tools for ourselves.
> We shall master his machinery and his inventions,
>   his skills, his medicine, his planning.
> But we'll retain our beauty
> And still be Indian.

Some Indians, like myself, walk always in two worlds, trying to maintain the perspective of both and to draw unto ourselves the best of both. This is not always done with ease, yet it is the course that must be walked by all American Indian children growing up today. It will be harder for them than it was for me, because the gap between the traditional Indian lifeway and the new technological society is far greater than was the gap between rural and city life in the earlier part of the century. Some of the traits and values that are the very core of contemporary American society are totally alien to their Indian upbringing. They must learn to live by the new code, yet their heritage cautions them against foolishly abandoning the basic values of the old.

VOCABULARY

1. Define the following words as Bennett uses them in his essay: prototypes, largesse, paternalism, assimilation, mores, tenor.
2. If you are unfamiliar with any other words in this essay, check them in a dictionary and then define them in your own words.

CONTENT

1. What differences does Bennett cite between the Indians of today and the Indians of yesterday?
2. What effects have the changes within their cultures had on the new Indians?
3. In what ways do Indians differ from other ethnic groups according to Bennett?
4. What is the importance of education to the Indian today?
5. Review Kennedy's "A Nation of Nations" (page 20). How do you think Indians would respond to the idea that the United States is a nation of nations?

RHETORIC

1. How does Bennett organize his comparison and contrast? What other type of organization might he have used?
2. How do Bennett's diction* and style* influence your understanding of the new Indians and the old Indians?
3. What is Bennett's purpose in including the brief poem he quotes?

READING AND WRITING SUGGESTIONS

1. Read a Native American creation account, such as "Creation of the Yakima World" from *Literature of the American Indian*. Write a brief essay discussing how the Yakima Indian view of creation differs from the Judeo-Christian view.

---

* Definitions of all terms marked with an asterisk may be found in the Glossary.

2. Noting Bennett's idea of "Americans *and* Indians," choose any ethnic group you wish and write a comparison and contrast essay showing the meaning of Bennett's comment: "Some Indians, like myself, walk always in two worlds, trying to maintain the perspective of both and to draw unto ourselves the best of both."

FROM POPPING THE QUESTION TO POPPING THE PILL

Margaret Mead

Margaret Mead (1901–1978), renowned cultural anthropologist, held honorary degrees from twelve universities. She was in demand as a speaker and lecturer and taught at some of the country's great universities, including Stanford, the University of California, Harvard, and Yale. Mead was the author or editor of twenty-nine books, of which Coming of Age in Samoa, *published in 1928, is generally considered her classic work. In recent years, she turned her attention to problems and changes in American culture, and became an authority on life in contemporary society. In the following essay, which appeared in* McCall's *in April 1976, Mead examines the customs surrounding modern courtship and marriage, comparing and contrasting these rituals with the customs of the past.*

There have been major changes in attitudes toward courtship and marriage among those middle-class, educated Americans who are celebrated in the media and who are style setters for American life. Courtship was once a regular part of American life; it was a long period, sometimes lasting for many years, and also a tentative one, during which a future husband or wife could still turn back but during which their relationship became more and more exclusive and socially recognized. Courtship both preceded the announcement of an engagement and followed the announcement, although a broken engagement was so serious that it could be expected to throw the girl into a depression from which she might never recover.

There were definite rules governing the courtship period, from the "bundling" permitted in early New England days, when young couples slept side by side with all their clothes on, to strict etiquette that prescribed what sort of gifts a man might give his fiancée in circles where expensive presents were customary. Gifts had to be either immediately consumable, like candy or flowers, or indestructible, like diamonds—which could be given back, their value unimpaired, if there was a rift in the relationship. Objects that could be damaged by use, like gloves and furs, were forbidden. A gentleman might call for a lady in a cab or in his own equipage, but it was regarded as inappropriate for him to pay for her train fare if they went on a journey.

How much chaperoning was necessary, and how much privacy the courting couple was allowed, was a matter of varying local custom. Long walks home through country lanes after church and sitting up in the parlor after their elders had retired for the night may have been permitted, but the bride was expected to be a virgin at marriage. The procedure for breaking off an engagement, which included the return of letters and photographs, was a symbolic way of stating that an unconsummated relationship could still be erased from social memory.

The wedding day was the highest point in a girl's life—a day to which she looked forward all her unmarried days and to which she looked back for the rest of her life. The splendor of her wedding, the elegance of dress and veil, the cutting of the cake, the departure amid a shower of rice and confetti, gave her an accolade of which no subsequent event could completely rob her. Today people over 50 years of age still treat their daughter's wedding this way, prominently displaying the photographs of the occasion. Until very recently, all brides' books prescribed exactly the same ritual they had prescribed 50 years before. The etiquette governing wedding presents—gifts that were or were not appropriate, the bride's maiden initials on her linen—was also specified. For the bridegroom the wedding represented the end of his free, bachelor days, and the bachelor dinner the night before the wedding symbolized this loss of freedom. A woman who did not marry—even if she had the alibi of a fiancé who had been killed in war or had abilities and charm and money of her own—was always at a social disadvantage, while an eligible bachelor was sought after by hostess after hostess.

Courtship ended at the altar, as the bride waited anxiously for the bridegroom who might not appear or might have forgotten the ring. Suppliant gallantry was replaced overnight by a reversal of roles, the wife now becoming the one who read her husband's every frown with anxiety lest she displease him.

This set of rituals established a rhythm between the future husband and wife and between the two sets of parents who would later become co-grandparents. It was an opportunity for mistakes to be corrected; and if the parents could not be won over, there was, as a last resort, elopement, in which the young couple proclaimed their desperate attraction to each other by flouting parental blessing. Each part of the system could be tested out for a marriage that was expected to last for life. We have very different ways today.

Since World War I, changes in relationships between the sexes have been occurring with bewildering speed. The automobile presented a challenge to chaperonage that American adults met by default. From then on, except in ceremonial and symbolic ways, chaperonage disappeared, and a style of premarital relationship was set up in which the onus was put on the girl to refuse inappropriate requests, while each young man declared his suitability by asking for favors that he did not expect to receive. The disappearance of chaperonage was facilitated by the greater freedom of middle-aged women, who began to envy their daughters' freedom, which they had never had. Social forms went through a whole series of rapid changes: The dance with formal partners and programs gave way to occasions in which mothers, or daughters, invited many more young men than girls, and the popular girl hardly circled the dance floor twice in the same man's arms. Dating replaced courtship—not as a prelude to anything but rather as a way of demonstrating popularity. Long engagements became increasingly unfashionable, and a series of more tentative commitments became more popular. As college education became the norm for millions of young people, "pinning" became a common stage before engagement. The ring was likely to appear just before the wedding day. And during the 1950s more and more brides got married while pregnant—but they still wore the long white veil, which was a symbol of virginity.

In this conservative, security-minded decade love became less important than marriage, and lovers almost disappeared from parks and riverbanks as young people threatened each other: "Either you marry me now, or I'll marry someone else." Courtship and dating were embraced by young people in lower grades in school, until children totally unready for sex were enmeshed by the rituals of pairing off. Marriage became a necessity for everyone, for boys as well as for girls: Mothers worried if their sons preferred electronic equipment or chess to girls and pushed their daughters relentlessly into marriage. Divorce became more and more prevalent, and people who felt their marriages were failing began to worry about whether they ought to get a divorce, divorce becoming a duty to an unfulfilled husband or to children exposed to an unhappy marriage. Remarriage was expected, until finally, with men dying earlier than women, there were no men left to marry. The United States became the most married country in the world. Children, your own or adopted, were just as essential, and the suburban life-style—each nuclear family isolated in its own home, with several children, a station wagon and a country-club membership—became the admired life-style, displayed in magazines for the whole world to see.

By the early sixties there were signs of change. We discovered we were running out of educated labor, and under the heading of self-fulfillment educated married women were being tempted back into the labor market. Young people began to advocate frankness and honesty, rebelling against the extreme hypocrisy of the 1950s, when religious and educational institutions alike connived to produce pregnancies that would lead to marriage. Love as an absorbing feeling for another person was rediscovered as marriage as a goal for every girl and boy receded into the back ground.

A series of worldwide political and ecological events facilitated these changes. Freedom for women accompanied agitation for freedom for blacks, for other minorities, for the Third World, for youth, for gay people. Zero-population growth became a goal, and it was no longer unfashionable to admit one did not plan to have children, or perhaps even to marry. The marriage age rose a little, the number of children fell a little. The enjoyment of pornography and the use of obscenity became the self-imposed obligation of the emancipated women. Affirmative action catapulted many unprepared women into executive positions. Men, weary of the large families of the '50s, began to desert them; young mothers, frightened by the prospect of being deserted, pulled up stakes and left their suburban split-levels to try to make it in the cities. "Arrangements," or public cohabitation of young people with approval and support from their families, college deans and employers, became common.

By the early 1970s the doomsters were proclaiming that the family was dead. There were over 8,000,000 single-parent households, most of them headed by poorly paid women. There were endless discussions of "open marriages," "group marriages," communes in which the children were the children of the group, and open discussion of previously taboo subjects, including an emphasis on female sexuality. Yet most Americans continued to live as they always had, with girls still hoping for a permanent marriage and viewing "arrangements" as stepping-stones to marriage. The much-publicized behavior of small but conspicuous groups filtered through the layers of society, so that the freedoms claimed by college youth were being claimed five years later by blue-collar youth; "swinging" (mate swapping) as a pastime of a bored upper-middle-class filtered down.

Perhaps the most striking change of all is that courtship is no longer a prelude to consummation. In many levels of contemporary society, sex relations require no prelude at all; the courtship that exists today tends to occur between a casual sex encounter and a later attempt by either the man or the woman to turn it into a permanent relationship. Courtship is also seen as an act in which either sex can take the lead. Women are felt to have an alternative to marriage, as once they had in the Middle Ages, when convent life was the choice of a large part of the population. Weddings are less conventional, although new conventions, like reading from Kahlil Gibran's *The Prophet*, spread very quickly. There is also a growing rebellion against the kind of town planning and housing that isolate young couples from the help of older people and friends that they need.

But the family is not dead. It is going through stormy times, and millions of children are paying the penalty of current disorganization, experimentation and discontent. In the process, the adults who should never marry are sorting themselves out. Marriage and parenthood are being viewed as a vocation rather than as the duty of every human being. As we seek more human forms of existence, the next question may well be how to protect our young people from a premature, pervasive insistence upon precocious sexuality, sexuality that contains neither love nor delight.

The birthrate is going up a little; women are having just as many babies as before, but having them later. The rights of fathers are being discovered and placed beside the rights of mothers. Exploitive and commercialized abortion mills are being questioned, and the Pill is proving less a panacea than was hoped. In a world troubled by economic and political instability, unemployment, highjacking, kidnapping and bombs, the preoccupation with private decisions is shifting to concern about the whole of humankind.

Active concern for the world permits either celibacy *or* marriage, but continuous preoccupation with sex leaves no time for anything else. As we used to say in the '20s, promiscuity, like free verse, is lacking in structure.

VOCABULARY

1. Most of the words in Mead's essay are probably familiar to you. What does this suggest about Mead's approach to writing?

2. If you are unfamiliar with any words in this essay, check them in a dictionary and then define them in your own words.

CONTENT

1. Mead maintains that over several generations major changes have occurred in attitudes toward courtship and marriage and the customs that surround these two institutions.

   a. What are some attitudes and customs that have remained the same?

   b. What are some attitudes and customs that have changed?

c. Discuss some events that have facilitated or accompanied changes that have occurred.

2. Do you think Porter ("The Necessary Enemy," page 106) would feel that the changes in courtship and marriage customs are positive or negative changes? Explain your answer.

3. Consider the trends that Mead presents in relation to your own generation's courtship and marriage experiences.

   a. How do your experiences differ from your parents' experiences? from your grandparents' experiences?

   b. Which set of experiences would you rather have: your generation's, your parents', or your grandparents'? Explain your answer.

RHETORIC

1. Mead spoke the way she wrote. Do you think her style* contributed to her popularity as a writer and speaker? Explain.

2. What ways of life do the two idioms* in the title connote*?

3. How would you describe the tone* of Mead's essay? Would you have predicted that tone from the essay's title*? Why or why not?

4. Mead uses amusing parallelism* in her title*.

   a. Why do you think she chose this title*?

   b. Do you think she would have used the same title if she had submitted her essay to the *Journal of Anthropological Research* or *Scientific American*? Explain.

   c. Is it fair to use a catchy title* to get people to read a serious work? Why or why not?

5. a. How does Mead organize her comparison and contrast?

   b. What transitional devices* does she use to move from one point to another?

   c. What other ways might she have organized the information?

6. Does Mead's last paragraph pertain to her thesis*, or do you think it serves only as a vehicle for her joke? Explain.

---

*Definitions of all terms marked with an asterisk may be found in the Glossary.

READING AND WRITING SUGGESTIONS

1. Do some research on courtship and marriage attitudes and customs in the United States and an Eastern nation. Then write an essay comparing and contrasting the attitudes and customs of the two countries.

2. Read an article or a book about life in the future, such as Alvin Toffler's *Future Shock.* Relate the information in Mead's essay about the present and the past with your reading about the future, and write an essay comparing and contrasting courtship and marriage customs in the three time periods—past, present, future.

PART TWO

DESCRIPTION

The word *description* comes from the Latin *describere,* meaning "to write about." Because description is an essential part of all writing, it is a tool of the other modes of discourse as well as a mode of discourse in its own right. The function of description is to portray feelings like love, abstract ideas like justice, or physical realities like objects, places, events, or persons as they are perceived through the five senses—smell, taste, vision, hearing, and touch.

There are two types of description. *Objective* description, sometimes called *realistic* description, depicts a subject as a camera would—as impartially and completely as possible. For example, you might objectively describe a chair this way: "the family's battered old wooden rocking chair, which was covered with chipped red paint." *Subjective* description, often called *impressionistic* description, involves the writer's interpretation and response to the subject under discussion. Depicting the family's old rocking chair subjectively, you might write, "It was obvious that the rocking chair had served the family well. Its seat and back were battered by the endless succession of children, parents, and grandparents who had sought comfort in its gentle motion. Its red paint, which had once brightened the corner of the kitchen where the chair stood, was now chipped and faded." As you might expect, many descriptive essays include both subjective and objective passages.

Figures of speech, which stimulate and appeal to the imagination, are an essential ingredient of effective description. We have many different forms of figurative language[1] but the most commonly used are similes, metaphors, and personification. *Similes* use the words "like" or "as" to make direct comparisons: "He was as sly and secretive as a cat." *Metaphors* make comparisons without prepositions or conjunctions by suggesting a likeness or analogy between one object and another: "He was a large bulldog of a man." *Personification* endows inanimate objects or abstract ideas with human attributes: "The restless sea tossed sleeplessly."

In writing description we must keep four things in mind—the point of view, the dominant mood, the details to be included, and the order of presentation of these details.

---

1. For example, Harding in his introduction to *The Variorum Walden* demonstrates that Thoreau used twenty-eight different types of figurative language in *Walden*.

THE SPARROW

Ivan Sergeyevich Turgenev

Ivan Sergeyevich Turgenev (1818–1883), one of the great nineteenth-century Russian writers, was born in Orel, Russia. His father was a retired cavalry officer, his mother a wealthy landowner whose ill treatment of her servants and her children impressed Turgenev deeply. As a child, Turgenev was educated by private tutors, studied at Moscow University, and later graduated from St. Petersburg University. Although he started his literary career as a poet, a collection of essays established his reputation. This collection, entitled A Sportsman's Notebook, *depicts life in Russia in the 1840s. Turgenev also wrote novels concerning social problems in Russia. His essay "The Sparrow" demonstrates the simplicity of his style, as well as his talent for observing and recording details precisely.*

I returned home from the chase, and wandered through an alley in my garden. My dog bounded before me.

Suddenly he checked himself, and moved forward cautiously, as if he scented game.

I glanced down the alley, and perceived a young sparrow with a yellow beak, and down upon its head. He had fallen out of the nest (the wind was shaking the beeches in the alley violently), and lay motionless and helpless on the ground, with his little, unfledged wings extended.

The dog approached it softly, when suddenly an old sparrow, with a black breast, quitted a neighboring tree, dropped like a stone right before the dog's nose, and, with ruffled plumage, and chirping desperately and pitifully, sprang twice at the open, grinning mouth.

He had come to protect his little one at the cost of his own life. His little body trembled all over, his voice was hoarse, he was in an agony—he offered himself.

The dog must have seemed a gigantic monster to him. But, in spite of that, he had not remained safe on his lofty bough. A Power stronger than his own will had forced him down.

Treasure stood still and turned away. . . . It seemed as if he also felt this Power.

I hastened to call the discomfited dog back and went away with a feeling of respect.

Yes, smile not! I felt a respect for this heroic little bird, and for the depth of his paternal love.

Love, I reflected, is stronger than death and the fear of death; it is love alone that supports and animates all.

VOCABULARY

1. Define the following words as Turgenev uses them in his essay: perceived, unfledged, quitted, discomfited.
2. If you are unfamiliar with any other words in this essay, check them in a dictionary and then define them in your own words.
3. Turgenev uses some words that a twentieth-century writer might not use. What are these words and what synonyms* might we substitute for them?

CONTENT

1. Summarize in your own words the moral Turgenev draws from the events in his essay.
2. What does Turgenev mean by "A Power stronger than his own will had forced him down"?
3. Do you think this account of a bird's love for its young is typical of parental love and protection in all species, including the human race? Describe any instances you know of that seem to indicate a failure of this kind of instinctive love in people or animals.
4. What is anthropomorphism*? How does Turgenev apply this device to his description of the old sparrow's motives and Treasure's reactions?

RHETORIC

1. Even in this brief essay, Turgenev uses sensory details extensively. Cite three or four instances in which he describes a sight or sound with particular vividness.
2. What is the essay's thesis*? Where is it most clearly stated? What effect does its location have on your understanding of Turgenev's message?

---

* Definitions of all terms marked with an asterisk may be found in the Glossary.

3. What device does Turgenev use in the sixth paragraph to dramatize the bravery of the old sparrow?
4. Is "The Sparrow" an example of objective description* or subjective description*? What is the basis for your judgment? What would the essay be like if Turgenev had used the other kind of description?

READING AND WRITING SUGGESTIONS

1. Write an essay about a dog or cat you have known, describing its appearance, its special traits, and one event which shows its distinctive personality.
2. Read Sheila Burnford's *The Incredible Journey*, one of Farley Mowat's novels of animal life, or a story which treats the world of animals anthropomorphically*. Write a brief essay describing the relationships between the animals in the work you select.

---

*Definitions of all terms marked with an asterisk may be found in the Glossary.

THREE DAYS TO SEE

Helen Keller

Helen Keller (1880–1968) came to be known the world over for her achievements, despite the fact that an early childhood illness left her blind and deaf. Her teacher, Anne Sullivan, helped Keller's world come alive by teaching her to communicate. Keller's courage in overcoming her handicaps has been recorded in her books The Story of My Life *and* The World I Live In *and in the theater, cinema, and television versions of* The Miracle Worker. *The following essay, published in* Atlantic Monthly *in 1933, is a moving account of what Keller thinks she would experience if she were given three days to see.*

All of us have read thrilling stories in which the hero had only a limited and specified time to live. Sometimes it was as long as a year; sometimes as short as twenty-four hours. But always we were interested in discovering just how the doomed man chose to spend his last days or his last hours. I speak, of course, of free men who have a choice, not condemned criminals whose sphere of activities is strictly delimited.

Such stories set us thinking, wondering what we should do under similar circumstances. What events, what experiences, what associations should we crowd into those last hours as mortal beings? What happiness should we find in reviewing the past, what regrets?

Sometimes I have thought it would be an excellent rule to live each day as if we should die tomorrow. Such an attitude would emphasize sharply the values of life. We should live each day with a gentleness, a vigor, and a keenness of appreciation which are often lost when time stretches before us in the constant panorama of more days and months and years to come. There are those, of course, who would adopt the epicurean motto of "Eat, drink, and be merry," but most people would be chastened by the certainty of impending death.

In stories, the doomed hero is usually saved at the last minute by some stroke of fortune, but almost always his sense of values is changed. He becomes more appreciative of the meaning of life and its permanent spiritual values. It has often been noted that those who live, or have lived, in the shadow of death bring a mellow sweetness to everything they do.

Most of us, however, take life for granted. We know that one day we must die, but usually we picture that day as far in the future. When we are in buoyant health, death is all but unimaginable. We seldom think of it. The days stretch out in an endless vista. So we go about our petty tasks, hardly aware of our listless attitude toward life.

The same lethargy, I am afraid, characterizes the use of all our faculties and senses. Only the deaf appreciate hearing, only the blind realize the manifold blessings that lie in sight. Particularly does this observation apply to those who have lost sight and hearing in adult life. But those who have never suffered impairment of sight or hearing seldom make the fullest use of these blessed faculties. Their eyes and ears take in all sights and sounds hazily, without concentration and with little appreciation. It is the same old story of not being grateful for what we have until we lose it, of not being conscious of health until we are ill.

I have often thought it would be a blessing if each human being were stricken blind and deaf for a few days at some time during his early adult life. Darkness would make him more appreciative of sight; silence would teach him the joys of sound.

Now and then I have tested my seeing friends to discover what they see. Recently I was visited by a very good friend who had just returned from a long walk in the woods, and I asked her what she had observed. "Nothing in particular," she replied. I might have been incredulous had

I not been accustomed to such responses, for long ago I became convinced that the seeing see little.

How was it possible, I asked myself, to walk for an hour through the woods and see nothing worthy of note? I who cannot see find hundreds of things to interest me through mere touch. I feel the delicate symmetry of a leaf. I pass my hands lovingly about the smooth skin of a silver birch, or the rough shaggy bark of a pine. In spring I touch the branches of trees hopefully in search of a bud, the first sign of awakening Nature after her winter's sleep. I feel the delightful, velvety texture of a flower, and discover its remarkable convolutions, and something of the miracle of Nature is revealed to me. Occasionally, if I am fortunate, I place my hand gently on a small tree and feel the happy quiver of a bird in full song. I am delighted to have the cool waters of a brook rush through my open fingers. To me a lush carpet of pine needles or spongy grass is more welcome than the most luxurious Persian rug. To me the pageant of seasons is a thrilling and unending drama, the action of which streams through my finger tips.

At times my heart cries out with longing to see all these things. If I can get so much pleasure from mere touch, how much more beauty must be revealed by sight. Yet, those who have eyes apparently see little. The panorama of color and action which fills the world is taken for granted. It is human, perhaps, to appreciate little that which we have and to long for that which we have not, but it is a great pity that in the world of light the gift of sight is used only as a mere convenience rather than as a means of adding fullness to life.

If I were the president of a university I should establish a compulsory course in "How to Use Your Eyes." The professor would try to show his pupils how they could add joy to their lives by really seeing what passes unnoticed before them. He would try to awake their dormant and sluggish faculties.

Perhaps I can best illustrate by imagining what I should most like to see if I were given the use of my eyes, say, for just three days. And while I am imagining, suppose you, too, set your mind to work on the problem of how you would use your own eyes if you had only three more days to see. If with the oncoming darkness of the third night you knew that the sun would never rise for you again, how would you spend those three precious intervening days? What would you most want to let your gaze rest upon?

I, naturally, should want most to see the things which have become dear to me through my years of darkness. You, too, would want to let your eyes rest long on the things that have become dear to you so that you could take the memory of them with you into the night that loomed before you.

If, by some miracle I were granted three seeing days, to be followed by a relapse into darkness, I should divide the period into three parts.

On the first day, I should want to see the people whose kindness and gentleness have made my life worth living. First I should like to gaze long upon the face of my dear teacher, Mrs. Anne Sullivan Macy, who came to me when I was a child and opened the outer world to me. I should want not merely to see the outline of her face, so that I could cherish it in my memory, but to study that face and find in it the living evidence of the sympathetic tenderness and patience with which she accomplished the difficult task of my education. I should like to see in her eyes that strength of character which has enabled her to stand firm in the face of difficulties, and that compassion for all humanity which she has revealed to me so often.

I do not know what it is to see into the heart of a friend through that "window of the soul," the eye. I can only "see" through my finger tips the outline of a face. I can detect laughter, sorrow, and many other obvious emotions. I know my friends from the feel of their faces. But I cannot really picture their personalities by touch. I know their personalities, of course, through other means, through the thoughts they express to me, through whatever of their actions are revealed to me. But I am denied that deeper understanding of them which I am sure would come through sight of them, through watching their reactions to various expressed thoughts and circumstances, through noting the immediate and fleeting reactions of their eyes and countenance.

Friends who are near to me I know well, because through the months and years they reveal themselves to me in all their phases; but of casual friends I have only an incomplete impression, an impression gained from a handclasp, from spoken words which I take from their lips with my finger tips, or which they tap into the palm of my hand.

How much easier, how much more satisfying it is for you who can see to grasp quickly the essential qualities of another person by watching the subtleties of expression, the quiver of a muscle, the flutter of a hand. But does it ever occur to you to use your sight to see into the inner nature of a friend or acquaintance? Do not most of you seeing people grasp casually the outward features of a face and let it go at that?

For instance, can you describe accurately the faces of five good friends? Some of you can, but many cannot. As an experiment, I have questioned husbands of long standing about the color of their wives' eyes, and often they express embarrassed confusion and admit they do not know. And, incidentally, it is a chronic complaint of wives that their husbands do not notice new dresses, new hats, and changes in household arrangements.

The eyes of seeing persons soon become accustomed to the routine of their surroundings, and they actually see only the startling and spectacular.

But even in viewing the most spectacular sights the eyes are lazy. Court records reveal every day how inaccurately "eyewitnesses" see. A given event will be "seen" in several different ways by as many witnesses. Some see more than others, but few see everything that is within the range of their vision.

Oh, the things that I should see if I had the power of sight for just three days!

The first day would be a busy one. I should call to me all my dear friends and look long into their faces, imprinting upon my mind the outward evidences of the beauty that is within them. I should let my eyes rest, too, on the face of a baby, so that I could catch a vision of the eager, innocent beauty which precedes the individual's consciousness of the conflicts which life develops.

And I should like to look into the loyal, trusting eyes of my dogs—the grave, canny little Scottie, Darkie, and the stalwart, understanding Great Dane, Helga, whose warm, tender, and playful friendships are so comforting to me.

On that busy first day I should also view the small simple things of my home. I want to see the warm colors in the rugs under my feet, the pictures on the walls, the intimate trifles that transform a house into home. My eyes would rest respectfully on the books in raised type which I have read, but they would be more eagerly interested in the printed books which seeing people can read, for during the long night of my life the books I have read and those which have been read to me have built themselves into a great shining lighthouse, revealing to me the deepest channels of human life and the human spirit.

In the afternoon of that first seeing day, I should take a long walk in the woods and intoxicate my eyes on the beauties of the world of Nature, trying desperately to absorb in a few hours the vast splendor which is constantly unfolding itself to those who can see. On the way home from my woodland jaunt my path would lie near a farm so that I might see the patient horses plowing in the field (perhaps I should see only a tractor!) and the serene content of men living close to the soil. And I should pray for the glory of a colorful sunset.

When dusk had fallen, I should experience the double delight of being able to see by artificial light, which the genius of man has created to extend the power of his sight when Nature decrees darkness.

In the night of that first day of sight, I should not be able to sleep, so full would be my mind of the memories of the day.

The next day—the second day of sight—I should arise with the dawn and see the thrilling miracle by which night is transformed into day. I should behold with awe the magnificent panorama of light with which the sun awakens the sleeping earth.

This day I should devote to a hasty glimpse of the world, past and present. I should want to see the pageant of man's progress, the kaleidoscope of the ages. How can so much be compressed into one day? Through the museums, of course. Often I have visited the New York Museum of Natural History to touch with my hands many of the objects there exhibited, but I have longed to see with my eyes the condensed history of the earth and its inhabitants displayed there—animals and the races of men pictured in their native environment; gigantic carcasses of dinosaurs and mastodons which roamed the earth long before man appeared, with his tiny stature and powerful brain, to conquer the animal kingdom; realistic presentations of the processes of evolution in animals, in man, and in the implements which man has used to fashion for himself a secure home on this planet; and a thousand and one other aspects of natural history.

I wonder how many readers of this article have viewed this panorama of the face of living things as pictured in that inspiring museum. Many, of course, have not had the opportunity, but I am sure that many who have had the opportunity have not made use of it. There, indeed, is a place to use your eyes. You who see can spend many fruitful days there, but I, with my imaginary three days of sight, could only take a hasty glimpse, and pass on.

My next stop would be the Metropolitan Museum of Art, for just as the Museum of Natural History reveals the material aspects of the world, so does the Metropolitan show the myriad facets of the human spirit. Throughout the history of humanity the urge to artistic expression has been almost as powerful as the urge for food, shelter, and procreation. And here, in the vast chambers of the Metropolitan Museum, is unfolded before me the spirit of Egypt, Greece, and Rome, as expressed in their art. I know well through my hands the sculptured gods and goddesses of the ancient Nile-land. I have felt copies of Parthenon friezes, and I have sensed the rhythmic beauty of charging Athenian warriors. Apollos and Venuses and the Wingèd Victory of Samothrace are friends of my finger tips. The gnarled, bearded features of Homer are dear to me, for he, too, knew blindness.

My hands have lingered upon the living marble of Roman sculpture as well as that of later generations. I have passed my hands over a plaster cast of Michelangelo's inspiring and heroic Moses; I have sensed the power of Rodin; I have been awed by the devoted spirit of Gothic wood carving. These arts which can be touched have meaning for me, but even they were meant to be seen rather than felt, and I can only guess at the beauty which remains hidden from me. I can admire the simple lines of a Greek vase, but its figured decorations are lost to me.

So on this, my second day of sight, I should try to probe into the soul of man through his art. The things I knew through touch I should now see. More splendid still, the whole magnificent world of painting would be opened to me, from the Italian Primitives, with their serene religious devotion, to the Moderns, with their feverish visions. I should look deep into the canvases of Raphael, Leonardo da Vinci, Titian, Rembrandt. I should want to feast my eyes upon the warm colors of Veronese, study the mysteries of El Greco, catch a new vision of Nature from Corot. Oh, there is so much rich meaning and beauty in the art of the ages for you who have eyes to see!

Upon my short visit to this temple of art I should not be able to review a fraction of that great world of art which is open to you. I should be able to get only a superficial impression. Artists tell me that for a deep and true appreciation of art one must educate the eye. One must learn through experience to weigh the merits of line, of composition, of form and color. If I had eyes, how happily would I embark upon so fascinating a study! Yet I am told that, to many of you who have eyes to see, the world of art is a dark night, unexplored and unilluminated.

It would be with extreme reluctance that I should leave the Metropolitan Museum, which contains the key to beauty—a beauty so neglected. Seeing persons, however, do not need a Metropolitan to find this key to beauty. The same key lies waiting in smaller museums, and in books on the shelves of even small libraries. But naturally, in my limited time of imaginary sight, I should choose the place where the key unlocks the greatest treasures in the shortest time.

The evening of my second day of sight I should spend at a theater or at the movies. Even now I often attend theatrical performances of all sorts, but the action of the play must be spelled into my hand by a companion. But how I should like to see with my own eyes the fascinating figure of Hamlet, or the gusty Falstaff amid colorful Elizabethan trappings! How I should like to follow each movement of the graceful Hamlet, each strut of the hearty Falstaff! And since I could see only one play, I should be confronted by a many-horned dilemma, for there are scores of plays I should want to see. You who have eyes can see any you like. How many of you, I wonder, when you gaze at a play, a movie, or any spectacle, realize and give thanks for the miracle of sight which enables you to enjoy its color, grace, and movement?

I cannot enjoy the beauty of rhythmic movement except in a sphere restricted to the touch of my hands. I can vision only dimly the grace of a Pavlova, although I know something of the delight of rhythm, for often I can sense the beat of music as it vibrates through the floor. I can well imagine that cadenced motion must be one of the most pleasing sights in the world. I have been able to gather something of this by tracing with my fingers the lines in sculptured marble; if this static grace can be so lovely, how much more acute must be the thrill of seeing grace in motion.

One of my dearest memories is of the time when Joseph Jefferson allowed me to touch his face and hands as he went through some of the gestures and speeches of his beloved Rip Van Winkle. I was able to catch thus a meager glimpse of the world of drama, and I shall never forget the delight of that moment. But, oh, how much I must miss, and how much pleasure you seeing ones can derive from watching and hearing the interplay of speech and movement in the unfolding of a dramatic performance! If I could see only one play, I should know how to picture in my mind the action of a hundred plays which I have read or had transferred to me through the medium of the manual alphabet.

So, through the evening of my second imaginary day of sight, the great figures of dramatic literature would crowd sleep from my eyes.

The following morning, I should again greet the dawn, anxious to discover new delights, for I am sure that, for those who have eyes which really see, the dawn of each day must be a perpetually new revelation of beauty.

This, according to the terms of my imagined miracle, is to be my third and last day of sight. I shall have no time to waste in regrets or longings; there is too much to see. The first day I devoted to my friends, animate and inanimate. The second revealed to me the history of man and Nature. Today I shall spend in the workaday world of the present, amid the haunts of men going about the business of life. And where can one find so many activities and conditions of men as in New York? So the city becomes my destination.

I start from my home in the quiet little suburb of Forest Hills, Long Island. Here, surrounded by green lawns, trees, and flowers, are neat little houses, happy with the voices and movements of wives and children, havens of peaceful rest for men who toil in the city. I drive across the lacy structure of steel which spans the East River, and I get a new and startling vision of the power and ingenuity of the mind of man. Busy boats chug and scurry about the river—racy speed boats, stolid, snorting tugs. If I had long days of sight ahead, I should spend many of them watching the delightful activity upon the river.

I look ahead, and before me rise the fantastic towers of New York, a city that seems to have stepped from the pages of a fairy story. What an awe-inspiring sight, these glittering spires, these vast banks of stone and steel—structures such as the gods might build for themselves! This animated picture is a part of the lives of millions of people every day. How many, I wonder, give it so much as a second glance? Very few, I fear. Their eyes are blind to this magnificent sight because it is so familiar to them.

I hurry to the top of one of those gigantic structures, the Empire State Building, for there, a short time ago, I "saw" the city below through the eyes of my secretary. I am anxious to compare my fancy with reality. I am sure I should not be disappointed in the panorama spread out before me, for to me it would be a vision of another world.

Now I begin my rounds of the city. First, I stand at a busy corner, merely looking at people, trying by sight of them to understand something of their lives. I see smiles, and I am happy. I see serious determination, and I am proud. I see suffering, and I am compassionate.

I stroll down Fifth Avenue. I throw my eyes out of focus so that I see no particular object but only a seething kaleidoscope of color. I am certain that the colors of women's dresses moving in a throng must be a gorgeous spectacle of which I should never tire. But perhaps if I had sight I should be like most other women—too interested in styles and the cut of individual dresses to give much attention to the splendor of color in the mass. And I am convinced, too, that I should become an inveterate window shopper, for it must be a delight to the eye to view the myriad articles of beauty on display.

From Fifth Avenue I make a tour of the city—to Park Avenue, to the slums, to factories, to parks where children play. I take a stay-at-home trip abroad by visiting the foreign quarters. Always my eyes are open wide to all the sights of both happiness and misery so that I may probe deep and add to my understanding of how people work and live. My heart is full of the images of people and things. My eye passes lightly over no single trifle; it strives to touch and hold closely each thing its gaze rests upon. Some sights are pleasant, filling the heart with happiness; but some are miserably pathetic. To these latter I do not shut my eyes, for they, too, are part of life. To close the eye on them is to close the heart and mind.

My third day of sight is drawing to an end. Perhaps there are many serious pursuits to which I should devote the few remaining hours, but I am afraid that on the evening of that last day I should again run away to the theater, to a hilariously funny play, so that I might appreciate the overtones of comedy in the human spirit.

At midnight my temporary respite from blindness would cease, and permanent night would close in on me again. Naturally in those three short days I should not have seen all I wanted to see. Only when darkness had again descended upon me should I realize how much I had left unseen. But my mind would be so crowded with glorious memories that I should have little time for regrets. Thereafter the touch of every object would bring a flowing memory of how that object looked.

Perhaps this short outline of how I should spend three days of sight does not agree with the program you would set for yourself if you knew that you were about to be stricken blind. I am, however, sure that if you actually faced that fate your eyes would open to things you had never seen before, storing up memories for the long night ahead. You would use your eyes as never before. Everything you saw would become dear to you. Your eyes would touch and embrace every object that came within your range of vision. Then, at last, you would really see, and a new world of beauty would open itself before you.

I who am blind can give one hint to those who see—one admonition to those who would make full use of the gift of sight: Use your eyes as if tomorrow you would be stricken blind. And the same method can be applied to the other senses. Hear the music of voices, the song of a bird, the mighty strains of an orchestra, as if you would be stricken deaf tomorrow. Touch each object you want to touch as if tomorrow your tactile sense would fail. Smell the perfume of flowers, taste with relish each morsel, as if tomorrow you could never smell and taste again. Make the most of every sense; glory in all the facets of pleasure and beauty which the world reveals to you through the several means of contact which Nature provides. But of all the senses, I am sure that sight must be the most delightful.

VOCABULARY

1. Define the following words as Keller uses them in her essay: buoyant, vista, impairment, symmetry, dormant, tactile, facets, parthenon, friezes, myriad.
2. If you are unfamiliar with any other words in this essay, check them in a dictionary and then define them in your own words.
3. What is a "many-horned dilemma"?

CONTENT

1. If Keller were given an opportunity to see for three days, what general plan would she follow for each day?
2. Follow Keller's suggestion that you "set your mind to work on the problem of how you would use your own eyes if you had only three more days to see."
   a. Answer her question, "If with the oncoming darkness of the third night you knew that the sun would never rise for you again, how would you spend those three precious intervenig days? What would you most want to let your gaze rest upon?"
   b. How do your priorities differ from Keller's?

3. Keller speaks of the joy of being able to see the faces of friends, and then questions whether many people with sight can describe accurately the faces of five good friends. Try to describe the faces of two good friends.
4. Keller stresses how we waste the precious hours of our lives on essentially unimportant things. Through the ages, thinkers have repeatedly made this point.
   a. Why do people find it so difficult to savor the moment? to concentrate on the essentials in life?
   b. What can we do to prevent ourselves from becoming so unhappy over trivialities?
5. Review Bertrand Russell's essay, "A Life Worth Living" (page 45). What similarities with Russell do you see in Keller's philosophy of living?

RHETORIC

1. State Keller's thesis* in your own words.
2. How many of the early paragraphs in the essay are actually part of the introduction*? What is the value of these introductory paragraphs in setting the tone* of the essay?
3. What is Keller attempting to do in her two closing* paragraphs?
4. Keeping in mind Keller's limitations, explain the effect her use of figurative language* has on the essay as a whole.
5. Do you find any evidence of sentimental appeal* in Keller's essay? If so, is it justified? Why or why not?

READING AND WRITING SUGGESTIONS

1. Helen Keller indicates that she would use her first day of seeing to look upon those whose "kindness and gentleness and companionship have made my life worth living." Describe one person who has made your life worth living.
2. Read an article or a book about the life of Franklin D. Roosevelt or some other individual who achieved success and fame in spite of a

---

*Definitions of all terms marked with an asterisk may be found in the Glossary.

handicap. Write a brief essay about the spirit and determination which helped this individual succeed in life.

3. "It is the same old story of not being grateful for what we have until we lose it, of not being conscious of health until we are ill." Using this statement by Keller as your thesis, write an essay in which you describe how to appreciate something before it is lost.

THE PRESENT

Annie Dillard

Annie Dillard (1945–) was born in Pittsburgh, Pennsylvania, and completed her undergraduate and graduate work at Hollins College. Since 1973, she has been a contributing editor to Harper's. *Her writing has also appeared in a wide variety of magazines including* Atlantic Monthly, Sports Illustrated, Cosmopolitan, *and* American Scholar. *Dillard's best-known work is* Pilgrim at Tinker Creek *(1974), from which the following selection is taken. Notice the author's careful attention to detail.*

Catch it if you can.

It is early March. I am dazed from a long day of interstate driving homeward; I pull in at a gas station in Nowhere, Virginia, north of Lexington. The young boy in charge ("Chick 'at oll?") is offering a free cup of coffee with every gas purchase. We talk in the glass-walled office while my coffee cools enough to drink. He tells me, among other things, that the rival gas station down the road, whose FREE COFFEE sign is visible from the interstate, charges you fifteen cents if you want your coffee in a Styrofoam cup, as opposed, I guess, to your bare hands.

All the time we talk, the boy's new beagle puppy is skidding around the office, sniffing impartially at my shoes and at the wire rack of folded maps. The cheerful human conversation wakes me, recalls me, not to a normal consciousness, but to a kind of energetic readiness. I step outside, followed by the puppy.

I am absolutely alone. There are no other customers. The road is vacant, the interstate is out of sight and earshot. I have hazarded into a new corner of the world, an unknown spot, a Brigadoon[1]. Before me extends a low hill trembling in yellow brome, and behind the hill, filling the sky, rises an enormous mountain ridge, forested, alive and awesome with brilliant blown lights. I have never seen anything so tremulous and live. Overhead, great strips and chunks of cloud dash to the northwest in a gold rush. At my back the sun is setting—how can I not have noticed before that the sun is setting? My mind has been a blank slab of black asphalt for hours, but that doesn't stop the sun's wild wheel. I set my coffee beside me on the curb; I smell loam on the wind; I pat the puppy; I watch the mountain.

My hand works automatically over the puppy's fur, following the line of hair under his ears, down his back, inside his forelegs, along his hot-skinned belly.

Shadows lope along the mountain's rumpled flanks; they elongate like root tips, like lobes of spilling water, faster and faster. A warm purple pigment pools in each ruck and tuck of the rock; it deepens and spreads, boring crevasses, canyons. As the purple vaults and slides, it tricks out the unleafed forest and rumpled rock in gilt, in shape-shifting patches of glow. These gold lights veer and retract, shatter and glide in a series of dazzling splashes, shrinking, leaking, exploding. The ridge's bosses and hummocks sprout bulging from its side; the whole mountain looms miles closer; the light warms and reddens; the bare forest folds and pleats itself like living protoplasm before my eyes, like a running chart, a wildly scrawling oscillograph on the present moment. The air cools; the puppy's skin is hot. I am more alive than all the world.

This is it, I think, this is it, right now, the present, this empty gas station, here, this western wind, this tang of coffee on the tongue, and I am patting the puppy, I am watching the mountain. And the second I verbalize this awareness in my brain, I cease to see the mountain or feel the puppy. I am opaque, so much black asphalt. But at the same second, the second I know I've lost it, I also realize that the puppy is still squirming on his back under my hand. Nothing has changed for him. He draws his legs down to stretch the skin taut so he feels every fingertip's stroke along his furred and arching side, his flank, his flung-back throat.

I sip my coffee. I look at the mountain, which is still doing its tricks, as you look at a still-beautiful face belonging to a person who was once your lover in another country years ago: with fond nostalgia, and recognition, but no real feelings save a secret astonishment that you are now

---

1. Brigadoon refers to a Scottish town which disappeared in 1747. The legend is that the town comes back to life one day every century.

strangers. Thanks. For the memories. It is ironic that the one thing that all religions recognize as separating us from our creator—our very self-consciousness—is also the one thing that divides us from our fellow creatures. It was a bitter birthday present from evolution, cutting us off at both ends. I get in the car and drive home.

Catch it if you can. The present is an invisible electron; its lightning path traced faintly on a blackened screen is fleet, and fleeing, and gone.

That I ended this experience prematurely for myself—that I drew scales over my eyes between me and the mountain and gloved my hand between me and the puppy—is not the only point. After all, it would have ended anyway. I've never seen a sunset or felt a wind that didn't. The levitating saints came down at last, and their two feet bore real weight. No, the point is that not only does time fly and do we die, but that in these reckless conditions we live at all, and are vouchsafed, for the duration of certain inexplicable moments, to know it.

VOCABULARY

1. Define the following words as Dillard uses them in her essay: brome, tremulous, loam, oscillograph, opaque, vouchsafed.
2. If you are unfamiliar with any other words in this essay, check them in a dictionary and then define them in your own words.

CONTENT

1. What does Dillard mean by the sentence, "The levitating saints came down at last, and their two feet bore real weight"?
2. Dillard speaks of separations—from the puppy, from "our creator" and from "our fellow creatures." What causes these separations? Why does Dillard consider them a "bitter present from evolution"?
3. In your opinion, is Dillard happy or unhappy in "this moment of awareness"? Explain.
4. Dillard decries our separation from the immediate beauty and essence of life as does Keller in "Three Days to See" (page 139). How does Dillard's suggestion about the reason for this separation differ from Keller's?

RHETORIC

1. How does the way in which Dillard states her thesis* contribute to our understanding of her message?

2. Dillard's essay contains two paragraphs that are one sentence long. What is the effect of this technique?
3. Why do you think Dillard uses a sentence fragment in the third from the last paragraph?
4. Dillard uses sights, sounds, smells, and actions to describe the mood of the fleeting moment. Cite an example of her careful use of detail for each of these cateories.
5. Dillard's last paragraph is complex and abstract*. Paraphrase its meaning in simpler and more concrete* words.
6. What does Dillard suggest with the place, "Nowhere, Virginia," the boy's marked dialect, and the allusion to Brigadoon?

READING AND WRITING SUGGESTIONS

1. Describe an experience in your life during which you were acutely aware of the fleeting moment. Set the scene with the same attention to detail that Dillard does.
2. Read Emily Dickinson's poem "A Light Exists in Spring." How does the subject matter and the mood of Dickinson's poem compare with those of Dillard's essay?

---

*Definitions of all terms marked with an asterisk may be found in the Glossary.

ANNE FRANK: THE TRIUMPH OF FAITH OVER EXPERIENCE

George F. Will

George F. Will (1914–) is a syndicated columnist and contributing editor to Newsweek *magazine. He graduated from Trinity College, attended Magdalen College, Oxford, and received a Ph.D. degree from Princeton University. A number of Will's essays from* Newsweek *and* The Washington Post *have been published in a book entitled* The Pursuit of Happiness and Other Sobering Thoughts. *The following essay, written in 1976, is from that collection.*

Amsterdam, the Netherlands—This coastal city of placid canals, a city hard won from a turbulent sea, this most bourgeois city, has a distinctive and agreeable architecture that is evidence of the inventiveness of the human spirit when challenged by the tax collector. Many houses are very deep but very narrow, so built because, for years, real estate taxes were based on the width of a building's canal frontage.

To solve the lighting problems created by this deep backward extension of row houses, some houses were built almost as two houses, with a small passageway connecting the front house with a back annex, and a small, light courtyard between them. Not all such houses have back annexes, and in those that do the annex can be hidden by concealing (with, for example, a bookcase) the entrance to the annex.

The four-story house on the canal at 263 Prinsengracht is typical. But because history touched it, hard, it is a shrine of sorts, a symbol of the triumph of faith over experience.

"8–9–10 July 1942. We put on heaps of clothes as if we were going to the North Pole, the sole reason being to take clothes with us. No Jew in our situation would have dreamed of going out with a suitcase full of clothing. . . . So we walked in the pouring rain . . . each with a school satchel and shopping bag filled to the brim. . . . We got sympathetic looks from people on the way to work. You could see by their faces how sorry they were they couldn't offer us a lift: the gaudy yellow star spoke for itself. . . . When we arrived at the Prinsengracht, Miep took us quickly upstairs and into the 'Secret Annexe.' She closed the door behind us and we were alone."

They lived behind the bookcase-that-was-a-door until August 4, 1944, when someone told the Gestapo that Dr. Otto Frank's family, and some others, eight in all, were hiding there. The Gestapo deported the inhabitants, one of whom, Dr. Frank's fifteen-year-old daughter, left behind three notebooks.

Great men's war memoirs tell the story of making history. But the most widely read book of the Second World War, Anne Frank's diary, is a view of history from the receiving end.

"6 June 1944 . . . the best part of the invasion is that I have the feeling that friends are approaching. . . . I may yet be able to go back to school in September. . . . 15 July 1944 . . . in spite of everything I still believe that people are really good at heart."

After the August 4 arrest, the Franks were sent to Auschwitz. A survivor says Anne, unlike most prisoners, retained her capacity for tears: there was, for example, the time the Hungarian children had to stand naked in the rain for half a day because they were brought too soon to the gas chamber.

At Auschwitz her head was shaved: The Reich needed women's hair for (among other things) packing around pipe joints in U-boats. Then for no knowable reason the Thousand-Year Reich shipped the fifteen-year-old girl to the Bergen-Belsen concentration camp. She died there in March 1945, shortly before the camp was liberated. She probably died of typhus, but no one really knows, because she was just another wraith-like person in the mud behind the wire.

A year earlier she had written: "23 February 1944 . . . Nearly every morning I go to the attic. . . . From my favorite spot on the floor I look up at the blue sky. . . . 'As long as this exists,' I thought, 'and I may live to see it, this sunshine, the cloudless skies, while this lasts, I cannot be unhappy.' . . . Riches can all be lost, but that happiness in your own heart can only be veiled, and it will still bring you happiness as long as you live. As long as you can look up fearlessly into the heavens."

Today visitors climb the ladder-like steps to see the attic where, from that window, Anne Frank looked up into the Dutch sky. Recently someone climbed to the top of those sad steps, pulled a pencil from his pocket and signed the woodwork: "D. E. Gomez, Leadville, Colo., January, 1976." Let the record show that the war made Western Europe safe for Gomez and his pencil.

VOCABULARY

1. Define the following words as Will uses them in his essay: placid, turbulent, bourgeois.

2. If you are unfamiliar with any other words in this essay, check them in a dictionary and then define them in your own words.

CONTENT

1. What does Will mean by his assertion that Anne Frank's diary was "a view of history from the receiving end"?
2. What effect is Will striving for with his reference to the "Thousand-Year Reich"?
3. Does your reaction to D. E. Gomez's action differ from Will's? Explain.
4. While Anne Frank's life was restricted as a result of political circumstances, Helen Keller's life was limited by her physical disabilities (refer to "Three Days to See," page 139). In what similar ways were these two individuals able to rise above the limitations imposed upon them?

RHETORIC

1. What characteristics of description does this essay contain?
2. How does Will move back and forth in time? Did you find the total effect confusing or dramatic? Explain.
3. What techniques does Will use to create a picture of Anne Frank?
4. Describe the impact of Will's closing*.

READING AND WRITING SUGGESTIONS

1. Read Anne Frank's diary, and then write a journal entry of your own briefly describing your feelings about your life, the people around you, and the values you hold important.
2. Look specifically at the February and March 1944 entries in Anne Frank's diary. Write a descriptive essay showing how, amidst the threat of death, Anne and her friend Peter were concerned with some of the same things all adolescents are concerned with.

---

*Definitions of all terms marked with an asterisk may be found in the Glossary.

ON THE FAR SIDE OF PAIN

George A. Sheehan

George A. Sheehan (1918–), a graduate of the State University of New York's College of Medicine in Brooklyn, is now a practicing physician in Red Bank, New Jersey. His specialty is internal medicine. In this essay, published in Runner's World *magazine in 1977, Sheehan describes the pain which trained athletes endure in order to excel at their sports.*

For the trained athlete, pain is his major enemy. Already disciplined to the long training schedule, the curtailment of social life and the separation from other interests, the athlete even at the top of his powers still must endure pain beyond his imagination and capacity if he wishes to get maximal performance.

"Your stomach feels as though it's going to fall out," writes Don Schollander;[1] "every kick hurts like hell—and suddenly you hear a shrill internal scream. Then you have a choice. Most swimmers back away. If you push through the pain barrier into real agony, you're a champion."

Runners have told of the same tortures. The muscles gradually hardening up into painful leaden stumps. The breath shortening to convulsive gasps. The chest filled with dry fire. The stomach threatening to explode in agony.

And again the difference between athletes is the peculiar ability—Roger Bannister[2] describes it as a capacity for mental excitement—which enables the runner to ignore or overcome discomfort and pain.

"It is this psychological factor—beyond the ken of physiology—which sets the razor's edge between victory and defeat," Bannister says, "and which determines how closely an athlete comes to the absolute limits of performance."

VOCABULARY

1. Define the following words as Sheehan uses them in his essay: curtailment, maximal, leaden, convulsive, ken.

---

1. American Olympic swimming champion. At age 18 became first swimmer in history of Olympics to win four gold medals in a single Olympiad.
2. English runner and first person to run the mile in less than four minutes.

2. If you are unfamiliar with any other words in this essay, check them in a dictionary and then define them in your own words.

CONTENT

1. Why do you think athletes are willing to curtail their social lives, to subject themselves to rigorous training schedules, and even to endure pain?
2. The most tangible symbol of a nonprofessional athlete's success is often a medal or trophy. Discuss how the following quotation relates to Sheehan's essay: "A medal is a label by which we distinguish the man who is unnatural enough to put the needs of civilization before the needs of survival. A medal is an award, not a reward."—A. T. W. Simeons
3. To excel in any activity—whether it be in art, music, law, sports, or business—a person must make certain sacrifices. What sacrifices do you think you will be asked to make in your chosen profession? Will you be willing to make them? Why?
4. Recall Maya Angelou's "Hope" (page 102) and comment on how Sheehan's observations about the physical and psychological factors in running might be applied to Joe Louis's championship boxing match.
5. Sheehan describes that "peculiar ability" of the athlete which allows him to forge ahead in spite of pain and discomfort. Read Plimpton's "The American Tradition of Winning" (page 64). How would Plimpton account for this ability? Does he see a different motivating factor than Sheehan sees?

RHETORIC

1. What is the thesis* of this brief essay? Is it implied or stated?
2. Does Sheehan use objective description* or subjective description*? If he had used the other kind of description, what would the effect have been?
3. Cite three examples of figurative language* in Sheehan's essay. How do these examples contribute to your understanding of the pain an athlete must endure?

---

*Definitions of all terms marked with an asterisk may be found in the Glossary.

READING AND WRITING SUGGESTIONS

1. Read an article or a book about a famous athlete, such as *Tarkenton* by Jim Klobuchar and Fran Tarkenton, and describe the personal qualities of the athlete and the sacrifices he or she made to get to the top.
2. Write an essay describing a particularly exhilarating athletic event in which you were either a participant or a spectator. Describe the spectators, the athletes, and the excitement of the competition.

THE APPLE TREE

John Galsworthy

John Galsworthy (1867–1933), the well-known English novelist, playwright, and social critic, attended Harrow and Oxford. He was admitted to the bar, and for a time he worked and traveled for his father's company. Galsworthy published numerous novels, over two dozen plays, and several collections of essays and poems. He is best known for The Forsyte Saga, *the history of an upper-middle-class family. In 1932 Galsworthy received the Nobel Prize for Literature. The following selection, in which he describes an orchard at night, was first published in 1916.*

It was nearly eleven that night when Ashurst put down the pocket *Odyssey* which for half an hour he had held in his hands without reading, and slipped through the yard down to the orchard. The moon had just risen, very golden, over the hill, and like a bright, powerful, watching spirit peered through the bars of an ash tree's half-naked boughs. In among the apple trees it was still dark, and he stood making sure of his direction, feeling the rough grass with his feet. A black mass close behind him stirred with a heavy grunting sound, and three large pigs settled down again close to each other, under the wall. He listened. There was no wind, but the stream's burbling, whispering chuckle had gained twice its daytime strength. One bird, he could not tell what, cried "Pip—pip," "Pip—pip," with perfect monotony; he could hear a night-jar spinning very far off; an owl hooting. Ashurst moved a step or two, and again halted, aware of a dim, living whiteness all round his head. On the dark, unstirring trees innumerable flowers and buds all soft and blurred were being bewitched to life by the creeping moonlight. He had the oddest feeling of actual companionship, as if a million white moths or spirits had floated in and settled between dark sky and darker ground, and were opening and shutting their wings on a level with his eyes. In the bewildering, still, scentless beauty of that moment he almost lost memory of why he had come to the orchard. The flying glamour which had clothed the earth all day had not gone now that night had fallen, but only changed into this new form. He moved on through the thicket of stems and boughs covered with that live, powdering whiteness, till he reached the big apple tree. No mistaking that, even in the dark, nearly twice the height and size of any other, and leaning out towards the open meadows and the stream. Under the thick branches he stood still again, to listen. The same sounds exactly, and a faint grunting from the sleepy pigs. He put his hands on the dry, almost warm tree trunk, whose rough, mossy surface gave forth a peaty scent at his touch. Would she come—would she? And among these quivering, haunted, moon-witched trees he was seized with doubts of everything! All was unearthly here, fit for no earthly lovers; fit only for god and goddess, faun and nymph—not for him and this little country girl. Would it not be almost a relief if she did not come? But all the time he was listening. And still that unknown bird went "Pip—pip," "Pip—pip," and there rose the busy chatter of the little trout stream, whereon the moon was flinging glances through the bars of her tree-prison. The blossom on a level with his eyes seemed to grow more living every moment, seemed with its mysterious white beauty more and more a part of his suspense. He plucked a fragment and held it close—three blossoms. Sacrilege to pluck fruit-tree blossom—soft, sacred, young blossom—and throw it away! Then suddenly he heard the gate close, the pigs stirring again and grunting; and leaning against the trunk, he pressed his hands to its mossy sides behind him, and held his breath. She might have been a spirit threading the trees, for all the noise she made! Then he saw her quite close—her dark form part of a little tree, her white face part of its blossom; so still, and peering towards him. He whispered: "Megan!" and held out his hands.

VOCABULARY

1. Define the following words as Galsworthy uses them in his essay: peaty, faun, nymph, sacrilege.
2. If you are unfamiliar with any other words in this essay, check them in a dictionary and then define them in your own words.

CONTENT

1. What kind of an evening is described in Galsworthy's essay? How is it portrayed in his description?
2. What is Ashurst's state of mind? How does Galsworthy indicate this?
3. Galsworthy hints at a conflict in Ashurst's relationship with Megan. What is this conflict? Beginning with the first line of the essay, show how this conflict is suggested.
4. Does this essay call to mind an experience from your past—for example, a first date, or a secret meeting? If so, describe the experience.
5. Review Margaret Mead's "From Popping the Question to Popping the Pill" (page 128). Considering the trends that Mead presents in relation to the setting described here, what do you think young people have lost or gained from the changes in dating customs?

RHETORIC

1. Does Galsworthy's title* reflect the subtlety and complexity of his essay? What other titles might he have used?
2. Cite examples of especially effective words and phrases that help set the essay's mood of tranquillity.
3. What specific words and phrases contribute to a mood of excitement or expectancy?
4. Find an example of onomatopoeia* (the formation of a word that imitates the sound associated with it), and two or three examples of alliteration* (the repetition of initial sounds in neighboring words or syllables). How do these two devices enhance the effectiveness of Galsworthy's essay?

READING AND WRITING SUGGESTIONS

1. Write a brief descriptive essay in which you continue Galsworthy's story, describing a scene that might have transpired between Ashurst and Megan.

---

*Definitions of all terms marked with an asterisk may be found in the Glossary.

2. Write a brief essay describing a secret rendezvous between two young lovers today. Where might they meet? What book might the young man be reading? What sounds might he hear while waiting?

MARY WHITE

William Allen White

William Allen White (1868–1944) was owner and editor of the Emporia Gazette *from 1895 until his death. He is the author of several novels and biographies, but he is best known for his contributions to newspapers and magazines. One editorial, "To an Anxious Friend," won him a Pulitzer prize in 1922. The essay "Mary White," which appeared in the Emporia* Gazette *March 15, 1921, is a description of White's daughter, who was killed in a fall from a horse.*

The Associated Press reports carrying the news of Mary White's death declared that it came as the result of a fall from a horse. How she would have hooted at that! She never fell from a horse in her life. Horses have fallen on her and with her—"I'm always trying to hold 'em in my lap," she used to say. But she was proud of few things, and one was that she could ride anything that had four legs and hair. Her death resulted not from a fall, but from a blow on the head which fractured her skull, and the blow came from the limb of an overhanging tree on the parking.

The last hour of her life was typical of its happiness. She came home from a day's work at school, topped off by a hard grind with the copy on the High School Annual, and felt that a ride would refresh her. She climbed into her khakis, chattering to her mother about the work she was doing, and hurried to get her horse and be out on the dirt roads for the country air and radiant green fields of the spring. As she rode through the town on an easy gallop she kept waving at passers-by. She knew everyone in town. For a decade the little figure with the long pig-tail and the red hair ribbon has been familiar on the streets of Emporia, and she got in the way of speaking to those who nodded at her. She passed the Kerrs, walking the horse, in front of the Normal Library, and waved at them; passed another friend a few hundred feet further on, and waved at her. The horse was walking and, as she turned into North Merchant Street she took off her cowboy hat, and the horse swung into a lope. She passed the Tripletts and waved her cowboy hat at them, still moving gaily north on Merchant Street. A Gazette carrier passed—a High School boy friend—and she waved at him, but with her bridle hand; the horse veered quickly; plunged into the parking where the low-hanging limb faced her, and, while she still looked back waving, the blow came. But she did not fall from the horse; she slipped off, dazed a bit, staggered and fell in a faint. She never quite recovered consciousness.

But she did not fall from the horse, neither was she riding fast. A year or so ago she used to go like the wind. But that habit was broken, and she used the horse to get into the open to get fresh, hard exercise, and to work off a certain surplus energy that welled up in her and needed a physical outlet. That need has been in her heart for years. It was back of the impulse that kept the dauntless, little brown-clad figure on the streets and country roads of this community and built into a strong, muscular body what had been a frail and sickly frame during the first years of her life. But the riding gave her more than a body. It released a gay and hardy soul. She was the happiest thing in the world. And she was happy because she was enlarging her horizon. She came to know all sorts and conditions of men; Charley O'Brien, the traffic cop, was one of her best friends. W. L. Holtz, the Latin teacher, was another. Tom O'Connor, farmer-politician, and Rev. J. H. J. Rice, preacher and police judge, and Frank Beach, music master, were her special friends, and all the girls, black and white, above the track and below the track, in Pepville and Stringtown, were among her acquaintances. And she brought home riotous stories of her adventures. She loved to rollick; persiflage was her natural expression at home. Her humor was a continual bubble of joy. She seemed to think in hyperbole and metaphor. She was mischievous without malice, as full of faults as an old shoe. No angel was Mary White, but an easy girl to live with, for she never nursed a grouch five minutes in her life.

With all her eagerness for the out-of-doors she loved books. On her table when she left her room were a book by Conrad, one by Galsworthy, *Creative Chemistry* by E. E. Slossom, and a Kipling book. She read Mark Twain, Dickens and Kipling before she was ten—all of their writings. Wells and Arnold Bennett particularly amused and diverted her. She was entered as a student in Wellesley in 1922; was assistant editor of the High School Annual this year, and in line for election to the editorship of the Annual next year. She was a member of the executive committee of the High School YWCA.

Within the last two years she had begun to be moved by an ambition to draw. She began as most children do by scribbling in her school books, funny pictures. She bought cartoon magazines and took a course—rather casually, naturally, for she was, after all, a child with no strong purposes—and this year she tasted the first fruits of success by having her pictures accepted by the High School Annual. But the thrill of delight she got when Mr. Ecord, of the Normal Annual, asked her to do the cartooning for that book this spring, was too beautiful for words. She fell to her work with all her enthusiastic heart. Her drawings were accepted, and her pride—always repressed by a lively sense of the ridiculousness of the figure she was cutting—was a really gorgeous thing to see. No successful artist ever drank a deeper draught of satisfaction than she took from the little fame her work was getting among her school-fellows. In her glory, she almost forgot her horse—but never her car.

For she used the car as a jitney bus. It was her social life. She never had a "party" in all her nearly seventeen years—wouldn't have one; but she never drove a block in the car in her life that she didn't begin to fill the car with pick-ups! Everybody rode with Mary White—white and black, old and young, rich and poor, men and women. She liked nothing better than to fill the car full of long-legged High School boys and an occasional girl, and parade the town. She never had a "date," nor went to a dance, except once with her brother, Bill, and the "boy proposition" didn't interest her—yet. But young people—great spring-breaking, varnish-cracking, fender-bending, door-sagging carloads of "kids" gave her great pleasure. Her zests were keen. But the most fun she ever had in her life was acting as chairman of the committee that got up the big turkey dinner for the poor folks at the county home; scores of pies, gallons of slaw; jam, cakes, preserves, oranges and a wilderness of turkey were loaded in the car and taken to the county home. And, being of a practical turn of mind, she risked her own Christmas dinner by staying to see that the poor folks actually got it all. Not that she was a cynic; she disliked to tempt folks. While there she found a blind colored uncle, very old, who could do nothing but make rag rugs, and she rustled up from her school friends rags enough to keep him busy for a season. The last engagement she tried to make was to take the guests at the county home out for a car ride. And the last endeavor of her life was to try to get a rest room for colored girls in the High School. She found one girl reading in the toilet, because there was no better place for a colored girl to loaf, and it inflamed her sense of injustice and she became a nagging harpy to those who, she thought, could remedy the evil. The poor she had always with her, and was glad of it. She hungered and thirsted for righteousness; and was the most impious creature in the world. She joined the Congregational Church without consulting her parents; not particularly for her soul's good. She never had a thrill of piety in her life, and would have hooted at a "testimony." But even as a little child she felt the church was an agency for helping people to more of life's abundance, and she wanted to help. She never wanted help for herself.

Clothes meant little to her. It was a fight to get a new rig on her; but eventually a harder fight to get it off. She never wore a jewel and had no ring but her High School class ring, and never asked for anything but a wrist watch. She refused to have her hair up; though she was nearly seventeen. "Mother," she protested, "you don't know how much I get by with, in my braided pigtails, that I could not with my hair up." Above every other passion of her life was her passion not to grow up, to be a child. The tom-boy in her, which was big, seemed to loathe to be put away forever in skirts. She was a Peter Pan, who refused to grow up.

Her funeral yesterday at the Congregational Church was as she would have wished it; no singing, no flowers save the big bunch of red roses from her Brother Bill's Harvard classmen—Heavens, how proud that would have made her! And the red roses from the Gazette force—in vases at her head and feet. A short prayer, Paul's beautiful essay on "Love" from the Thirteenth Chapter of First Corinthians, some remarks about her democratic spirit by her friend, John H. J. Rice, pastor and police judge, which she would have deprecated if she could, a prayer sent down for her by her friend, Carl Nau, and opening the service the slow, poignant movement from Beethoven's Moonlight Sonata, which she loved, and closing the service a cutting from the joyously melancholy first movement of Tschaikowski's Pathetic Symphony, which she liked to hear in certain moods on the phonograph; then the Lord's Prayer by her friends in the High School.

That was all.

For her pall-bearers only her friends were chosen: her Latin teacher, W. L. Holtz; her High School principal, Rice Brown; her doctor, Frank Foncannon; her friend, W. W. Finney; her pal at the Gazette office, Walter Hughes; and her brother, Bill. It would have made her smile to know that her friend, Charley O'Brien, the traffic cop, had been transferred from Sixth and Commercial to the corner near the church to direct her friends who came to bid her good-by.

A rift in the clouds in a gray day threw a shaft of sunlight upon her coffin as her nervous, energetic little body sank to its last sleep. But the soul of her, the glowing, gorgeous, fervent soul of her, surely was flaming in eager joy upon some other dawn.

VOCABULARY

1. Define the following words as White uses them in his essay: rollick, persiflage, harpy, loathe, deprecate, poignant, fervent, riotous.
2. If you are unfamiliar with any other words in this essay, check them in a dictionary and then define them in your own words.

CONTENT

1. In the opening paragraph and later in his essay, White emphasizes that Mary White did not fall from her horse. Why do you think he is so concerned about this distinction between Mary's falling from the horse and her slipping off after receiving a blow to the head?
2. What qualities belonging to his daughter does White describe in the second and third paragraphs of his essay? How are these qualities reaffirmed later in the essay?
3. How does White deal with his grief? Support your answers with evidence from the essay.
4. Barber, in "Four Types of Presidents" (p. 40), asserts that we can depict the essence of most people according to their active or passive response to life and their positive or negative feelings about what they do. Use these two dimensions to explain the essence of Mary White.

RHETORIC

1. White uses several figurative* words and phrases to paint a picture of what Mary was like. Which touched you the most and gave you the clearest picture of Mary's appearance and character?
2. How does White describe Mary's speech? Quote an example. What does White's description of Mary's speech indicate about the kind of person she was?
3. Notice how many sentences White begins with a conjunction. What is the effect of this?
4. Near the end of the essay White uses a one sentence paragraph, "That was all." What effect does this achieve?
5. Assess the function and the effectiveness of the last paragraph. How does this paragraph complement the image of Mary that White creates?

READING AND WRITING SUGGESTIONS

1. All of us, at one point or another, are faced with the death of a family member or close friend. In a brief essay, describe such an experience

---

*Definitions of all terms marked with an asterisk may be found in the Glossary.

in your own life. Use the experience, as White did, not as an end in itself, but as a way to characterize the life of the essay's subject.

2. Read Theodore Roethke's poem "Elegy to Jane," about the death of a young student in a horseback riding incident. Comment on the similarities or differences between Roethke's poem and White's essay in terms of the incident treated and the writer's tone.

PART THREE

ARGUMENT

The purpose of argument as a mode of discourse is to convince the reader to accept the writer's viewpoint on an issue. There are two forms of argument: *logical argument,* which appeals to the reason or intellect of the reader, and *persuasive argument,* which appeals primarily to the reader's emotions. Needless to say, many strong arguments combine these two forms in a single essay.

Logical argument uses three methods to develop a strong and convincing position—induction, deduction, and analogy. *Induction* presents a series of facts or truths that lead to a larger general truth. If, for example, you wanted to argue inductively that the Loch Ness Monster does not exist, you would begin your essay by stating the facts supporting your position: that no one has ever seen Nessie at close range, that photographs and films purporting to show the monster are blurred and indistinct, and that a recent scientific expedition using sophisticated equipment failed to detect any sign of the creature. You would then close your argument with the generalization that the Loch Ness Monster does not, therefore, exist.

Deduction, on the other hand, begins with a generalization about an entire class and applies that generalization to a specific member of the class. For example, you might begin a deductive argument by stating and attempting to prove the generalization that no monsters exist on earth. Once you had shown that Nessie is, indeed, a monster, you could then argue that the creature does not exist. The problems inherent in this type of argument are apparent in this example; to prove your point you would have to show not only that Nessie is a member of the class, monster, but also that your generalization about the class—no monsters exist on earth—is true.

Analogy, the third method of development, employs the reasoning that if two or more things share certain proven similarities, then they will probably be similar in other respects. To use the monster example once again, you might say that since King Kong and Nessie are both monsters, and King Kong does not exist, then Nessie also does not exist. As the example illustrates, however, analogy can easily be misused, for few ideas or things are exactly alike. If the two things being compared are only superficially similar, the analogy may be false, or at best weak, leading to an unreliable or untenable conclusion.

As mentioned earlier, *persuasive argument,* unlike logical argument, appeals to the emotions of the reader. Rather than depending on a specific type of reasoning as a method for developing a proposition, persuasive argument relies particularly on strength of language to convince the reader of the truth of a proposition. Persuasive argument is seldom effective, however, if it is not supported by logic; even the most elegant of phrases will not convince the reader who sees that the argument simply does not make sense.

The force of an argument always depends on the nature of the evidence given to support the proposition. This evidence must be both accurate and sufficient to prove the point, and the authorities quoted in support of the argument must be qualified in the subject area being discussed. Writers—and readers—of argument must be aware of logical fallacies which weaken a discussion; the most common of these are non sequiturs, post hoc ergo propter hoc reasoning, ad hominem attacks, begging the question, overgeneralization, and special pleading. If you are not familiar with these logical fallacies, consult the Glossary for definitions. Also, refer to Shulman's "Love is a Fallacy" (page 54) for humorous illustrations of each.

THE STOCKHOLM ADDRESS

William Faulkner

William Faulkner (1879–1962), one of the greatest modern American writers, was born in New Albany, Mississippi. In 1918 he enlisted in the Royal Canadian Air Force, and after the war ended, he enrolled at the University of Mississippi for two years. Faulkner spent most of his life in the small Mississippi town of Oxford, the model for fictional Yoknapatawpha County, which served as the setting for much of his writing. Among Faulkner's best-known works are The Sound and the Fury, Light in August, *and* As I Lay Dying. *On December 10, 1950, in Stockholm, Sweden, Faulkner was awarded the Nobel Prize for Literature. In response, he gave the brief but eloquent address that follows.*

I feel that this award was not made to me as a man, but to my work—a life's work in the agony and sweat of the human spirit, not for glory and least of all for profit, but to create out of the materials of the human spirit something which did not exist before. So this award is only mine in trust. It will not be difficult to find a dedication for the money part of it commensurate with the purpose and significance of its origin. But I would like to do the same with the acclaim too, by using this moment as a pinnacle from which I might be listened to by the young men and women already dedicated to the same anguish and travail, among whom is already that one who will some day stand here where I am standing.

Our tragedy today is a general and universal physical fear so long sustained by now that we can even bear it. There are no longer problems of the spirit. There is only the question: When will I be blown up? Because of this, the young man or woman writing today has forgotten the problems of the human heart in conflict with itself which alone can make good writing because only that is worth writing about, worth the agony and the sweat.

He must learn them again. He must teach himself that the basest of all things is to be afraid; and, teaching himself that, forget it forever, leaving no room in his workshop for anything but the old verities and truths of the heart, the old universal truths lacking which any story is ephemeral and doomed—love and honor and pity and pride and compassion and sacrifice. Until he does so, he labors under a curse. He writes not of love but of lust, of defeats in which nobody loses anything of value, of victories without hope and, worst of all, without pity or compassion. His griefs grieve on no universal bones, leaving no scars. He writes not of the heart but of the glands.

Until he relearns these things, he will write as though he stood among and watched the end of man. I decline to accept the end of man. It is easy enough to say that man is immortal simply because he will endure: that when the last ding-dong of doom has clanged and faded from the last worthless rock hanging tideless in the last red and dying evening, that even then there will still be one more sound: that of his puny inexhaustible voice, still talking. I refuse to accept this. I believe that man will not merely endure: he will prevail. He is immortal, not because he alone among creatures has an inexhaustible voice, but because he has a soul, a spirit capable of compassion and sacrifice and endurance. The poet's, the writer's, duty is to write about these things. It is his privilege to help man endure by lifting his heart, by reminding him of the courage and honor and hope and pride and compassion and pity and sacrifice which have been the glory of his past. The poet's voice need not merely be the record of man, it can be one of the props, the pillars to help him endure and prevail.

VOCABULARY

1. Define the following words as Faulkner uses them in his address: commensurate, pinnacle, anguish, travail, verities, ephemeral.

2. Faulkner uses three key words in his address: *immortal, endure*, and *prevail*. Define these words by pointing out the differences in their meanings. What is the total, or combined, effect of these words?

CONTENT

1. What does Faulkner regard as the "old universal truths"? Explain why you agree or disagree with him.
2. Are Faulkner's remarks still relevant today—more than thirty years after he delivered his address—or has the world situation changed significantly?
3. What does Faulkner mean by the last sentence in paragraph three, "He writes not of the heart but of the glands"?
4. In your own words state what Faulkner sees as the duty of young writers.
5. Faulkner talks about the glory of man's past, a present filled with fear, and a future in which man can prevail. Review Russell's "A Life Worth Living" (page 45).
   a. Do Russell and Faulkner agree on what makes life worth living?
   b. Do the two see the task of the poet or the writer in the same way? Explain.

RHETORIC

1. Faulkner's address dwells on two related themes, one concerning young writers and one concerning the fate of humanity. Describe Faulkner's two themes in greater detail, and explain how he weaves them together in his address. To whom is the statement addressed?
2. How does Faulkner support his position that "man will prevail"? Is his argument primarily rational* or emotional*? At what point does it become clear which type of argument he will use?
3. Find an example of a metaphor*, a simile*, of alliteration*, and of metonomy* in Faulkner's address. What effect do these have on your understanding of his message?
4. Which in your opinion is primarily responsible for the tone* of Faulkner's message—its style or its content? Explain.
5. What repeated phrases provide a link between paragraphs one and two? Point out instances of repetition* and parallelism* in paragraphs three and four.

---

*Definitions of all terms marked with an asterisk may be found in the Glossary.

READING AND WRITING SUGGESTIONS

1. Write an essay in which you argue what the role of the writer should be in today's world.
2. Faulkner says that "our tragedy today is a general and universal physical fear." Do you agree or disagree with Faulkner on this point? Write a brief essay in which you support your position.
3. Imagine that you have won an international prize for something that you have accomplished. Using Faulkner's speech as a model, write an acceptance speech in which you address an issue that you feel is of vital significance to humanity's future.
4. Read Faulkner's *Light in August* and write a brief essay discussing how well Faulkner himself lives up to the goals he advocates for writers in "The Stockholm Address." Use specific details to support your argument.

IS IT TIME TO STOP LEARNING?

David S. Saxon

David S. Saxon (1920–) earned a Ph.D. in physics from the Massachusetts Institute of Technology. He has held a number of teaching and administrative positions in higher education and is currently president of the University of California. In the following essay, which appeared in Newsweek *in 1976, Saxon argues for a continuing emphasis on higher education in modern American society.*

A strange new term has recently crept into our national vocabulary: overeducation. It is a term that would have confounded most Americans in every generation up to this Bicentennial year. For them, education was a social necessity to be provided, an individual good to be sought and an end to be sacrificed for. The only limits were the abilities and aspirations of students and the resources of the community.

What has happened in society today that gives rise to talk of overeducation? Have we actually reached and even passed the socially useful and individually rewarding limits of learning in America? Or have we somehow mislaid our proper measure of the broader values of education in a democratic society?

Let's examine this curious new term, overeducation. Overeducation for *what?* For a full and satisfying life? For a lifetime of changing careers in a rapidly changing world? For active participation in the affairs of a modern democratic government?

No, the term generally means that a person has received more learning, or other learning, than is required for his or her first major job. It may be a perfectly valid description of a person's education in relation to that particular circumstance. But that circumstance, though important, is not the whole of life. And the tendency to measure the value of education against this single, limited yardstick is disastrously shortsighted for both the individual and society.

Measures of Education

Throughout our history, American education has been built to other measures, and the results have had a tremendous influence on the nation's development. One such measure has been the need for leadership based on ability and talent rather than rank. The Pilgrims, after just sixteen years of colonizing the New World wilderness, established Harvard College, declaring that "one of the next things we longed for, and looked after was to advance learning and perpetuate it to posterity; dreading to leave an illiterate ministry to the churches, when our present ministers shall lie in the dust." And Thomas Jefferson called for the education of "youth of talent" without regard for their social or economic status as "the keystone of the arch of our government."

Another measure has been the importance of universal education to a democratic society. Benjamin Franklin wrote that "nothing is of more importance for the public weal, than to firm and train up youth in wisdom and virtue. Wise and good men are, in my opinion, the strength of a state; much more so than riches and arms." A third measure has been the advantage of merging the practical and liberal arts. When Abraham Lincoln signed the land-grant college legislation of 1862, he set America on its course toward a distinctive model of higher education, not for the few but for the many, not as a cloister but as the active partner of agriculture and industry and all the other segments of a developing society.

And when Johns Hopkins University in 1876 joined undergraduate education with the most advanced graduate instruction and research, American education was extending its reach toward the farthest frontiers of scientific and scholarly discovery.

Building to these measures has produced in America an educational system that is in many ways unparalleled in history, and this is a healthy perspective from which to view our present shortcomings and the problems that lie ahead.

Certainly education in the United States is unmatched in its accessibility to the highest levels for the broadest cross-section of the citizenry, though we have much farther to go in this respect. Our total educational structure is unequaled in its diversity—public and private institutions, religious and secular, local and statewide—and this rich diversity is our protection against control or conformity in the realm of ideas. And nowhere else has there been a more rapid transfer of scholarly discoveries through basic research to practical application.

But have we now, finally, reached the useful limit of our educational resources for many of our citizens? Can we now say to some of them, "You won't need any more formal learning for *your* role in society"? And to *which* Americans shall we say that their future working careers or their cultural horizons or their prospects for civic or political leadership don't seem to warrant the cost of a broad education beyond their immediate occupational needs?

Cultivating Potential

I am painfully aware that academic leaders have themselves too often resorted to strictly economic appeals for support because these seemed easier to explain and justify than the less tangible purposes of learning. We have too often promised more than we could deliver on investments in research, and so have invited disappointed expectations and some disillusion with what education can offer in exchange for its considerable cost. But neither education nor society in general will benefit from a continuing rebuff for these sins.

To the extent that the level of education and society's ability to put it to use are out of balance, then what a peculiarly negative solution—what a tragic waste of human potential—to limit education and learning. Wouldn't it make far better sense to concentrate on how to use the full capacity of all of our citizens?

We need that capacity now. I think we are more in need of wisdom today than at most earlier stages of our history. A broad liberal education is not the only ingredient of wisdom, but it is an essential one. We need all the knowledge we can muster to meet our technological and scientific problems. We need all the accumulated experience and understanding of humanity we can absorb to meet our social problems. And I believe we can ill afford the risk of foreclosing the maximum cultivation of that knowledge and understanding simply because it seems not to be required for immediate vocational purposes.

America's vision for 200 years has been longer than that. Overeducation is an idea whose time must never come.

VOCABULARY

1. Define the following words as Saxon uses them in his essay: confounded, perpetuate, posterity, keystone, weal, cloister, secular.
2. If you are unfamiliar with any other words in this essay, check them in a dictionary and then define them in your own words.

CONTENT

1. Summarize Saxon's reasons for our needing wisdom more today than we did at earlier periods in our history. Add a reason of your own.
2. What are Saxon's arguments against the trend away from liberal, broad-based education to education that is vocational or job-oriented?
3. How would you respond if someone told you that you had to stop attending school because you wouldn't need any more formal learning for your role in society?
4. Answer Saxon's question, "And to *which* Americans shall we say that their future working careers or their cultural horizons or their prospects for civic or political leadership don't seem to warrant the cost of a broad education beyond their immediate occupational needs?" As you answer, remember that intelligence tests and scholastic aptitude tests are coming under increasingly heavy criticism for being biased—especially against people from nonacademic environments.

RHETORIC

1. Does Saxon use logical argument or persuasive argument? Would his background lead you to expect the kind of argument he uses?
2. Why does Saxon go into such detail in showing the importance of education in the development of the United States?
3. Why do you think Saxon uses headings in his essay? Did they help you in any way?
4. In a well-constructed essay, the title*, introduction*, thesis*, supporting ideas*, and closing* are integrated into a unified and coherent

whole. Explain how Saxon achieves unity* and coherence* beginning with the title and concluding with his last two-sentence paragraph.

READING AND WRITING SUGGESTIONS

1. Design and then defend your plan for the ideal university. What kind of students would you want the university to attract? What subjects would be taught there? What methods of teaching would be used?
2. Read John W. Gardner's *Excellence* or a similar book on American education and write a brief essay in which you attack or defend the author's point of view.
3. Write an argumentative essay on the topic, "Every American Has (Does Not Have) a Right to a College Education," or the topic, "Every American Has (Does Not Have) a Need for a College Education."

---

*Definitions of all terms marked with an asterisk may be found in the Glossary.

A MODEST PROPOSAL

for Preventing the Children of Poor People in Ireland from Being a Burden to Their Parents or Country, and for Making Them Beneficial to the Public

Jonathan Swift

Jonathan Swift (1667–1745) was a master satirist of eighteenth-century England. His most famous work, Gulliver's Travels, *was written in 1726 and depicted people as petty, spiteful, malicious, despicable creatures. The following essay reflects Swift's indignation against man's inhumanity to man, exhibited in this instance in the English government's treatment of the Irish people. Swift's essay is a famous example of irony, a comic device in which the true meaning is the opposite of what is literally expressed.*

It is a melancholy object to those who walk through this great town[1] or travel in the country, when they see the streets, the roads, and cabin doors, crowded with beggars of the female-sex, followed by three, four, or six children, all in rags and importuning every passenger for an alms. These mothers, instead of being able to work for their honest livelihood, are forced to employ all their time in strolling to beg sustenance for their helpless infants, who, as they grow up, either turn thieves for want of work, or leave their dear native country to fight for the Pretender in Spain, or sell themselves to the Barbadoes.[2]

I think it is agreed by all parties that this prodigious number of children in the arms, or on the backs, or at the heels of their mothers, and frequently of their fathers, is in the present deplorable state of the kingdom a very great additional grievance; and therefore whoever could find out a fair, cheap, and easy method of making these children sound, useful members

1. Dublin.
2. The Pretender was James Francis Edward Stuart (1688–1766), son of the deposed Catholic king of England, James II. Many Irishmen escaped their poverty by contracting as servants in the Barbadoes and other islands in the West Indies.

of the commonwealth would deserve so well of the public as to have his statue set up for a preserver of the nation.

But my intention is very far from being confined to provide only for the children of professed beggars; it is of a much greater extent, and shall take in the whole number of infants at a certain age who are born of parents in effect as little able to support them as those who demand our charity in the streets.

As to my own part, having turned my thoughts for many years upon this important subject, and maturely weighed the several schemes of other projectors, I have always found them grossly mistaken in their computation. It is true, a child just dropped from its dam may be supported by her milk for a solar year, with little other nourishment; at most not above the value of two shillings, which the mother may certainly get, or the value in scraps, by her lawful occupation of begging; and it is exactly at one year old that I propose to provide for them in such a manner as instead of being a charge upon their parents or the parish, or wanting food and raiment for the rest of their lives, they shall on the contrary contribute to the feeding, and partly to the clothing, of many thousands.

There is likewise another great advantage in my scheme, that it will prevent those voluntary abortions, and that horrid practice of women murdering their bastard children, alas, too frequent among us, sacrificing the poor innocent babes, I doubt, more to avoid the expense than the shame, which would move tears and pity in the most savage and inhuman breast.

The number of souls in this kingdom being usually reckoned one million and a half, of these I calculate there may be about two hundred thousand couples whose wives are breeders; from which number I subtract thirty thousand couples who are able to maintain their own children, although I apprehend there cannot be so many under the present distresses of the kingdom; but this being granted, there will remain a hundred and seventy thousand breeders. I again subtract fifty thousand for those women who miscarry, or whose children die by accident or disease within the year. There only remain a hundred and twenty thousand children of poor parents annually born. The question therefore is, how this number shall be reared and provided for, which, as I have already said, under the present situation of affairs, is utterly impossible by all the methods hitherto proposed. For we can neither employ them in handicraft nor agriculture; we neither build houses (I mean in the country) nor cultivate land. They can very seldom pick up a livelihood by stealing till they arrive at six years old, except where they are of towardly parts; although I confess they learn the rudiments much earlier, during which time they can however be looked upon only as probationers, as I have been informed by a principal gentleman in the county of Cavan, who protested to me that he never knew above one or two instances under the age of six, even in a part of the kingdom so renowned for the quickest proficiency in that art.

I am assured by our merchants that a boy or girl before twelve years old is no salable commodity; and even when they come to this age they will not yield above three pounds, or three pounds and a half a crown at most on the Exchange; which cannot turn to account either to the parents or the kingdom, the charge of nutriment and rags having been at least four times that value.

I shall now therefore humbly propose my own thoughts, which I hope will not be liable to the least objection.

I have been assured by a very knowing American of my acquaintance in London, that a young healthy child well nursed is at a year old a most delicious, nourishing, and wholesome food, whether stewed, roasted, baked, or boiled; and I make no doubt that it will equally serve in a fricassee or a ragout.

I do therefore humbly offer it to public consideration that of the hundred and twenty thousand children, already computed, twenty thousand may be reserved for breed, whereof only one fourth part to be males, which is more than we allow to sheep, black cattle, or swine; and my reason is that these children are seldom the fruits of marriage, a circumstance not much regarded by our savages, therefore one male will be sufficient to serve four females. That the remaining hundred thousand may at a year old be offered in sale to the persons of quality and fortune through the kingdom, always advising the mother to let them suck plentifully in the last month, so as to render them plump and fat for a good table. A child will make two dishes at an entertainment for friends; and when the family dines alone, the fore or hind quarter will make a reasonable dish, and seasoned with a little pepper or salt will be very good boiled on the fourth day, especially in winter.

I have reckoned upon a medium that a child just born will weigh twelve pounds, and in a solar year if tolerably nursed increaseth to twenty-eight pounds.

I grant this food will be somewhat dear, and therefore very proper for landlords, who, as they have already devoured most of the parents, seem to have the best title to the children.

Infant's flesh will be in season throughout the year, but more plentiful in March, and a little before and after. For we are told by a grave author, an eminent French physician,[3] that fish being a prolific diet, there are more children born in Roman Catholic countries about nine months after Lent than at any other season; therefore, reckoning a year after Lent, the markets

3. Rabelais.

will be more glutted than usual, because the number of popish infants is at least three to one in this kingdom; and therefore it will have one other collateral advantage, by lessening the number of Papists among us.

I have already computed the charge of nursing a beggar's child (in which list I reckon all cottagers, laborers, and four fifths of the farmers) to be about two shillings per annum, rags included; and I believe no gentleman would repine to give ten shillings for the carcass of a good fat child, which, as I have said, will make four dishes of excellent nutritive meat, when he hath only some particular friend or his own family to dine with him. Thus the squire will learn to be a good landlord, and grow popular among the tenants; the mother will have eight shillings net profit, and be fit for work until she produces another child.

Those who are more thrifty (as I must confess the times require) may flay the carcass; the skin of which artificially dressed will make admirable gloves for the ladies, and summer boots for fine gentlemen.

As to our city of Dublin, shambles may be appointed for this purpose in the most convenient parts of it, and butchers we may be assured will not be wanting; although I rather recommend buying the children alive, and dressing them hot from the knife as we do roasting pigs.

A very worthy person, a true lover of his country, and whose virtues I highly esteem, was lately pleased in discoursing on this matter to offer a refinement upon my scheme. He said that many gentlemen of this kingdom having of late destroyed their deer, he conceived that the want of venison might be well supplied by the bodies of young lads and maidens, not exceeding fourteen years of age nor under twelve, so great a number of both sexes in every county being now ready to starve for want of work and service; and these to be disposed of by their parents, if alive, or otherwise by their nearest relations. But with due deference to so excellent a friend and so deserving a patriot, I cannot be altogether in his sentiments; for as to the males, my American acquaintance assured me from frequent experience that their flesh was generally tough and lean, like that of our schoolboys, by continual exercise, and their taste disagreeable; and to fatten them would not answer the charge. Then as to the females, it would, I think with humble submission, be a loss to the public, because they soon would become breeders themselves: and besides, it is not improbable that some scrupulous people might be apt to censure such a practice (although indeed very unjustly) as a little bordering upon cruelty; which, I confess, hath always been with me the strongest objection against any project, how well soever intended.

But in order to justify my friend, he confessed that this expedient was put into his head by the famous Psalmanazar, a native of the island Formosa, who came from thence to London above twenty years ago, and in conversation told my friend that in his country when any young person happened to be put to death, the executioner sold the carcass to persons of quality as a prime dainty; and that in his time the body of a plump girl of fifteen, who was crucified for an attempt to poison the emperor, was sold to his Imperial Majesty's prime minister of state, and other great mandarins of the court, in joints from the gibbet, at four hundred crowns. Neither indeed can I deny that if the same use were made of several plump young girls in this town, who without one single groat to their fortunes cannot stir abroad without a chair, and appear at the playhouse and assemblies in foreign fineries which they never will pay for, the kingdom would not be the worse.

Some persons of a desponding spirit are in great concern about that vast number of poor people who are aged, diseased, or maimed, and I have been desired to employ my thoughts what course may be taken to ease the nation of so grievous an encumbrance. But I am not in the least pain upon that matter, because it is very well known that they are every day dying and rotting by cold and famine, and by filth and vermin, as fast as can be reasonably expected. And as to the younger laborers, they are now in almost as hopeful a condition. They cannot get work, and consequently pine away for want of nourishment to a degree that if at any time they are accidentally hired to common labor, they have not strength to perform it; and thus the country and themselves are happily delivered from the evils to come.

I have too long digressed, and therefore shall return to my subject. I think the advantages by the proposal which I have made are obvious and many, as well as of the highest importance.

For first, as I have already observed, it would greatly lessen the number of Papists, with whom we are yearly overrun, being the principal breeders of our nation as well as our most dangerous enemies; and who stay at home on purpose to deliver the kingdom to the Pretender, hoping to take their advantage by the absence of so many good Protestants, who have chosen rather to leave their country than to stay at home and pay tithes against their conscience to an Episcopal curate.

Secondly, the poorer tenants will have something valuable of their own, which by law may be made liable to distress, and help to pay their landlord's rent, their corn and cattle being already seized and money a thing unknown.

Thirdly, whereas the maintenance of an hundred thousand children, from two years old and upwards, cannot be computed at less than ten shillings a piece per annum, the nation's stock will be thereby increased fifty thousand pounds per annum, besides the profit of a new dish introduced to the tables of all gentlemen of fortune in the kingdom who have any refinement in taste. And the money will circulate among ourselves, the goods being entirely of our own growth and manufacture.

Fourthly, the constant breeders, besides the gain of eight shillings sterling per annum by the sale of their children, will be rid of the charge of maintaining them after the first year.

Fifthly, this food would likewise bring great custom to taverns, where the vintners will certainly be so prudent as to procure the best receipts for dressing it to perfection, and consequently have their houses frequented by all the fine gentlemen, who justly value themselves upon their knowledge in good eating; and a skillful cook, who understands how to oblige his guests, will contrive to make it as expensive as they please.

Sixthly, this would be a great inducement to marriage, which all wise nations have either encouraged by rewards or enforced by laws and penalties. It would increase the care and tenderness of mothers toward their children, when they were sure of a settlement for life to the poor babes, provided in some sort by the public, to their annual profit instead of expense. We should see an honest emulation among the married women, which of them could bring the fattest child to the market. Men would become as fond of their wives during the time of their pregnancy as they are now of their mares in foal, their cows in calf, or sows when they are ready to farrow; nor offer to beat or kick them (as is too frequent a practice) for fear of a miscarriage.

Many other advantages might be enumerated. For instance, the addition of some thousand carcasses in our exportation of barreled beef, the propagation of swine's flesh, and improvement in the art of making good bacon, so much wanted among us by the great destruction of pigs, too frequent at our tables, which are no way comparable in taste or magnificence to a well-grown, fat, yearling child, which roasted whole will make a considerable figure at a lord mayor's feast or any other public entertainment. But this and many others I omit, being studious of brevity.

Supposing that one thousand families in this city would be constant customers for infants' flesh, besides others who might have it at merry meetings, particularly weddings and christenings, I compute that Dublin would take off annually about twenty-thousand carcasses, and the rest of the kingdom (where probably they will be sold somewhat cheaper) the remaining eighty thousand.

I can think of no one objection that will possibly be raised against this proposal, unless it should be urged that the number of people will be thereby much lessened in the kingdom. This I freely own, and it was indeed one principal design in offering it to the world. I desire the reader will observe, that I calculate my remedy for this one individual kingdom of Ireland and for no other that ever was, is, or I think ever can be upon earth. Therefore let no man talk to me of other expedients: of taxing our absentees at five shillings a pound: of using neither clothes nor household furniture except what is of our own growth and manufacture: of utterly rejecting the materials and instruments that promote foreign luxury: of curing the expensiveness of pride, vanity, idleness, and gaming in our women: of introducing a vein of parismony, prudence, and temperance: of learning to love our country, in the want of which we differ even from Laplanders and the inhabitants of Topinamboo[4]: of quitting our animosities and factions, nor acting any longer like the Jews, who were murdering one another at the very moment their city was taken: of being a little cautious not to sell our country and conscience for nothing: of teaching landlords to have at least one degree of mercy toward their tenants: lastly, of putting a spirit of honesty, industry, and skill into our shopkeepers: who, if a resolution could now be taken to buy only our native goods, would immediately unite to cheat and exact upon us in the price, the measure, and the goodness, nor could ever yet be brought to make one fair proposal of just dealing, though often and earnestly invited to it.

Therefore I repeat, let no man talk to me of these and the like expedients, till he hath at least some glimpse of hope that there will ever be some hearty and sincere attempt to put them in practice.

But as to myself, having been wearied out for many years with offering vain, idle, visionary thoughts, and at length utterly despairing of success, I fortunately fell upon this proposal, which, as it is wholly new, so it hath something solid and real, of no expense and little trouble, full in our own power, and whereby we can incur no danger in disobliging England. For this kind of commodity will not bear exportation, the flesh being of too tender a consistence to admit a long continuance in salt, although perhaps I could name a country which would be glad to eat up our whole nation without it.

After all, I am not so violently bent upon my own opinion as to reject any offer proposed by wise men, which shall be found equally innocent, cheap, easy, and effectual. But before something of that kind shall be advanced in contradicton to my scheme, and offering a better, I desire the author or authors will be pleased maturely to consider two points. First, as things now stand, how they will be able to find food and raiment for an hundred thousand useless mouths and backs. And secondly, there being a round million of creatures in human figure throughout this kingdom, whose sole subsistence put into a common stock would leave them in debt two millions of pounds sterling, adding those who are beggars by profession to the bulk of farmers, cottagers, and laborers, with their wives and children who are beggars in effect; I desire those politicians who dislike my overture, and may perhaps be so bold to attempt an answer, that they will first ask the parents of these mortals whether they would not at this

4. Jungle region.

day think it a great happiness to have been sold for food at a year old in the manner I prescribe, and thereby have avoided such a perpetual scene of misfortunes as they have since gone through by the oppression of landlords, the impossibility of paying rent without money or trade, the want of common sustenance, with neither house nor clothes to cover them from the inclemencies of the weather, and the most inevitable prospect of entailing the like or greater miseries upon their breed forever.

I profess, in the sincerity of my heart, that I have not the least personal interest in endeavoring to promote this necessary work, having no other motive than the public good of my country, by advancing our trade, providing for infants, relieving the poor, and giving some pleasure to the rich. I have no children by which I can propose to get a single penny; the youngest being nine years old, and my wife past childbearing.

VOCABULARY

1. Define the following words as Swift uses them in this essay: importuning, prodigious, deplorable, rudiments, fricassee, ragout, mandarins, gibbet, groat, encumbrance, vermin, emulation, farrow, propagation, parsimony, inclemencies.
2. If you are unfamiliar with any other words in this essay, check them in a dictionary and then define them in your own words.
3. In "Politics and the English Language," George Orwell advises against using a long word where a short one will do. Find at least eight long words Swift uses and suggest a shorter one for each.

CONTENT

1. What problem is Swift proposing to solve? What are its roots?
2. What arguments does he give to support his proposal?
3. Why doesn't Swift's proposal apply to people who are aged, diseased, or maimed?
4. Swift condemns eighteenth-century England and a social climate that allows the rich to exploit the poor. Do the wealthy still prey upon the poor? Do the poor fare better now? Defend your answer.
5. Do you think that satire* can be offensive if one is very close to the issue? For example, what would be the current reaction to Swift's

---

*Definitions of all terms marked with an asterisk may be found in the Glossary.

proposal in countries such as India where overpopulation and poverty are widespread?

6. What specific changes do you think Swift was really trying to bring about when he wrote this essay?

RHETORIC

1. Although both Swift and Saxon (in "Is It Time to Stop Learning?" page 173) address social problems, their tone* differs markedly. Explain the difference and discuss why you think one is more effective than the other.
2. What does this essay's title* contribute to your understanding of Swift's tone* and message?
3. Cite at least six statements that illustrate the satirical* nature of this essay. For example, "a child just dropped from the dam."
4. Swift concludes his essay by summarizing his six arguments for his proposal. Does this make his proposal more or less worthy of acceptance? Why?
5. Does Swift engage in overkill? Defend your answer.

READING AND WRITING SUGGESTIONS

1. Irony* is saying the opposite or almost the opposite of what you mean, for example, saying "It's a *lovely* day" when it's raining and cold. Write a satirical essay on some serious subject such as capital punishment, the legalization of marijuana, abortion, or euthanasia. Remember to exaggerate your position almost to the point of absurdity, or at least until your reader will know what side you are on. At the same time maintain your ironic tone.
2. Read Charles McGlashan's *History of the Donner Party,* a true story of pioneers traveling to California and the horror and despair that transpired when they were marooned in the snowy Sierra in the winter of 1846–47. Or read a more recent account of actual cannibalism in Piers Paul Read's *Alive: The Story of the Andes Survivors.* Summarize the account and discuss whether the circumstances justified the cannibalism described.

---

*Definitions of all terms marked with an asterisk may be found in the Glossary.

THE RIGHT TO DIE

Norman Cousins

Norman Cousins (1912–) was born in New Jersey. After studying at Columbia University, he began his career as the education editor of the New York Evening Post. *For many years, he was the literary and managing editor of the* Saturday Review of Literature, *and he is best known for his weekly editorials on a great variety of subjects. Cousins is the author and editor of a number of books, including* Anatomy of an Illness *and collections of* Saturday Review *essays, many of which he wrote. In this* Saturday Review *essay from 1975, Cousins presents a brief and compassionate argument in support of the right to choose one's own time of death.*

The world of religion and philosophy was shocked recently when Henry P. Van Dusen and his wife ended their lives by their own hands. Dr. Van Dusen had been president of Union Theological Seminary; for more than a quarter-century he had been one of the luminous names in Protestant theology. He enjoyed world status as a spiritual leader. News of the self-inflicted death of the Van Dusens, therefore, was profoundly disturbing to all those who attach a moral stigma to suicide and regard it as a violation of God's laws.

Dr. Van Dusen had anticipated this reaction. He and his wife left behind a letter that may have historic significance. It was very brief, but the essential point it made is now being widely discussed by theologians and could represent the beginning of a reconsideration of traditional religious attitudes toward self-inflicted death. The letter raised a moral issue: does an individual have the obligation to go on living even when the beauty and meaning and power of life are gone?

Henry and Elizabeth Van Dusen had lived full lives. In recent years, they had become increasingly ill, requiring almost continual medical care. Their infirmities were worsening, and they realized they would soon become completely dependent for even the most elementary needs and functions. Under these circumstances, little dignity would have been left in life. They didn't like the idea of taking up space in a world with too many mouths and too little food. They believed it was a misuse of medical science to keep them technically alive.

They therefore believed they had the right to decide when to die. In making that decision, they weren't turning against life as the highest value; what they were turning against was the notion that there were no circumstances under which life should be discontinued.

An important aspect of human uniqueness is the power of free will. In his books and lectures, Dr. Van Dusen frequently spoke about the exercise of this uniqueness. The fact that he used his free will to prevent life from becoming a caricature of itself was completely in character. In their letter, the Van Dusens sought to convince family and friends that they were not acting solely out of despair or pain.

The use of free will to put an end to one's life finds no sanction in the theology to which Pitney Van Dusen was committed. Suicide symbolizes discontinuity; religion symbolizes continuity, represented at its quintessence by the concept of the immortal soul. Human logic finds it almost impossible to come to terms with the concept of non-existence. In religion, the human mind finds a larger dimension and is relieved of the ordeal of a confrontation with non-existence.

Even without respect to religion, the idea of suicide has been abhorrent throughout history. Some societies have imposed severe penalties on the families of suicides in the hope that the individual who sees no reason to continue his existence may be deterred by the stigma his self-destruction would inflict on loved ones. Other societies have enacted laws prohibiting suicide on the grounds that it is murder. The enforcement of such laws, of course, has been an exercise in futility.

Customs and attitudes, like individuals themselves, are largely shaped by the surrounding environment. In today's world, life can be prolonged by science far beyond meaning or sensibility. Under these circumstances, individuals who feel they have nothing more to give to life, or to receive from it, need not be applauded, but they can be spared our condemnation.

The general reaction to suicide is bound to change as people come to understand that it may be a denial, not an assertion, of moral or religious ethics to allow life to be extended without regard to decency or pride. What moral or religious purpose is celebrated by the annihilation of the human spirit in the triumphant act of keeping the body alive? Why are so many people more readily appalled by an unnatural form of dying than by an unnatural form of living?

"Nowadays," the Van Dusens wrote in their last letter, "it is difficult to die. We feel that this way we are taking will become more usual and acceptable as the years pass.

"Of course, the thought of our children and our grandchildren makes us sad, but we still feel that this is the best way and the right way to go. We are both increasingly weak and unwell and who would want to die in a nursing home?

"We are not afraid to die. . . ."

Pitney Van Dusen was admired and respected in life. He can be admired and respected in death. "Suicide," said Goethe, "is an incident in human life which, however much disputed and discussed, demands the sympathy of every man, and in every age must be dealt with anew."

Death is not the greatest loss in life. The greatest loss is what dies inside us while we live. The unbearable tragedy is to live without dignity or sensitivity.

VOCABULARY

1. Define the following words as Cousins uses them in his essay: stigma, quintessence, abhorrent, appalled.
2. If you are unfamiliar with any other words in this essay, check them in a dictionary and then define them in your own words.

CONTENT

1. What arguments does Cousins put forth to justify the Van Dusens' right to take their own lives? Are they convincing arguments? Could people generalize these arguments to justify committing suicide in the face of any difficult circumstances, for example, emotional problems?
2. Why is attempted suicide against the law in some states? In your opinion, are *legal* prohibitions against suicide justified?
3. What are your views on suicide? Why do you think you hold these views? Explain why you agree or disagree with Cousins' conclusion about suicide.
4. What do you think Goethe meant when he said that suicide "in every age must be dealt with anew"?
5. In your opinion is there a difference between passive euthanasia (allowing someone to die) and mercy killing? Are the two equally moral or immoral? Defend your answer.

RHETORIC

1. What is the thesis* of this essay? Where is it most clearly stated?

---

*Definitions of all terms marked with an asterisk may be found in the Glossary.

2. Does Cousins' title* clearly indicate his thesis*? Would "The Right to Commit Suicide Under Some Circumstances" be a more accurate title? Would it be more effective? Why or why not?
3. Does Cousins build his argument on logical* or emotional* grounds?
4. Cousins uses two kinds of figurative language* in his first paragraph. What are they? What do they mean?
5. Describe the essay's tone*. What effect does the last paragraph have in contributing to this tone?

READING AND WRITING SUGGESTIONS

1. Suicide is the second highest cause of death among college students. Give this fact some thought, and write a brief essay explaining why you think this is the case.
2. Every society has its own way of dealing with death. Read a book on the subject, such as Jessica Mitford's *The American Way of Death* or Elizabeth Kubler-Ross's *On Death and Dying,* and write an argumentative essay defending or attacking America's way of dealing with death. Discuss such aspects of the subject as the cost of funerals, the custom of displaying the corpse, and the construction of elaborate memorial monuments.
3. One of the basic social issues of our age is capital punishment. Read Norman Mailer's *The Executioner's Song,* an account of Gary Gilmore's execution, at his own request, by a Utah firing squad. Write an argumentative essay in which you answer one of these two questions:
    a. Is capital punishment a kind of mercy killing?
    b. Gary Gilmore attempted suicide while he was in the Utah prison. He was rushed to the hospital and extraordinary steps taken to save his life. Many times death row prisoners are under 24-hour guard to prevent suicide. Why might condemned prisoners want to commit suicide, and why does society want to prevent such suicide?

---

*Definitions of all terms marked with an asterisk may be found in the Glossary.

A LETTER TO ALFRED

Flannery O'Connor

Flannery O'Connor (1925–1964) was born in Savannah, Georgia, to an old Catholic family. She lived most of her life in Milledgeville, where she attended Georgia State College for Women. O'Connor died at the age of thirty-nine from lupus, a disease she inherited from her father. In her relatively short life, she wrote a number of novels and short stories, four of which were published after her death. Among her best known works are Wise Blood, A Good Man Is Hard to Find, The Violent Bear It Away, *and* Everything That Rises Must Converge.

The selection below is taken from The Habit of Being *(1979), a collection of Flannery O'Connor's letters compiled and edited by a friend after O'Connor's death. Some letters legitimately can be considered essays if they adhere to one idea, are expressive of the people who write them, and say what seems to them important and worth consideration. Such is the case in the following letter written to Alfred Corn, a student at Emory University, in reply to a letter he wrote O'Connor after she lectured to his class.*

30 May 62

I think that this experience you are having of losing your faith, or as you think, of having lost it, is an experience that in the long run belongs to faith; or at least it can belong to faith if faith is still valuable to you, and it must be or you would not have written me about this.

I don't know how the kind of faith required of a Christian living in the 20th century can be at all if it is not grounded on this experience that you are having right now of unbelief. This may be the case always and not just in the 20th century. Peter said, "Lord, I believe. Help my unbelief." It is the most natural and most human and most agonizing prayer in the gospels, and I think it is the foundation prayer of faith.

As a freshman in college you are bombarded with new ideas, or rather pieces of ideas, new frames of reference, an activation of the intellectual life which is only beginning, but which is already running ahead of your lived experience. After a year of this, you think you cannot believe. You are just beginning to realize how difficult it is to have faith and the measure of a commitment to it, but you are too young to decide you don't have faith just because you feel you can't believe. About the only way we know whether we believe or not is by what we do, and I think from your letter that you will not take the path of least resistance in this matter and simply decide that you have lost your faith and that there is nothing you can do about it.

One result of the stimulation of your intellectual life that takes place in a college is usually a shrinking of the imaginative life. This sounds like a paradox, but I have often found it to be true. Students get so bound up with difficulties such as reconciling the clashing of so many different faiths such as Buddhism, Mohammedanism, etc., that they cease to look for God in other ways. Bridges once wrote Gerard Manley Hopkins and asked him to tell him how he, Bridges, could believe. He must have expected from Hopkins a long philosophical answer. Hopkins wrote back, "Give alms." He was trying to say to Bridges that God is to be experienced in Charity (in the sense of love for the divine image in human beings). Don't get so entangled with intellectual difficulties that you fail to look for God in this way.

The intellectual difficulties have to be met, however, and you will be meeting them for the rest of your life. When you get a reasonable hold on one, another will come to take its place. At one time, the clash of the different world religions was a difficulty for me. Where you have absolute solutions, however, you have no need of faith. Faith is what you have in the absence of knowledge. The reason this clash doesn't bother me any longer is because I have got, over the years, a sense of the immense sweep of creation, of the evolutionary process in everything, of how incomprehensible God must necessarily be to be the God of heaven and earth. You can't fit the Almighty into your intellectual categories. I might suggest that you look into some of the works of Pierre Teilhard de Chardin (*The Phenomenon of Man* et al.). He was a paleontologist—helped to discover Peking man—and also a man of God. I don't suggest you go to him for answers but for different questions, for that stretching of the imagination that you need to make you a sceptic in the face of much that you are learning, much of which is new and shocking but which when boiled down becomes less so and takes its place in the general scheme of things. What kept me a sceptic in college was precisely my Christian faith. It always said: wait, don't bite on this, get a wider picture, continue to read.

If you want your faith, you have to work for it. It is a gift, but for very few is it a gift given without any demand for equal time devoted to its cultivation. For every book you read that is anti-Christian, make it your business to read one that presents the other side of the picture; if one isn't satisfactory read others. Don't think that you have to abandon reason to be a Christian. A book that might help you is *The Unity of Philosophical*

Experience by Etienne Gilson. Another is Newman's *The Grammar of Assent.* To find out about faith, you have to go to the people who have it and you have to go to the most intelligent ones if you are going to stand up intellectually to agnostics and the general run of pagans that you are going to find in the majority of people around you. Much of the criticism of belief that you find today comes from people who are judging it from the standpoint of another and narrower discipline. The Biblical criticism of the 19th century, for instance, was the product of historical disciplines. It has been entirely revamped in the 20th century by applying broader criteria to it, and those people who lost their faith in the 19th century because of it, could better have hung on in blind trust.

Even in the life of a Christian, faith rises and falls like the tides of an invisible sea. It's there, even when he can't see it or feel it, if he wants it to be there. You realize, I think, that it is more valuable, more mysterious, altogether more immense than anything you can learn or decide upon in college. Learn what you can, but cultivate Christian scepticism. It will keep you free—not free to do anything you please, but free to be formed by something larger than your own intellect or the intellects of those around you.

I don't know if this is the kind of answer that can help you, but any time you care to write to me, I can try to do better.

VOCABULARY

1. Define the following words as O'Connor uses them: paradox, incomprehensible, paleontologist, Peking man, sceptic, agnostics, pagan, revamped.
2. If you are unfamiliar with any other words in this selection, check them in a dictionary and then define them in your own words.

CONTENT

1. What suggestions does O'Connor make to Alfred to help him sustain his faith?
2. What does the author mean when she says, "About the only way we know whether we believe or not is by what we do"?
3. Do you agree that one thing that takes place in college is "a shrinking of the imaginative life"? Do you agree with reasons O'Connor gives for this statement? Why or why not?
4. O'Connor sums up her advice to Alfred by telling him to "cultivate

Christian scepticism." What does she mean? Do you think this is good advice? Explain.

5. Review Cousins' "The Right to Die" (page 187). Suppose Dr. Van Dusen had written to Flannery O'Connor telling her of the plan he and his wife had for taking their lives. What do you think O'Connor's response would have been?

RHETORIC

1. Does O'Connor's opening paradox* help convey the crux of her argument? Explain. Where else does she use a paradox*?
2. Is the author's argument logical* or persuasive*? Cite examples to support your answer.
3. Is the simile* in the next to the last paragraph effective? Why or why not? Suggest other similes* she could have used.
4. What is the tone* of O'Connor's letter to Alfred? How did she achieve this tone*?

READING AND WRITING SUGGESTIONS

1. What is your most deeply held belief? Write an argumentative essay defending it.
2. Suppose you are Alfred and received O'Connor's letter. Write a response, agreeing or disagreeing with her arguments.
3. Read any one of the works mentioned in O'Connor's selection and write an essay relating it to her advice to Alfred.

---

*Definitions of all terms marked with an asterisk may be found in the Glossary.

DARWIN'S CONCLUSION ON HIS THEORY AND RELIGION

Charles Robert Darwin

Charles Robert Darwin (1809–1882) was born in Shrewsbury, England. Although he ultimately achieved fame as a naturalist and author, he first studied medicine at Edinburgh University and later transferred to Cambridge, where he studied for the ministry. When he was twenty-two, however, he was appointed naturalist on the H.M.S. Beagle, *and this five-year sailing expedition prepared him for his lifework in the study of the evolution of species. In 1859, Darwin's great work,* The Origin of Species, *was published. Darwin's theory of evolution brought him wide renown, but it also caused a storm of controversy. In the essay that follows, Darwin defends his theory, asserting that no conflict exists between it and religion.*

I see no good reason why the views given in this volume should shock the religious feelings of any one. It is satisfactory, as showing how transient such impressions are, to remember that the greatest discovery ever made by man, namely, the law of the attraction of gravity, was also attacked by Leibnitz, "as subversive of natural, and inferentially of revealed, religion." A celebrated author and divine has written to me that "he has gradually learned to see that it is just as noble a conception of the Deity to believe that he created a few original forms, capable of self-development into other and needful forms, as to believe that he required a fresh act of creation to supply the voids caused by the action of his laws."

Why, it may be asked, until recently did nearly all the most eminent living naturalists and geologists disbelieve in the mutability of species? It cannot be asserted that organic beings in a state of nature are subject to no variation; it cannot be proved that the amount of variation in the course of long ages is a limited quantity; no clear distinction has been, or can be, drawn between species and well-marked varieties. It cannot be maintained that species when intercrossed are invariably sterile, and varieties invariably fertile; or that sterility is a special endowment and sign of creation. The belief that species were immutable productions was almost unavoidable as long as the history of the world was thought to be of short duration; and now that we have acquired some idea of the lapse of time, we are too apt to assume, without proof, that the geological record is so perfect that it would have afforded us plain evidence of the mutation of species, if they had undergone mutation. . . .

Authors of the highest eminence seem to be fully satisfied with the view that each species has been independently created. To my mind it accords better with what we know of the laws impressed on matter by the Creator, that the production and extinction of the past and present inhabitants of the world should have been due to secondary causes, like those determining the birth and death of the individual. When I view all beings not as special creations, but as the lineal descendants of some few beings which lived long before the first bed of the Cambrian system was deposited, they seem to me to become ennobled. Judging from the past, we may safely infer that not one living species will transmit its unaltered likeness to a distant futurity. And of the species now living very few will transmit progeny of any kind to a far distant futurity; for the manner in which all organic beings are grouped shows that the greater number of species in each genus, and all the species in many genera, have left no descendants, but have become utterly extinct. We can so far take a prophetic glance into futurity as to foretell that it will be the common and widely spread species, belonging to the larger and dominant groups within each class, which will ultimately prevail and procreate new and dominant species. As all the living forms of life are the lineal descendants of those which lived long before the Cambrian epoch, we may feel certain that the ordinary succession by generation has never once been broken, and that no cataclysm has desolated the whole world. Hence we may look with some confidence to a secure future of great length. And as natural selection works solely by and for the good of each being, all corporeal and mental endowments will tend to progress towards perfection.

It is interesting to contemplate a tangled bank, clothed with many plants of many kinds, with birds singing on the bushes, with various insects flitting about, and with worms crawling through the damp earth, and to reflect that these elaborately constructed forms, so different from each other, and dependent upon each other in so complex a manner, have all been produced by laws acting around us. These laws, taken in the largest sense, being growth with reproduction; inheritance, which is almost implied by reproduction; variability from the indirect and direct action of the conditions of life, and from use and disuse; a ration of increase so high as to lead to a struggle for life, and as a consequence to natural selection, entailing divergence of character and the extinction of less improved forms. Thus, from the war of nature, from famine and death, the most exalted object which we are capable of conceiving, namely, the production of the higher animals, directly follows. There is grandeur in this view of life, with its several powers, having been originally breathed by the Creator into a few forms or into one; and that, whilst this planet has gone cycling on according to the fixed law of gravity, from so simple a beginning endless forms most beautiful and most wonderful have been, and are being evolved.

VOCABULARY

1. Define the following words as Darwin uses them in his essay: transient, subversive, eminent, mutability, mutation, lineal, progeny, cataclysm, corporeal, genus.
2. If you are unfamiliar with any other words in this essay, check them in a dictionary and then define them in your own words.
3. What is the Cambrian system? the Cambrian epoch?

CONTENT

1. Summarize the points Darwin makes in his theory of evolution and in his defense of his theory.
2. In "Those Crazy Ideas" (page 29), Asimov discusses the way Darwin arrived at his theory of evolution. Does Asimov's account strengthen or weaken your view of Darwin? Explain.
3. Is Darwin optimistic or pessimistic about the future of life forms in general? of specific life forms?
4. Why do you think that so many people of Darwin's time were offended and outraged by his theory of evolution?
5. What is your personal view of Darwin's theory of evolution?
6. Darwin becomes quite eloquent in his final two sentences. Are his comments consistent with Faulkner's assertion, "I believe that man will not merely endure; he will prevail"? Which author's statement is more effective? Why?

RHETORIC

1. What is Darwin's thesis*? Is it stated or implied?

---

*Definitions of all terms marked with an asterisk may be found in the Glossary.

2. To what use does Darwin put the two quotations in his first paragraph?
3. What kind of argument* does Darwin use to arrive at his theory of evolution? What kind of argument does he use to defend his theory?
4. Understanding Darwin's ideas requires close reading. Is this because of his subject or his style*? Explain.

READING AND WRITING SUGGESTIONS

1. Imagine that you have been asked to appear before a church group either to defend or to attack Darwin's theory of evolution. Write an outline of the arguments you would use to support your position.
2. The famous Scopes trial, conducted in 1925, climaxed a controversy over the teaching of the theory of evolution in Tennessee's schools. Read about the events which led up to the trial and review the trial's outcome. Then write a brief essay in which you describe the issues involved in the trial and discuss whether you think a similar controversy could develop today.

*Definitions of all terms marked with an asterisk may be found in the Glossary.

WHAT THIS COUNTRY NEEDS IS A GOOD BAD-WRITING COURSE

Elizabeth Pope

Elizabeth Pope (1917–) is professor of English at Mills College in Oakland, California, a position she has held since 1944. Dr. Pope wrote this essay for the student newspaper, The Mills Stream, *November 23, 1976. It was later carried in a slightly different form in the* Los Angeles Times.

While I have the utmost admiration for the splendid job which the staff of English-1 is doing, I sometimes wonder whether the faculty would not do better to give up their unremitting efforts to teach good writing and start trying to teach Bad Writing instead.

To judge by what I see all around me, there is an enormous demand for Bad Writing in practically every field—political, educational, sociological, academic, commercial—and many Mills students already show a pronounced flair for it. In a democratic society, the will of the majority must ultimately prevail; and in a time like this, the students should be doing all they can to fit themselves for jobs in the real world.

It is obviously too soon to speculate about the endless possibilities which would then open up: the English major with an emphasis on anti-creative writing; the sophomore survey course covering the best bad writers from Andreas Capellanus to Richard Milhous Nixon; advanced de-composition; the many independent studies that might be made of certain poets and novelists who are now understandably neglected but who at least have never been picked bare like Shakespeare or Joyce.

For the moment, however, all I wish to do is to make some very modest proposals, to suggest a few tentative rules for writing the Basic Bad Paper, which is after all the foundation stone on which everything else must rest.

Rule 1: Never take chances by giving your real opinion. Give the professor back his own instead. Many birds are fed by "regurgitation"—that is, by bits of half-digested food—so why shouldn't he (she) be?

Rule 2: If you *must* give your real opinion, never mind whether it's reasonable, fair, intelligent or supported by the evidence. It's yours, and that's all that matters.

Rule 3: When writing literary criticism, never assume that the professor is already familiar with the plot of the novel or the play. Begin by telling him all about it. If the novel is unusually lengthy, like *Moby Dick*, or the play unusually complicated, like *The Way of the World*, it may take so long to go over it that you may find yourself without the time or energy to say anything more by the time you reach Page 20.

Rule 4: Never make it easy for the reader to follow your argument by supplying him with sign-posts like "but," "however," "furthermore," "on the other hand," and so forth.

Rule 5: Never just say a thing once and be done with it. Repeat yourself. Don't say "a beige coat"; say "a coat beige in color."

Rule 6: Never use a short exact word when you can use a long vague one instead. The long vague word not only sounds more impressive, but will make it harder for your reader to understand exactly what you mean. Don't say "rape" or "riot" when you can say "incident"; don't say "beat" when you can say "negative reinforcement." All four-letter words are in general to be avoided, except for the word "seem." Don't say "it's raining"—always say, "It seems to be raining."

Rule 7: Never check your paper carefully for misspelled words, typographical errors or erroneous punctuation. While this sort of thing won't actually ruin your argument, it will irritate and distract your reader like a pebble in his shoe, or grit in his food, and keep him from concentrating on what it is you really have to say.

Rule 8: If all else fails, and you *must* say something interesting, type it with a worn-out pale gray ribbon, preferably on semi-transparent flimsy paper. Then at least you can be sure that nobody will be able to read it with any comfort or pleasure.

Rule 9: Never forget James Thurber's magnificent slogan, the watchword of this pioneer movement: "Don't get it right. Just get it written."

VOCABULARY

1. Define the following words as Pope uses them in her essay: unremitting, decomposition, erroneous.
2. Does Pope follow her own Rule 6 in her essay? Explain.

CONTENT

1. Why does Pope think this country needs a good bad-writing course?
2. Who is Pope criticizing in Rule 1? Is her criticism justified? Defend your answer.

3. Would Godwin (see "The Watcher at the Gates," page 9) agree or disagree with Thurber's "Don't get it right. Just get it written"? Defend your answer.

RHETORIC

1. Why does Pope capitalize "Bad Writing" in her first two paragraphs?
2. At what point does it become obvious that Pope's essay is a satire*?
3. Why do you think so many people use long or vague words instead of short exact words? When, if ever, do you do this?
4. For her closing*, Pope quotes a James Thurber pun. Explain why this is or is not an effective ending to the essay.

READING AND WRITING SUGGESTIONS

1. In an argumentative essay defend or attack this statement: "In a democratic society the will of the majority must ultimately prevail."
2. Read George Orwell's essay "Politics and the English Language" and contrast his writing rules with Pope's.

---

*Definitions of all terms marked with an asterisk may be found in the Glossary.

THE LIFELINE OF THE RACE

John W. Gardner

John W. Gardner (1912–) was born in Los Angeles and received a doctorate in psychology from the University of California. After teaching at Connecticut College for Women and Mt. Holyoke College, he joined the Carnegie Foundation and, in 1955, became its president. Under his leadership, the Foundation sponsored many studies pertaining to education in America. He is especially concerned about maintaining standards of excellence in a time of mass education. His book Excellence: Can We Be Equal and Excellent Too? *speaks to this concern. From 1965 to 1968, Gardner was Secretary of Health, Education and Welfare. In 1970 he announced the formation of Common Cause, a nonpartisan citizen's lobby which he continues to serve as a board member. In addition to* Excellence, *his writings include* Self-Renewal: The Individual and The Innovative Society *and* In Common Cause. *The following selection is from Gardner's latest book,* Morale *(1978). In this selection Gardner examines the attitudes and values that make possible, or thwart, the regeneration of society.*

The most powerful moving forces in history are not societies—which are forever decaying—but highly motivated people and their ideas of what is worth living for and striving for.

Every year tens of millions of Americans come to the nation's capital to visit our national shrines. Day after day one sees them streaming through the Lincoln Memorial, the Washington Monument, the Capitol. But the spirit of the nation does not reside in the physical structures. It is in the minds of the citizens who come to look at the structures. That is where a vital society begins; and, if it ends, that is where it ends. If they stop believing, if they lose faith, if they stop caring, the monuments will be meaningless piles of stone, and the nation will be as lifeless as the stones. There will still be the land and a lot of people milling around; but the venture that began with the Declaration of Independence, the venture familiarly known as America, will be dead.

It need not happen. But it could. The task of the moment is to re-create a motivated society. If we fail in that, forget the rest. When a society disintegrates, you may be sure that its animating ideas and ideals died first in the minds of men and women.

The Unknowable Future

A Chinese proverb says, "To prophesy is extremely difficult—especially with respect to the future." A nineteenth-century horse breeder foresaw the day when transportation would be wholly revolutionized by the breeding of a horse that could run at a pace of fifty miles an hour indefinitely. The Wright brothers thought that invention of the airplane would bring an end to all wars, because under observation from the air no military force could maneuver secretly.

If it's hard to know the shape of things to come, it's virtually impossible to design social arrangements for that unknown future. It is tempting to imagine that we can draw neat blueprints of a society that will serve future generations, but we cannot. This truth is ignored to the point of comedy by many of the earnest voices that tell us how to reconstruct our society. There's a chronic shortage of people who can solve our problems here and now, but never a shortage of people who will tell us how to design our society for an unpredictable future. They woefully underestimate the imponderables of social change, especially now, when its swift flow threatens the continuities of human experience in ways we can hardly imagine.

We cannot design today the institutions for a future we cannot foretell. The best we can do is to foster the kinds of men and women who can cope with the future as it unfolds, who are capable of facing new realities as they emerge without forgetting the continuities in our tradition and our longer-term aspirations as a free people. If we are to create a society for the transitions ahead that is worthy of our heritage of freedom, our surest resource will be men and women of courage and conviction who carry within themselves a sense of what is important for the human future, a sense of what makes societies vital and humane.

A System That Evolves

With the old ways losing their hold and new ways yet to be shaped, it will be useful to remember that the time-honored customs and arrangements of a society—its institutions—have never been the solid foundation that they are widely assumed to be. They are creations of the human mind, forever changing.

We might find contemporary changes less disturbing if we reflected on the profound transformations that have already occurred in our own history. When the British colonized North America, they assumed that they could transport their institutions and attitudes to these shores more or less intact; but before the seventeenth century ended, the North American colonists had created a strikingly new way of life. They had developed attitudes and social arrangements that made the Revolution almost inevitable. That was the first America. It wasn't born in 1776; that's when it was old enough to leave home. It underwent marked changes, particularly with the emergence of Jacksonian democracy, but from beginning to end it was rural, essentially preindustrial, overwhelmingly Protestant, and relatively insulated from the rest of the world. Then in the mid-nineteenth century the first America slowly disappeared; and a very different society took shape as the powerful stirrings of industrialism began their transforming work. The second America was increasingly urban, secular, industrial, heavily salted with immigrants, pursuing ardently the revolutions in communication and transportation, and immensely exhilarated by its own growth. The third America, which came in with Franklin D. Roosevelt, was acutely conscious of social issues and committed to use the power of the federal government to resolve those issues. It was also internationalist and—ultimately—enormously preoccupied with the arts of war. (I have sketched the three Americas in grossly oversimplified terms, but the reader will recognize the underlying reality of profound social change.)

Now we are undergoing another transition. We cannot know what the next America will be like; but no one who reflects on the profound alterations—economic, political, and social—that accompanied past transitions can doubt that "the American system"—so often piously regarded as immutable—is in fact changing continuously, all the while retaining powerful continuities of character and spirit.

The Lifeline of the Race

It isn't enough to tell people that they must be equal to the challenges the future will bring. The contemporary mind asks, "Why? What makes it worthwhile? What can I believe? What can I admire and take sustenance from?"

The question isn't easily answered. Around the individual today swirls a bewildering jumble of faiths, heresies, and unbelief. It's hard for any thoughtful person to observe, in Cardinal Newman's words, "the defeat of good, the success of evil . . . the pervading idolatries, the corruptions" and still find ground for moral striving.

It isn't only the modern mind that has had difficulty with such questions. More than 2000 years ago, Ecclesiastes, who had a boundless capacity to be disappointed by the world, was particularly troubled that one cannot expect just rewards in this life. It concerned him that the wise man fares no better than the fool, the righteous no better than the wicked. The race is not to the swift: "Time and chance happeneth to them all."

It is true that there is no assurance of reward for effort or wisdom or talent or virtue, at least not in the terms that the world commonly reckons rewards—money, status, acclaim, pleasure, or power. Sensible people grasp that reality fairly early.

So why bother to meet any standards of behavior? Why strive to diminish human suffering? Why combat injustice? For some the answer may lie in being true to their religious convictions; for others, in expressing their allegiance to a moral order (however they may conceive it); for still others, simply in trying to be true to what humans can be at their best.

"Trying to be true to what humans can be at their best." The words are deceptively simple, but the idea has great power. Humans have shown themselves capable of degradation as well as nobility, of cruelty as well as kindness, of greed as well as generosity. To pretend that the darker side of human nature dissolves under the cleansing rays of idealism is to delude oneself. Yet even in those moments of history when corruption and degradation seemed wholly triumphant, there were some men and women who continued stubbornly to seek justice and liberty and a world that honored the worth and dignity of each person; there were those who strove for excellence; there were those who tried to create a more humane environment for those around them. Some left their names in the history books, others were well known in their time and place but are unknown to us; and some were perhaps never heard of beyond their neighborhood. You have known such people. Some have bettered the lives of millions of persons, others may have helped only a few among their immediate family and friends. It doesn't matter.

An enduring basis for moral commitment is to affirm our allegiance to those men and women, to associate ourselves with the human spirit striving for the best. To remind ourselves that they existed, is a message of solidarity for every seriously striving person.

There is no evidence that humans can perfect themselves or their societies. But their impulse to try accounts for the best moments in humankind's stormy history. People of various religions and philosophical views explain the impulse in varying terminology, but few deny that it exists. The impulse may be layered over, ignored, or smothered by worldliness and cynicism; but it is there—and, in some people, inextinguishable. We draw our spiritual strength from just those people, even though most of them are unknown to us. They are the bearers of the spirit, the lifeline of the race, stretching back through the centuries.

Continuities of the Spirit

All of us celebrate our values in our behavior. The way we act and conduct our lives says something to others—perhaps something reprehensible, perhaps something encouraging. We are teaching by example—bad lessons or good. Each of us is saying—in our behavior—"This is one thing of which humankind is capable." We are allying ourselves with those who have exalted humankind or with those who have degraded it. All those who set standards for themselves, rear their children responsibly, strengthen the bonds of community, do their work creditably and accept individual responsibility are building the common future. It is the universal ministry.

This is a heartening truth for those people who wish to assist in the regeneration of values but can't imagine how they can possibly influence this huge and complex society. They are not as powerless as they believe. No one can measure the contagion of ideas, values, and aspirations as expressed in the lives and acts of individual men and women. That contagion produces continuities in social behavior that are not readily discernible. We are familiar with the continuities evident in the influence of great teachers, prophets, and philosophers, but we have given little thought to the moral and spiritual lineage of everyday human interaction. We couldn't possibly name the many people who have influenced us, sometimes through a single exemplary act. As they influenced us, others influenced them. Those living today will influence others. The web of influence reaches back through the generations, stretching over centuries a skein of incomparable delicacy and strength. That moral and spiritual lineage, often preserved at great cost, is an antidote to the cynicism so often generated by the contemporary inflated self, which seeks all meaning in its own aches and itches.

VOCABULARY

1. Define the following words as Gardner uses them in this selection: animating, immutable, sustenance, pervading, idolatry, reprehensible, contagion, lineage, skein, antidote.
2. If you are unfamiliar with any other words in this selection, check them in a dictionary and then define them in your own words.
3. Define Jacksonian democracy.

CONTENT

1. What are the "three Americas" that Gardner describes? What is the purpose of this description?

2. After admitting that there "is no assurance of reward for effort or wisdom or talent or virtue," Gardner goes on to suggest several reasons for moral striving. What are they?
3. Do you agree with Gardner's suggestion that self-absorption causes cynicism? Explain your answer.
4. In what ways do you personally feel responsible to assist in what Gardner refers to as the regeneration of values?
5. How do Gardner's arguments for moral regeneration compare with Bertrand Russell's ideas of success in "A Life Worth Living" (page 45)?

RHETORIC

1. What is Gardner's thesis*? What effect does his repetition of the thesis have?
2. Does Gardner use logic* or persuasion* to build his argument? Explain.
3. Gardner uses several direct quotations in this selection. How do they affect his argument?
4. Does Gardner's use of headings as a transitional device* make this selection easier to read and understand? State the main idea* under each heading.

READING AND WRITING SUGGESTIONS

1. Write an argumentative essay agreeing or disagreeing with Gardner's optimism about humanity.
2. In a brief essay, describe how someone on a day-to-day basis or in "a single exemplary act" influenced your life.
3. When William Sloane Coffin, Jr., left the chaplaincy of Yale University to take part in the "Freedom Rides" of the 1960s, he was severely criticized. Read *Once to Every Man, A Memoir,* in which he explains the formation and living out of his values. Then write an essay defending or attacking his actions.

---

*Definitions of all terms marked with an asterisk may be found in the Glossary.

PART FOUR

NARRATION

Narration is the mode of discourse that presents a sequence of events occurring over a period of time. Narrative essays may be factual or impressionistic. *Factual narratives* deal with historical events—ranging from the sinking of the *Titanic* to a real episode in the writer's childhood. *Imaginative narratives* focus on highly imaginative or fictional events—for example, extraterrestrial beings' first arrival on earth. But whether a narrative is factual or impressionistic, it is distinguished from the other three modes of discourse in that it presents the thesis indirectly by showing it rather than directly by telling about it.

Narration may be dramatized, generalized, or summarized. *Dramatized narration* shows characters in action, portraying them as vividly as possible and often presenting dialogue to heighten the immediacy of the scene. *Generalized narration* maintains a greater distance from the subject, describing and presenting it in a more subdued and contemplative manner. *Summarized narration* condenses generalized narration, presenting a sequence of events briefly and concisely.

Narrative writing should employ the sound rhetorical and logical procedures essential to the other modes of discourse. In addition, the writer should pay particular attention to sequential coherence, point of view, and dialogue. To achieve sequential coherence, the writer must decide whether to adopt a strict chronological approach—recounting events as they happened in time—or to create a different temporal approach—perhaps giving the story's conclusion first and then showing the events that led up to it. The method used depends on the writer's purpose and the nature of the material being presented.

To achieve a consistent viewpoint, the writer must decide whether to give a first-person or a third-person account of an event and must maintain this point of view throughout the essay. Point of view has a strong effect on an essay's emphasis: a first-person narrative is generally more personal, revealing in-depth reactions to an event, whereas a third-person narrative tends to be more objective and allows the writer to explore the private thoughts, feelings, motives, and activities of one or more characters in as much detail as desired.

When presenting dialogue, the writer must demonstrate a good ear, choosing vocabulary and speech patterns to suit the character speaking. No matter how interesting a dialogue may be, no one will find it convincing if the truck driver who is speaking sounds like a teenage girl or if a small child sounds like a college-educated adult.

One further note: each essay in this selection is essentially a narrative—that is, most of the essay is a story, demonstrating an idea. Often writers use stories or anecdotes merely as support for their central thesis, presenting them as examples which point up the truth of their thesis. Such essays are classified elsewhere in this volume in the sections on exposition, description, and argument.

SHOOTING AN ELEPHANT

George Orwell

George Orwell (1903–1950) was the pseudonym of Eric Blair, an English writer who was born the son of a minor customs official in India. Orwell was educated in England, but he returned to southern Asia as a young man and served with the Imperial Police in Burma. Both as a man and as a writer, he strongly criticized totalitarian societies. His questioning of totalitarianism can be seen in his books Animal Farm, *a political satire, and* 1984, *a grim vision of what the future might be like in a highly regimented society. In "Shooting an Elephant," taken from his book* Shooting an Elephant and Other Essays, *published in 1950, Orwell explores the internal conflicts of a man caught between private conviction and public pressure.*

In Moulmein, in Lower Burma, I was hated by large numbers of people—the only time in my life that I have been important enough for this to happen to me. I was sub-divisional police officer of the town, and in an aimless, petty kind of way anti-European feeling was very bitter. No one had the guts to raise a riot, but if a European woman went through the bazaars alone somebody would probably spit betel juice over her dress. As a police officer I was an obvious target and was baited whenever it seemed safe to do so. When a nimble Burman tripped me up on the football field and the referee (another Burman) looked the other way, the crowd yelled with hideous laughter. This happened more than once. In the end the sneering yellow faces of young men that met me everywhere, the insults hooted after me when I was at a safe distance, got badly on my nerves. The young Buddhist priests were the worst of all. There were several thousands of them in the town and none of them seemed to have anything to do except stand on street corners and jeer at Europeans.

All this was perplexing and upsetting. For at that time I had already made up my mind that imperialism was an evil thing and the sooner I chucked up my job and got out of it the better. Theoretically—and secretly, of course—I was all for the Burmese and all against their oppressors, the British. As for the job I was doing, I hated it more bitterly than I can perhaps make clear. In a job like that you see the dirty work of Empire at close quarters. The wretched prisoners huddling in the stinking cages of the lock-ups, the grey, cowed faces of the long-term convicts, the scarred buttocks of the men who had been flogged with bamboos—all these oppressed me with an intolerable sense of guilt. But I could get nothing into perspective. I was young and ill-educated and I had had to think out my problems in the utter silence that is imposed on every Englishman in the East. I did not even know that the British Empire is dying, still less did I know that it is a great deal better than the younger empires that are going to supplant it. All I knew was that I was stuck between my hatred of the empire I served and my rage against the evil-spirited little beasts who tried to make my job impossible. With one part of my mind I thought of the British Raj[1] as an unbreakable tyranny, as something clamped down, *in saecula saeculorum,*[2] upon the will of prostrate peoples; with another part I thought that the greatest joy in the world would be to drive a bayonet into a Buddhist priest's guts. Feelings like these are the normal by-products of imperialism; ask any Anglo-Indian official, if you can catch him off duty.

One day something happened which in a round-about way was enlightening. It was a tiny incident in itself, but it gave me a better glimpse than I had had before of the real nature of imperialism—the real motives for which despotic governments act. Early one morning the sub-inspector at a police station the other end of the town rang me up on the 'phone and said that an elephant was ravaging the bazaar. Would I please come and do something about it? I did not know what I could do, but I wanted to see what was happening and I got on to a pony and started out. I took my rifle, an old .44 Winchester and much too small to kill an elephant, but I thought the noise might be useful *in terrorem.*[3] Various Burmans stopped me on the way and told me about the elephant's doings. It was not, of course, a wild elephant, but a tame one which had gone "must."[4] It had been chained up, as tame elephants always are when their attack of "must" is due, but on the previous night it had broken its chain and escaped. Its mahout,[5] the only person who could manage it when it was in that state, had set out in pursuit, but had taken the wrong direction and was now twelve hours' journey away, and in the morning the elephant had suddenly reappeared in the town. The Burmese population had no weapons and were quite helpless against it. It had already destroyed somebody's bamboo hut; killed a cow and raided some fruit-stalls and devoured

1. Reign.
2. A Latin phrase meaning "forever and ever" or "for all eternity."
3. Latin for "as a means of provoking fright; an instrument of terror."
4. A period of frenzy occurring in elephants during the mating season.
5. Trainer and rider.

the stock; also it had met the municipal rubbish van, and, when the driver jumped out and took to his heels, had turned the van over and inflicted violences upon it.

The Burmese sub-inspector and some Indian constables were waiting for me in the quarter where the elephant had been seen. It was a very poor quarter, a labyrinth of squalid bamboo huts, thatched with palm-leaf, winding all over a steep hillside. I remember that it was a cloudy, stuffy morning at the beginning of the rains. We began questioning the people as to where the elephant had gone, and, as usual, failed to get any definite information. That is invariably the case in the East; a story always sounds clear enough at a distance, but the nearer you get to the scene of events the vaguer it becomes. Some of the people said that the elephant had gone in one direction, some said that he had gone in another, some professed not even to have heard of an elephant. I had almost made up my mind that the whole story was a pack of lies, when we heard yells a little distance away. There was a loud, scandalized cry of "Go away, child! Go away this instant" and an old woman with a switch in her hand came around the corner of a hut, violently shooing away a crowd of naked children. Some more women followed, clicking their tongues and exclaiming; evidently there was something that the children ought not to have seen. I rounded the hut and saw a man's dead body sprawling in the mud. He was an Indian, a black Dravidian coolie, almost naked, and he could not have been dead many minutes. The people said that the elephant had come suddenly upon him round the corner of the hut, caught him with its trunk, put its foot on his back and ground him into the earth. This was the rainy season and the ground was soft, and his face had scored a trench a foot deep and a couple of yards long. He was lying on his belly with arms crucified and head sharply twisted to one side. His face was coated with mud, the eyes wide open, the teeth bared and grinning with an expression of unendurable agony. (Never tell me, by the way, the dead look peaceful. Most of the corpses I have seen looked devilish.) The friction of the great beast's foot had stripped the skin from his back as neatly as one skins a rabbit. As soon as I saw the dead man I sent an orderly to a friend's house nearby to borrow an elephant rifle. I had already sent back the pony, not wanting it to go mad with fright and throw me if it smelled the elephant.

The orderly came back in a few minutes with a rifle and five cartridges, and meanwhile some Burmans had arrived and told us that the elephant was in the paddy fields below, only a few hundred yards away. As I started forward practically the whole population of the quarter flocked out of the houses and followed me. They had seen the rifle and were all shouting excitedly that I was going to shoot the elephant. They had not shown much interest in the elephant when he was merely ravaging their homes, but it was different now that he was going to be shot. It was a bit of fun to them, as it would be to an English crowd; besides they wanted the meat. It made me vaguely uneasy. I had no intention of shooting the elephant—I had merely sent for the rifle to defend myself if necessary—and it is always unnerving to have a crowd following you. I marched down the hill, looking and feeling a fool, with the rifle over my shoulder and an ever-growing army of people jostling at my heels. At the bottom, when you got away from the huts, there was a metalled road and beyond that a miry waste of paddy fields a thousand yards across, not yet ploughed but soggy from the first rains and dotted with coarse grass. The elephant was standing eight yards from the road, his left side towards us. He took not the slightest notice of the crowd's approach. He was tearing up bunches of grass, beating them against his knees to clean them and stuffing them into his mouth.

I had halted on the road. As soon as I saw the elephant I knew with perfect certainty that I ought not to shoot him. It is a serious matter to shoot a working elephant—it is comparable to destroying a huge and costly piece of machinery—and obviously one ought not to do it if it can possibly be avoided. And at that distance, peacefully eating, the elephant looked no more dangerous than a cow. I thought then and I think now that his attack of "must" was already passing off; in which case he would merely wander harmlessly about until the mahout came back and caught him. Moreover, I did not in the least want to shoot him. I decided that I would watch him for a little while to make sure that he did not turn savage again, and then go home.

But at that moment I glanced round at the crowd that had followed me. It was an immense crowd, two thousand at the least and growing every minute. It blocked the road for a long distance on either side. I looked at the sea of yellow faces above the garish clothes—faces all happy and excited over this bit of fun, all certain that the elephant was going to be shot. They were watching me as they would watch a conjurer about to perform a trick. They did not like me, but with the magical rifle in my hands I was momentarily worth watching. And suddenly I realized that I should have to shoot the elephant after all. The people expected it of me and I had got to do it; I could feel their two thousand wills pressing me forward, irresistibly. And it was at this moment, as I stood there with the rifle in my hands, that I first grasped the hollowness, the futility of the white man's dominion in the East. Here was I, the white man with his gun, standing in front of the unarmed native crowd—seemingly the leading actor of the piece; but in reality I was only an absurd puppet pushed to and fro by the will of those yellow faces behind. I perceived in this moment that when the white man turns tyrant it is his own freedom that he destroys. He becomes a sort of hollow, posing dummy, the conventionalized figure of a sahib.[6] For it is the condition of his rule that he shall spend his life in trying to impress the "natives," and so in every crisis he has got to do what the "natives" expect of him. He wears a mask, and his face grows to fit it. I had got to shoot the elephant. I had committed myself to doing it when I sent for the rifle. A sahib has got to act like a sahib; he has got to appear resolute, to know his own mind and do definite things. To come all that way, rifle in hand, with two thousand people marching at my heels, and then to trail feebly away, having done nothing—no, that was impossible. The crowd would laugh at me. And my whole life, every white man's life in the East, was one long struggle not to be laughed at.

But I did not want to shoot the elephant. I watched him beating his bunch of grass against his knees, with that preoccupied grandmotherly air that elephants have. It seemed to me that it would be murder to shoot him. At that age I was not squeamish about killing animals, but I had never shot an elephant and never wanted to. (Somehow it always seems worse to kill a *large* animal.) Besides, there was the beast's owner to be considered. Alive, the elephant was worth at least a hundred pounds; dead, he would only be worth the value of his tusks, five pounds, possibly. But I had got to act quickly. I turned to some experienced-looking Burmans who had been there when we arrived, and asked them how the elephant had been behaving. They all said the same thing: he took no notice of you if you left him alone, but he might charge you if you went too close to him.

It was perfectly clear to me what I ought to do. I ought to walk up to within, say, twenty-five yards of the elephant and test his behavior. If he charged I could shoot, if he took no notice of me it would be safe to leave him until the mahout came back. But also I knew that I was going to do no such thing. I was a poor shot with a rifle and the ground was soft mud into which one would sink at every step. If the elephant charged and I missed him, I should have about as much chance as a toad under a steamroller. But even then I was not thinking particularly of my own skin, only of the watchful yellow faces behind. For at that moment, with the crowd watching me, I was not afraid in the ordinary sense, as I would have been if I had been alone. A white man mustn't be frightened in front of "natives"; and so, in general, he isn't frightened. The sole thought in my mind was that if anything went wrong those two thousand Burmans would see me pursued, caught, trampled on and reduced to a grinning corpse like that Indian up the hill. And if that happened it was quite probable that some

6. Master; an Indian form of respect used when addressing a Britisher.

of them would laugh. That would never do. There was only one alternative. I shoved the cartridges into the magazine and lay down on the road to get a better aim.

The crowd grew very still, and a deep, low, happy sigh, as of people who see the theatre curtain go up at last, breathed from innumerable throats. They were going to have their bit of fun after all. The rifle was a beautiful German thing with cross-hair sights. I did not then know that in shooting an elephant one would shoot to cut an imaginary bar running from ear-hole to ear-hole. I ought, therefore, as the elephant was sideways on, to have aimed straight at his earhole; actually I aimed several inches in front of this, thinking the brain would be further forward.

When I pulled the trigger I did not hear the bang or feel the kick—one never does when a shot goes home—but I heard the devilish roar of glee that went up from the crowd. In that instant, in too short a time, one would have thought, even for the bullet to get there, a mysterious, terrible change had come over the elephant. He neither stirred nor fell, but every line on his body had altered. He looked suddenly stricken, shrunken, immensely old, as though the frightful impact of the bullet had paralyzed him without knocking him down. At last, after what seemed a long time—it might have been five seconds, I dare say—he sagged flabbily to his knees. His mouth slobbered. An enormous senility seemed to have settled upon him. One could have imagined him thousands of years old. I fired again into the same spot. At the second shot he did not collapse but climbed with desperate slowness to his feet and stood weakly upright, with legs sagging and head drooping. I fired a third time. That was the shot that did it for him. You could see the agony of it jolt his whole body and knock the last remnant of strength from his legs. But in falling he seemed for a moment to rise, for as his hind legs collapsed beneath him he seemed to tower upwards like a huge rock toppling, his trunk reaching skywards like a tree. He trumpeted, for the first and only time. And then down he came, his belly towards me, with a crash that seemed to shake the ground even where I lay.

I got up. The Burmans were already racing past me across the mud. It was obvious that the elephant would never rise again, but he was not dead. He was breathing very rhythmically with long rattling gasps, his great mound of a side painfully rising and falling. His mouth was wide open—I could see far down into the caverns of pale pink throat. I waited a long time for him to die, but his breathing did not weaken. Finally I fired my two remaining shots into the spot where I thought his heart must be. The thick blood welled out of him like red velvet, but still he did not die. His body did not even jerk when the shots hit him, the tortured breathing continued without a pause. He was dying, very slowly and in great agony, but in some world remote from me where not even a bullet could damage him further. I felt that I had got to put an end to that dreadful noise. It seemed dreadful to see the great beast lying there, powerless to move and yet powerless to die, and not even to be able to finish him. I sent back for my small rifle and poured shot after shot into his heart and down his throat. They seemed to make no impression. The tortured gasps continued as steadily as the ticking of a clock.

In the end I could not stand it any longer and went away. I heard later that it took him half an hour to die. Burmans were bringing dahs[7] and baskets even before I left, and I was told they had stripped his body almost to the bones by the afternoon.

Afterwards, of course, there were endless discussions about the shooting of the elephant. The owner was furious, but he was only an Indian and could do nothing. Besides, legally I had done the right thing, for a mad elephant has to be killed, like a mad dog, if its owner fails to control it. Among the Europeans opinion was divided. The older men said I was right, the younger men said it was a damn shame to shoot an elephant for killing a coolie, because an elephant was worth more than any damn Coringhee coolie. And afterwards I was very glad that the coolie had been killed; it put me legally in the right and it gave me a sufficient pretext for shooting the elephant. I often wondered whether any of the others grasped that I had done it solely to avoid looking a fool.

VOCABULARY

1. Define the following words as Orwell uses them in his essay: betel, imperialism, prostrate, despotic, squalid, paddy, garish, conjurer, senility, pretext.
2. If you are unfamiliar with any other words in this essay, check them in a dictionary and then define them in your own words.

CONTENT

1. In narration a story is told not just for itself but also for a purpose. What is Orwell's stated purpose in this story?
2. Explain the meaning of the following phrases in the context of the essay as a whole.
   a. "He wears a mask, and his face grows to fit it."
   b. ". . . you see the dirty work of Empire at close quarters."

---

7. Crude litters much in use for transport throughout the East.

3. How does Orwell feel about imperialism? about the Burmese natives? about the other English officers? Cite examples to support each judgment.

4. Did the protagonist think he *ought* to shoot the elephant? What reasons did he give for his conclusion?

5. Have you ever done something you didn't want to do in order to avoid looking foolish? If so, what was it you did and how did you feel afterward?

6. Review Hemingway's essay "Bull Fighting" (page 78). Compare the attitude of the crowd toward the bull fight with the attitude of the Burmans toward the fate of the elephant.

RHETORIC

1. Is Orwell's essay dramatized, generalized, or summarized narration? Explain your answer.

2. What is the tone* of this narrative? Does Orwell sound more like a member speaking in the House of Commons or like one civil servant talking to another over drinks in a club? How does Orwell achieve this effect?

3. How do the two introductory paragraphs which precede the story about the elephant foreshadow* what comes later in the story?

4. In another essay—"Politics and the English Language"—Orwell offers the following advice: "Never use a metaphor, simile, or other figure of speech you are used to seeing in print" and "Never use a long word where a short one will do." In "Shooting an Elephant," does Orwell follow his own advice? Support your answers with examples.

READING AND WRITING SUGGESTIONS

1. Consider Orwell's sentence, "When a white man turns tyrant it is his own freedom that he destroys." Although Orwell is referring specifically to white men in a colonial context, the sentence can be generalized to apply to all people. For example, Booker T. Washington said, "To keep a man in the ditch you have to get down there with him and stay there." Write a narrative essay about a person to whom these generalizations apply.

---

*Definitions of all terms marked with an asterisk may be found in the Glossary.

2. Read about a fictional character, such as Captain Vere in Herman Melville's *Billy Budd*, who acts from a sense of duty to a system even when that duty conflicts with what he or she thinks is right. Write a narrative essay describing the internal tensions such a person must feel.

SHAME

Dick Gregory

Dick Gregory (1923–), well-known comedian and entertainer, was born in St. Louis and attended Southern Illinois University, where he was named an outstanding athlete in 1953. He was a leader in antiwar and civil rights activities during the 1960s. His books include From the Back of the Bus; What's Happening; Dick Gregory's Political Primer; The Myths of American History; *and* Dick Gregory's Natural Diet for Folks Who Eat: Cookin' with Mother Nature. *In this essay, taken from his autobiography* Nigger *(1964), Gregory explores a humiliating experience he suffered in his childhood.*

I never learned hate at home, or shame. I had to go to school for that. I was about seven years old when I got my first big lesson. I was in love with a little girl named Helene Tucker, a light-complexioned little girl with pigtails and nice manners. She was always clean and she was smart in school. I think I went to school then mostly to look at her. I brushed my hair and even got me a little old handkerchief. It was a lady's handkerchief, but I didn't want Helene to see me wipe my nose on my hand. The pipes were frozen again, there was no water in the house, but I washed my socks and shirt every night. I'd get a pot, and go over to Mister Ben's grocery store, and stick my pot down into his soda machine. Scoop out some chopped ice. By evening the ice melted to water for washing. I got sick a lot that winter because the fire would go out at night before the clothes were dry. In the morning I'd put them on, wet or dry, because they were the only clothes I had.

Everybody's got a Helene Tucker, a symbol of everything you want. I loved her for her goodness, her cleanness, her popularity. She'd walk down my street and my brothers and sisters would yell, "Here comes Helene," and I'd rub my tennis sneakers on the back of my pants and wish my hair wasn't so nappy and the white folks' shirt fit me better. I'd run out on the street. If I knew my place and didn't come too close, she'd wink at me and say hello. That was a good feeling. Sometimes I'd follow her all the way home, and shovel the snow off her walk and try to make friends with her Momma and her aunts. I'd drop money on her stoop late at night on my way back from shining shoes in the taverns. And she had a Daddy, and he had a good job. He was a paper hanger.

I guess I would have gotten over Helene by summertime, but something happened in that classroom that made her face hang in front of me for the next twenty-two years. When I played the drums in high school it was for Helene and when I broke track records in college it was for Helene and when I started standing behind microphones and heard applause I wished Helene could hear it, too. It wasn't until I was twenty-nine years old and married and making money that I finally got her out of my system. Helene was sitting in that classroom when I learned to be ashamed of myself.

It was on a Thursday. I was sitting in the back of the room, in a seat with a chalk circle drawn around it. The idiot's seat, the troublemaker's seat.

The teacher thought I was stupid. Couldn't spell, couldn't read, couldn't do arithmetic. Just stupid. Teachers were never interested in finding out that you couldn't concentrate because you were so hungry, because you hadn't had any breakfast. All you could think about was noontime, would it ever come? Maybe you could sneak into the cloakroom and steal a bite of some kid's lunch out of a coat pocket. A bite of something. Paste. You can't really make a meal out of paste, or put it on bread for a sandwich, but sometimes I'd scoop a few spoonfuls out of the paste jar in the back of the room. Pregnant people get strange tastes. I was pregnant with poverty. Pregnant with dirt and pregnant with smells that made people turn away, pregnant with cold and pregnant with shoes that were never bought for me, pregnant with five other people in my bed and no Daddy in the next room, and pregnant with hunger. Paste doesn't taste too bad when you're hungry.

The teacher thought I was a troublemaker. All she saw from the front of the room was a little black boy who squirmed in his idiot's seat and made noises and poked the kids around him. I guess she couldn't see a kid who made noises because he wanted someone to know he was there.

It was on a Thursday, the day before the Negro payday. The eagle always flew on Friday. The teacher was asking each student how much his father would give to the Community Chest. On Friday night, each kid would get the money from his father, and on Monday he would bring it to the school. I decided I was going to buy me a Daddy right then. I had money in my pocket from shining shoes and selling papers, and whatever Helene Tucker pledged for her Daddy I was going to top it. And I'd hand the money right in. I wasn't going to wait until Monday to buy me a Daddy.

I was shaking, scared to death. The teacher opened her book and started calling out names alphabetically.

"Helene Tucker?"

"My daddy said he'd give two dollars and fifty cents."

"That's very nice, Helene. Very, very nice indeed."

That made me feel pretty good. It wouldn't take too much to top that. I had almost three dollars in dimes and quarters in my pocket. I stuck my hand in my pocket and held onto the money, waiting for her to call my name. But the teacher closed her book after she called everybody else in the class.

I stood up and raised my hand.

"What is it now?"

"You forgot me."

She turned toward the blackboard. "I don't have time to be playing with you, Richard."

"My Daddy said he'd . . ."

"Sit down, Richard, you're disturbing the class."

"My Daddy said he'd give . . . fifteen dollars."

She turned around and looked mad. "We are collecting the money for you and your kind, Richard Gregory. If your Daddy can give fifteen dollars you have no business being on relief."

"I got it right now, I got it right now, my Daddy gave it to me to turn in today, my Daddy said . . ."

"And furthermore," she said, looking right at me, her nostrils getting big and her lips getting thin and her eyes opening wide, "we know you don't have a Daddy."

Helene Tucker turned around, her eyes full of tears. She felt sorry for me. Then I couldn't see her too well because I was crying, too.

"Sit down, Richard."

And I always thought the teacher kind of liked me. She always picked me to wash the blackboard on Friday, after school. That was a big thrill, it made me feel important. If I didn't wash it, come Monday the school might not function right.

"Where are you going, Richard?"

I walked out of school that day, and for a long time I didn't go back very often. There was shame there.

Now there was shame everywhere. It seemed like the whole world had been inside that classroom, everyone had heard what the teacher had said, everyone had turned around and felt sorry for me. There was shame in going to the Worthy Boys Annual Christmas Dinner for you and your kind, because everybody knew what a worthy boy was. Why couldn't they just call it the Boys Annual Dinner; why'd they have to give it a name? There was shame in wearing the brown and orange and white plaid mackinaw the welfare gave to three thousand boys. Why'd it have to be the same for everybody so when you walked down the street the people could see you were on relief? It was a nice warm mackinaw and it had a hood, and my Momma beat me and called me a little rat when she found out I stuffed it in the bottom of a pail full of garbage way over on Cottage Street. There was shame in running over to Mister Ben's at the end of the day and asking for his rotten peaches, there was shame in asking Mrs. Simmons for a spoonful of sugar, there was shame in running out to meet the relief truck. I hated that truck, full of food for you and your kind. I ran into the house and hid when it came. And then I started to sneak through alleys, to take the long way home so the people going into White's Eat Shop wouldn't see me. Yeah, the whole world heard the teacher that day, we all know you don't have a Daddy.

It lasted for a while, this kind of numbness. I spent a lot of time feeling sorry for myself. And then one day I met this wino in a restaurant. I'd been out hustling all day, shining shoes, selling newspapers, and I had goo-gobs of money in my pocket. Bought me a bowl of chili for fifteen cents, and a cheeseburger for fifteen cents, and a Pepsi for five cents, and a piece of chocolate cake for ten cents. That was a good meal. I was eating when this old wino came in. I love winos because they never hurt anyone but themselves.

The old wino sat down at the counter and ordered twenty-six cents worth of food. He ate it like he really enjoyed it. When the owner, Mister Williams, asked him to pay the check, the old wino didn't lie or go through his pocket like he suddenly found a hole.

He just said: "Don't have no money."

The Owner yelled: "Why in hell you come in here and eat my food if you don't have no money? That food cost me money."

Mister Williams jumped over the counter and knocked the wino off his stool and beat him over the head with a pop bottle. Then he stepped back and watched the wino bleed. Then he kicked him. And he kicked him again.

I looked at the wino with blood all over his face and I went over. "Leave him alone, Mister Williams. I'll pay the twenty-six cents."

The wino got up, slowly, pulling himself up to the stool, then up to the counter, holding on for a minute until his legs stopped shaking so bad. He looked at me with pure hate. "Keep your twenty-six cents. You don't have to pay, not now. I just finished paying for it."

He started to walk out, and as he passed me, he reached down and touched my shoulder. "Thanks, sonny, but it's too late now. Why didn't you pay it before?"

I was pretty sick about that. I waited too long to help another man.

VOCABULARY

1. Define the following words as Gregory uses them in this selection: nappy, stoop, mackinaw.
2. If you are unfamiliar with any other words in this selection, check them in a dictionary and then define them in your own words.

CONTENT

1. Gregory states that "everybody's got a Helene Tucker, a symbol of everything you want."
   a. What was Helene a symbol of for Gregory? What is the impact in this essay of using such a symbol?
   b. Why was Gregory so upset by being shamed in front of Helene and by her pity for him?
   c. What did having Helene as a symbol cause Gregory to do? What happened that enabled him to let her go?
2. Recall an event that made you feel shame. Would you be able to write about it and publish it for everyone to read?
3. The important leadership Gregory has exerted in the struggle for black people's civil rights may have been influenced by the trauma and need he experienced as a child.
   a. If this is the case, is the good he has done worth the price he paid?
   b. Might he still have achieved as much in adulthood if he had not experienced the shame that he did?
4. How was Gregory's teacher like the instructor Langer describes in "The Human Use of Language" (page 96)?
5. How does the impact of Gregory's lesson compare with the impact of the lesson Franklin learned in his childhood ("The Whistle," page 121)?

RHETORIC

1. What is the effect of the three introductory paragraphs which precede Gregory's account of the events in the narrative beginning in the fourth paragraph?
2. Why do you think Gregory uses sentence fragments in this selection?
3. Describe the rhetorical effect of Gregory's use of the word "pregnant" in paragraph five.
4. How would you describe the essay's tone*? How does Gregory communicate this tone?
5. After the central narrative ends, Gregory devotes the last nine paragraphs to an account of his experience with a wino. What does this anecdote* contribute to the total essay?

READING AND WRITING SUGGESTIONS

1. Write a narrative essay showing what might have occurred if Gregory's teacher had responded to him in an understanding way. How might he have felt and acted subsequently?
2. Read a book about a deprived childhood, such as Jonathan Kozol's *Death at an Early Age*, which illustrates Gregory's powerful image of "a kid who made noises because he wanted someone to know he was there." Write an essay describing what humiliation can do to a child already uncertain of his or her own self-worth.

---

*Definitions of all terms marked with an asterisk may be found in the Glossary.

A CHILD'S DREAM OF A STAR

Charles Dickens

Charles Dickens (1812–1870) was born in England to a poor family. When he was twelve his father was taken to debtor's prison, leaving Dickens to support himself. The humiliation associated with his poverty and his father's arrest stayed with him throughout his life, and many of his novels are concerned with unhappy children, as well as social injustice of all kinds. Dickens' vivid portrayal of the poor living conditions endured by the lower classes did much to influence the wealthier classes of Victorian England to examine the social problems of their day. The Pickwick Papers, A Christmas Carol, Oliver Twist, The Old Curiosity Shop, David Copperfield, A Tale of Two Cities *and* Great Expectations *are among his most famous works. The following essay, "A Child's Dream of a Star," illustrates Dickens' use of overstatement, repetition, imagery, figurative language, and emotional appeal.*

There was once a child, and he strolled about a good deal, and thought of a number of things. He had a sister, who was a child too, and his constant companion. These two used to wonder all day long. They wondered at the beauty of the flowers; they wondered at the height and blueness of the sky; they wondered at the depth of the bright water; they wondered at the goodness and the power of God who made the lovely world.

They used to say to one another sometimes, Supposing all the children upon earth were to die, would the flowers, and the water, and the sky be sorry? They believed they would be sorry. For, said they, the buds are the children of the flowers; and the little playful streams that gambol down the hillsides are the children of the water; and the smallest bright specks playing at hide and seek in the sky all night must surely be the children of the stars; and they would all be grieved to see their playmates, the children of men, no more.

There was one clear, shining star that used to come out in the sky before the rest, near the church spire, above the graves. It was larger and more beautiful, they thought, than all the others, and every night they watched for it, standing hand in hand at a window. Whoever saw it first cried out, "I see the star!" And often they cried out both together, knowing so well when it would rise, and where. So they grew to be such friends with it, that, before lying down in their beds, they always looked out once again to bid it good-night; and when they were turning round to sleep they used to say, "God bless the star!"

But while she was still very young, oh very, very young, the sister drooped, and came to be so very weak that she could no longer stand in the window at night; and then the child looked sadly out by himself, and when he saw the star, turned round and said to the patient, pale face on the bed, "I see the star!" and then a smile would come upon the face, and a little weak voice used to say, "God bless my brother and the star!"

And so the time came all too soon! when the child looked out alone, and when there was no face on the bed; and when there was a little grave among the graves, not there before; and when the star made long rays down toward him, as he saw it through his tears.

Now, these rays were so bright, and they seemed to make such a shining way from earth to heaven, that when the child went to his solitary bed, he dreamed about the star; and dreamed that, lying where he was, he saw a train of people taken up that sparkling road by angels. And the star, opening, showed him a great world of light, where many more such angels waited to receive them.

All these angels, who were waiting, turned their beaming eyes upon the people who were carried up into the star; and soon came out from the long rows in which they stood, and fell upon the people's necks, and kissed them tenderly, and went away with them down avenues of light, and were so happy in their company, that lying in his bed he wept for joy.

But there were many angels who did not go with them, and among them one he knew. The patient face that once had lain upon the bed was glorified and radiant, but his heart found out his sister among all the host.

His sister's angel lingered near the entrance of the star, and said to the leader among those who had brought the people thither:—

"Is my brother come?"

And he said "No."

She was turning hopefully away, when the child stretched out his arms and cried, "O sister, I am here! Take me!" and then she turned her beaming eyes upon him, and it was night; and the star was shining in the room, making long rays down toward him as he saw it through his tears.

From that hour forth, the child looked out upon the star as on the home he was to go to, when his time should come; and he thought that he did not belong to the earth alone, but to the star too, because of his sister's angel gone before.

There was a baby born to be a brother to the child; and while he was so little that he never yet had spoken a word, he stretched his tiny form out on his bed, and died.

Again the child dreamed of the open star, and of the company of angels, and the train of people, and the rows of angels with their beaming eyes all turned upon those people's faces.

Said his sister's angel to the leader:—

"Is my brother come?"

And he said, "Not that one, but another."

As the child beheld his brother's angel in her arms, he cried, "O sister, I am here! Take me!" And she turned and smiled upon him, and the star was shining.

He grew to be a young man, and was busy at his books when an old servant came to him and said:—

"Thy mother is no more. I bring her blessings on her darling son!"

Again at night he saw the star, and all that former company. Said his sister's angel to the leader:—

"Is my brother come?"

And he said, "Thy mother!"

A mighty cry of joy went forth through all the star, because the mother was re-united to her two children. And he stretched out his arms and cried, "O mother, sister, and brother, I am here! Take me!" And they answered him, "Not yet," and the star was shining.

He grew to be a man, whose hair was turning gray, and he was sitting in his chair by his fireside, heavy with grief, and with his face bedewed with tears, when the star opened once again.

Said his sister's angel to the leader:—

"Is my brother come?"

And he said, "Nay, but his maiden daughter."

And the man who had been the child saw his daughter, newly lost to him, a celestial creature among those three, and he said, "My daughter's head is on my sister's bosom, and her arm is around my mother's neck, and at her feet there is the baby of old time, and I can bear the parting from her, God be praised!"

And the star was shining.

Thus the child came to be an old man, and his once smooth face was wrinkled, and his steps were slow and feeble, and his back was bent. And one night as he lay upon his bed, his children standing round, he cried, as he had cried so long ago:—

"I see the star!"

They whispered to one another, "He is dying."

And he said, "I am. My age is falling from me like a garment, and I move toward the star as a child. And O my Father, now I thank thee that it has so often opened, to receive those dear ones who await me!"

And the star was shining; and it shines upon his grave.

VOCABULARY

1. Define the following words as Dickens uses them in his essay: gambol, drooped, thither, bedewed, celestial.
2. Which words or expressions in this essay reflect the fact that it is a nineteenth-century work?

CONTENT

1. Describe the character of the brother and sister.
2. What are the feelings of the brother as he passes from youth to old age?
3. Who is the "leader" whom Dickens mentions?
4. Does Dickens imply that life will triumph over death? Explain your answer.
5. Review "Mary White" by William Allen White (page 162). Compare White's attitude toward life and death with the attitude held by the brother in Dickens' essay.

RHETORIC

1. What is Dickens' thesis* in this essay?
2. List three examples of figurative language* in this essay. What effect do they have on your understanding of the narrative?
3. Dickens uses a chronological approach to achieve sequential coherence. How could you change the sequence to use flashback*? What effect would this have on the narrative?
4. The question "Is my brother come?" is asked several times in the essay. At its most specific level, it is simply an inquiry about the brother. But what deeper level of meaning* does Dickens intend with this question?
5. What mood* does Dickens' dialogue* create?

---

*Definitions of all terms marked with an asterisk may be found in the glossary.

READING AND WRITING SUGGESTIONS

1. Write a narrative essay describing an incident from your own childhood that had a dramatic effect on your ideas about life and death. Focus on feelings as much as on facts in your narrative.
2. Read or recall one of Dickens' stories or novels and write a brief narrative essay describing the history of one of the characters in the work you select.

SEPARATING

JOHN UPDIKE

John Updike (1932–), whose father was a teacher and whose mother was an author, was born in Shillington, Pennsylvania. He graduated summa cum laude from Harvard University. Updike's literary talent was recognized early, and while still in his twenties he won a Guggenheim Fellowship and the Rosenthal Award of the National Institute of Arts and Letters. Subsequently, he received an O. Henry Prize Story Award and a National Book Award. Although he has written poetry, essays, and short stories, Updike has achieved greatest fame with his novels, including Rabbit Redux, Couples, *and* The Coup. *In "Separating," which first appeared in the June 23, 1975, issue of* The New Yorker, *Updike explores a man's conflict and desolation in separating himself from his past.*

The day was fair. Brilliant. All that June the weather had mocked the Maples' internal misery with solid sunlight—golden shafts and cascades of green in which their conversations had wormed unseeing, their sad murmuring selves the only stain in Nature. Usually by this time of the year they had acquired tans; but when they met their elder daughter's plane on her return from a year in England they were almost as pale as she, though Judith was too dazzled by the sunny opulent jumble of her native land to notice. They did not spoil her homecoming by telling her immediately. Wait a few days, let her recover from jet lag, had been one of their formulations, in that string of gray dialogues—over coffee, over cocktails, over Cointreau—that had shaped the strategy of their dissolution, while the earth performed its annual stunt of renewal unnoticed beyond their closed windows. Richard had thought to leave at Easter; Joan had insisted they wait until the four children were at last assembled, with all exams passed and ceremonies attended, and the bauble of summer to console them. So he had drudged away, in love, in dread, repairing screens, getting the mowers sharpened, rolling and patching their new tennis court.

The court, clay, had come through its first winter pitted and windswept bare of redcoat. Years ago the Maples had observed how often, among their friends, divorce followed a dramatic home improvement, as if the marriage were making one last twitchy effort to live; their own worst crisis had come amid the plaster dust and exposed plumbing of a kitchen renovation. Yet, a summer ago, as canary-yellow bulldozers gaily churned a grassy, daisy-dotted knoll into a muddy plateau, and a crew of pigtailed young men raked and tamped clay into a plane, this transformation did not strike them as ominous, but festive in its impudence; their marriage could rend the earth for fun. The next spring, waking each day at dawn to a sliding sensation as if the bed were being tipped, Richard found the barren tennis court, its net and tapes still rolled in the barn, an environment congruous with his mood of purposeful desolation, and the crumbling of handfuls of clay into cracks and holes (dogs had frolicked on the court in a thaw; rivulets had evolved trenches) an activity suitably elemental and interminable. In his sealed heart he hoped the day would never come.

Now it was here. A Friday. Judith was reacclimated; all four children were assembled, before jobs and camps and visits again scattered them. Joan thought they should be told one by one. Richard was for making an announcement at the table. She said, "I think just making an announcement is a cop-out. They'll start quarrelling and playing to each other instead of focussing. They're each individuals, you know, not just some corporate obstacle to your freedom."

"O.K., O.K., I agree." Joan's plan was exact. That evening, they were giving Judith a belated welcome-home dinner, of lobster and champagne. Then, the party over, they, the two of them, who nineteen years before would push her in a baby carriage along Tenth Street to Washington Square, were to walk her out of the house, to the bridge across the salt creek, and tell her, swearing her to secrecy. Then Richard Jr., who was going directly from work to a rock concert in Boston, would be told, either late when he returned on the train or early Saturday morning before he went off to his job; he was seventeen and employed as one of a golf-course maintenance crew. Then the two younger children, John and Margaret, could, as the morning wore on, be informed.

"Mopped up, as it were," Richard said.

"Do you have any better plan? That leaves you the rest of Saturday to answer any questions, pack, and make your wonderful departure."

"No," he said, meaning he had no better plan, and agreed to hers, though it had an edge of false order, a plea for control in the semblance of its achievement, like Joan's long chore lists and financial accountings and, in the days when he first knew her, her too copious lecture notes. Her plan turned one hurdle for him into four—four knife-sharp walls, each with a sheer blind drop on the other side.

All spring he had been morbidly conscious of insides and outsides, of barriers and partitions. He and Joan stood as a thin barrier between the children and the truth. Each moment was a partition, with the past on one side and the future on the other, a future containing this unthinkable *now*. Beyond four knifelike walls a new life for him waited vaguely. His skull cupped a secret, a white face, a face both frightened and soothing, both strange and known, that he wanted to shield from tears, which he felt all about him, solid as the sunlight. So haunted, he had become obsessed with battening down the house against his absence, replacing screens and sash cords, hinges and latches—a Houdini making things snug before his escape.

The lock. He had still to replace a lock on one of the doors of the screened porch. The task, like most such, proved more difficult than he had imagined. The old lock, aluminum frozen by corrosion, had been deliberately rendered obsolete by manufacturers. Three hardware stores had nothing that even approximately matched the mortised hole its removal (surprisingly easy) left. Another hole had to be gouged, with bits too small and saws too big, and the old hole fitted with a block of wood—the chisels dull, the saw rusty, his fingers thick with lack of sleep. The sun poured down, beyond the porch, on a world of neglect. The bushes already needed pruning, the windward side of the house was shedding flakes of paint, rain would get in when he was gone, insects, rot, death. His family, all those he would lose, filtered through the edges of his awareness as he struggled with screw holes, splinters, opaque instructions, minutiae of metal.

Judith sat on the porch, a princess returned from exile. She regaled them with stories of fuel shortages, of bomb scares in the Underground, of Pakistani workmen loudly lusting after her as she walked past on her way to dance school. Joan came and went, in and out of the house, calmer than she should have been, praising his struggles with the lock as if this were one more and not the last of their chain of shared chores. The younger of his sons, John, now at fifteen suddenly, unwittingly handsome, for a few minutes held the rickety screen door while his father clumsily hammered and chiselled, each blow a kind of sob in Richard's ears. His younger daughter, having been at a slumber party, slept on the porch hammock through all the noise—heavy and pink, trusting and forsaken. Time, like the sunlight, continued relentlessly; the sunlight slowly slanted. Today was one of the longest days. The lock clicked, worked. He was through. He had a drink; he drank it on the porch, listening to his daughter. "It was so sweet," she was saying, "during the worst of it, how all the butcher's and bakery shops kept open by candlelight. They're all so plucky and cute. From the papers, things sounded so much worse here—people shooting people in gas lines, and everybody freezing."

Richard asked her, "Do you still want to live in England forever?" *Forever:* the concept, now a reality upon him, pressed and scratched at the back of his throat.

"No," Judith confessed, turning her oval face to him, its eyes still childishly far apart, but the lips set as over something succulent and satisfactory. "I was anxious to come home. I'm an American." She was a woman. They had raised her; he and Joan had endured together to raise her, alone of the four. The others had still some raising left in them. Yet it was the thought of telling Judith—the image of her, their first baby, walking between them arm in arm to the bridge—that broke him. The partition between himself and the tears broke. Richard sat down to the celebratory meal with the back of his throat aching; the champagne, the lobster seemed phases of sunshine; he saw them and tasted them through tears. He blinked, swallowed, croakily joked about hay fever. The tears would not stop leaking through; they came not through a hole that could be plugged but through a permeable spot in a membrane, steadily, purely, endlessly, fruitfully. They became, his tears, a shield for himself against these others—their faces, the fact of their assembly, a last time as innocents, at a table where he sat the last time as head. Tears dropped from his nose as he broke the lobster's back; salt flavored his champagne as he sipped it; the raw clench at the back of his throat was delicious. He could not help himself.

His children tried to ignore his tears. Judith, on his right, lit a cigarette, gazed upward in the direction of her too energetic, too sophisticated exhalation; on her other side, John earnestly bent his face to the extraction of the last morsels—legs, tail segments—from the scarlet corpse. Joan, at the opposite end of the table, glanced at him surprised, her reproach displaced by a quick grimace, of forgiveness, or of salute to his superior gift of strategy. Between them, Margaret, no longer called Bean, thirteen and large for her age, gazed from the other side of his pane of tears as if into a shop-window at something she coveted—at her father, a crystalline heap of splinters and memories. It was not she, however, but John who, in the kitchen, as they cleared the plates and carapaces away, asked Joan the question: *"Why is Daddy crying?"*

Richard heard the question but not the murmured answer. Then he heard Bean cry, "Oh, no-oh!"—the faintly dramatized exclamation of one who had long expected it.

John returned to the table carrying a bowl of salad. He nodded tersely at his father and his lips shaped the conspiratorial words "She told."

"Told what?" Richard asked aloud, insanely.

The boy sat down as if to rebuke his father's distraction with the example of his own good manners and said quietly, "The separation."

Joan and Margaret returned; the child, in Richard's twisted vision, seemed diminished in size, and relieved, relieved to have had the boogeyman at last proved real. He called out to her—the distances at the table had grown immense—"You knew, you always knew," but the clenching at the back of his throat prevented him from making sense of it. From afar he heard Joan talking, levelly, sensibly, reciting what they had prepared: it was a separation for the summer, an experiment. She and Daddy both agreed it would be good for them; they needed space and time to think; they liked each other but did not make each other happy enough, somehow.

Judith, imitating her mother's factual tone, but in her youth off-key, too cool, said, "I think it's silly. You should either live together or get divorced."

Richard's crying, like a wave that has crested and crashed, had become tumultuous; but it was overtopped by another tumult, for John, who had been so reserved, now grew larger and larger at the table. Perhaps his younger sister's being credited with knowing set him off. "Why didn't you *tell* us?" he asked, in a large round voice quite unlike his own. "You should have *told* us you weren't getting along."

Richard was startled into attempting to force words through his tears. "We *do* get along, that's the trouble, so it doesn't show even to us—" "That we do not love each other" was the rest of the sentence; he couldn't finish it.

Joan finished for him, in her style. "And we've always, *especially,* loved our children."

John was not mollified. "What do you care about *us*?" he boomed. "We're just little things you *had*." His sisters' laughing forced a laugh from him, which he turned hard and parodistic: "Ha ha *ha*." Richard and Joan realized simultaneously that the child was drunk, on Judith's homecoming champagne. Feeling bound to keep the center of the stage, John took a cigarette from Judith's pack, poked it into his mouth, let it hang from his lower lip, and squinted like a gangster.

"You're not little things we had," Richard called to him. "You're the whole point. But you're grown. Or almost."

The boy was lighting matches. Instead of holding them to his cigarette (for they had never seen him smoke; being "good" had been his way of setting himself apart), he held them to his mother's face, closer and closer, for her to blow out. Then he lit the whole folder—a hiss and then a torch, held against his mother's face. Prismed by his tears, the flame filled Richard's vision; he didn't know how it was extinguished. He heard Margaret say, "Oh stop showing off," and saw John, in response, break the cigarette in two and put the halves entirely into his mouth and chew, sticking out his tongue to display the shreds to his sister.

Joan talked to him, reasoning—a fountain of reason, unintelligible. "Talked about it for years . . . our children must help us . . . Daddy and I both want . . ." As the boy listened, he carefully wadded a paper napkin into the leaves of his salad, fashioned a ball of paper and lettuce, and popped it into his mouth, looking around the table for the expected laughter. None came. Judith said, "Be mature," and dismissed a plume of smoke.

Richard got up from this stifling table and led the boy outside. Though the house was in twilight, the outdoors still brimmed with light, the long waste light of high summer. Both laughing, he supervised John's spitting out the lettuce and paper and tobacco into the pachysandra. He took him by the hand—a square gritty hand, but for its softness a man's. Yet, it held on. They ran together up into the field, past the tennis court. The raw banking left by the bulldozers was dotted with daisies. Past the court and a flat stretch where they used to play family baseball stood a soft green rise glorious in the sun, each weed and species of grass distinct as illumination on parchment. "I'm sorry, so sorry," Richard cried. "You were the only one who ever tried to help me with all the goddam jobs around this place."

Sobbing, safe within his tears and the champagne, John explained, "It's not just the separation, it's the whole crummy year, I *hate* that school, you can't make any friends, the history teacher's a scud."

They sat on the crest of the rise, shaking and warm from their tears but easier in their voices, and Richard tried to focus on the child's sad year—the weekdays long with homework, the weekends spent in his room with model airplanes, while his parents murmured down below, nursing their separation. How selfish, how blind, Richard thought; his eyes felt scoured. He told his son, "We'll think about getting you transferred. Life's too short to be miserable."

They had said what they could, but did not want the moment to heal, and talked on, about the school, about the tennis court, whether it would ever again be as good as it had been that first summer. They walked to inspect it and pressed a few more tapes more firmly down. A little stiltedly, perhaps trying to make too much of the moment, to prolong it, Richard led the boy to the spot in the field where the view was best, of the metallic blue river, the emerald marsh, the scattered islands velvet with shadow in the low light, the white bits of beach far away. “See,” he said. “It goes on being beautiful. It’ll be here tomorrow.”

“I know,” John answered, impatiently. The moment had closed.

Back in the house, the others had opened some white wine, the champagne being drunk, and still sat at the table, the three females, gossiping. Where Joan sat had become the head. She turned, showing him a tearless face, and asked, “All right?”

“We’re fine,” he said, resenting it, though relieved, that the party went on without him.

In bed she explained, “I couldn’t cry I guess because I cried so much all spring. It really wasn’t fair. It’s your idea, and you made it look as though I was kicking you out.”

“I’m sorry,” he said. “I couldn’t stop. I wanted to but couldn’t.”

“You *didn’t* want to. You loved it. You were having your way, making a general announcement.”

“I love having it over,” he admitted. “God, those kids were great. So brave and funny.” John, returned to the house, had settled to a model airplane in his room, and kept shouting down to them, “I’m O.K. No sweat.” “And the way,” Richard went on, cozy in his relief, “they never questioned the reasons we gave. No thought of a third person. Not even Judith.”

“That *was* touching,” Joan said.

He gave her a hug. “You were great too. Thank you.” Guiltily, he realized he did not feel separated.

“You still have Dickie to do,” she told him. These words set before him a black mountain in the darkness; its cold breath, its near weight affected his chest. Of the four children Dickie was most nearly his conscience. Joan did not need to add, “That’s one piece of your dirty work I won’t do for you.”

“I know. I’ll do it. You go to sleep.”

Within minutes, her breathing slowed, became oblivious and deep. It was quarter to midnight. Dickie’s train from the concert would come in at one-fourteen. Richard set the alarm for one. He had slept atrociously for weeks. But whenever he closed his lids some glimpse of the last hours scorched them—Judith exhaling toward the ceiling in a kind of aversion, Bean’s mute staring, the sunstruck growth of the field where he and John had rested. The mountain before him moved closer, moved within him; he was huge, momentous. The ache at the back of his throat felt stale. His wife slept as if slain beside him. When, exasperated by his hot lids, his crowded heart, he rose from bed and dressed, she awoke enough to turn over. He told her then, “If I could undo it all, I would.”

“Where would you begin?” she asked. There was no place. Giving him courage, she was always giving him courage. He put on shoes without socks in the dark. The children were breathing in their rooms, the downstairs was hollow. In their confusion they had left lights burning. He turned off all but one, the kitchen overhead. The car started. He had hoped it wouldn't. He met only moonlight on the road; it seemed a diaphanous companion, flickering in the leaves along the roadside, haunting his rear-view mirror like a pursuer, melting under his headlights. The center of town, not quite deserted, was eerie at this hour. A young cop in uniform kept company with a gang of T-shirted kids on the steps of the bank. Across from the railroad station, several bars kept open. Customers, mostly young, passed in and out of the warm night, savoring summer's novelty. Voices shouted from cars as they passed; an immense conversation seemed in progress. Richard parked and in his weariness put his head on the passenger seat, out of the commotion and wheeling lights. It was as when, in the movies, an assassin grimly carries his mission through the jostle of a carnival—except the movies cannot show the precipitous, palpable slope you cling to within. You cannot climb back down; you can only fall. The synthetic fabric of the car seat, warmed by his cheek, confided to him an ancient, distant scent of vanilla.

A train whistle caused him to lift his head. It was on time; he had hoped it would be late. The slender drawgates descended. The bell of approach tingled happily. The great metal body, horizontally fluted, rocked to a stop, and sleepy teen-agers disembarked, his son among them. Dickie did not show surprise that his father was meeting him at this terrible hour. He sauntered to the car with two friends, both taller than he. He said "Hi" to his father and took the passenger's seat with an exhausted promptness that expressed gratitude. The friends got into the back, and Richard was grateful; a few minutes' postponement would be won by driving them home.

He asked, "How was the concert?"

"Groovy," one boy said from the back seat.

"It bit," the other said.

"It was O.K.," Dickie said, moderate by nature, so reasonable that in his childhood the unreason of the world had given him headaches, stomach aches, nausea. When the second friend had been dropped off at his dark house, the boy blurted, "Dad, my eyes are killing me with hay fever! I'm out there cutting that mothering grass all day!"

"Do we still have those drops?"

"They didn't do any good last summer."

"They might this." Richard swung a U-turn on the empty street. The drive home took a few minutes. The mountain was here, in his throat. "Richard," he said, and felt the boy, slumped and rubbing his eyes, go tense at his tone. "I didn't come to meet you just to make your life easier. I came because your mother and I have some news for you, and you're a hard man to get ahold of these days. It's sad news."

"That's O.K." The reassurance came out soft, but quick, as if released from the tip of a spring.

Richard had feared that his tears would return and choke him, but the boy's manliness set an example, and his voice issued forth steady and dry. "It's sad news, but it needn't be tragic news, at least for you. It should have no practical effect on your life, though it's bound to have an emotional effect. You'll work at your job, and go back to school in September. Your mother and I are really proud of what you're making of your life; we don't want that to change at all."

"Yeah," the boy said lightly, on the intake of his breath, holding himself up. They turned the corner; the church they went to loomed like a gutted fort. The home of the woman Richard hoped to marry stood across the green. Her bedroom light burned.

"Your mother and I," he said, "have decided to separate. For the summer. Nothing legal, no divorce yet. We want to see how it feels. For some years now, we haven't been doing enough for each other, making each other as happy as we should be. Have you sensed that?"

"No," the boy said. It was an honest, unemotional answer: true or false in a quiz.

Glad for the factual basis, Richard pursued, even garrulously, the details. His apartment across town, his utter accessibility, the split vacation arrangements, the advantages to the children, the added mobility and variety of the summer. Dickie listened, absorbing. "Do the others know?"

Richard described how they had been told.

"How did they take it?"

"The girls pretty calmly. John flipped out; he shouted and ate a cigarette and made a salad out of his napkin and told us how much he hated school."

His brother chuckled. "He did?"

"Yeah. The school issue was more upsetting for him than Mom and me. He seemed to feel better for having exploded."

"He did?" The repetition was the first sign that he was stunned.

"Yes. Dickie, I want to tell you something. This last hour, waiting for your train to get in, has been about the worst of my life. I hate this. *Hate* it. My father would have died before doing it to me." He felt immensely lighter, saying this. He had dumped the mountain on the boy. They were home. Moving swiftly as a shadow, Dickie was out of the car, through the bright kitchen. Richard called after him, "Want a glass of milk or anything?"

"No thanks."

"Want us to call the course tomorrow and say you're too sick to work?"

"No, that's all right." The answer was faint, delivered at the door to his room; Richard listened for the slam of a tantrum. The door closed normally. The sound was sickening.

Joan had sunk into that first deep trough of sleep and was slow to awake. Richard had to repeat, "I told him."

"What did he say?"

"Nothing much. Could you go say good night to him? Please."

She left their room, without putting on a bathrobe. He sluggishly changed back into his pajamas and walked down the hall. Dickie was already in bed, Joan was sitting beside him, and the boy's bedside clock radio was murmuring music. When she stood, an inexplicable light—the moon?—outlined her body through the nightie. Richard sat on the warm place she had indented on the child's narrow mattress. He asked him, "Do you want the radio on like that?"

"It always is."

"Doesn't it keep you awake? It would me."

"No."

"Are you sleepy?"

"Yeah."

"Good. Sure you want to get up and go to work? You've had a big night."

"I want to."

Away at school this winter he had learned for the first time that you can go short of sleep and live. As an infant he had slept with an immobile, sweating intensity that had alarmed his babysitters. As the children aged, he became the first to go to bed, earlier for a time than his younger brother and sister. Even now, he would go slack in the middle of a television show, his sprawled legs hairy and brown. "O.K. Good boy, Dickie, listen. I love you so much, I never knew how much until now. No matter how this works out, I'll always be with you. Really."

Richard bent to kiss an averted face but his son, sinewy, turned and with wet cheeks embraced him and gave him a kiss, on the lips, passionate as a woman's. In his father's ear he moaned one word, the crucial, intelligent word: *"Why?"*

Why. It was a whistle of wind in a crack, a knife thrust, a window thrown open on emptiness. The white face was gone, the darkness was featureless. Richard had forgotten why.

VOCABULARY

1. Define the following words as Updike uses them in his essay: congruous, semblance, mortised, carapaces, parodistic, mollified, diaphanous, precipitous, palpable, garrulously.
2. If you are unfamiliar with any other words in this essay, check them in a dictionary and then define them in your own words.

CONTENT

1. Richard does chores like "a Houdini making things snug before his escape." What is Richard trying to escape?
2. Describe the reaction of each member of the Maple family to the separation.
3. Updike presents the events in his essay primarily from Richard's viewpoint. Retell the narrative from Joan's point of view*.
4. Speculate on what you think might have happened next had the narration continued. State the reasons for your prediction.

RHETORIC

1. Updike describes Richard's mood as one of "purposeful desolation." Does this phrase describe the tone* of the entire essay? Support your answer with details.
2. What form of narration does Updike use in his essay: dramatized, generalized, or summarized? Would one of the other forms more effectively present the ideas and feelings he seeks to portray? Why or why not?
3. Select two or three examples of figurative language* and indicate what they contribute to the meaning and tone of Updike's essay.
4. The observation, "Time, like the sunlight, continued relentlessly; The sunlight slowly slanted," reflects the fast and inevitable movement of events toward the conclusion Richard dreads. Identify other examples of Updike's diction* which are charged with meaning. Interpret your examples.

READING AND WRITING SUGGESTIONS

1. Read a book, such as Avery Corman's *Kramer vs. Kramer,* about the breakup of a family with a young child. Then write a narrative essay about the breakup from the child's point of view.
2. In an earlier essay ("From Popping the Question to Popping the Pill," page 128), Margaret Mead said of the family: ". . . millions of children are paying the penalty of current disorganization, experimentation, and discontent." Write an essay suggesting ways in which this situation might be improved.

---

*Definitions of all terms marked with an asterisk may be found in the Glossary.

MY FURTHEST-BACK PERSON—"THE AFRICAN"

Alex Haley

Alex Haley (1921–), upon retiring from the Coast Guard in 1959, decided to become a free-lance writer. He took an apartment in Greenwich Village and devoted his full energies to writing. Seventeen years of struggle followed. With the publication of Roots *in October 1976, Haley gained immediate fame. Combined with the televised mini-series,* Roots *was widely proclaimed as the most important civil rights event since the 1965 march on Selma.* Roots *spurred black people's search for their identity and has been the catalyst for a broad-based movement among all peoples to seek their origins. The following account of how Haley researched and wrote* Roots *appeared in* The New York Times *on July 16, 1972.*

My Grandma Cynthia Murray Palmer lived in Henning, Tenn. (pop. 500), about 50 miles north of Memphis. Each summer as I grew up there, we would be visited by several women relatives who were mostly around Grandma's age, such as my Great Aunt Liz Murray who had taught in Oklahoma, and Great Aunt Till Merriwether from Jackson, Tenn., or their considerably younger niece, Cousin Georgia Anderson from Kansas City, Kan., and some others. Always after the supper dishes had been washed, they would go out to take seats and talk in the rocking chairs on the front porch, and I would scrunch down, listening, behind Grandma's squeaky chair, with the dusk deepening into night and the lightning bugs flickering on and off above the now shadowy honeysuckles. Most often they talked about our family—the story had been passed down for generations—until the whistling blur of lights of the southbound Panama Limited train *whooshing* through Henning at 9:05 P.M. signaled our bedtime.

So much of their talking of people, places and events I didn't understand: For instance, what was an "Ol' Massa," an "Ol' Missus" or a "plantation"? But early I gathered that white folks had done lots of bad things to our folks, though I couldn't figure out why. I guessed that all that they talked about had happened a long time ago, as now or then Grandma or another, speaking of someone in the past, would excitedly thrust a finger toward me, exclaiming, "Wasn't big as *this* young 'un!" And it would astound me that anyone as old and grey-haired as they could relate to my age. But in time my head began both a recording and picturing of the more graphic scenes they would describe, just as I also visualized David killing Goliath with his slingshot, Old Pharaoh's army drowning, Noah and his ark, Jesus feeding that big multitude with nothing but five loaves and two fishes, and other wonders that I heard in my Sunday school lessons at our New Hope Methodist Church.

The furthest-back person Grandma and the others talked of—always in tones of awe, I noticed—they would call "The African." They said that some ship brought him to a place that they pronounced "Naplis." They said that then some "Mas' John Waller" bought him for his plantation in "Spotsylvania County, Va." This African kept on escaping, the fourth time trying to kill the "hateful po' cracker" slave-catcher, who gave him the punishment choice of castration or of losing one foot. This African took a foot being chopped off with an ax against a tree stump, they said, and he was about to die. But his life was saved by "Mas' John's" brother—"Mas William Waller," a doctor, who was so furious about what had happened that he bought the African for himself and gave him the name "Toby."

Crippling about, working in "Mas' William's" house and yard, the African in time met and mated with "the big house cook named Bell," and there was born a girl named Kizzy. As she grew up her African daddy often showed her different kinds of things, telling her what they were in his native tongue. Pointing at a banjo, for example, the African uttered, *"ko"*; or pointing at a river near the plantation, he would say, *"Kamby Bolong."* Many of his strange words started with a *"k"* sound, and the little, growing Kizzy learned gradually that they identified different things.

When addressed by other slaves as "Toby," the master's name for him, the African said angrily that his name was *"Kin-tay."* And as he gradually learned English, he told young Kizzy some things about himself—for instance, that he was not far from his village, chopping wood to make himself a drum, when four men had surprised, overwhelmed, and kidnaped him.

So Kizzy's head held much about her African daddy when at age 16 she was sold away onto a much smaller plantation in North Carolina. Her new "Mas' Tom Lea" fathered her first child, a boy she named George. And Kizzy told her boy all about his African grandfather. George grew up to be such a gamecock fighter that he was called "Chicken George," and people would come from all over and "bet big money" on his cockfights. He mated with Matilda, another of Lea's slaves; they had seven children, and he told them the stories and strange sounds of their African great-grandfather. And one of those children, Tom, became a blacksmith who was bought away by a "Mas' Murray" for his tobacco plantation in Alamance County, N.C.

Tom mated there with Irene, a weaver on the plantation. She also bore seven children, and Tom now told them all about their African great-great-grandfather, the faithfully passed-down knowledge of his sounds and stories having become by now the family's prideful treasure.

The youngest of that second set of seven children was a girl, Cynthia, who became my maternal Grandma (which today I can only see as fated). Anyway, all of this is how I was growing up in Henning at Grandma's, listening from behind her rocking chair as she and the other visiting old women talked of that African (never then comprehended as *my* great-great-great-great-grandfather) who said his name was *"Kin-tay,"* and said *"ko"* for banjo, *"Kamby Bolong"* for river, and a jumble of other *"k"*-beginning sounds that Grandma privately muttered, most often while making beds or cooking, and who also said that near his village he was kidnaped while chopping wood to make himself a drum.

The story had become nearly as fixed in my head as in Grandma's by the time Dad and Mama moved me and my two younger brothers, George and Julius, away from Henning to be with them at the small black agricultural and mechanical college in Normal, Ala., where Dad taught.

To compress my next 25 years: When I was 17 Dad let me enlist as a mess boy in the U.S. Coast Guard. I became a ship's cook out in the South Pacific during World War II, and at night down by my bunk I began trying to write sea adventure stories, mailing them off to magazines and collecting rejection slips for eight years before some editors began purchasing and publishing occasional stories. By 1949 the Coast Guard had made me its first "journalist"; finally with 20 years' service, I retired at the age of 37, determined to make a full time career of writing. I wrote mostly magazine articles; my first book was "The Autobiography of Malcolm X."

Then one Saturday in 1965 I happened to be walking past the National Archives building in Washington. Across the interim years I had thought of Grandma's old stories—otherwise I can't think what diverted me up the Archives' steps. And when a main reading room desk attendant asked if he could help me, I wouldn't have dreamed of admitting to him some curiosity hanging on from boyhood about my slave forebears. I kind of bumbled that I was interested in census records of Alamance County, North Carolina, just after the Civil War.

The microfilm rolls were delivered, and I turned them through the machine with a building sense of intrigue, viewing in different census takers' penmanship an endless parade of names. After about a dozen microfilmed rolls, I was beginning to tire, when in utter astonishment I looked upon the names of Grandma's parents: Tom Murray, Irene Murray . . . older sisters of Grandma's as well—every one of them a name that I'd heard countless times on her front porch.

It wasn't that I hadn't believed Grandma. You just *didn't* not believe my Grandma. It was simply so uncanny actually seeing those names in print and in official U.S. Government records.

During the next several months I was back in Washington whenever possible, in the Archives, the Library of Congress, the Daughters of the American Revolution Library. (Whenever black attendants understood the idea of my search, documents I requested reached me with miraculous speed.) In one source or another during 1966 I was able to document at least the highlights of the cherished family story. I would have given anything to have told Grandma, but, sadly, in 1949 she had gone. So I went and told the only survivor of those Henning front-porch storytellers: Cousin Georgia Anderson, now in her 80s in Kansas City, Kan. Wrinkled, bent, not well herself, she was so overjoyed, repeating to me the old stories and sounds; they were like Henning echoes: "Yeah, boy, that African say his name was '*Kin-tay*'; he say the banjo was '*ko,*' and the river '*Kamby-Bolong,*' an' he was off choppin some wood to make his drum when they grabbed 'im!" Cousin Georgia grew so excited we had to stop her, calm her down, "You go 'head, boy! Your grandma an' all of 'em—they up there watching what you do!"

That week I flew to London on a magazine assignment. Since by now I was steeped in the old, in the past, scarcely a tour guide missed me—I was awed at so many historical places and treasures I'd heard of and read of. I came upon the Rosetta stone in the British Museum, marveling anew at how Jean Champollion, the French archeologist, had miraculously deciphered its ancient demotic and hieroglyphic texts . . .

The thrill of that just kept hanging around in my head. I was on a jet returning to New York when a thought hit me. Those strange, unknown-tongue sounds, always part of our family's old story . . . they were obviously bits of our original African "*Kin-tay*'s" native tongue. What specific tongue? Could I somehow find out?

Back in New York, I began making visits to the United Nations Headquarters lobby; it wasn't hard to spot Africans. I'd stop any I could, asking if my bits of phonetic sounds held any meaning for them. A couple of dozen Africans quickly looked at me, listened, and took off—understandably dubious about some Tennesseean's accent alleging "African" sounds.

My research assistant, George Sims (we grew up together in Henning), brought me some names of ranking scholars of African linguistics. One was particularly intriguing: a Belgian- and English-educated Dr. Jan Vansina; he had spent his early career living in West African villages, studying and tape-recording countless oral histories that were narrated by certain very old African men; he had written a standard textbook, "The Oral Tradition."

So I flew to the University of Wisconsin to see Dr. Vansina. In his living room I told him every bit of the family story in the fullest detail that I could remember it. Then, intensely, he queried me about the story's relay across the generations, about the gibberish of *"k"* sounds Grandma had fiercely muttered to herself while doing her housework, with my brothers and me giggling beyond her hearing at what we had dubbed "Grandma's noises."

Dr. Vansina, his manner very serious, finally said, "These sounds your family has kept sound very probably of the tongue called 'Mandinka.' "

I'd never heard of any "Mandinka." Grandma just told of the African saying *"ko"* for banjo, or *"Kamby Bolong"* for a Virginia river.

Among Mandinka stringed instruments, Dr. Vansina said, one of the oldest was the *"kora."*

"Bolong," he said was clearly Mandinka for "river." Preceded by *"Kamby,"* it very likely meant "Gambia River."

Dr. Vansina telephoned an eminent Africanist colleague, Dr. Philip Curtin. He said that the phonetic *"Kin-tay"* was correctly spelled *"Kinte,"* a very old clan that had originated in Old Mali. The Kinte men traditionally were blacksmiths, and the women were potters and weavers.

I knew I must get to the Gambia River.

The first native Gambian I could locate in the U.S. was named Ebou Manga, then a junior attending Hamilton College in upstate Clinton, N.Y. He and I flew to Dakar, Senegal, then took a smaller plane to Yundum Airport, and rode a van to Gambia's capital, Bathurst. Ebou and his father assembled eight Gambia government officials. I told them Grandma's stories, every detail I could remember, as they listened intently, then reacted. " *'Kamby Bolong'* of course is Gambia River!" I heard. "But more clue is your forefather's saying his name was *'Kinte.'* " Then they told me something I would never even have fantasized—that in places in the back country lived very old men, commonly called *griots,* who could tell centuries of the histories of certain very old family clans. As for *Kintes,* they pointed out to me on a map some family villages, Kinte-Kundah, and Kinte-Kundah Janneh-Ya, for instance.

The Gambian officials said they would try to help me. I returned to New York dazed. It is embarrassing to me now, but despite Grandma's stories, I'd never been concerned much with Africa, and I had the routine images of African people living mostly in exotic jungles. But a compulsion now laid hold of me to learn all I could, and I began devouring books about Africa, especially about the slave trade. Then one Thursday's mail contained a letter from one of the Gambian officials, inviting me to return there.

Monday I was back in Bathurst. It galvanized me when the officials said that a *griot* had been located who told the *Kinte* clan history—his name was Kebba Kanga Fofane. To reach him, I discovered, required a modified safari: renting a launch to get upriver, two land vehicles to carry supplies by a roundabout land route, and employing finally 14 people, including three interpreters and four musicians, since a *griot* would not speak the revered clan histories without background music.

The boat Baddibu vibrated upriver, with me acutely tense: Were these Africans maybe viewing me as but another of the pith-helmets? After about two hours, we put in at James Island, for me to see the ruins of the once British-operated James Fort. Here two centuries of slave ships had loaded thousands of cargoes of Gambian tribespeople. The crumbling stones, the deeply oxidized swivel cannon, even some remnant links of chain seemed all but impossible to believe. Then we continued upriver to the left-bank village of Albreda, and there put ashore to continue on foot to Juffure, village of the *griot*. Once more we stopped, for me to see *toubob kolong*, "the white man's well," now almost filled in, in a swampy area with abundant, tall, saw-toothed grass. It was dug two centuries ago to "17 men's height deep" to insure survival drinking water for long-driven, famishing coffles of slaves.

Walking on, I kept wishing that Grandma could hear how her stories had led me to the *"Kamby Bolong."* (Our surviving story teller Cousin Georgia died in a Kansas City hospital during this same morning, I would learn later.) Finally, Juffure village's playing children, sighting us, flashed an alert. The 70-odd people came rushing from their circular, thatch-roofed, mud-walled huts, with goats bounding up and about, and parrots squawking from up in the palms. I sensed him in advance somehow, the small man amid them, wearing a pillbox cap and an off-white robe—the *griot*. Then the interpreters went to him, as the villagers thronged around me.

And it hit me like a gale wind: every one of them, the whole crowd, was *jet black*. An enormous sense of guilt swept me—a sense of being some kind of hybrid . . . a sense of being impure among the pure. It was an awful sensation.

The old *griot* stepped away from my interpreters and the crowd quickly swarmed around him—all of them buzzing. An interpreter named A. B. C. Salla came to me; he whispered: "Why they stare at you so, they have never seen here a black American." And that hit me: I was symbolizing for them twenty-five millions of us they had never seen. What did they think of me—of us?

Then abruptly the old *griot* was briskly walking toward me. His eyes boring into mine, he spoke in Mandinka, as if instinctively I should understand—and A. B. C. Salla translated:

"Yes . . . we have been told by the forefathers . . . that many of us from this place are in exile . . . in that place called America . . . and in other places."

I suppose I physically wavered, and they thought it was the heat; rustling whispers went through the crowd, and a man brought me a low stool. Now the whispering hushed—the musicians had softly begun playing *kora* and *balafon,* and a canvas sling lawn seat was taken by the *griot,* Kebba Kanga Fofane, aged 75 "rains" (one rainy season each year). He seemed to gather himself into a physical rigidity, and he began speaking the *Kinte* clan's ancestral oral history; it came rolling from his mouth across the next hours . . . 17th- and 18th-century *Kinte* lineage details, predominantly what men took wives; the children they "begot," in the order of their births; those children's mates and children.

Events frequently were dated by some proximate singular physical occurrence. It was as if some ancient scroll were printed indelibly within the *griot's* brain. Each few sentences or so, he would pause for an interpreter's translation to me. I distill here the essence:

The *Kinte* clan began in Old Mali, the men generally blacksmiths ". . . who conquered fire," and the women potters and weavers. One large branch of the clan moved to Mauretania from where one son of the clan, Kairaba Kunta Kinte, a Moslem Marabout holy man, entered Gambia. He lived first in the village of Pakali N'Ding; he moved next to Jiffarong village; ". . . and then he came here, into our own village of Juffure."

In Juffure, Kairaba Kunta Kinte took his first wife, ". . . a Mandinka maiden, whose name was Sireng. By her, he begot two sons, whose names were Janneh and Saloum. Then he got a second wife, Yaisa. By her, he begot a son, Omoro."

The three sons became men in Juffure. Janneh and Saloum went off and founded a new village, Kinte-Kundah Janneh-Ya. "And then Omoro, the youngest son, when he had 30 rains, took as a wife a maiden, Binta Kebba.

"And by her, he begot four sons—Kunta, Lamin, Suwadu, and Madi . . ."

Sometimes, a "begotten," after his naming, would be accompanied by some later-occurring detail, perhaps as ". . . in time of big water (flood), he slew a water buffalo." Having named those four sons, now the *griot* stated such a detail.

"About the time the king's soldiers came, the eldest of these four sons, Kunta, when he had about 16 rains, went away from this village, to chop wood to make a drum . . . and he was never seen again . . ."

Goose-pimples the size of lemons seemed to pop all over me. In my knapsack were my cumulative notebooks, the first of them including how in my boyhood, my Grandma, Cousin Georgia and the others told of the

African *"Kin-tay"* who always said he was kidnapped near his village—while chopping wood to make a drum . . .

I showed the interpreter, he showed and told the *griot,* who excitedly told the people; they grew very agitated. Abruptly then they formed a human ring, encircling me, dancing and chanting. Perhaps a dozen of the women carrying their infant babies rushed in toward me, thrusting the infants into my arms—conveying, I would later learn, "the laying on of hands . . . through this flesh which is us, we are you, and you are us." The men hurried me into their mosque, their Arabic praying later being translated outside: "Thanks be to Allah for returning the long lost from among us." Direct descendants of Kunta Kinte's blood brothers were hastened, some of them from nearby villages, for a family portrait to be taken with me, surrounded by actual ancestral sixth cousins. More symbolic acts filled the remaining day.

When they would let me leave, for some reason I wanted to go away over the African land. Dazed, silent in the bumping Land Rover, I heard the cutting staccato of talking drums. Then when we sighted the next village, its people came thronging to meet us. They were all—little naked ones to wizend elders—waving, beaming, amid a cacophony of crying out; and then my ears identified their words: *"Meester Kinte! Meester Kinte!"*

Let me tell you something: I am a man. But I remember the sob surging up from my feet, flinging up my hands before my face and bawling as I had not done since I was a baby . . . the jet-black Africans were jostling, staring . . . I didn't care, with the feelings surging. If you really knew the odyssey of us millions of black Americans, if you really knew how we came in the seeds of our forefathers, captured, driven, beaten, inspected, bought, branded, chained in foul ships, if you really knew, you needed weeping . . .

Back home, I knew that what I must write, really, was our black saga, where any individual's past is the essence of the millions'. Now flat broke, I went to some editors I knew, describing the Gambian miracle, and my desire to pursue the research; Doubleday contracted to publish, and Reader's Digest to condense the projected book; then I had advances to travel further.

What ship brought Kinte to Grandma's " 'Naplis" (Annapolis, Md., obviously)? The old *griot's* time reference to "king's soldiers" sent me flying to London. Feverish searching at last identified, in British Parliament records, "Colonel O'Hare's Forces," dispatched in mid-1767 to protect the then British-held James Fort whose ruins I'd visited. So Kunta Kinte was down in some ship probably sailing later that summer from the Gambia River to Annapolis.

Now I feel it was fated that I had taught myself to write in the U.S. Coast Guard. For the sea dramas I had concentrated on had given me years of experience searching among yellowing old U.S. maritime records. So now in English 18th Century marine records I finally tracked ships reporting themselves in and out to the Commandant of the Gambia River's James Fort. And then early one afternoon I found that a Lord Ligonier under a Captain Thomas Davies had sailed on the Sabbath of July 5, 1767. Her cargo: 3,265 elephants' teeth, 3,700 pounds of beeswax, 800 pounds of cotton, 32 ounces of Gambian gold, and 140 slaves; her destination: "Annapolis."

That night I recrossed the Atlantic. In the Library of Congress the Lord Ligonier's arrival was one brief line in "Shipping In The Port of Annapolis—1748–1775." I located the author, Vaughan W. Brown, in his Baltimore brokerage office. He drove to Historic Annapolis, the city's historical society, and found me further documentation of her arrival on Sept. 29, 1767. (Exactly two centuries later, Sept. 29, 1967, standing, staring seaward from an Annapolis pier, again I knew tears.) More help came in the Maryland Hall of Records. Archivist Phebe Jacobsen found the Lord Ligonier's arriving customs declaration listing, "98 Negroes"—so in her 86-day crossing, 42 Gambians had died, one among the survivors being 16-year-old Kunta Kinte. Then the microfilmed Oct. 1, 1767, Maryland Gazette contained, on page two, an announcement to prospective buyers from the ship's agents, Daniel of St. Thos. Jenifer and John Ridout (the Governor's secretary): "from the River GAMBIA, in AFRICA . . . a cargo of choice, healthy SLAVES . . ."

VOCABULARY

1. Define the following words as Haley uses them in his essay: demotic, hieroglyphic, phonetic, linguistics, griots, coffles, eminent, proximate, staccato, cacophony.
2. If you are unfamiliar with any other words in this essay, check them in a dictionary and then define them in your own words.

CONTENT

1. What stages does Haley go through in his search for his roots?
2. Haley moves backward and forward in time as he describes his forebears. Reorganize his information into a strict chronological outline starting with Kunta Kinte's forebears and concluding with Haley.

3. What does the African villagers' reaction to Haley's discoveries suggest about human nature in general?
4. Kennedy ("A Nation of Nations," page 20) and Bennett ("The New Indians and Old Indians," page 124) celebrate the contributions of particular groups to the American way of life. Following their ideas, identify important contributions blacks have made.

RHETORIC

1. Haley's story about his search for roots follows one sequence and his story about his family's history follows another. Describe each sequence. How do the two sequences differ?
2. Identify three metaphors* and idioms* in Haley's essay.
3. "I was symbolizing for them twenty-five millions of us they had never seen . . . I knew that what I must write, really, was our black saga, where any individual's past is the essence of the millions'." What do these comments indicate about the levels of meaning* Haley is trying to express in *Roots*?
4. Haley's is a factual narrative. How would the deeper levels of meaning* have been affected if he had used an imaginative narrative?

READING AND WRITING SUGGESTIONS

1. Read *The Autobiography of Miss Jane Pittman* by Ernest Gaines. How does Gaines' account of the pain and triumph which Jane Pittman experienced compare with what Haley's family experienced after arriving in this country?
2. Write a narrative essay describing as much as you can about your own family's roots.

---

*Definitions of all terms marked with an asterisk may be found in the Glossary.

THE DEATH OF THE MOTH

Virginia Woolf

Virginia Woolf (1882–1941), the distinguished British author, wrote her first novel, The Voyage Out, *in 1915. She continued to write until her suicide at her home in Sussex, England. Other works by Woolf include* Mrs. Dalloway, To the Lighthouse, Orlando, The Waves, *and* The Years, *the latter acclaimed by critics to be her masterpiece. "The Death of the Moth" is the title essay of a collection of Woolf's work published shortly after her death.*

Moths that fly by day are not properly to be called moths; they do not excite that pleasant sense of dark autumn nights and ivy-blossom which the commonest yellow underwing asleep in the shadow of the curtain never fails to rouse in us. They are hybrid creatures, neither gay like butterflies nor sombre like their own species. Nevertheless the present specimen, with his narrow hay-coloured wings, fringed with a tassel of the same colour, seemed to be content with life. It was a pleasant morning, mid-September, mild, benignant, yet with a keener breath than that of the summer months. The plough was already scoring the field opposite the window, and where the share had been, the earth was pressed flat and gleamed with moisture. Such vigour came rolling in from the fields and the down beyond that it was difficult to keep the eyes strictly turned upon the book. The rooks too were keeping one of their annual festivities; soaring round the tree-tops until it looked as if a vast net with thousands of black knots in it has been cast up into the air; which, after a few moments sank slowly down upon the trees until every twig seemed to have a knot at the end of it. Then, suddenly, the net would be thrown into the air again in a wider circle this time, with the utmost clamour and vociferation, as though to be thrown into the air and settle slowly down upon the tree-tops were a tremendously exciting experience.

The same energy which inspired the rooks, the ploughmen, the horses, and even, it seemed, the lean bare-backed downs, sent the moth fluttering from side to side of his square of the window-pane. One could not help watching him. One was, indeed, conscious of a queer feeling of pity for him. The possibilities of pleasure seemed that morning so enormous and so various that to have only a moth's part in life, and a day moth's at that, appeared a hard fate, and his zest in enjoying his meagre opportunities to the full, pathetic. He flew vigorously to one corner of his compartment, and, after waiting there a second, flew across to the other. What remained for him but to fly to a third corner and then to a fourth? That was all he could do, in spite of the size of the downs, the width of the sky, the far-off smoke of houses, and the romantic voice, now and then, of a steamer out at sea. What he could do he did. Watching him, it seemed as if a fiber, very thin but pure, of the enormous energy of the world had been thrust into his frail and diminutive body. As often as he crossed the pane, I could fancy that a thread of vital light became visible. He was little or nothing but life.

Yet, because he was so small, and so simple a form of the energy that was rolling in at the open window and driving its way through so many narrow and intricate corridors in my own brain and in those of other human beings, there was something marvelous as well as pathetic about him. It was as if someone had taken a tiny bead of pure life and decking it as lightly as possible with down and feathers, had set it dancing and zigzagging to show us the true nature of life. Thus displayed one could not get over the strangeness of it. One is apt to forget all about life, seeing it humped and bossed and garnished and cumbered so that it has to move with the greatest circumspection and dignity. Again, the thought of all that life might have been had he been born in any other shape caused one to view his simple activities with a kind of pity.

After a time, tired by his dancing apparently, he settled on the window ledge in the sun, and the queer spectacle being at an end, I forgot about him. Then, looking up, my eye was caught by him. He was trying to resume his dancing, but seemed either so stiff or so awkward that he could only flutter to the bottom of the window-pane; and when he tried to fly across it he failed. Being intent on other matters I watched these futile attempts for a time without thinking, unconsciously waiting for him to resume his flight, as one waits for a machine, that has stopped momentarily, to start again without considering the reason for its failure. After perhaps a seventh attempt he slipped from the wooden ledge and fell, fluttering his wings, on to his back on the window-sill. The helplessness of his attitude roused me. It flashed upon me that he was in difficulties; he could no longer raise himself; his legs struggled vainly. But, as I stretched out a pencil, meaning to help him to right himself, it came over me that the failure and awkwardness were the approach of death. I laid the pencil down again.

The legs agitated themselves once more. I looked as if for the enemy against which he struggled. I looked out of doors. What had happened there? Presumably it was midday, and work in the fields had stopped. Stillness and quiet had replaced the previous animation. The birds had taken themselves off to feed in the brooks. The horses stood still. Yet the power was there all the same, massed outside indifferent, impersonal, not attending to anything in particular. Somehow it was opposed to the little hay-coloured moth. It was useless to try to do anything. One could only watch the extraordinary efforts made by those tiny legs against an oncoming doom which could, had it chosen, have submerged an entire city, not merely a city, but masses of human beings; nothing, I knew, had any chance against death. Nevertheless after a pause of exhaustion the legs fluttered again. It was superb this last protest, and so frantic that he succeeded at last in righting himself. One's sympathies, of course, were all on the side of life. Also, when there was nobody to care or to know, this gigantic effort on the part of an insignificant little moth, against a power of such magnitude, to retain what no one else valued or desired to keep, moved one strangely. Again, somehow, one saw life, a pure bead. I lifted the pencil again, useless though I knew it to be. But even as I did so, the unmistakable tokens of death showed themselves. The body relaxed, and instantly grew stiff. The struggle was over. The insignificant little creature now knew death. As I looked at the dead moth, this minute wayside triumph of so great a force over so mean an antagonist filled me with wonder. Just as life had been strange a few minutes before, so death was now as strange. The moth having righted himself now lay most decently and uncomplainingly composed. O yes, he seemed to say, death is stronger than I am.

VOCABULARY

1. Define the following words as Woolf uses them in her essay: rook, benignant, clamour, vociferation, diminutive, circumspection.
2. If you are unfamiliar with any other words in this essay, check them in a dictionary and then define them in your own words.

CONTENT

1. According to Woolf, what is the true nature of life? of death?
2. Woolf portrays the moth against a background teeming with life.
    a. What impact does the moth's life and death have on that background?
    b. How much impact do you think Woolf feels that most people's living and dying have on the flow of life?
3. In Woolf's opinion, why is it so easy for us to fail to see the true nature of life?

4. In "The Stockholm Address" (page 170), Faulkner states, "I believe that man will not merely endure: he will prevail." Do you think that Woolf would have agreed? Why or why not?

5. Some of Woolf's contemporaries developed the motto "Living well is the best revenge." What do you think they meant? Do you think that Woolf agreed? Why or why not?

RHETORIC

1. For what does Woolf use the moth as a metaphor*? Why do you think she chose a moth's existence as the vehicle for making her point?

2. How does Woolf use personification* and metaphor* in describing the rooks' activities?

3. Is Woolf's narrative factual or impressionistic? What sequence does she use to describe the events that take place?

4. Woolf frequently makes use of contrasts. For example, in the first paragraph she portrays the moth as a poor thing who nevertheless is content with life; in the second paragraph she shows that he couldn't do much but "what he could do he did."

    a. Identify two more examples of Woolf's use of contrasts.

    b. What point do you think Woolf is trying to make by this use of contrasts?

READING AND WRITING SUGGESTIONS

1. In the third paragraph Woolf comments, "One is apt to forget all about life, seeing it humped and bossed and garnished and cumbered so that it has to move with the greatest circumspection and dignity." Write a narrative essay applying her idea to your own life.

2. Review "The Right to Die" by Norman Cousins (page 187) or Dylan Thomas's poem "Do Not Go Gently Into That Good Night." Write a brief narrative essay stating your opinion on how much we should struggle to save a doomed life.

---

*Definitions of all terms marked with an asterisk may be found in the Glossary.

A DISSERTATION UPON ROAST PIG

Charles Lamb

Charles Lamb (1775–1834), English essayist, critic, and poet, overcame many obstacles to pursue his career as a writer. After receiving only seven years of formal education, he became a clerk at the age of fifteen. He was confined to an insane asylum for a brief period when he was twenty-one, and, a few months after his release, his sister was committed for life to an insane asylum for the murder of their mother. Lamb obtained his sister's release by pledging to care for her, and from that time onward he spent much of his time tending to her needs. Working together, Lamb and his sister produced Tales from Shakespeare *and* Poetry for Children. *Despite Lamb's fear that his sister's psychotic episodes would recur, his writing is often cheerful and humorous. "A Dissertation upon Roast Pig," one of the most highly praised of Lamb's many fine essays, provides an excellent example of his use of humor and satire.*

Mankind, says a Chinese manuscript, which my friend M. was obliging enough to read and explain to me, for the first seventy thousand ages ate their meat raw, clawing or biting it from the living animal, just as they do in Abyssinia to this day. This period is not obscurely hinted at by their great Confucius in the second chapter of his "Mundane Mutations," where he designates a kind of golden age by the term Cho-fang, literally the Cooks' holiday. The manuscript goes on to say that the art of roasting, or rather broiling (which I take to be the elder brother) was accidentally discovered in the manner following. The swineherd, Ho-ti, having gone out into the woods one morning, as his manner was, to collect mast for his hogs, left his cottage in the care of his eldest son Bo-bo, a great lubberly boy, who being fond of playing with fire, as younkers of his age commonly are, let some sparks escape into a bundle of straw, which kindling quickly spread the conflagration over every part of their poor mansion, till it was reduced to ashes. Together with the cottage (a sorry antediluvian makeshift of a building, you may think it), what was of much more importance, a fine litter of new-farrowed pigs, no less than nine in number, perished. China pigs have been esteemed a luxury all over the East from the remotest periods that we read of. Bo-bo was in the utmost consternation, as you may think, not so much for the sake of the tenement, which his father and he could easily build up again with a few dry branches, and the labor of an hour or two, at any time, as for the loss of the pigs. While he was thinking what he should say to his father, and wringing his hands over the smoking remnants of one of those untimely sufferers, an odor assailed his nostrils, unlike any scent which he had before experienced. What could it proceed from?—not from the burnt cottage—he had smelt that smell before—indeed this was by no means the first accident of the kind which had occurred through the negligence of this unlucky young firebrand. Much less did it resemble that of any known herb, weed, or flower. A premonitory moistening at the same time overflowed his nether lip. He knew not what to think. He next stooped down to feel the pig, if there were any signs of life in it. He burnt his fingers, and to cool them he applied them in his booby fashion to his mouth. Some of the crumbs of the scorched skin had come away with his fingers, and for the first time in his life (in the world's life indeed, for before him no man had known it) he tasted—crackling! Again he felt and fumbled at the pig. It did not burn him so much now, still he licked his fingers from a sort of habit. The truth at length broke into his slow undersanding that it was the pig that smelt so, and the pig that tasted so delicious; and, surrendering himself up to the newborn pleasure, he fell to tearing up whole handfuls of the scorched skin with the flesh next it, and was cramming it down his throat in his beastly fashion, when his sire entered amid the smoking rafters, armed with a retributory cudgel, and, finding how affairs stood, began to rain blows upon the young rogue's shoulders as thick as hailstones, which Bo-bo heeded not any more than if they had been flies. The tickling pleasure which he experienced in his lower regions had rendered him quite callous to any inconveniences he might feel in those remote quarters. His father might lay on, but he could not beat him from his pig till he had fairly made an end of it, when, becoming a little more sensible of his situation, something like the following dialogue ensued:—

"You graceless whelp, what have you got there devouring? Is it not enough that you have burnt me down three houses with your dog's tricks, and be hanged to you, but you must be eating fire, and I know not what—what have you got there, I say?"

"Oh, father, the pig, the pig, do come and taste how nice the burnt pig eats!"

The ears of Ho-ti tingled with horror. He cursed his son, and he cursed himself that ever he should beget a son that should eat burnt pig.

Bo-bo, whose scent was wonderfully sharpened since morning, soon raked out another pig, and fairly rending it asunder, thrust the lesser half by main force into the fists of Ho-ti, still shouting out, "Eat, eat, eat the burnt pig, father, only taste—O Lord!"—with such like barbarous ejaculations, cramming all the while as if he would choke.

Ho-ti trembled in every joint while he grasped the abominable thing, wavering whether he should not put his son to death for an unnatural young monster, when the crackling scorching his fingers, as it had done his son's, and applying the same remedy to them, he, in his turn, tasted some of its flavor, which, make what sour mouths he would for a pretense, proved not altogether displeasing to him. In conclusion (for the manuscript here is a little tedious) both father and son fairly sat down to the mess, and never left off till they had despatched all that remained of the litter.

Bo-bo was strictly enjoined not to let the secret escape, for the neighbors would certainly have stoned them for a couple of abominable wretches, who could think of improving upon the good meat which God had sent them. Nevertheless, strange stories got about. It was observed that Ho-ti's cottage was burnt down now more frequently than ever. Nothing but fires from this time forward. Some would break out in broad day, others in the nighttime. As often as the sow farrowed, so sure was the house of Ho-ti to be in a blaze; and Ho-ti himself, which was the more remarkable, instead of chastising his son, seemed to grow more indulgent to him than ever. At length they were watched, the terrible mystery discovered, and father and son summoned to take their trial at Pekin, then an inconsiderable assize town. Evidence was given, the obnoxious food itself produced in court, and verdict about to be pronounced, when the foreman of the jury begged that some of the burnt pig, of which the culprits stood accused, might be handed into the box. He handled it, and they all handled it, and burning their fingers as Bo-bo and his father had done before them, and nature prompting to each of them the same remedy, against the face of all the facts, and the clearest charge which judge had ever given—to the surprise of the whole court, townsfolk, strangers, reporters, and all present—without leaving the box, or any manner of consultation whatever, they brought in a simultaneous verdict of Not Guilty.

The judge, who was a shrewd fellow, winked at the manifest iniquity of the decision; and, when the court was dismissed, went privily, and bought up all the pigs that could be had for love or money. In a few days his lordship's town house was observed to be on fire. The thing took wing, and now there was nothing to be seen but fires in every direction. Fuel and pigs grew enormously dear all over the district. The insurance offices one and all shut up shop. People built slighter and slighter every day, until it was feared that the very science of architecture would in no long time be lost to the world. Thus this custom of firing houses continued, till in process of time, says my manuscript, a sage arose, like our Locke, who made a discovery that the flesh of swine, or, indeed, of any other animal, might be cooked (burnt as they called it) without the necessity of consuming a whole house to dress it. Then first began the rude form of a gridiron. Roasting by the string, or spit, came in a century or two later, I forget in whose dynasty. By such slow degrees, concludes the manuscript, do the most useful, and seemingly the most obvious arts, make their way among mankind.

Without placing too implicit faith in the account above given, it must be agreed that if a worthy pretext for so dangerous an experiment as setting houses on fire (especially in these days) could be assigned in favor of any culinary object, that pretext and excuse might be found in roast pig.

Of all the delicacies in the whole *mundus edibilis,*[1] I will maintain it to be the most delicate—*princeps obsoniorum.*[2]

I speak not of your grown porkers—things between pig and pork—those hobbydehoys—but a young and tender suckling—under a moon old—guiltless as yet of the sty—with no original speck of the *amor immunditiae,*[3] the hereditary failing of the first parent, yet manifest—his voice as yet not broken, but something between a childish treble and a grumble—the mild forerunner, or *praeludium,*[4] of a grunt.

He must be roasted. I am not ignorant that our ancestors ate them seethed, or boiled—but what a sacrifice of the exterior tegument!

There is no flavor comparable, I will contend, to that of the crisp, tawny, well-watched, not over-roasted crackling, as it is well called—the very teeth are invited to their share of the pleasure at this banquet in overcoming the coy, brittle resistance—with the adhesive oleaginous—oh, call it not fat—but an indefinable sweetness growing up to it—the tender blossoming of fat—fat cropped in the bud—taken in the shoot—in the first innocence—the cream and quintessence of child-pig's yet pure food—the lean, no lean, but a kind of animal manna—or, rather, fat and lean (if it must be so) so blended and running into each other that both together make but one ambrosian result, or common substance.

Behold him, while he is doing—it seemeth rather a refreshing warmth than a scorching heat that he is so passive to. How equably he twirleth round the string!—Now he is just done. To see the extreme sensibility of that tender age, he hath wept out his pretty eyes—radiant jellies—shooting stars!

See him in the dish, his second cradle, how meek he lieth!—wouldst thou have had this innocent grow up to the grossness and indocility which too often accompany maturer swinehood? Ten to one he would have proved

1. World of eating.
2. Prince of delight.
3. Love of filth.
4. Prelude.

a glutton, a sloven, an obstinate, disagreeable animal—wallowing in all manner of filthy conversation! From these sins he is happily snatched away—

> Ere sin could blight, or sorrow fade,
> Death came with timely care—

his memory is odoriferous—no clown curseth, while his stomach half rejecteth, the rank bacon—no coal heaver bolteth him in reeking sausages—he hath a fair sepulchre in the grateful stomach of the judicious epicure—and for such a tomb might be content to die.

He is the best of sapors. Pineapple is great. She is, indeed, almost too transcendent—a delight, if not sinful, yet so like to sinning, that really a tender-conscienced person would do well to pause—too ravishing for mortal taste, she woundeth and excoriateth the lips that approach her—like lovers' kisses, she biteth—she is a pleasure bordering on pain from the fierceness and insanity of her relish—but she stoppeth at the palate—she meddleth not with the appetite—and the coarsest hunger might barter her consistently for a mutton chop.

Pig—let me speak his praise—is no less provocative of the appetite than he is satisfactory to the criticalness of the censorious palate. The strong man may batten on him, and the weakling refuseth not his mild juices.

Unlike to mankind's mixed characters, a bundle of virtues and vices, inexplicably intertwisted, and not to be unraveled without hazard, he is—good throughout. No part of him is better or worse than another. He helpeth, as far as his little means extend, all around. He is the least envious of banquets. He is all neighbors' fare.

I am one of those who freely and ungrudgingly impart a share of the good things of this life which fall to their lot (few as mine are in this kind) to a friend. I protest I take as great an interest in my friend's pleasures, his relishes, and proper satisfactions, as in mine own. "Presents," I often say, "endear Absents." Hares, pheasants, partridges, snipes, barn-door chickens (those "tame villatic fowl"), capons, plovers, brawn, barrels of oysters, I dispense as freely as I receive them. I love to taste them, as it were, upon the tongue of my friend. But a stop must be put somewhere. One would not, like Lear, "give everything." I make my stand upon pig. Methinks it is an ingratitude to the Giver of all good flavors, to extra-domiciliate, or send out of the house, slightingly (under pretext of friendship, or I know not what), a blessing so particularly adapted, predestined, I may say, to my individual palate. It argues an insensibility.

I remember a touch of conscience in this kind at school. My good old aunt, who never parted from me at the end of a holiday without stuffing a sweetmeat, or some nice thing into my pocket, had dismissed me one evening with a smoking plum cake, fresh from the oven. On my way to school (it was over London Bridge) a gray-headed old beggar saluted me (I have no doubt at this time of day that he was a counterfeit). I had no pence to console him with, and in the vanity of self-denial, and the very coxcombry of charity, schoolboy-like, I made him a present of—the whole cake! I walked on a little, buoyed up, as one is on such occasions, with a sweet soothing of self-satisfaction; but before I had got to the end of the bridge my better feelings returned and I burst into tears, thinking how ungrateful I had been to my good aunt, to go and give her good gift away to a stranger that I had never seen before, and who might be a bad man for aught I knew; and then I thought of the pleasure my aunt would be taking in thinking that I—I myself, and not another—would eat her nice cake—and what should I say to her the next time I saw her—now naughty I was to part with her pretty present—and the odor of that spicy cake came back upon my recollection, and the pleasure and the curiosity I had taken in seeing her make it, and her joy when she sent it to the oven, and how disappointed she would feel that I had never had a bit of it in my mouth at last—and I blamed my impertinent spirit of almsgiving, and out-of-place hypocrisy of goodness, and, above all, I wished never to see the face again of that insidious, good-for-nothing, old gray imposter.

Our ancestors were nice in their method of sacrificing the tender victims. We read of pigs whipped to death with something of a shock, as we hear of any other obsolete custom. The age of discipline is gone by, or it would be curious to inquire (in a philosophical light merely) what effect this process might have towards intenerating and dulcifying a substance, naturally so mild and dulcet as the flesh of young pigs. It looks like refining a violet. Yet we should be cautious, while we condemn the inhumanity, how we censure the wisdom of the practice. It might impart a gusto.

I remember an hypothesis, argued upon by the young students, when I was at St. Omer's, and maintained with much learning and pleasantry on both sides, "Whether supposing that the flavor of a pig who obtained his death by whipping *(per flagellationem extremam)*[5] superadded a pleasure upon the palate of a man more intense than any possible suffering we can conceive in the animal, is man justified in using that method of putting the animal to death?" I forget the decision.

His sauce should be considered. Decidedly, a few bread crumbs, done up with his liver and brains, and a dash of mild sage. But, banish, dear Mrs. Cook, I beseech you, the whole onion tribe. Barbecue your whole hogs to your palate, steep them in shallots, stuff them out with plantations of the rank and guilty garlic; you cannot poison them, or make them stronger than they are—but consider, he is a weakling—a flower.

5. Through extreme whipping.

VOCABULARY

1. Define the following words as Lamb uses them in his essay: mast, antediluvian, farrowed, premonitory, nether, retributory, assize, tegument, quintessence, odoriferous, sepulchre, epicure, sapors, excoriate, censorious, batten, villatic, coxcombry, insidious, intenerating, dulcify.
2. If you are unfamiliar with any other words in this essay, check them in a dictionary and then define them in your own words.

CONTENT

1. "Unlike to mankind's mixed characters, a bundle of virtues and vices, inexplicably intertwisted, and not to be unraveled without hazard [the pig] is—good throughout." Look beyond the humor in this sentence and explain what it suggests about Lamb's attitude toward people. Find other places in the essay where Lamb shows the same attitude either openly or implicitly.
2. Discuss the idea of serendipity in the context of Ho-ti's and Bo-bo's discoveries.
3. Review Swift's "A Modest Proposal" (page 178). What similarities do you observe in Swift and Lamb's themes and their treatment of these themes?
4. McGhee, in "The Lost Art of Conversation" (page 15), outlines the qualities of a good conversationalist. Do you think Lamb would qualify? Support your answer with examples.

RHETORIC

1. Compare the introduction* to the essay with its conclusion* and decide whether this beginning and ending would lead you to predict that the essay would be well organized.
2. How does Lamb's anecdote* about the aunt, the gray-headed beggar, and the plum cake relate to his thesis*? Could he have omitted the anecdote without weakening the essay?
3. What are the characteristics of Lamb's style* and diction*? Do these characteristics make him easy or difficult to understand?
4. Examine the passages you found most amusing and describe how Lamb makes them humorous.

---

*Definitions of all terms marked with an asterisk may be found in the Glossary.

READING AND WRITING SUGGESTIONS

1. Using Lamb's tongue-in-cheek style, write a narrative essay describing your feelings about a favorite food.

2. Read an encyclopedia article about Charles Goodyear's accidental discovery of the vulcanization process after long years of fruitless experimentation. Write a narrative essay on the workings of chance, focusing on this incident in Goodyear's life.

PART FIVE

ESSAYS FOR INDEPENDENT ANALYSIS

SIMPLE TRUTHS

William J. Bennett

William J. Bennett (1943–) is director of the National Humanities Center, Research Triangle Park, North Carolina. He received his B.A. from Williams College, his Ph.D. from the University of Texas, and a law degree from Harvard. Dr. Bennett is co-author of Counting by Race, *a book about the Baake case. He has also written articles for* The Wall Street Journal, Commentary, *and* Encounter. *This essay appeared in the January 7, 1980 issue of* Newsweek.

Earlier in this century, Justice Oliver Wendell Holmes wrote: "At this time we need education in the obvious more than investigation of the obscure." Holmes was right, and what he said is still true. For some reason, Americans seem more and more fascinated by the obscure. Many of us want to be captivated by the difficult and bizarre. Some intellectuals make their living by creating obscurities for the rest of us to puzzle over. A friend of mine who is a humanities professor says that in many university courses perfectly sober students pay a lot of money to trade horse sense for moonshine.

Now, I do not wish to disparage the joy of working one's mind on complex matters. These are pleasures for the intellect, and discoveries and insights are gained by wrestling with tough problems. It is the tendency or wish to make *everything* difficult that bothers me. It bothers me because it makes a casualty of simple truths. Simple truths are simply and utterly true no matter how many mental somersaults one turns to deny them and cast them as problems. I want to preserve simple truths because they are valuable. They can be held on to through thick and thin; simple truths are handles for the mind to grasp in a world in which everything is called confusing and many things are.

Simple truths should be granted, not to discourage people from thinking, but to encourage them to start thinking about the many things that are truly difficult. All plans—public policies, choices of career—need foundations, and somewhere in the foundations there are simple truths. Once they are discovered, one can move on. But to ponder and debate forever, questioning and doubting simple truths, is not a sign of sophistication or profundity. Sometimes doubt is in fact only a delaying tactic, an avoidance of the responsibility that comes with recognizing that some things are simply true.

It has become fashionable to say that everything is more difficult than it appears, but some things are simpler than they appear. So I submit a short list of simple truths which, interestingly enough, many people nowadays don't believe:

1. America is a great country. By comparison with its own past, or the past and present of any country, there is simply no doubt about this. Look at personal freedom, wealth, efforts to help the poor, efforts to help other countries, educational institutions, religious and artistic vitality and health. As one person has put it, in the story of misery and inhumanity that is history, the American achievement is striking. Is improvement needed? Yes. Does this dislodge the simple truth? No.

2. Travel is not the way to "find yourself." Rangoon, Tahiti, the Australian outback, Rome, Paris and the Canary Islands offer many satisfactions, but finding the meaning of one's life is not one of them. With the exception of Saint Paul and a few others, mankind cannot count on being lucky enough to get the decisive word on itself while touring. What's queer about this simple truth is that despite the general acknowledgment of it, people continue to pack up and go in search of what most often can be found most readily at home, usually by facing up to one's shortcomings, possibilities and responsibilities. The harder one looks for The Answer in faraway places, the more elusive and distant it becomes. Wherever and whatever The Answer is (if it is anywhere at all), it tends not to be found on cruises.

3. Sex changes things between people. Despite Playboy and other advocates of unencumbered sexuality, sex is more than, and more complicated than, what it is sometimes taken to be: merely a "natural" thing to do, a desire to be indulged whenever one wishes and an act of the same order and consequence as having dinner, sending flowers or going for a walk. This idea, far from a simple truth, is a simple-minded error. It is an error because sexual intimacy, with rare exceptions, is not a matter of the juxtaposition of bodies. It involves people as persons and persons are complex: they have needs, histories and souls. Sex may or may not make a relationship better, but it certainly makes it different.

4. Civilization's values are learned. Children are not born with an instinct for democracy or citizenship. Civility, probity, a disinterested concern for the well-being of others are not part of the natural order. Efforts must be made by each generation of adults, for each generation of children, to bring them to an understanding of a spiritual inheritance that is their birthright but that doesn't come with birth. Free, responsible, thoughtful people do not emerge naturally or by accident. Rather, such people are the result of the intentions and efforts of parents, teachers, communities and society at large. This requires that at all times we consciously nurture and support those institutions, practices and traditions that move civilization along and provide new participants in it.

5. The best enjoyment follows work. Relaxation, vacation, leisure beckon to us constantly from television, magazines, and the neighbors' slide shows. But as anyone who has tried it knows, unabated leisure and "relaxation" soon become boring. There are few pleasures as satisfying as the joy of good work, and the best relaxation is rooted in the knowledge that a job has been well done.

6. Sincerity is not the test of truth. How deeply one believes something is not a test of its truth. If something is dubious, believing it "harder" doesn't make it any truer. Sincerity, like conscience, is a reliable guide to action or belief only when it is conjoined with intelligence. No fact was ever altered by believing it wasn't one, no matter how sincerely.

7. No one who is 16 has ever been 40, but everyone who is 40 was once 16. This truth escapes the notice of almost all adolescents and many parents. Although the world has changed in 2,400 years, the perspective of a 16-year-old today is still a lot more like the perspective of a 16-year-old in Plato and Aristotle's time than it is like the perspective of a 40-year-old today. In all periods of human history, there are certain things most people learn from experience. Some of this lore can be passed on to the young. But this can occur only if the 40-year-olds will consider their experience and speak of it, and if the 16-year-olds will listen. The 16-year-olds will not listen unless efforts are made to get their attention.

Casting everything in doubt is at once a luxury and a danger. When simple truths are put in doubt, we should not be surprised to find ourselves mired in endless and fruitless debate. To say that some truths are simple is not to say they are unimportant. One of the most important lessons we can learn is that we deny simple truths at some peril to ourselves and to what we hold dear.

SURRENDER AS THE NOBLE COURSE

Andrew M. Greeley

Andrew M. Greeley (1928–) a Roman Catholic priest, is a sociologist, educator, and writer. He is currently director of the Center for the Study of American Pluralism in Chicago, lecturer in sociology at the University of Chicago, and professor of higher education at the University of Illinois in Chicago. Greeley is the author of more than twenty books, many of them commentaries on current American life. One of his special concerns is young people. His book Strangers in the House: Catholic Youth in America *is a collection of essays in which he examines factors in the American culture which lead to apathy among youth.* And the Young Shall See Visions *and* Letters to Nancy *deal with problems of religious belief, love and marriage, and other questions common to young people. In the essay that follows, Greeley discusses the vulnerability that is an inevitable part of close relationships.*

The trouble with intimacy is that it means vulnerability. Everyone wants intimacy but few of us are very good at vulnerability. We pay lip service to "openness" and "trust," but usually these are mask words which we use to hide ourselves and to keep others at bay. Get too close to me and I'll beat you over the head with my openness and trust.

With the vocabulary provided by Freud and his followers, and the time provided by increased leisure and life expectancy, our generation is the first in history to set out self-consciously and in massive numbers to search for the joys of intimacy. But there is no evidence that we have much progressed over our predecessors in our skills at vulnerability. We attempt to make bricks, despite the biblical lesson on the subject, without straw.

How much authentic vulnerability—as opposed to the synthetic kind acquired on encounter weekends—have you observed on the expressway to intimacy?

The vulnerable person is strong enough to risk getting hurt—not pointlessly, not irrationally, not as an inverted defense mechanism; but as a part of a reasonable if not altogether rational risk. He can give himself to another human being not like a dive bomber crashing into an aircraft carrier or like a Mack truck crumpling a Volkswagen, but rather in a gentle and subtle process by which the other is invited, indeed seduced, to give himself in return.

How many such people do you know?

The vulnerable person takes a chance on having his heart broken. He strips himself of his defenses (not completely, not suddenly, not traumatically, but slowly, like an accomplished burlesque dancer) in the hope that when the other sees him as he is, the other will find him irresistible. In such a defenseless position, he can very easily be hurt, badly hurt.

Furthermore, he *will* be hurt. The lesson of all our experience is that the vulnerable person does indeed have his heart broken, he is indeed ridiculed, rejected, made a fool of. Sometimes the pain of such a heartbreak is healed as reconciliation restores the violated intimacy. But only the most naive believe that all stories have happy endings (though only the most cynical believe that none do). Some broken hearts remain broken.

Yet the deadly paradox of intimacy is that either we strip away our defenses in a continuing process or we will build them up in a similar process. We either let the other get closer to us and thus get closer to him or we push each other away. There is no middle ground. When push comes to shove, most of us push instead of surrendering.

In our pseudosophistication we try to persuade ourselves that we are no longer troubled by the shame of physical nudity. It is an act that normally does not work. But physical nakedness is a symbol—indeed a "sacrament" (in the old sense of a revealing insight)—of psychological nakedness. We are "shamed" when we take off our clothes because we have nothing left under which to hide, nothing to protect our weaknesses and deficiencies, we are defenseless, easily hurt. Psychic nakedness is much more terrifying—and hence much less frequently attempted. For if the other can see us as we are, then we are open to being destroyed by him.

So we hedge our bets and protect our own apparent worthlessness. The cynical "Why take the chance?"—rarely spoken but more rarely ignored—dominates our emotional life. We cover our fear with a barrage of words claiming that we are not afraid. It is all the other people who claim to be "open and trusting" who are kidding themselves.

The theologians used to call this fear of the other "original sin." The name may be out of fashion, but the reality is not. Blessed be he who does not take chances for he will not be hurt. Woe to him who risks giving his whole self, for he surely will be hurt.

But then it may be worth it. And the name of that thought, according to the old theologians, was Grace.

ON THE MEANING OF WORK

Robert Coles

Robert Coles (1918–) was born in Kansas City, Missouri. He received his B.A. and M.A. from the University of Illinois and his Ph.D. from the University of North Carolina. His work in marketing research at the Westinghouse Electric Corporation and as an industrial economist with the Federal Reserve Bank has led to his writing a number of booklets and articles on merchandising, advertising, and management. In this essay, Coles presents some characteristics we need to consider when we define work.

In early December of 1934 a serious and scholarly young French lady, about to turn twenty-six, took a job in a factory at the outskirts of Paris. Day after day she operated a drill, used a power press, and turned a crank handle. From doing so Simone Weil became tired and sad, but she persisted—and all the while kept a "factory journal." In time she moved to another factory, there to pack cartons under distinctly unfavorable circumstances. She felt cramped, pushed, and in general badly used, even as her co-workers did; eventually she was fired. Still undaunted, she found employment in the well-known Renault works, the pride of industrial France. She lived in a world of machines and shop stewards and intense heat and long working days. She saw men and women hurt and insulted, men and women grow weak and bitter and weary. She also saw men and women struggle hard to find what joy and humor they could amid these long stretches of dangerous and exhausting work. Enraged, at a loss to know what she thought and believed to be true, she kept at her job. She also kept asking her co-workers to share their thoughts with her.

Simone Weil was a moral philosopher, a theologian, some would say. She had no interest in studying factory life sociologically or analyzing the psychological "adjustment" of workers to their jobs. Nor was she trying to see how "the other half" lives for one or another reason. She had in mind no shocking news stories as she worked week after week, month after month. She was not out to prove that the modern worker is "exploited" or on the verge of joining some "revolution"—or alternatively, happy beyond anyone's comprehension but his own. Though her mind was capable of constructing its fair share of abstractions, she sensed the danger of doing so. An intellectual, she profoundly distrusted, even scorned, the dozens and dozens of writers and scholars and theorists who wrote with assurance about the workingman and his lot. Instead she wanted to place herself in the very midst of what interested her, there to learn from concrete experience—and only later would she stop and ask herself what she *believed*, what she had to *say*, about subjects like "the effect of work on the worker," subjects that she well knew a mind like hers was tempted to seize and probe and dissect without the slightest exposure to a Renault factory building, let alone those who work inside it.

Eventually she would carry her experiences to the countryside; she learned to pick crops, plow the land, tend animals, and in general live the life of a peasant—to the point that she unnerved her hosts. She was no snob, no condescending "observer" bent on picking up a few facts, establishing a reputation of sorts, then hurrying off so as to cash in on the time spent "out there." The people with whom she stayed (at Bourges, about 100 miles due south of Paris) later remarked upon their guest's ability to cut through the barriers that naturally went to separate her from them—"and put herself at our level."

In fact Simone Weil wanted to do more than "understand" others, or make them feel that she was stooping ever so gracefully. She saw factory workers and field hands as her brothers and sisters, out of a deep and certainly religious need to do so, a longing she described (for herself and for the rest of us) in *The Need for Roots,* written toward the end of her short yet intense life. (She died in 1943 at the age of thirty-three.) In the book she emphasizes that we need desperately—indeed die spiritually if we do not have—a community, one whose life, whose values and customs and traditions, whose *sanction,* a person doesn't so much think about as take for granted. If that is not very original and surprising, Miss Weil's notion of what a "community" is, or ought to be, goes much further; she sees us as always wanting to be in touch with others, not only our immediate families or more distant kin or our neighbors but those we work with, with whom we spend well over half our waking hours. For her, economists and political scientists (not to mention politicians), as well as psychologists and sociologists, all too often fail to grasp the true rhythms in life. True, they point out how much money we have or don't have, how much power one or another "class" has; or else they emphasize the lusts and rages we feel and try to express or subdue. Meanwhile, all over the world millions and millions of men and women (yes, and children) mark their lives by working, resting from work as best they can, and going back to work—until they die. And for Simone Weil it is with such day-to-day experiences that one who wants to comprehend man's nature and society's purposes ought to start.

Though she got on well with her fellow workers in several factories and on a farm, and though she held off at all times from extending cheap pity to those men and women, or condescension masked as moral outrage, or contempt dressed up as radical theory, she had to set down what she saw and heard. That is to say, she had to list the various kinds of suffering she saw among France's workers:

> We must change the system concerning concentration of attention during working hours, the types of stimulants which make for the overcoming of laziness or exhaustion—and which at present are merely fear and extra pay—the type of obedience necessary, the far too small amount of initiative, skill and thought demanded of workmen, their present exclusion from any imaginative share in the work of the enterprise as a whole, their sometimes total ignorance of the value, social utility, and destination of the things they manufacture, and the complete divorce between working life and family life. The list could well be extended.

She went on to do so; she extended her list and spelled out how life goes for millions of workmen in what she called "our industrial prisons"—where (she well knew) men are glad to be, rather than go hungry or be idle. But she was not primarily a social critic; perhaps more than anything else she was a visionary, hence easily written off as impractical—but uncannily able to say things starkly and prophetically and with apparent naiveté, which more cautious and "realistic" men only in time would come to see as indeed significant. So she noted how frightened and sullen her co-workers became, how drained they felt by the end of the day, how tempted they were to make minor mistakes, slow down, even at times cause considerable damage to the plant in which they worked or to the products they were turning out. Why is it so, she asked—why must men (in both America and Russia—that is, under capitalism and Communism alike) work in such huge, cold, impersonal places, and feel so fortunate (such is their vulnerability, their fear, their insecurity) for having even that kind of opportunity? The answer, no doubt, is that efficiency demands it; in a modern industrial nation mass production has to take place in large factories. Yet, in the France of the 1930s, Miss Weil saw what we in America are now beginning to notice and worry about: the dangers which a cult of efficiency and productivity, unqualified by ethical if not spiritual considerations, can present us with. She saw how much her worker friends needed one another, how hard they tried to enjoy one another's company, notwithstanding all the factory rules and regulations. She saw how tempted they were to stay off the job, to feign illness or offer some other excuse that enabled them to take at least this day off. She saw how greedy and thoughtless an industrial empire can become: land, water, air, raw materials, the lives of people—everything is grist for those modern mills of ours, which in turn are defended as necessary for our "advanced civilization," while all the while we cough and hold our noses and our ears and see about us an increasingly bleak and contaminated land, and feel upset as well, at a loss, and more than a little angry. The words and phrases are familiar, indeed have become clichés: absenteeism, ecological disaster, alienation, dehumanization, the loss of a sense of community.

Simone Weil sensed in her intuitive way that something was wrong, that a new order of attention must be given to the ordinary working man—whether he wears a blue collar or a white one—to his need for fellowship and dignity as well as money, to his struggle for meaning as well as possessions.

Working people with whom I have talked make quite clear the ways they feel cornered, trapped, lonely, pushed around at work, and, as Simone Weil kept on emphasizing, confused by a sense of meaninglessness. These feelings, I have noticed, often take the form of questions—and I will take the liberty of paraphrasing some of them that I have heard: What am I doing that *really matters*? What is the point to it all—not life, as some philosophers say, but the specific, tangible things I do or make? What would I do if I had a real choice—something which I doubt I ever will have? Is there some other, some better way to work? Might we not break up these large factories and offices, work closer to our homes, closer to one another as workers—and work together on something that is not a fragment of this, a minor part of that, but is whole and significant and recognizable as important in our lives?

If those were "romantic" inquiries for a much-troubled and fussy and brilliant French religious philosopher and political essayist in the 1930s, they may not be altogether impractical for us today. The workers I have heard may not speak as Simone Weil did; but like her they are able to be obsessed by the riddles and frustrations that life presents—and like her, they can spot trouble when it is in front of them, literally in the air, the dangerously contaminated air. As never before, our industrial societies are now being forced to look inward, so to speak, to become aware of the implications of our policies, among them those followed by the thousands of businesses which employ millions of workers. No doubt in the 1930s a skeptic could easily have made light of Simone Weil's concern that the French landscape outside various giant factories was in several ways being defaced. No doubt today what she (and over the decades many, many workers) wanted done inside those factories can still seem impractical. But that word "impractical" is one that history has taught us to think twice about. One generation's impracticality has a way of becoming another's urgent necessity.

ON BEING A POSSIBILIST

Max Lerner

Max Lerner (1902–), journalist and scholar, was born in White Russia and brought to the United States at the age of five. He completed his B.A. at Yale, his M.A. at Washington University, and his Ph.D. at the Brookings Graduate School of Economics and Government. Lerner began his career as assistant editor of the Encyclopedia of Social Sciences, *of which he later became managing editor. He has been a member of the faculty or a visiting lecturer at a number of colleges and universities, including Sarah Lawrence, Harvard, Brandeis, and the United States International University. Among Lerner's major works are* Actions and Passions: Notes on the Multiple Revolution of Our Time, The Age of Overkill: A Preface to World Politics, *and* America and Its Discontents. *His newspaper column is syndicated throughout the United States and many foreign countries.*

In a time such as ours, when man acts like a wolf to man, it may seem more than a little absurd to question the prevailing gloom. Yet I want to break a lance in defense of the possible.

In my teaching, lecturing and column writing, I get a question thrust at me constantly: "Are you an optimist or a pessimist?" At times I get impatient. Do they think this is Wall Street, where you are bullish or bearish about stocks you can't control? Our destiny as a people rests not in our stars but in ourselves. I am neither optimist nor pessimist. I am a possibilist.

To believe either that everything is bound to work out or that nothing will ever work out is equally an exercise in mindlessness. There are no blank-check guarantees that we will survive and prosper, and no inevitability that we won't. I believe in the possible. More options are open for us than we dare admit. Everything depends on our collective intelligence in making choices, and our will to carry them out.

The prevailing view is that all our options have narrowed. I don't believe it. There is a sense of being trapped—the feeling that nothing we do makes much difference. Which leads to frantic group pressures and single-issue politics, or to the cynical rejection of all forms of public life and to a wallowing in our egos.

Let's face it. We used up our resources, polluted our environment and laid staggering burdens on our government. Which means we must now place limits on our desires, needs, greeds. The historians call it the Age of Limits.

Civil-Rights Movement

But it is equally an Age of Breakthroughs which compensate for the narrowed options. It is hard to see this because the limits are concrete and urgent while the breakthroughs are less visible.

But they are nonetheless real. I ask the black students in my seminars: would you rather have come of age in the years before the civil-rights movement—or now? I ask the women of every age: would you rather be living in the days of male power and swagger, with slim options for jobs and careers and meager life chances—or now?

I ask the professionals—the athletes, film and TV performers, photographers, playwrights, musicians, architects, writers, artists of every kind: would you rather have plied your craft before the large audiences were opened up to you—or now?

I ask the young scientists, the doctors and researchers, teachers, law and medical students, staff workers, young business executives: would you rather have lived and worked before the great breakthroughs of the knowledge revolution—or now?

I ask the code breakers who deviate from the narrow social norms of the past, and who have found new life-styles: would you rather have lived before society accepted your lifeways, and before the breakthroughs that gave you a new identity—or now?

I say to the chronologically aging who still feel young in spirit: would you rather have lived out your years at a time when elderly Americans were shunted aside and were held to have lost their capacity to function creatively—or now?

I hold with Freud that civilizations are caught between the twin gods, Eros and Thanatos—love and death, the life-affirming and life-denying principles. I find the conventional terms like "liberal" and "conservative" less and less useful. What counts is whether we are on the side of life affirmations or life denials. If I have to belong to a party, I am of the party of Eros, not of Thanatos.

I am no believer in automatic progress. I have experienced too much to wear blinders readily. But I can point to the real revolutions in process—in research, in access to life chances, in sexual attitudes, in awareness of the phases of the life cycle, in values and life-styles. The '60s were the most revolutionary decade in American history. The revolutions of the '70s—and those to come in the '80s—were and will be less dramatic and visible but they may prove deeper.

An Age of Trade-offs

We have too long allowed ourselves to be blinkered by the naysayers of our time. An Age of Limits can also be an Age of Trade-offs. As a possibilist I believe there are practical ways to resolve conflicts by contriving trade-offs in which you swap something marginal or formal to achieve what neither camp can do without. We see it done every day in the Supreme Court decisions, which give trade-offs the authority of law. I have to add, however, that you can't trade off the essential life principle for a death principle.

I am even aware of the uprootings and unravelings which threaten the cultural health of America. Every society has them, but ours seem to be piling up—the fragmenting of life, the battering of the family, the erosion of work, the breaking of connections, the intensity of pressure-group and single-issue politics, the imperial ego, the conspiracy hunting, the cult of the image, the moral relativism, the ethics of "anything goes," the refusal to see anything in life as sacred.

Yet, to counter this, America for me, even today, is the world's most revolutionary culture. It is in a phase of rapid change which belies the familiar charge of decay. In every area of thought and action, those who know most testify to the stunning, almost unimaginable transformations they are witnessing in their fields. How then can the civilization as a whole be stagnant or dying?

Inner Changes

The great event of the twentieth century—greater than the Russian or Chinese revolutions—has been America's defining of itself as a complex civilization, growing and enduring amidst the wrack of change. People around the world recognize it. They want to come here—by boat, by plane, by swimming, by cutting the barbed wire at the frontiers, by sneaking in. Their instinct is sounder than the self-hating doubts of some intellectuals.

The violences and excesses, the uprootings and unravelings of our culture are best seen as the agonizing inner changes of a social organism as it moves toward a higher degree of complexity. They are evidences not of a senile but of a still-adolescent society, not of a dying civilization but of one that has not wholly found itself. If America dies, it will not be of a running down of energies but of an explosion of energies.

Call this the manifesto of a possibilist. When I am asked whether America has come to the end of its tether, my answer is that of the lyric in "Porgy and Bess": "It ain't necessarily so." I believe, as yeasayers have insisted from Walt Whitman to Thomas Wolfe to our own day, that the true discovery of America still lies ahead.

THE MOUNTAIN OF MISERIES

Joseph Addison

Joseph Addison (1672–1719), one of England's greatest essayists, exerted a strong influence on English public opinion in the eighteenth century. After graduating with honors from Oxford, Addison entered politics, and eventually became secretary of state. The son of a clergyman, he was recognized as a man of lofty character who was concerned about purity and uprightness. Many of his essays depict the virtues—simplicity and good nature—which Addison demonstrated in his own life and which he valued in others. Addison's fame rests primarily on his contributions to the Tatler *and the* Spectator, *two newspapers which carried political, social, and literary news of the period. In the following essay, taken from the* Spectator, *Addison describes the scene that might transpire if people were given a chance to trade their own miseries for the miseries of others.*

Qui fit, Maecenas, ut nemo, quam sibi sortem
Seu ratio dederit, seu fors objecerit, illa
Contentus vivat: laudet diversa sequentes?

—*Hor.* Sat. i., Lib. I. I.

Whence is't, Maecenas, that so few approve
The state they're placed in, and incline to rove;
Whether against their will by fate impos'd,
Or by consent and prudent choice espous'd?

—*Horneck*

It is a celebrated thought of Socrates, that if all the misfortunes of mankind were cast into a public stock, in order to be equally distributed among the whole species, those who now think themselves the most unhappy would prefer the share they are already possessed of before that which would fall to them by such a division. Horace has carried this thought a great deal further in the motto of my paper, which implies that the hardships or misfortunes we lie under are more easy to us than those of any other person would be, in case we could change conditions with him.

As I was ruminating upon these two remarks, and seated in my elbow chair, I insensibly fell asleep; when, on a sudden, methought there was a proclamation made by Jupiter that every mortal should bring in his griefs and calamities, and throw them together in a heap. There was a large plain appointed for this purpose. I took my stand in the centre of it, and saw with a great deal of pleasure the whole human species marching one after another, and throwing down their several loads, which immediately grew up into a prodigious mountain, that seemed to rise above the clouds.

There was a certain lady of a thin airy shape, who was very active in this solemnity. She carried a magnifying glass in one of her hands, and was clothed in a loose flowing robe, embroidered with several figures of fiends and spectres, that discovered themselves in a thousand chimerical shapes, as her garment hovered in the wind. There was something wild and distracted in her looks. Her name was Fancy. She led up every mortal to the appointed place, after having very officiously assisted him in making up his pack, and laying it upon his shoulders. My heart melted within me to see my fellow-creatures groaning under their respective burdens, and to consider that prodigious bulk of human calamities which lay before me.

There were, however, several persons who gave me great diversion upon this occasion. I observed one bringing in a fardel very carefully concealed under an old embroidered cloak, which, upon his throwing it into the heap, I discovered to be Poverty. Another, after a great deal of puffing, threw down his luggage, which, upon examining, I found to be his wife.

There were multitudes of lovers saddled with very whimsical burdens composed of darts and flames; but, what was very odd, though they sighed as if their hearts would break under these bundles of calamities, they could not persuade themselves to cast them into the heap, when they came up to it; but, after a few faint efforts, shook their heads, and marched away as heavy laden as they came. I saw multitudes of old women throw down their wrinkles, and several young ones who stripped themselves of a tawny skin. There were very great heaps of red noses, large lips, and rusty teeth. The truth of it is, I was surprised to see the greatest part of the mountain made up of bodily deformities. Observing one advancing towards the heap with a larger cargo than ordinary upon his back, I found upon his near approach that it was only a natural hump, which he disposed of, with great joy of heart, among this collection of human miseries. There were likewise distempers of all sorts, though I could not but observe that there were many more imaginary than real. One little packet I could not but take notice of, which was a complication of all the diseases incident to human nature, and was in the hand of a great many fine people: this was called the spleen. But what most of all surprised me was, a remark I made, that there was not a single vice or folly thrown into the whole heap; at which I was very much astonished, having concluded within myself that every one would take this opportunity of getting rid of his passions, prejudices, and frailties.

I took notice in particular of a very profligate fellow, who I did not question came loaded with his crimes; but upon searching into his bundle I found that instead of throwing his guilt from him, he had only laid down his memory. He was followed by another worthless rogue, who flung away his modesty instead of his ignorance.

When the whole race of mankind had thus cast their burdens, the phantom which had been so busy on this occasion, seeing me an idle Spectator of what had passed, approached towards me. I grew uneasy at her presence, when of a sudden she held her magnifying glass full before my eyes. I no sooner saw my face in it, but was startled at the shortness of it, which now appeared to me in its utmost aggravation. The immoderate breadth of the features made me very much out of humor with my own countenance, upon which I threw it from me like a mask. It happened very luckily that one who stood by me had just before thrown down his visage, which it seems was too long for him. It was indeed extended to a most shameful length; I believe the very chin was, modestly speaking, as long as my whole face. We had both of us an opportunity of mending ourselves; and all the contributions being now brought in, every man was at liberty to exchange his misfortunes for those of another person. But as there arose many new incidents in the sequel of my vision, I shall reserve them for the subject of my next paper.

Quid causae est, merito quin illis Jupiter ambas
Iratus buccas inflet, neque se fore posthac
Tam facilem dicat, votis ut prabeat aurem?

—*Hor.* Sat. i., Lib. I., 20.

Were it not just that Jove, provok'd to heat,
Should drive these triflers from the hallow'd seat,
And unrelenting stand when they entreat?

—*Horneck.*

In my last paper I gave my reader a sight of that mountain of miseries which was made up of those several calamities that afflict the minds of men. I saw with unspeakable pleasure the whole species thus delivered from its sorrows; though at the same time, as we stood around the heap, and surveyed the several materials of which it was composed, there was scarcely a mortal in this vast multitude, who did not discover what he thought the pleasures of life, and wondered how the owners of them ever came to look upon them as burdens and grievances.

As we were regarding very attentively this confusion of miseries, this chaos of calamity, Jupiter issued out a second proclamation, that every one was now at liberty to exchange his affliction, and to return to his habitation with any such other bundle as should be delivered to him.

Upon this, Fancy began again to bestir herself, and, parceling out the whole heap with incredible activity, recommended to every one his particular packet. The hurry and confusion at this time was not to be expressed. Some observations, which I made upon this occasion, I shall communicate to the public. A venerable gray-headed man, who had laid down the colic, and who, I found, wanted an heir to his estate, snatched up an undutiful son that had been thrown into the heap by his angry father. The graceless youth, in less than a quarter of an hour, pulled the old gentleman by the beard, and had liked to have knocked his brains out; so that meeting the true father, who came towards him with a fit of the gripes, he begged him to take his son again, and give him back his colic; but they were incapable either of them to recede from the choice they had made. A poor galley slave, who had thrown down his chains, took up the gout in their stead, but made such wry faces, that one might easily perceive he was no great gainer by the bargain. It was pleasant enough to see the several exchanges that were made, for sickness against poverty, hunger against want of appetite, and care against pain.

The female world were very busy among themselves in bartering for features: one was trucking a lock of gray hairs for a carbuncle, another was making over a short waist for a pair of round shoulders, and a third cheapening a bad face for a lost reputation; but on all these occasions there was not one of them who did not think the new blemish, as soon as she had got it into her possession, much more disagreeable than the old one. I made the same observation on every other misfortune or calamity which every one in the assembly brought upon himself in lieu of what he had parted with. Whether it be that all the evils which befall us are in some measure suited and proportioned to our strength, or that every evil becomes more supportable by our being accustomed to it, I shall not determine.

I could not from my heart forbear pitying the poor hump-backed gentleman mentioned in the former paper, who went off a very well-shaped person with a stone in his bladder; nor the fine gentleman who had struck up this bargain with him, that limped through a whole assembly of ladies, who used to admire him, with a pair of shoulders peeping over his head.

I must not omit my own particular adventure. My friend with a long visage had no sooner taken upon him my short face, but he made such a grotesque figure in it that as I looked upon him I could not forbear laughing at myself, insomuch that I put my own face out of countenance. The poor gentleman was so sensible of the ridicule that I found he was ashamed of what he had done; on the other side, I found that I myself had no great reason to triumph, for as I went to touch my forehead I missed the place, and clapped my finger upon my upper lip. Besides, as my nose was exceeding prominent, I gave it two or three unlucky knocks as I was playing my hand about my face, and aiming at some other part of it. I saw two other gentlemen by me who were in the same ridiculous circumstances. These had made a foolish swap between a couple of thick bandy legs and two long trapsticks that had no calves to them. One of these looked like a man walking upon stilts, and was so lifted up into the air, above his ordinary height, that his head turned round with it; while the other made such awkward circles, as he attempted to walk, that he scarcely knew how to move forward upon his new supporters. Observing him to be a pleasant kind of fellow, I stuck my cane in the ground, and told him I would lay him a bottle of wine that he did not march up to it on a line, that I drew for him, in a quarter of an hour.

The heap was at last distributed among the two sexes, who made a most piteous sight, as they wandered up and down under the pressure of their several burdens. The whole plain was filled with murmurs and complaints, groans and lamentations. Jupiter at length, taking compassion on the poor mortals, ordered them a second time to lay down their loads, with a design to give every one his own again. They discharged themselves with a great deal of pleasure; after which, the phantom who had led them into such gross delusions was commanded to disappear. There was sent in her stead a goddess of a quite different figure; her motions were steady and composed, and her aspect serious but cheerful. She every now and then cast her eyes towards heaven, and fixed them upon Jupiter; her name was Patience. She had no sooner placed herself by the Mount of Sorrows, but, what I thought very remarkable, the whole heap sunk to such a degree that it did not appear a third part so big as it was before. She afterwards returned every man his own proper calamity, and, teaching him how to bear it in the most commodious manner, he marched off with it contentedly, being very well pleased that he had not been left to his own choice as to the kind of evils which fell to his lot.

Besides the several pieces of morality to be drawn out of this Vision, I learnt from it never to repine at my own misfortunes, or to envy the happiness of another, since it is impossible for any man to form a right judgment of his neighbor's sufferings; for which reason also I have determined never to think too lightly of another's complaints, but to regard the sorrows of my fellow-creatures with sentiments of humanity and compassion.

THE LIBERATED WOMAN

Susan Sontag

Susan Sontag (1933–), novelist, short story writer, critic, and essayist, was born in New York City. She received her bachelor's degree from the University of Chicago, and two master's degrees—one in English and one in philosophy—from Harvard. Sontag has taught or been a visiting lecturer at a number of colleges and universities, including City College of New York, Columbia, and Rutgers. Among her best-known works are Against Interpretation and Other Essays *and* On Photography. *Her short stories, reviews, and essays have appeared in* Atlantic Monthly, American Review, Nation, *and* Harper's. *The selection below first appeared in* Partisan Review *and was written in response to a questionnaire sent Sontag by the editors of* Libra, *a Spanish quarterly. In her essay Sontag answers one of the questions posed to her by the* Libra *editors.*

How do you, who are precisely a liberated woman, experience the attitude of men toward you?

I would never describe myself as a liberated woman. Of course, things are never as simple as *that*. But I have always been a feminist.

When I was five years old, I day-dreamed about becoming a biochemist and winning the Nobel Prize. (I had just read a biography of Madame Curie.) I stuck with chemistry until the age of ten, when I decided I would become a doctor. At fifteen, I knew I was going to be a writer. That is to say: from the beginning it never even occurred to me that I might be prevented from doing things in "the world" because I was born female. Perhaps because I spent most of my sickly childhood reading and in my chemistry laboratory in the empty garage, growing up in a very provincial part of the United States with a family life so minimal that it could be described as subnuclear, I was curiously innocent of the very existence of a barrier. When, at fifteen, I left home to go to a university, and then took up various careers, the relations that I had with men in my professional life seemed to me, with some exceptions, cordial and untroubled. So I went on not knowing there was a problem. I didn't even know I was a feminist, so unfashionable was that point of view at the time, when I married at the age of seventeen and kept my own name; it seemed to me an equally "personal" act of principle on my part, when I divorced my husband seven years later, to have indignantly rejected my lawyer's automatic bid for alimony, even though I was broke, homeless, and jobless at that moment and I had a six-year-old child to support.

Now and then, people I met would allude to the supposed difficulties of being both independent and a woman; I was always surprised—and sometimes annoyed, because, I thought, they were being obtuse. The problem didn't exist for me—except in the envy and resentment I occasionally felt from other women, the educated, jobless, home stranded wives of the men with whom I worked. I was conscious of being an exception, but it hadn't ever seemed hard to be an exception; and I accepted the advantages I enjoyed as my right. I know better now.

My case is not uncommon. Not so paradoxically, the position of a "liberated" woman in a liberal society where the vast majority of women are *not* liberated can be embarrassingly easy. Granted a good dose of talent and a certain cheerful or merely dogged lack of self-consciousness, one can even escape (as I did) the initial obstacles and derision that are likely to afflict a woman who insists on autonomy. It will not seem so hard for such a woman to lead an independent life; she may even reap some professional advantages from being a woman, such as greater visibility. Her good fortune is like the good fortune of a few blacks in a liberal but still racist society. Every liberal grouping (whether political, professional or artistic) needs its token woman.

What I have learned in the last five years—helped by the women's movement—is to situate my own experience in a certain *political* perspective. My good fortune is really beside the point. What does it prove? Nothing.

Any already "liberated" woman who complacently accepts her privileged situation participates in the oppression of other women. I accuse the overwhelming majority of women with careers in the arts and sciences, in the liberal professions, and in politics of doing just that.

I have often been struck by how misogynistic most successful women are. They are eager to say how silly, boring, superficial, or tiresome they find other women, and how much they prefer the company of men. Like most men, who basically despise and patronize women, most "liberated" women don't like or respect other women. If they don't fear them as sexual rivals, they fear them as professional rivals—wishing to guard their special status as women admitted into largely all-male professional worlds. Most women who pass as being "liberated" are shameless Uncle Toms, eager to flatter their men colleagues, becoming their accomplices in putting down other, less accomplished women, dishonestly minimizing the difficulties they themselves have run into because of being women. The implication of their behavior is that all women can do what they have done, if only they would exert themselves; that the barriers put up by men are flimsy; that it is mainly women themselves who hold themselves back. This simply is not true.

The first responsibility of a "liberated" woman is to lead the fullest, freest, and most imaginative life she can. The second responsibility is her solidarity with other women. She may live and work and make love with men. But she has no right to represent her situation as simpler, or less suspect, or less full of compromises than it really is. Her good relations with men must not be bought at the price of betraying her sisters.

CHANNELLED WHELK

Anne Morrow Lindbergh

Anne Morrow Lindbergh (1906–) was born in Englewood, New Jersey. While her father, Dwight Morrow, was the American ambassador to Mexico, Charles Lindbergh visited Mexico City on a goodwill tour following his solo flight across the Atlantic. He and Anne Morrow met at this time and were later married. The Lindberghs were the central figures in a highly publicized family tragedy involving the kidnapping and death of their baby. Anne Morrow Lindbergh has written several best-sellers, both in prose and poetry. Among her best-known works are North to the Orient, Listen! The Wind, *and* Gift from the Sea, *an introspective study of the problems of women. In this essay, she discusses the difficulty of attaining inner harmony in the midst of the distractions and complexities of daily life.*

The shell in my hand is deserted. It once housed a whelk, a snail-like creature, and then temporarily, after the death of the first occupant, a little hermit crab, who has run away, leaving his tracks behind him like a delicate vine on the sand. He ran away, and left me his shell. It was once a protection to him. I turn the shell in my hand, gazing into the wide open door from which he made his exit. Had it become an encumbrance? Why did he run away? Did he hope to find a better home, a better mode of living? I too have run away, I realize, I have shed the shell of my life, for these few weeks of vacation.

But his shell—it is simple; it is bare, it is beautiful. Small, only the size of my thumb, its architecture is perfect, down to the finest detail. Its shape, swelling like a pear in the center, winds in a gentle spiral to the pointed apex. Its color, dull gold, is whitened by a wash of salt from the sea. Each whorl, each faint knob, each criss-cross vein in its egg-shell texture, is as clearly defined as on the day of creation. My eye follows with delight the outer circumference of that diminutive winding staircase up which this tenant used to travel.

My shell is not like this, I think. How untidy it has become! Blurred with moss, knobby with barnacles, its shape is hardly recognizable any more. Surely, it had a shape once. It has a shape still in my mind. What is the shape of my life?

The shape of my life today starts with a family. I have a husband, five children and a home just beyond the suburbs of New York. I have also a craft, writing, and therefore work I want to pursue. The shape of my life, is, of course, determined by many other things; my background and childhood, my mind and its education, my conscience and its pressures, my heart and its desires. I want to give and take from my children and husband, to share with friends and community, to carry out my obligations to man and to the world, as a woman, as an artist, as a citizen.

But I want first of all—in fact, as an end to these other desires—to be at peace with myself. I want a singleness of eye, a purity of intention, a central core to my life that will enable me to carry out these obligations and activities as well as I can. I want, in fact—to borrow from the language of the saints—to live "in grace" as much of the time as possible. I am not using this term in a strictly theological sense. By grace I mean an inner harmony, essentially spiritual, which can be translated into outward harmony. I am seeking perhaps what Socrates asked for in the prayer from the *Phaedrus* when he said, "May the outward and inward man be at one." I would like to achieve a state of inner spiritual grace from which I could function and give as I was meant to in the eye of God.

Vague as this definition may be, I believe most people are aware of periods in their lives when they seem to be "in grace" and other periods when they feel "out of grace," even though they may use different words to describe these states. In the first happy condition, one seems to carry all one's tasks before one lightly, as if borne along on a great tide; and in the opposite state one can hardly tie a shoestring. It is true that a large part of life consists in learning a technique of tying the shoestring, whether one is in grace or not. But there are techniques of living too; there are even techniques in the search for grace. And techniques can be cultivated. I have learned by some experience, by many examples, and by the writings of countless others before me, also occupied in the search, that certain environments, certain modes of life, certain rules of conduct are more conducive to inner and outer harmony than others. There are, in fact, certain roads that one may follow. Simplification of life is one of them.

I mean to lead a simple life, to choose a simple shell I can carry easily—like a hermit crab. But I do not. I find that my frame of life does not foster simplicity. My husband and five children must make their way in the world. The life I have chosen as wife and mother entrains a whole caravan of complications. It involves a house in the suburbs and either household drudgery or household help which wavers between scarcity and non-existence for most of us. It involves food and shelter; meals, planning, marketing, bills, and making the ends meet in a thousand ways. It involves not only the butcher, the baker, the candlestickmaker but countless other experts to keep my modern house with its modern "simplifications" (electricity, plumbing, refrigerator, gas-stove, oil-burner, dish-washer, radios, car, and numerous other labor-saving devices) functioning properly. It involves health; doctors, dentists, appointments, medicine, cod-liver oil, vitamins, trips to the drugstore. It involves education, spiritual, intellectual, physical; schools, school conferences, car-pools, extra trips for basketball or orchestra practice; tutoring; camps, camp equipment and transportation. It involves clothes, shopping, laundry, cleaning, mending, letting skirts down and sewing buttons on, or finding someone else to do it. It involves friends, my husband's, my children's, my own, and endless arrangements to get together; letters, invitations, telephone calls and transportation hither and yon.

For life today in America is based on the premise of ever-widening circles of contact and communication. It involves not only family demands, but community demands, national demands, international demands on the good citizen, through social and cultural pressures, through newspapers, magazines, radio programs, political drives, charitable appeals, and so on. My mind reels with it. What a circus act we women perform every day of our lives. It puts the trapeze artist to shame. Look at us. We run a tight rope daily, balancing a pile of books on the head. Baby-carriage, parasol, kitchen chair, still under control. Steady now!

This is not the life of simplicity but the life of multiplicity that the wise men warn us of. It leads not to unification but to fragmentation. It does not bring grace; it destroys the soul. And this is not only true of my life, I am forced to conclude; it is the life of millions of women in America. I stress America, because today, the American woman more than any other has the privilege of choosing such a life. Woman in large parts of the civilized world has been forced back by war, by poverty, by collapse, by the sheer struggle to survive, into a smaller circle of immediate time and space, immediate family life, immediate problems of existence. The American woman is still relatively free to choose the wider life. How long she will hold this enviable and precarious position no one knows. But her particular situation has a significance far above its apparent economic, national or even sex limitations.

For the problem of the multiplicity of life not only confronts the American woman, but also the American man. And it is not merely the concern of the American as such, but of our whole modern civilization, since life in America today is held up as the ideal of a large part of the rest of the world. And finally, it is not limited to our present civilization, though we are faced with it now in an exaggerated form. It has always been one of the pitfalls of mankind. Plotinus was preaching the dangers of multiplicity of the world back in the third century. Yet, the problem is particularly and essentially woman's. Distraction is, always has been, and probably always will be, inherent in woman's life.

For to be a woman is to have interests and duties, raying out in all directions from the central mother-core, like spokes from the hub of a wheel. The pattern of our lives is essentially circular. We must be open to all points of the compass; husband, children, friends, home, community; stretched out, exposed, sensitive like a spider's web to each breeze that blows, to each call that comes. How difficult for us, then, to achieve a balance in the midst of these contradictory tensions, and yet how necessary for the proper functioning of our lives. How much we need, and how arduous of attainment is that steadiness preached in all rules for holy living. How desirable and how distant is the ideal of the contemplative, artist, or saint—the inner inviolable core, the single eye.

With a new awareness, both painful and humorous, I begin to understand why the saints were rarely married women. I am convinced it has nothing inherently to do, as I once supposed, with chastity or children. It has to do primarily with distractions. The bearing, rearing, feeding and educating of children; the running of a house with its thousand details; human relationships with their myriad pulls—woman's normal occupations in general run counter to creative life, or contemplative life, or saintly life. The problem is not merely one of *Woman and Career, Woman and the Home, Woman and Independence*. It is more basically: how to remain whole in the midst of the distractions of life; how to remain balanced, no matter what centrifugal forces tend to pull one off center; how to remain strong, no matter what shocks come in at the periphery and tend to crack the hub of the wheel.

What is the answer? There is no easy answer, no complete answer. I have only clues, shells from the sea. The bare beauty of the channelled whelk tells me that one answer, and perhaps a first step, is in simplification of life, in cutting out some of the distractions. But how? Total retirement is not possible. I cannot shed my responsibilities. I cannot permanently inhabit a desert island. I cannot be a nun in the midst of family life. I would not want to be. The solution for me, surely, is neither in total renunciation of the world, nor in total acceptance of it. I must find a balance somewhere, or an alternating rhythm between these two extremes; a swinging of the pendulum between solitude and communion, between retreat and return. In my periods of retreat, perhaps I can learn something to carry back into my worldly life. I can at least practice for these two weeks the simplification of outward life, as a beginning. I can follow this superficial clue, and see where it leads. Here, in beach living, I can try.

One learns first of all in beach living the art of shedding; how little one can get along with, not how much. Physical shedding to begin with, which then mysteriously spreads into other fields. Clothes, first. Of course, one needs less in the sun. But one needs less anyway, one finds suddenly. One does not need a closet-full, only a small suitcase-full. And what a relief it is! Less taking up and down of hems, less mending, and—best of all—less worry about what to wear. One finds one is shedding not only clothes—but vanity.

Next, shelter. One does not need the airtight shelter one has in winter in the North. Here I live in a bare sea-shell of a cottage. No heat, no telephone, no plumbing to speak of, no hot water, a two-burner oil stove, no gadgets to go wrong. No rugs. There were some, but I rolled them up the first day; it is easier to sweep the sand off a bare floor. But I find I don't bustle about with unnecessary sweeping and cleaning here. I am no longer aware of the dust. I have shed my Puritan conscience about absolute tidiness and cleanliness. Is it possible that, too, is a material burden? No curtains. I do not need them for privacy; the pines around my house are enough protection. I want the windows open all the time, and I don't want to worry about rain. I begin to shed my Martha-like anxiety about many things. Washable slipcovers, faded and old—I hardly see them; I don't worry about the impression they make on other people. I am shedding pride. As little furniture as possible; I shall not need much. I shall ask into my shell only those friends with whom I can be completely honest. I find I am shedding hypocrisy in human relationships. What a rest that will be! The most exhausting thing in life, I have discovered, is being insincere. That is why so much of social life is exhausting; one is wearing a mask. I have shed my mask.

I find I live quite happily without those things I think necessary in winter in the North. And as I write these words, I remember, with some shock at the disparity in our lives, a similar statement made by a friend of mine in France who spent three years in a German prison camp. Of course, he said, qualifying his remark, they did not get enough to eat, they were sometimes atrociously treated, they had little physical freedom. And yet, prison life taught him how little one can get along with, and what extraordinary spiritual freedom and peace such simplification can bring. I remember again, ironically, that today more of us in America than anywhere else in the world have the luxury of choice between simplicity and complication of life. And for the most part we, who could use simplicity, choose complication. War, prison, survival periods, enforce a form of simplicity on man. The monk and the nun choose it of their own free will. But if one accidentally finds it, as I have for a few days, one finds also the serenity it brings.

Is it not rather ugly, one may ask? One collects material possessions not only for security, comfort or vanity, but for beauty as well. Is your sea-shell house not ugly and bare? No, it is beautiful, my house. It is bare, of course, but the wind, the sun, the smell of the pines blow through its bareness. The unfinished beams in the roof are veiled by cobwebs. They are lovely, I think, gazing up at them with new eyes; they soften the hard lines of the rafters as grey hairs soften the lines on a middle-aged face. I no longer pull out grey hairs or sweep down cobwebs. As for the walls, it is true they looked forbidding at first. I felt cramped and enclosed by their blank faces. I wanted to knock holes in them, to give them another dimension with pictures or windows. So I dragged home from the beach grey arms of driftwood, worn satin-smooth by wind and sand. I gathered trailing green vines with floppy red-tipped leaves. I picked up the whitened skeletons of conchshells, their curious hollowed-out shapes faintly reminiscent of abstract sculpture. With these tacked to walls and propped up in corners, I am satisfied. I have a periscope out to the world. I have a window, a view, a point of flight from my sedentary base.

I am content. I sit down at my desk, a bare kitchen table with a blotter, a bottle of ink, a sand dollar to weight down one corner, a clam shell for a pen tray, the broken tip of a conch, pink-tinged, to finger, and a row of shells to set my thoughts spinning.

I love my sea-shell of a house. I wish I could live in it always. I wish I could transport it home. But I cannot. It will not hold a husband, five children and the necessities and trappings of daily life. I can only carry back my little channelled whelk. It will sit on my desk in Connecticut, to remind me of the ideal of a simplified life, to encourage me in the game I played on the beach. To ask how little, not how much, can I get along with. To say—is it necessary?—when I am tempted to add one more accumulation to my life, when I am pulled toward one more centrifugal activity.

Simplification of outward life is not enough. It is merely the outside. But I am starting with the outside. I am looking at the outside of a shell, the outside of my life—the shell. The complete answer is not to be found on the outside, in an outward mode of living. This is only a technique, a road to grace. The final answer, I know, is always inside. But the outside can give a clue, can help one to find the inside answer. One is free, like the hermit crab, to change one's shell.

Channelled whelk, I put you down again, but you have set my mind on a journey, up an inwardly winding spiral staircase of thought.

A DEBT TO DICKENS

Pearl S. Buck

Pearl S. Buck (1892–1973), the daughter of Presbyterian missionaries, was taken to China as a young child and spent most of her early years there. After graduating from Randolph-Macon Woman's College in Virginia, she returned to China and married a missionary. Buck won international fame and a Pulitzer Prize for her book The Good Earth, *the story of a Chinese peasant and his wife struggling for land and security. Other works by Buck include* Sons, A House Divided, Fighting Angel, *and* The Exile. *She received the Nobel Prize for Literature in 1938. The following essay is a moving account of Pearl Buck's early life in China and of the comfort and companionship she found at that time in the works of Charles Dickens.*

I have long looked for an opportunity to pay a certain debt which I have owed since I was seven years old. Debts are usually burdens, but this is no ordinary debt, and it is no burden, except as the feeling of warm gratitude may ache in one until it is expressed. My debt is to an Englishman, who long ago in China rendered an inestimable service to a small American child. That child was myself and that Englishman was Charles Dickens. I know no better way to meet my obligation than to write down what Charles Dickens did in China for an American child.

First, you must picture to yourself that child, living quite solitary in a remote Chinese countryside, in a small mission bungalow perched upon a hill among the rice fields in the valleys below. In the near distance wound that deep, treacherous, golden river, the Yangtse, and some of the most terrifying and sinister, as well as the most delightful and exciting moments of that child's life, were spent beside the river. She loved to crawl along its banks upon the rocks or upon the muddy flats and watch for the lifting of the huge four-square nets that hung into the moving yellow flood, and see out of that flood come perhaps again and again an empty net, but sometimes great flashing, twisting silver bodies of fish. She lingered beside villages of boat folk, and saw them live, the babies tied to a rope and splashing in the shallower waters. But she saw babies dead thrown into the deep waters. She wandered small and alien among the farm folk in the earthen houses among the fields. She accepted a bowl of rice and cabbage often at meal time and sat among the peasants on the threshing floor about the door and ate, usually in silence, listening and listening, answering their kindly, careless questions, bearing with shy, painful smiles their kind, teasing laughter at her yellow curls and unfortunate blue eyes, which they thought so ugly. She was, she knew, very alien. Upon the streets of the great city where sometimes she went she learned to accept the cry of foreign devil, and to realize she was a foreign devil. Once when she was very, very small, before she knew better, she turned as worms will, and flung back a word she had learned among the boat folk when they quarrelled. It was a word so wicked that the youth who called her foreign devil ran howling with terror, and thereafter she went more contentedly, not using the word any more because of its great wickedness, but knowing she had it to use if she needed it very much.

She grew from a very tiny child into a bigger child, still knowing she was alien. However kindly the people about her might be, and they were much more often kind than not, she knew that she was foreign to them. And she wondered very much about her own folk and where they were and how they looked and at what they played. But she did not know. In the bungalow were her parents, very busy, very, very busy, and when she had learned her lessons in the morning quickly, they were too busy to pay much heed to her and so she wandered about a great deal, seeing and learning all sorts of things. She had fun. But very often she used to wonder, "Where are the other children like me? What is it like in the country where they live?" She longed very much, I can remember, to have some of them to play with. But she never had them.

To this small, isolated creature there came one day an extraordinary accident. She was an impossibly voracious reader. She would like to have had children's books, but there were none, and so she read everything—Plutarch's Lives and Fox's *Martyrs*, the Bible, church history, and the hot spots in Jonathan Edwards's sermons, and conversations out of Shakespeare, and bits of Tennyson and Browning which she could not understand at all. Then one day she looked doubtfully at a long row of somber blue books on a very high shelf. They were quite beyond her reach. Later she discovered this was because they were novels. But being desperate she put a three-cornered bamboo stool on top of a small table and climbed up and stared at the bindings and in faded black titles she read *Oliver Twist*, by Charles Dickens. She was then a little past seven years old. It was a very hot August day, in the afternoon about three o'clock, when the household was asleep, all except the indefatigable parents, and they were very, very busy. She took *Oliver Twist* out of his place—it was fat and thick, for *Hard Times* was bound with it—and in great peril descended, and stopping in the pantry for a pocket full of peanuts, she made off to a secret corner of the veranda into which only a small, agile child could squeeze, and opened the closely printed pages of an old edition, and discovered her playmates.

How can I make you know what that discovery was to that small, lonely child? There in that corner above the country road in China, with vendors passing beneath me, I entered into my own heritage. I cannot tell you about those hours. I know I was roused at six o'clock by the call to my supper, and I looked about dazed, to discover the long rays of the late afternoon sun streaming across the valleys. I remember twice I closed the book and burst into tears, unable to bear the tragedy of Oliver Twist, and then opened it quickly again, burning to know more. I remember, most significant of all, that I forgot to touch a peanut, and my pocket was still quite full when I was called. I went to my supper in a dream, and read as late as I dared in my bed afterward, and slept with the book under my pillow, and woke again in the early morning. When *Oliver Twist* was finished, and after it *Hard Times,* I was wretched with indecision. I felt I must read it all straight over again, and yet I was voracious for that long row of blue books. What was in them? I climbed up again, finally, and put *Oliver Twist* at the beginning, and began on the next one, which was *David Copperfield.* I resolved to read straight through the row and then begin at the beginning once more and read straight through again.

This program I carried on consistently, over and over, for about ten years, and after that I still kept a Dickens book on hand, so to speak, to dip into and feel myself at home again. Today I have for him a feeling which I have for no other human soul. He opened my eyes to people, he taught me to love all sorts of people, high and low, rich and poor, the old and little children. He taught me to hate hypocrisy and pious mouthing of unctuous words. He taught me that beneath gruffness there may be kindness, and that kindness is the sweetest thing in the world, and goodness is the best thing in the world. He taught me to despise money grubbing. People today say he is obvious and sentimental and childish in his analysis of character. It may be so, and yet I have found people surprisingly like those he wrote about—the good a little less undiluted, perhaps, and the evil a little more mixed. And I do not regret that simplicity of his, for it had its own virtue. The virtue was of a great zest for life. If he saw everything black and white, it was because life rushed out of him strong and clear, full of love and hate. He gave me that zest, that immense joy in life and in people, and in their variety.

He gave me, too, my first real glimpse of a kindly English God, a sort of father, to whom the childlike and the humble might turn. There was no talk of hell in his books. He made Christmas for me, a merry, roaring English Christmas, full of goodies and plum puddings and merriment and friendly cheer. I went to his parties over and over again, for I had no others. I remember one dreadful famine winter the thing that kept me laughing and still a child was *Pickwick Papers*. I read it over and over, and laughed, as I still laugh, over the Wellers and the widow and Mr. Pickwick and all his merry company. They were as real to me as the sad folk outside the compound walls, and they saved me.

And he made me love England. I have no drop of English blood in my veins. I have German and Dutch and French ancestors, I was born in the United States of American parents, and I have spent my life in China. But part of me is English, for I love England with a peculiar, possessing love. I do possess something of England. When I went there years later, London was my city and the countryside I knew. I was not strange. The people were my own people, too. England is the mother of a certain part of my spirit. I can never take sides against England or the English. It is not only that we speak a common tongue and that we are the same race. There is far more than that. I know English people. I love English people. I have grown up among them. I am used to them. They have been my companions for many years. They are forever my friends. When several years ago in China there was a period of misunderstanding of certain British policies, I steadfastly refused to agree with the distrust expressed by some of my Chinese friends toward England. I was sure of the quality of the English people and of their integrity. What they said they would do, they would do. And they did. Their armies were peacefully withdrawn when the necessity of protection was over, they did not proceed to the conquest the Chinese thought was inevitable, and more than any Western power they have steadily shown their honesty of purpose toward the Chinese. After it was over, my Chinese friends said wondering, "You were right." And I replied, "I knew I was."

This is what Charles Dickens did for me. His influence I cannot lose. He has made himself a part of me forever.

WHY I WRITE

Joan Didion

Joan Didion (1935–) was born in California and began her career when she won Vogue *magazine's Prix de Paris award in her senior year of college. She later became an associate editor of* Vogue. *She is the author of two collections of essays,* Slouching Towards Bethlehem *and* The White Album, *and of three novels,* Run River, Play It As It Lays, *and* A Book of Common Prayer. *In this essay, Didion describes the characteristics of mind and personality that have made her a writer.*

Of course I stole the title for this talk, from George Orwell. One reason I stole it was that I like the sound of the words: *Why I Write.* There you have three short unambiguous words that share a sound, and the sound they share is this: *I I I*

In many ways writing is the act of saying *I*, of imposing oneself upon other people, of saying *listen to me, see it my way, change your mind.* It's an aggressive, even a hostile act. You can disguise its aggressiveness all you want with veils of subordinate clauses and qualifiers and tentative subjunctives, with ellipses and evasions—with the whole manner of intimating rather than claiming, of alluding rather than stating—but there's no getting around the fact that setting words on paper is the tactic of a secret bully, an invasion, an imposition of the writer's sensibility on the reader's most private space.

I stole the title not only because the words sounded right but because they seemed to sum up, in a no-nonsense way, all I have to tell you. Like many writers I have only this one "subject," this one "area": the act of writing. I can bring you no reports from any other front. I may have other interests: I am "interested," for example, in marine biology, but I don't flatter myself that you would come out to hear me talk about it. I am not a scholar. I am not in the least an intellectual, which is not to say that when I hear the word "intellectual" I reach for my gun, but only to say that I do not think in abstracts. During the years when I was an undergraduate at Berkeley I tried, with a kind of hopeless late-adolescent energy, to buy some temporary visa into the world of ideas, to forge for myself a mind that could deal with the abstract.

In short I tried to think. I failed. My attention veered inexorably back to the specific, to the tangible, to what was generally considered, by everyone I knew then and for that matter have known since, the peripheral. I would try to contemplate the Hegelian dialectic and would find myself concentrating instead on a flowering pear tree outside my window and the particular way the petals fell on my floor. I would try to read linguistic theory and would find myself wondering instead if the lights were on in the bevatron up the hill. When I say that I was wondering if the lights were on in the bevatron you might immediately suspect, if you deal in ideas at all, that I was registering the bevatron as a political symbol, thinking in shorthand about the military-industrial complex and its role in the university community, but you would be wrong. I was only wondering if the lights were on in the bevatron, and how they looked. A physical fact.

I had trouble graduating from Berkeley, not because of this inability to deal with ideas—I was majoring in English, and I could locate the house-and-garden imagery in *Portrait of a Lady* as well as the next person, "imagery" being by definition the kind of specific that got my attention—but simply because I had neglected to take a course in Milton. For reasons which now sound baroque I needed a degree by the end of that summer, and the English department finally agreed, if I would come down from Sacramento every Friday and talk about the cosmology of *Paradise Lost*, to certify me proficient in Milton. I did this. Some Fridays I took the Greyhound bus, other Fridays I caught the Southern Pacific's City of San Francisco on the last leg of its transcontinental trip. I can no longer tell you whether Milton put the sun or the earth at the center of his universe in *Paradise Lost*, the central question of at least one century and a topic about which I wrote 10,000 words that summer, but I can still recall the exact rancidity of the butter in the City of San Francisco's dining car, and the way the tinted windows on the Greyhound bus cast the oil refineries around Carquinez Straits into a grayed and obscurely sinister light. In short my attention was always on the periphery, on what I could see and taste and touch, on the butter, and the Greyhound bus. During those years I was traveling on what I knew to be a very shaky passport, forged papers: I knew that I was no legitimate resident in any world of ideas. I knew I couldn't think. All I knew then was what I couldn't do. All I knew then was what I wasn't, and it took me some years to discover what I was.

Which was a writer.

By which I mean not a "good" writer or a "bad" writer but simply a writer, a person whose most absorbed and passionate hours are spent arranging words on pieces of paper. Had my credentials been in order I would never have become a writer. Had I been blessed with even limited access to my own mind there would have been no reason to write. I write entirely to find out what I'm thinking, what I'm looking at, what I see and what it means. What I want and what I fear. Why did the oil refineries around Carquinez Straits seem sinister to me in the summer of 1956? Why have the night lights in the bevatron burned in my mind for twenty years? *What is going on in these pictures in my mind?*

When I talk about pictures in my mind I am talking, quite specifically, about images that shimmer around the edges. There used to be an illustration in every elementary psychology book showing a cat drawn by a patient in varying stages of schizophrenia. This cat had a shimmer around it. You could see the molecular structure breaking down at the very edges of the cat: the cat became the background and the background the cat, everything interacting, exchanging ions. People on hallucinogens describe the same perception of objects. I'm not a schizophrenic, nor do I take hallucinogens, but certain images do shimmer for me. Look hard enough, and you can't miss the shimmer. It's there. You can't think too much about these pictures that shimmer. You just lie low and let them develop. You stay quiet. You don't talk to many people and you keep your nervous system from shorting out and you try to locate the cat in the shimmer, the grammar in the picture.

Just as I meant "shimmer" literally I mean "grammar" literally. Grammar is a piano I play by ear, since I seem to have been out of school the year the rules were mentioned. All I know about grammar is its infinite power. To shift the structure of a sentence alters the meaning of that sentence, as definitely and inflexibly as the position of a camera alters the meaning of the object photographed. Many people know about camera angles now, but not so many know about sentences. The arrangement of the words matters, and the arrangement you want can be found in the picture in your mind. The picture dictates the arrangement. The picture dictates whether this will be a sentence with or without clauses, a sentence that ends hard or a dying-fall sentence, long or short, active or passive. The picture tells you how to arrange the words and the arrangement of the words tells you, or tells me, what's going on in the picture. *Nota bene:*

It tells you.

You don't tell it.

Let me show you what I mean by pictures in the mind. I began *Play It As It Lays* just as I have begun each of my novels, with no notion of "character" or "plot" or even "incident." I had only two pictures in my mind, more about which later, and a technical intention, which was to write a novel so elliptical and fast that it would be over before you noticed it, a novel so fast that it would scarcely exist on the page at all. About the pictures: the first was of white space. Empty space. This was clearly the picture that dictated the narrative intention of the book—a book in which anything that happened would happen off the page, a "white" book to which the reader would have to bring his or her own bad dreams—and yet this picture told me no "story," suggested no situation. The second picture did. This second picture was of something actually witnessed. A young woman with long hair and a short white halter dress walks through the casino at the Riviera in Las Vegas at one in the morning. She crosses the casino alone and picks up a house telephone. I watch her because I have heard her paged, and recognize her name: she is a minor actress I see around Los Angeles from time to time, in places like Jax and once in a gynecologist's office in the Beverly Hills Clinic, but have never met. I know nothing about her. Who is paging her? Why is she here to be paged? How exactly did she come to this? It was precisely this moment in Las Vegas that made *Play It As It Lays* begin to tell itself to me, but the moment appears in the novel only obliquely, in a chapter which begins:

"Maria made a list of things she would never do. She would never: walk through the Sands or Caesar's alone after midnight. She would never: ball at a party, do S-M unless she wanted to, borrow furs from Abe Lipsey, deal. She would never: carry a Yorkshire in Beverly Hills."

That is the beginning of the chapter and that is also the end of the chapter, which may suggest what I meant by "white space."

I recall having a number of pictures in my mind when I began the novel I just finished, *A Book of Common Prayer*. As a matter of fact one of these pictures was of that bevatron I mentioned, athough I would be hard put to tell you a story in which nuclear energy figured. Another was a newspaper photograph of a hijacked 707 burning on the desert in the Middle East. Another was the night view from a room in which I once spent a week with paratyphoid, a hotel room on the Colombian coast. My husband and I seemed to be on the Colombian coast representing the United States of America at a film festival (I recall invoking the name "Jack Valenti" a lot, as if its reiteration could make me well), and it was a bad place to have fever, not only because my indisposition offended our hosts but because every night in this hotel the generator failed. The lights went out. The elevator stopped. My husband would go to the event of the evening and make excuses for me and I would stay alone in this hotel room, in the dark. I remember standing at the window trying to call Bogotá (the telephone seemed to work on the same principle as the generator) and watching the night wind come up and wondering what I was doing eleven degrees off the equator with a fever of 103. The view from that window definitely figures in *A Book of Common Prayer*, as does the burning 707, and yet none of these pictures told me the story I needed.

The picture that did, the picture that shimmered and made these other images coalesce, was the Panama airport at 6 A.M. I was in this airport only once, on a plane to Bogotá that stopped for an hour to refuel, but the way it looked that morning remained superimposed on everything I saw until the day I finished *A Book of Common Prayer*. I lived in that airport for several years. I can still feel the hot air when I step off the plane, can see the heat already rising off the tarmac at 6 A.M. I can feel my skirt damp and wrinkled on my legs. I can feel the asphalt stick to my sandals. I remember the big tail of a Pan American plane floating motionless down at the end of the tarmac. I remember the sound of a slot machine in the waiting room. I could tell you that I remember a particular woman in the airport, an American woman, a *norteamericana*, a thin *norteamericana* about 40 who wore a big square emerald in lieu of a wedding ring, but there was no such woman there.

I put this woman in the airport later. I made this woman up, just as I later made up a country to put the woman in, and a family to run the country. This woman in the airport is neither catching a plane nor meeting one. She is ordering tea in the airport coffee shop. In fact she is not simply "ordering" tea but insisting that the water be boiled, in front of her, for twenty minutes. Why is this woman in this airport? Why is she going nowhere, where has she been? Where did she get that big emerald? What derangement, or disassociation, makes her believe that her will to see the water boiled can possibly prevail?

"She had been going to one airport or another for four months, one could see it, looking at the visas on her passport. All those airports where Charlotte Douglas's passport had been stamped would have looked alike. Sometimes the sign on the tower would say 'Bienvenidos' and sometimes the sign on the tower would say 'Bienvenue,' some places were wet and hot and others dry and hot, but at each of these airports the pastel concrete walls would rust and stain and the swamp off the runway would be littered with the fuselages of cannibalized Fairchild F-227's and the water would need boiling.

"I knew why Charlotte went to the airport even if Victor did not.

"I knew about airports."

These lines appear about halfway through *A Book of Common Prayer*, but I wrote them during the second week I worked on the book, long before I had any idea where Charlotte Douglas had been or why she went to airports. Until I wrote these lines I had no character called "Victor" in mind: the necessity for mentioning a name, and the name "Victor," occurred to me as I wrote the sentence. *I knew why Charlotte went to the airport* sounded incomplete. *I knew why Charlotte went to the airport even if Victor did not* carried a little more narrative drive. Most important of all, until I wrote these lines I did not know who "I" was, who was telling the story. I had intended until that moment that the "I" be no more than the voice of the author, a 19th-century omniscient narrator. But there it was:

"I knew why Charlotte went to the airport even if Victor did not.

"I knew about airports."

This "I" was the voice of no author in my house. This "I" was someone who not only knew why Charlotte went to the airport but also knew someone called "Victor." Who was Victor? Who was this narrator? Why was this narrator telling me this story? Let me tell you one thing about why writers write: had I known the answer to any of these questions I would never have needed to write a novel.

WHERE I LIVED, AND WHAT I LIVED FOR

Henry David Thoreau

Henry David Thoreau (1817–1862), the great American philosopher, poet, and naturalist, was born in Concord, Massachusetts. After graduating from Harvard, Thoreau worked for a while as a teacher. But, uncertain as to what he wanted to do with his life, he resigned his position and took on a series of odd jobs. From 1845 to 1847 Thoreau lived in a small cabin that he built for himself on the shores of Walden Pond near Concord, Massachusetts. He recorded his experiences in his best-known work, Walden, *a classic in American literature. The selection below, taken from* Walden, *highlights Thoreau's spirit of individualism and his lifelong passion for freedom.*

At a certain season of our life we are accustomed to consider every spot as the possible site of a house. I have thus surveyed the country on every side within a dozen miles of where I live. In imagination I have bought all the farms in succession, for all were to be bought, and I knew their price. I walked over each farmer's premises, tasted his wild apples, discoursed on husbandry with him, took his farm at his price, at any price, mortgaging it to him in my mind; even put a higher price on it,—took every thing but a deed of it—took his word for his deed, for I dearly love to talk,—cultivated it, and him too to some extent, I trust, and withdrew when I had enjoyed it long enough, leaving him to carry it on. This experience entitled me to be regarded as a sort of real-estate broker by my friends. Wherever I sat, there I might live, and the landscape radiated from me accordingly. What is a house but a *sedes*, a seat?—better if a country seat. I discovered many a site for a house not likely to be soon improved, which some might have thought too far from the village, but to my eyes the village was too far from it. Well, there I might live, I said; and there I did live, for an hour, a summer and a winter life; saw how I could let the years run off, buffet the winter through, and see the spring come in. The future inhabitants of this region, wherever they may place their houses, may be sure that they have been anticipated. An afternoon sufficed to lay out the land into orchard, woodlot, and pasture, and to decide what fine oaks or pines should be left to stand before the door, and whence each blasted tree could be seen to the best advantage; and then I let it lie, fallow perchance, for a man is rich in proportion to the number of things which he can afford to let alone.

My imagination carried me so far that I even had the refusal of several farms,—the refusal was all I wanted,—but I never got my fingers burned by actual possession. The nearest that I came to actual possession was when I bought the Hollowell Place, and had begun to sort my seeds, and collected materials with which to make a wheelbarrow to carry it on or off with; but before the owner gave me a deed of it, his wife—every man has such a wife—changed her mind and wished to keep it, and he offered me ten dollars to release him. Now, to speak the truth, I had but ten cents in the world, and it surpassed my arithmetic to tell, if I was that man who had ten cents, or who had a farm, or ten dollars, or all together. However, I let him keep the ten dollars and the farm too, for I had carried it far enough; or rather, to be generous, I sold him the farm for just what I gave for it, and, as he was not a rich man, made him a present of ten dollars, and still had my ten cents, and seeds, and materials for a wheelbarrow left. I found thus that I had been a rich man without any damage to my poverty. But I retained the landscape, and I have since annually carried off what it yielded without a wheelbarrow. With respect to landscapes,—

> I am monarch of all I *survey*,
> My right there is none to dispute.

I have frequently seen a poet withdraw, having enjoyed the most valuable part of a farm, while the crusty farmer supposed that he had got a few wild apples only. Why, the owner does not know it for many years when a poet has put his farm in rhyme, the most admirable kind of invisible fence, has fairly impounded it, milked it, skimmed it, and got all the cream, and left the farmer only the skimmed milk.

The real attractions of the Hollowell farm, to me, were: its complete retirement, being about two miles from the village, half a mile from the nearest neighbor, and separated from the highway by a broad field; its bounding on the river, which the owner said protected it by its fogs from frosts in the spring, though that was nothing to me; the gray color and ruinous state of the house and barn, and the dilapidated fences, which put such an interval between me and the last occupant; the hollow and lichen-covered apple trees, gnawed by rabbits, showing what kind of neighbors I should have; but above all, the recollection I had of it from my earliest voyages up the river, when the house was concealed behind a dense grove of red maples, through which I heard the house-dog bark. I was in haste to buy it, before the proprietor finished getting out some rocks, cutting down the hollow apple trees, and grubbing up some young birches which had sprung up in the pasture, or, in short, had made any more of his improvements. To enjoy these advantages I was ready to carry it on; like Atlas,[1] to take the world on my shoulders,—I never heard what compensation he received from that,—and do all those things which had no other motive or excuse but that I might pay for it and be unmolested in my possession of it; for I knew all the while that it would yield the most abundant crop of the kind I wanted if I could only afford to let it alone. But it turned out as I have said.

All that I could say, then, with respect to farming on a large scale, (I have always cultivated a garden), was, that I had had my seeds ready. Many think that seeds improve with age. I have no doubt that time discriminates between the good and the bad; and when at last I shall plant, I shall be less likely to be disappointed. But I would say to my fellows, once for all, As long as possible live free and uncommitted. It makes but little difference whether you are committed to a farm or the county jail.

Old Cato,[2] whose "De Re Rustica" is my "Cultivator," says,—and the only translation I have seen makes sheer nonsense of the passage,—"When you think of getting a farm, turn it thus in your mind, not to buy greedily; nor spare your pains to look at it, and do not think it enough to go round it once. The oftener you go the more it will please you, if it is good." I think I shall not buy greedily, but go round and round it as long as I live, and be buried in it first, that it may please me the more at last.

The present was my next experiment of this kind, which I propose to describe more at length; for convenience, putting the experience of two years into one. As I have said, I do not propose to write an ode to dejection,

---

1. A Greek god who carried the world and sky on his shoulders.
2. Marcus Porcius Cato, a Roman philosopher.

but to brag as lustily as chanticleer in the morning, standing on his roost, if only to wake my neighbors up.

When first I took up my abode in the woods, that is, began to spend my nights as well as days there, which, by accident, was on Independence Day, or the Fourth of July, 1845, my house was not finished for winter, but was merely a defence against the rain, without plastering or chimney, the walls being of rough, weather-stained boards, with wide chinks, which made it cool at night. The upright white hewn studs and freshly planed door and window casings gave it a clean and airy look, especially in the morning, when its timbers were saturated with dew, so that I fancied that by noon some sweet gum would exude from them. To my imagination it retained throughout the day more or less of this auroral character, reminding me of a certain house on a mountain which I had visited the year before. This was an airy and unplastered cabin, fit to entertain a travelling god, and where a goddess might trail her garments. The winds which passed over my dwelling were such as sweep over the ridges of mountains, bearing the broken strains, or celestial parts only, of terrestrial music. The morning wind forever blows, the poem of creation is uninterrupted; but few are the ears that hear it. Olympus[3] is but the outside of the earth everywhere.

The only house I had been the owner of before, if I except a boat, was a tent, which I used occasionally when making excursions in the summer, and this is still rolled up in my garret; but the boat, after passing from hand to hand, has gone down the stream of time. With this more substantial shelter about me, I had made some progress toward settling in the world. This frame, so slightly clad, was a sort of crystallization around me, and reacted on the builder. It was suggestive somewhat as a picture in outlines. I did not need to go outdoors to take the air, for the atmosphere within had lost none of its freshness. It was not so much within doors as behind a door where I sat, even in the rainiest weather. The Harivansa[4] says, "An abode without birds is like a meat without seasoning." Such was not my abode, for I found myself suddenly neighbor to the birds; not by having imprisoned one, but having caged myself near them. I was not only nearer to some of those which commonly frequent the garden and the orchard, but those wilder and more thrilling songsters of this forest which never, or rarely, serenade a villager,—the woodthrush, the veery, the scarlet tanager, the field-sparrow, the whippoorwill, and many others.

I was seated by the shore of a small pond, about a mile and a half south of the village of Concord and somewhat higher than it, in the midst of

---

3. The mythological home of the Greek gods.

4. A fifth-century Hindu religious epic.

an extensive wood between that town and Lincoln; and about two miles south of that our only field known to fame, Concord Battle Ground; but I was so low in the woods that the opposite shore, half a mile off, like the rest, covered with wood, was my most distant horizon. For the first week, whenever I looked out on the pond it impressed me like a tarn high up on the side of a mountain, its bottom far above the surface of other lakes, and, as the sun arose, I saw it throwing off its nightly clothing of mist, and here and there, by degrees, its soft ripples or its smooth reflecting surface was revealed, while the mists, like ghosts, were stealthily withdrawing in every direction into the woods, as at the breaking up of some nocturnal conventicle. The very dew seemed to hang upon the trees later into the day than usual, as on the sides of mountains.

This small lake was of most value as a neighbor in the intervals of a gentle rain-storm in August, when, both air and water being perfectly still, but the sky overcast, mid-afternoon had all the serenity of evening, and the wood-thrush sang around, and was heard from shore to shore. A lake like this is never smoother than at such a time; and the clear portion of the air above it being shallow and darkened by clouds, the water, full of light and reflections, becomes a lower heaven itself so much the more important. From a hill-top near by, where the wood had been recently cut off, there was a pleasing vista southward across the pond, through a wide indentation in the hills which form the shore there, where their opposite sides sloping toward each other suggested a stream flowing out in that direction through a wooded valley, but stream there was none. That way I looked between and over the near green hills to some distant and higher ones in the horizon, tinged with blue. Indeed, by standing on tiptoe I could catch a glimpse of some of the peaks of the still bluer and more distant mountain ranges in the northwest, those true-blue coins from heaven's own mint, and also of some portion of the village. But in other directions, even from this point, I could not see over or beyond the woods which surrounded me. It is well to have some water in your neighborhood, to give buoyancy to and float the earth. One value even of the smallest well is, that when you look into it you see that earth is not continent but insular. This is as important as that it keeps butter cool. When I looked across the pond from this peak toward the Sudbury meadows, which in time of flood I distinguished elevated perhaps by a mirage in their seething valley, like a coin in a basin, all the earth beyond the pond appeared like a thin crust insulated and floated even by this small sheet of intervening water, and I was reminded that this on which I dwelt was but *dry land*.

Though the view from my door was still more contracted, I did not feel crowded or confined in the least. There was pasture enough for my imagination. The low shrub-oak plateau to which the opposite shore arose stretched away toward the prairies of the West and the steppes of Tartary, affording ample room for all the roving families of men. "There are none happy in the world but beings who enjoy freely a vast horizon,"—said Damodara,[5] when his herds required new and larger pastures.

Both place and time were changed, and I dwelt nearer to those parts of the universe and to those eras in history which had most attracted me. Where I lived was as far off as many a region viewed nightly by astronomers. We are wont to imagine rare and delectable places in some remote and more celestial corner of the system, behind the constellation of Cassiopeia's Chair, far from noise and disturbance. I discovered that my house actually had its site in such a withdrawn, but forever new and unprofaned, part of the universe. If it were worth the while to settle in those parts near to the Pleiades or the Hyades, to Aldebaran or Altair,[6] then I was really there, or at an equal remoteness from the life which I had left behind, dwindled and twinkling with as fine a ray to my nearest neighbor, and to be seen only in moonless nights by him. Such was that part of creation where I had squatted:—

> There was a shepherd that did live,
> And held his thoughts as high
> As were the mounts whereon his flocks
> Did hourly feed him by.

What should we think of the shepherd's life if his flocks always wandered to higher pastures than his thoughts?

Every morning was a cheerful invitation to make my life of equal simplicity, and I may say innocence, with Nature herself. I have been as sincere a worshipper of Aurora[7] as the Greeks. I got up early and bathed in the pond; that was a religious exercise, and one of the best things which I did. They say that characters were engraven on the bathing tub of King Tching-thang[8] to this effect: "Renew thyself completely each day; do it again, and again, and forever again." I can understand that. Morning brings back the heroic ages. I was as much affected by the faint hum of a mosquito making its invisible and unimaginable tour through my apartment at earliest dawn, when I was sitting with door and windows open, as I could be by any trumpet that ever sang of fame. It was Homer's requiem; itself an Iliad and Odyssey in the air, singing its own wrath and wanderings. There was something cosmical about it; a standing adver-

5. A Hindu god.
6. Constellations and stars.
7. The goddess of the dawn.
8. Another name for Confucius.

tisement, till forbidden, of the everlasting vigor and fertility of the world. The morning, which is the most memorable season of the day, is the awakening hour. Then there is least somnolence in us; and for an hour, at least, some part of us awakes which slumbers all the rest of the day and night. Little is to be expected of that day, if it can be called a day, to which we are not awakened by our Genius, but by the mechanical nudgings of some servitor, are not awakened by our own newly acquired force and aspirations from within, accompanied by the undulations of celestial music, instead of factory bells, and a fragrance filling the air—to a higher life than we fell asleep from; and thus the darkness bear its fruit, and prove itself to be good, no less than the light. That man who does not believe that each day contains an earlier, more sacred, and auroral hour than he has yet profaned, has despaired of life, and is pursuing a descending and darkening way. After a partial cessation of his sensuous life, the soul of man, or its organs rather, are reinvigorated each day, and his Genius tries again what noble life it can make. All memorable events, I should say, transpire in morning time and in a morning atmosphere. The Vedas[9] say, "All intelligences awake with the morning." Poetry and art, and the fairest and most memorable of the actions of men, date from such an hour. All poets and heroes, like Memnon, are the children of Aurora, and emit their music at sunrise. To him whose elastic and vigorous thought keeps pace with the sun, the day is a perpetual morning. It matters not what the clocks say or the attitudes and labors of men. Morning is when I am awake and there is a dawn in me. Moral reform is the effort to throw off sleep. Why is it that men give so poor an account of their day if they have not been slumbering? They are not such poor calculators. If they had not been overcome with drowsiness, they would have performed something. The millions are awake enough for physical labor; but only one in a million is awake enough for effective intellectual exertion, only one in a hundred millions to a poetic or divine life. To be awake is to be alive. I have never yet met a man who was quite awake. How could I have looked him in the face?

We must learn to reawaken and keep ourselves awake, not by mechanical aids, but by an infinite expectation of the dawn, which does not forsake us in our soundest sleep. I know of no more encouraging fact than the unquestionable ability of man to elevate his life by a conscious endeavor. It is something to be able to paint a particular picture, or to carve a statue, and so to make a few objects beautiful; but it is far more glorious to carve and paint the very atmosphere and medium through which we look, which morally we can do. To affect the quality of the day, that is the highest of

---

9. Hindu religious scriptures.

the arts. Every man is tasked to make his life, even in its details, worthy of the contemplation of his most elevated and critical hour. If we refused, or rather used up, such paltry information as we get, the oracles would distinctly inform us how this might be done.

I went to the woods because I wished to live deliberately, to front only the essential facts of life, and see if I could not learn what it had to teach, and not, when I came to die, discover that I had not lived. I did not wish to live what was not life, living is so dear; nor did I wish to practise resignation, unless it was quite necessary. I wanted to live deep and suck out all the marrow of life, to live so sturdily and Spartan-like as to put to rout all that was not life, to cut a broad swath and shave close, to drive life into a corner, and reduce it to its lowest terms, and, if it proved to be mean, why then to get the whole and genuine meanness of it, and publish its meanness to the world; or if it were sublime, to know it by experience, and be able to give a true account of it in my next excursion. For most men, it appears to me, are in a strange uncertainty about it, whether it is of the devil or of God, and have *somewhat hastily* concluded that it is the chief end of man here to "glorify God and enjoy him forever."

Still we live meanly, like ants; though the fable tells us that we were long ago changed into men; like pygmies we fight with cranes; it is error upon error, and clout upon clout, and our best virtue has for its occasion a superfluous and evitable wretchedness. Our life is frittered away by detail. An honest man has hardly need to count more than his ten fingers, or in extreme cases he may add his ten toes, and lump the rest. Simplicity, simplicity, simplicity! I say, let your affairs be as two or three, and not a hundred or a thousand; instead of a million count half a dozen, and keep your accounts on your thumb nail. In the midst of this chopping sea of civilized life, such are the clouds and storms and quicksands and thousand-and-one items to be allowed for, that a man has to live, if he would not founder and go to the bottom and not make his port at all, by dead reckoning, and he must be a great calculator indeed who succeeds. Simplify, simplify. Instead of three meals a day, if it be necessary eat but one; instead of a hundred dishes, five; and reduce other things in proportion. Our life is like a German Confederacy, made up of petty states, with its boundary forever fluctuating, so that even a German cannot tell you how it is bounded at any moment. The nation itself, with all its so-called internal improvements, which, by the way, are all external and superficial, is just such an unwieldly and overgrown establishment, cluttered with furniture and tripped up by its own traps, ruined by luxury and heedless expense, by want of calculation and a worthy aim, as the million households in the land; and the only cure for it, as for them, is in a rigid economy, a stern and more than Spartan simplicity of life and elevation of purpose. It lives too fast. Men think that it is essential that the *Nation* have commerce, and export ice, and talk through a telegraph, and ride thirty miles an hour, without a doubt, whether *they* do or not; but whether we should live like baboons or like men, is a little uncertain. If we do not get out sleepers, and forge rails, and devote days and nights to the work, but go to tinkering upon our *lives* to improve *them,* who will build railroads? And if railroads are not built, how shall we get to heaven in season? But if we stay at home and mind our business, who will want railroads? We do not ride on the railroad; it rides upon us. Did you ever think what those sleepers are that underlie the railroad? Each one is a man, an Irishman, or Yankee man. The rails are laid on them, and they are covered with sand, and the cars run smoothly over them. They are sound sleepers, I assure you. And every few years a new lot is laid down and run over; so that, if some have the pleasure of riding on a rail, others have the misfortune to be ridden upon. And when they run over a man that is walking in his sleep, and supernumerary sleeper in the wrong position, and wake him up, they suddenly stop the cars, and make a hue and cry about it, as if this were an exception. I am glad to know that it takes a gang of men for every five miles to keep the sleepers down and level in their beds as it is, for this is a sign that they may sometime get up again.

Why should we live with such hurry and waste of life? We are determined to be starved before we are hungry. Men say that a stitch in time saves nine, and so they take a thousand stitches to-day to save nine to-morrow. As for *work*, we haven't any of any consequence. We have the Saint Vitus' dance, and cannot possibly keep our heads still. If I should only give a few pulls at the parish bell-rope, as for a fire, that is, without setting the bell, there is hardly a man on his farm in the outskirts of Concord, notwithstanding that press of engagements which was his excuse so many times that morning, nor a boy, nor a woman, I might almost say, but would forsake all and follow that sound, not mainly to save property from the flames, but, if we will confess the truth, much more to see it burn, since burn it must, and we, be it known, did not set it on fire,—or to see it put out, and have a hand in it, if that is done as handsomely; yes, even if it were the parish church itself. Hardly a man takes a half hour's nap after dinner, but when he wakes up he holds up his head and asks, "What's the news?" as if the rest of mankind had stood his sentinels. Some give directions to be waked every half hour, doubtless for no other purpose; and then, to pay for it, they tell what they have dreamed. After a night's sleep the news is as indispensable as the breakfast. "Pray tell me any thing new that has happened to a man anywhere on this globe,"—and he reads it over his coffee and rolls, that a man has had his eyes gouged out this morning on the Wachito River; never dreaming the while that he lives in the dark unfathomed mammoth cave of this world, and has but the rudiment of an eye himself.

For my part, I could easily do without the post-office. I think that there are very few important communications made through it. To speak critically, I never received more than one or two letters in my life—I wrote this some years ago—that were worth the postage. The penny-post is, commonly, an institution through which you seriously offer a man that penny for his thoughts which is so often safely offered in jest. And I am sure that I never read any memorable news in a newspaper. If we read of one man robbed, or murdered, or killed by accident, or one house burned, or one vessel wrecked, or one steamboat blown up, or one cow run over on the Western Railroad, or one mad dog killed, or one lot of grasshoppers in the winter—we never need read of another. One is enough. If you are acquainted with the principle, what do you care for a myriad instances and applications? To a philosopher all *news*, as it is called, is gossip, and they who edit and read it are old women over their tea. Yet not a few are greedy after this gossip. There was such a rush, as I hear, the other day at one of the offices to learn the foreign news by the last arrival, that several large squares of plate glass belonging to the establishment were broken by the pressure,—news which I seriously think a ready wit might write a twelvemonth, or twelve years, beforehand with sufficient accuracy. As for Spain, for instance, if you know how to throw in Don Carlos and the Infanta, and Don Pedro[10] and Seville and Granada, from time to time in the right proportions,—they may have changed the names a little since I saw the papers,—and serve up a bull-fight when other entertainments fail, it will be true to the letter, and give us as good an idea of the exact state or ruin of things in Spain as the most succinct and lucid reports under this head in the newspapers: and as for England, almost the last significant scrap of news from that quarter was the revolution of 1649; and if you have learned the history of her crops for an average year, you never need attend to that thing again, unless your speculations are of a merely pecuniary character. If one may judge who rarely looks into the newspapers, nothing new does ever happen in foreign parts, a French revolution not excepted.

What news! how much more important to know what that is which was never old! "Kieou-he-yu (great dignitary of the state of Wei) sent a man to Khoung-tseu to know his news. Khoung-tseu caused the messenger to be seated near him, and questioned him in these terms: What is your master doing? The messenger answered with respect: My master desires to diminish the number of his faults, but he cannot come to the end of them. The messenger being gone, the philosopher remarked: What a worthy messenger! What a worthy messenger!" The preacher, instead of

10. Nineteenth-century Spanish nobles.

vexing the ears of drowsy farmers on their day of rest at the end of the week,—for Sunday is the fit conclusion of an ill-spent week, and not the fresh and brave beginning of a new one,—with this one other draggle-tail of a sermon, should shout with thundering voice,—"Pause! Avast! Why so seeming fast, but deadly slow?"

Shams and delusions are esteemed for soundest truths, while reality is fabulous. If men would steadily observe realities only, and not allow themselves to be deluded, life, to compare it with such things as we know, would be like a fairy tale and the Arabian Nights' Entertainments. If we respected only what is inevitable and has a right to be, music and poetry would resound along the streets. When we are unhurried and wise, we perceive that only great and worthy things have any permanent and absolute existence,—that petty fears and petty pleasures are but the shadow of the reality. This is always exhilarating and sublime. By closing the eyes and slumbering, and consenting to be deceived by shows, men establish and confirm their daily life of routine and habit everywhere, which still is built on purely illusory foundations. Children, who play life, discern its true law and relations more clearly than men, who fail to live it worthily, but who think that they are wiser by experience, that is, by failure. I have read in a Hindoo book, that "there was a king's son, who, being expelled in infancy from his native city, was brought up by a forester, and, growing up to maturity in that state, imagined himself to belong to the barbarous race with which he lived. One of his father's ministers having discovered him, revealed to him what he was, and the misconception of his character was removed, and he knew himself to be a prince. So soul," continues the Hindoo philosopher, "from the circumstances in which it is placed, mistakes its own character, until the truth is revealed to it by some holy teacher, and then it knows itself to be *Brahme*."[11] I perceive that we inhabitants of New England live this mean life that we do because our vision does not penetrate the surface of things. We think that that *is* which *appears* to be. If a man should walk through this town and see only the reality, where, think you, would the "Mill-dam"[12] go to? If he should give us an account of the realities he beheld there, we should not recognize the place in his description. Look at a meeting-house, or a court-house, or a jail, or a shop, or a dwelling-house, and say what that thing really is before a true gaze, and they would all go to pieces in your account of them. Men esteem truth remote, in the outskirts of the system, behind the farthest star, before Adam and after the last man. In eternity there is indeed something true and sublime. But all these times and places and occasions are

---

11. Brahma, the Hindu creator.

12. Shopping area of Concord.

now and here. God himself culminates in the present moment, and will never be more divine in the lapse of all the ages. And we are enabled to apprehend at all what is sublime and noble only the perpetual instilling and drenching of the reality that surrounds us. The universe constantly and obediently answers to our conceptions; whether we travel fast or slow, the track is laid for us. Let us spend our lives in conceiving then. The poet or the artist never yet had so fair and noble a design but some of his posterity at least could accomplish it.

Let us spend one day as deliberately as Nature, and not be thrown off the track by every nutshell and mosquito's wing that falls on the rails. Let us rise early and fast, or break fast, gently and without perturbation; let company come and let company go, let the bells ring and the children cry—determined to make a day of it. Why should we knock under and go with the stream? Let us not be upset and overwhelmed in that terrible rapid and whirlpool called a dinner, situated in the meridian shallows. Weather this danger and you are safe, for the rest of the way is downhill. With unrelaxed nerves, with morning vigor, sail by it, looking another way, tied to the mast like Ulysses. If the engine whistles, let it whistle till it is hoarse for its pains. If the bell rings, why should we run? We will consider what kind of music they are like. Let us settle ourselves, and work and wedge our feet downward through the mud and slush of opinion, and prejudice, and tradition, and delusion, and appearance, that alluvion which covers the globe, through Paris and London, through New York and Boston and Concord, through Church and State, through poetry and philosophy and religion, till we come to a hard bottom and rocks in place, which we can call *reality*, and say, This is, and no mistake; and then begin again, having a *point d'appui*,[13] below freshet and frost and fire, a place where you might found a wall or a state, or set a lamp-post safely, or perhaps a gauge, not a Nilometer,[14] but a Realometer, that future ages might know how deep a freshet of shams and appearances had gathered from time to time. If you stand right fronting and face to face to a fact, you will see the sun glimmer on both its surfaces, as if it were a cimeter,[15] and feel its sweet edge dividing you through the heart and marrow, and so you will happily conclude your mortal career. Be it life or death, we crave only reality. If we are really dying, let us hear the rattle in our throats and feel cold in the extremities; if we are alive, let us go about our business.

Time is but the stream I go a-fishing in. I drink at it; but while I drink I see the sandy bottom and detect how shallow it is. Its thin current slides

---

13. Base.

14. A gauge used to measure the rise of the Nile River.

15. An outmoded spelling of *scimitar*, a sword with a curved blade.

away, but eternity remains. I would drink deeper; fish in the sky, whose bottom is pebbly with stars. I cannot count one. I know not the first letter of the alphabet. I have always been regretting that I was not as wise as the day I was born. The intellect is a cleaver; it discerns and rifts its way into the secret of things. I do not wish to be any more busy with my hands than is necessary. My head is hands and feet. I feel all my best faculties concentrated in it. My instinct tells me that my head is an organ for burrowing, as some creatures use their snout and fore-paws, and with it I would mine and burrow my way through these hills. I think that the richest vein is somewhere hereabouts; so by the divining-rod and thin rising vapors I judge; and here I will begin to mine.

GLOSSARY

Abstract Words/Concrete Words

An abstract word refers to something that cannot be seen, touched, or otherwise perceived by the senses (peace, freedom). A concrete word refers to something that can be seen, touched, or otherwise perceived by the senses (book, car).

Ad Hominem Attack

A method of avoiding the issue in argument by criticizing or attacking a person's character instead of dealing directly with the person's ideas.

Allegory

A type of narration in which characters and events symbolize abstract ideas. Often there is a moral aim.

Alliteration

The repetition of sounds, usually at the beginning of two or more words—for example, silent screen star, hale and hearty.

Analogy

A device to help one understand what is complex or unfamiliar by relating it to something simple or familiar. When used in argument, analogy is often questionable because even though two items may be alike in some ways, they are not necessarily alike in all ways.

Analysis

The process of breaking a whole into parts and showing their interrelationship in order to understand the nature of the whole.

Anecdote

A short narrative, usually humorous and of a real or imagined happening, used to illustrate a point.

Anthropomorphism

The attributing of human qualities to nonhuman things.

Antonyms

Words that have directly opposite meanings—for example, *love* and *hate*.

Appeals Based on Misleading Authority

Used in this sense, an authority can be someone who knows a great deal about a subject, or it can be a source of information, such as statistics, an encyclopedia, or the U.S. Constitution. Quoting an authority is common practice in legal and scholarly writings, but it can be misused in at least two ways: when the writer does not tell exactly who or what the authority is and how the evidence was obtained, and when the authority cited is not qualified to comment on the subject. The statement "Research reveals that children like baseball better than swimming," for example, invites the reader to ask what research is being alluded to and where it was obtained.

Argument

One of the four modes of discourse whose purpose is to persuade the reader to accept the writer's viewpoint on an issue.

Assumption of Proof by Failure to Find an Opposite Case

The assertion that something is true because there is no evidence that it is not true. Positive evidence is necessary to prove something; a mere demonstration that there is no evidence against a proposition does not prove that the proposition is true.

Avoiding the Question

Distracting the reader from the case in point by presenting material which is not relevant. Two devices commonly used in avoiding the question are the non sequitur and the ad hominem attack, each of which is defined in a separate entry in this glossary.

Argument

One of the four modes of discourse whose purpose is to persuade the reader to accept the writer's viewpoint on an issue.

Assumption of Proof by Failure to Find an Opposite Cause

The assertion that something is true because there is no evidence that it is not true. Positive evidence is necessary to prove something; a mere demonstration that there is no evidence against a proposition does not prove that the proposition is true.

Avoiding the Question

Distracting the reader from the case in point by presenting material which is not relevant. Two devices commonly used in avoiding the question are the non sequitur and the ad hominem attack, each of which is defined in a separate entry in this glossary.

Bandwagon Appeal

A method of encouraging a person to take a specific course of action on the grounds that everyone else is doing it.

Begging the Question

A logical fallacy in which part of what is to be proved (the conclusion) is already assumed to be true (the premise). The statement "Rembrandt was a greater artist than Eakins because people with good taste in art prefer Rembrandt" is an example of this fallacy, which often takes the form of circular argument.

Cause and Effect

A method of expository writing involving the examination of events that lead to a particular situation or the results that follow from a particular cause.

Chronological Order

A method of organization in which a narrative or the stages in a process are presented in the time order in which they occurred.

Circular Argument

A method of arguing the truth of a premise by restating the premise rather than giving evidence to show why it is true—for example, "You need a sense of humor to be happy because one's happiness depends on one's being able to see the funny side of things."

Classification

An expository method of development concerned with sorting members of a large group into categories on the basis of common or shared traits.

Cliché

An expression that has lost its impact and freshness because of overuse—for example, happy as a lark, dead as a doornail.

Closing

The conclusion of an essay. Some devices commonly used in closings are the reassertion of proof given in support of the thesis, a summary of the points made in the essay, a presentation of the implications or significance of the points made, and a statement of some deeper meaning hitherto undiscussed in the essay.

Coherence

The arrangement of ideas in such a way that they flow smoothly and logically. Some arrangements commonly used to achieve coherence are chronological order, spatial order, order of importance, order needed for comparison and contrast, induction, and deduction. Coherence may be increased through the use of transitional structures that help the reader follow the line of thought from one idea to the next.

Colloquial English or Colloquialism

Conversational or informal English as distinguished from formal language.

Comparison

A basic method of presenting ideas that identifies and emphasizes the similarities between things.

Concrete Words

See Abstract Words/Concrete Words.

Connotation

The meanings associated with a word apart from its explicit meaning, or denotation. For example, the word "yellow" *denotes* a color, but it also *connotes* cowardice.

Context

The setting in which an idea develops or an event occurs.

Contrast

A basic method of presenting ideas that identifies and emphasizes the differences between things.

Deadwood

Words that do not contribute to meaning or clarity. For example, "He teaches in the area of English" has no clearer meaning than "He teaches English."

Deduction

A form of argument in which a generalization is applied to a series of specific facts in order to prove the generalization; reasoning from the general to the particular.

Definition

The act of pinpointing the exact meaning of a term.

Denotation

The exact, literal meaning of a word.

Description

A mode of discourse whose function is to depict an object, place, person, or event as it is perceived through the five senses.

Dialogue

Passages in written material representing conversation between two or more people.

Diction

The choice of words used in talking or writing.

Dominant Mood

A technique used in descriptive writing to indicate the vantage point, angle, or set of attitudes from which the writer presents the material.

Dramatized Narration

A form of narration which shows characters in action.

Emphasis

The amount of stress given to specific areas. There are six main ways to give an idea emphasis:

—Position: In most essays, the ending is the most emphatic position, the beginning is the second most emphatic position, and the middle is the least emphatic position.

—Proportion: The greatest amount of space is generally given to the most important ideas.

—Repetition: Ideas to be emphasized are often repeated in order to establish their importance in the reader's mind.

—Typography: Italics, capital letters, and exclamation points may be used to show emphasis.

—Headnotes and titles: Headnotes and titles are often used to highlight ideas.

—Tagging: Phrases like "the most important" and "the crux of the matter" signal emphasis.

Euphemisms

Less direct or milder words substituted for words considered distasteful or offensive. For example, "sanitary landfill" is a euphemism for "garbage dump."

Example

An expository method of development in which the writer makes an abstraction meaningful by using an illustration.

Exclusion

The process of defining an entity by discussing characteristics it does not have; a synonym for *negation*.

Exposition

One of the four modes of discourse that employs a clear, straightforward presentation of ideas, usually to inform or explain.

Fable

A narrative in which animals speak and act like humans in order to illustrate a useful truth.

False Dilemma

A logical fallacy that involves two elements: the dilemma—equally unwanted choices—and falseness—choices that are not the only ones possible. An example of false dilemma is the question, "Does my suit look better than you expected it to look or does it look worse?"

False Sequence

Sometimes called *post hoc, ergo proper hoc reasoning,* this fallacy suggests that if one event follows another, the second event necessarily must be caused by the first event. An example of this type of reasoning is: "Most accidents happen within fifty miles of people's homes. Therefore, it is safer to drive on long trips than it is to drive around town." Logically, of course, most accidents happen near people's homes because people spend more time driving near home; there is no basis for the belief that it is safer to drive far from home.

Figurative Language

Language that carries a meaning different from the denotative meaning of the words. Figurative language is used to convey the sense or feeling of a situation rather than the objective facts. Some of the more commonly used kinds of figurative language are metaphors, similes, idioms, and personification. (Each type of figurative language is defined in a separate entry.)

Figures of Speech

See Figurative Language.

Flashback

The interruption of the chronological sequence of a narrative in order to portray an event which occured at an earlier time.

Foreshadowing

Giving a clue to an event that will occur later in a narrative.

General Language/Specific Language

General language is loose and imprecise, whereas specific language pinpoints meaning more exactly. For example, "The quarterback broke his ankle" is more specific than "The football player suffered an injury."

Generalized Narration

A type of narration in which the writer maintains a distance from the subject.

Hyperbole

Deliberate overstatement or exaggeration that is used to heighten the effect of a statement.

Idiom

An expression that has come to have a specific meaning through long usage. An idiom's meaning is not readily understandable from its grammatical structure or from the meanings of its parts. To "give in" to someone, for example, is an idiom.

Impressionistic Description

A type of descriptive writing that interprets and responds to what is being portrayed.

Induction

A form of argument in which specific facts lead to a larger general truth; reasoning from the particular to the general.

Informal English

The level of language that is used in ordinary conversation and in most books, articles, and newspapers.

Introduction

The beginning of an essay, often used to establish common ground with the readers, to attract their interest, or to serve as a keynote or setting for an essay. The introduction should relate directly to the thesis. Some devices commonly used in introductions are headnotes, anecdotes, straw men, statistics, allusions, rhetorical questions, and quotations.

Irony

The use of an expression in a humorous or sarcastic way that implies the exact opposite of the expression's literal meaning.

Jargon

Technical language used by specialists.

Levels of Meaning

The various levels at which the sense and implications of a literary work may be read. All works have a literal meaning—the actual sense of the words on the page—but beyond this, the characters, objects, and actions in a work often reflect a more general meaning—political, moral, spiritual, etc.—which applies beyond the specific case described in the work.

Loaded Words

Words associated with strong feelings that are used to appeal to readers' emotions.

Logic

The science of correct thinking based on established criteria and methods of reasoning.

Logical Argument

Argument that appeals to the reason or intellect of the reader.

Logical Fallacy

An error in reasoning. Some common fallacies are overgeneralization, assumption of proof by failure to find an opposite case, special pleading, avoiding the question, circular argument, the false dilemma, the false sequence, and the false analogy. (Each type of fallacy is defined in a separate entry.)

Major Proposition

See Proposition.

Maxim

A general truth or rule of conduct expressed in a concise manner.

Metaphor

A comparison between things that are essentially unrelated. The comparison is implied rather than directly stated, and, unlike simile, it is not introduced by "like" or "as." (See the introduction to Part II, Description.)

Methods of Reasoning

Procedures that are used in argument for organizing and weighing information. Three major methods of reasoning are induction, deduction, and analogy. (Each method is defined in a separate entry. See also the introduction to Part III, Argument.)

Metonymy

The naming of one thing for another because of their association through experience. For example, we call journalists the press and money bread.

Minor Proposition

See Proposition.

Misleading Statements

Statements that seem to say one thing when they really say a less desirable thing. For example, the statement "These fine limited editions have been presented to the Duke of Edinburgh" suggests that the Duke appreciates these items, and, therefore, that we should do so as well. However, the sentence only states that the editions were given to the Duke; it does not actually comment on his opinion of them.

Misleading Writing Style

A style deliberately used by an author to confuse readers or to divert their attention from a deficiency in the author's argument. Some devices commonly used to mislead readers are double negatives, irrelevant material, highly complex sentences and paragraphs, and difficult or extremely technical vocabulary.

Mixed Metaphor

A metaphor in which one figure of speech is combined incongruously with another—for example, "The *ship of state* is traveling a *rocky road*."

Mode of Discourse

A category of writing; traditionally, exposition, description, argumentation, and narration.

Monologue

A written passage representing the speech of a single person.

Narration

A mode of discourse that tells a story or presents a sequence of events over a period of time.

Negation

The process of defining an entity by discussing characteristics it does not have; known also as *exclusion*.

Non Sequitur

A statement that does not follow from the evidence given or does not relate to the question asked.

Objective Description

A style of descriptive writing that depicts a subject as a camera would—impartially and concretely.

Onomatopoeia

The formation of a word that imitates the sound associated with the action the word denotes—for example, the fire *sizzled*.

Overgeneralization

A generalization is a statement that applies to all cases in a specific class. An overgeneralization is a generalization which is not true for all cases, even though it may sound true. "All men were once boys" is a generalization because it applies to all cases in the class "men." "All men like to eat" is an overgeneralization because some men do not enjoy eating, even though they must eat in order to survive.

Parable

A short narrative, usually imagined, intended to convey a moral lesson.

Paradox

A statement that is true even though at first glance it seems contradictory, unbelievable, or absurd.

Parallelism

The expression of ideas that are equally important in the same grammatical form. For example, in the sentence "He enjoyed only two things: food and sleep," the words "food" and "sleep" are both nouns and, therefore, parallel in structure. In the sentence "He enjoyed only two things: eating and sleep," however, the parallelism is destroyed.

Patterns of Development

Organizational methods of expository writing. The most common are definition, classification, example, analysis, cause and effect, and comparison and contrast. (Each of these is defined in a separate entry.)

Personification

The attribution of human qualities to animals or inanimate objects—for example, "She's a great ship."

Persuasive Argument

A form of writing that appeals to the emotions of the reader.

Point of View

The position from which an author perceives and discusses a topic or relates a narrative.

Polysyndeton

Repetition of conjunctions such as *and, but, for*. For example, "They won fame and fortune and much goodwill." Because the King James version of the Bible uses much polysyndeton, the device often creates biblical overtones.

Post Hoc Ergo Propter Hoc Reasoning

In argument, the fallacy that one event necessarily causes another. Consider: "After Tim left the game, the team lost. I knew they couldn't win without him." Any number of other causes could have been responsible for the team's losing.

Pretentious Writing

Writing which is more expressive or learned than the situation demands. For example, "Prolixity simulates erudition" is a pretentious way of saying "Wordiness gives the appearance of high education."

Process Analysis

A special form of analysis that presents a process in a series of sequential steps.

Proposition

The point to be argued. A proposition may be an idea or a suggested course of action. The major proposition is the thesis—the main point to be considered—and the minor propositions are the points used to support the major proposition.

Rhetorical Question

A question to which no answer is expected—for example, "Who would not prefer freedom to slavery?"

Satire

A literary method that uses wit, irony, or sarcasm to ridicule human failings.

Sentimental Appeal

A method of argument in which the author attempts to convince readers of the truth of a proposition by appealing strictly to their emotions.

Simile

A figure of speech in which the words *like* or *as* are used to make direct comparisons between things that are essentially dissimilar.

Slang

Informal colloquial language—for example, the words *guy* and *cop*.

Slanted words

Words intentionally used to arouse the reader's emotions.

Slogans

Brief, striking phrases that are sometimes used in argument to arouse the reader's enthusiasm. They are often used to camouflage a lack of logical reasoning.

Special Pleading

The use of one set of standards to judge the author's side of the argument and another, often more exacting, set to judge the opposing point of view.

Specific Language

See General Language/Specific Language.

Straw Man

A logical fallacy in which the author introduces an easily demolished argument opposing his or her own point of view and then points out the errors in that argument.

Style

An author's individual way of writing—of using words, constructing sentences, and organizing ideas.

Subjective Description

A style of descriptive writing in which writers express their own impressions, interpretations, and responses.

Summarized Narration

A type of narrative writing that presents a sequence of events briefly and concisely.

Synonyms

Words that have the same or similar meanings.

Theme

See Thesis.

Thesis

The main idea or central point of the essay. It may be stated directly or implied. In nonfiction prose, the thesis may also be called the theme.

Title

A word, phrase, or sentence set off at the beginning of a literary work and often used to convey its main idea. A title may be explicit or general, and it may be accompanied by a subtitle which either extends or restricts its meaning.

Tone

The feeling or attitude an author conveys in a work. The tone of an essay may be humorous, angry, informal, scholarly, sarcastic, or matter of fact, among others, depending on how the author uses words and sentence patterns.

Transitional Structures

Devices that are used to give coherence and to show relationships among ideas in literary works. Five frequently used types of transitional structures are conjunctions, parallel structure, enumeration, ordered headings, and repetition of content.

Trite Expressions

Sometimes called clichés, trite expressions are those that have grown stale through frequent use.

Understatement

Use of language that is deliberately gentler, milder, weaker, or less sensational than the situation merits. For example, it is an understatement to call a civil war an "unpleasant situation."

Unity

The achievement of wholeness in an essay by using supporting ideas directly related to the thesis and by eliminating all irrelevant ideas.

Unsupported Inferences

Inferences are conclusions derived logically from specific given information. Authors make *unsupported* inferences when they draw conclusions from insufficient evidence.

Weak Analogy

An analogy in which the similarities between two things do not fully justify the comparison being drawn. See the introduction to Comparison and Contrast in Part I, Exposition.

Wordiness

The use of excess words, sometimes referred to as deadwood or talking around the point, that can be cut without affecting meaning.

BIBLIOGRAPHY

Angelou, Maya. *Gather Together in My Name*. New York: Random House, 1974.

———. *I Know Why the Caged Bird Sings*. New York: Random House, 1970.

———. *Singin' and Swingin' and Gettin' Merry Like Christmas*. New York: Random House, 1976.

Asimov, Isaac. *Fact and Fancy*. New York: Doubleday, 1962.

———. *In Memory Yet Green: The Autobiography of Isaac Asimov*. New York: Doubleday, 1979.

———. *Pebble in the Sky*. New York: Doubleday, 1950.

Baker, Russell. *All Things Considered*. Philadelphia: Lippincott, 1965.

———. *An American in Washington*. New York: Knopf, 1961.

———. *Poor Russell's Almanac*. New York: Doubleday, 1972.

Barber, James D. *Presidential Character: Predicting Performance in the White House*. Englewood Cliffs, N.J.: Prentice-Hall, 1977.

Bartlett, John. *Familiar Quotations*. Boston: Little, Brown, 1968.

Bombeck, Erma. *The Grass Is Always Greener over the Septic Tank*. New York: McGraw-Hill, 1976.

Buck, Pearl S. *The Exile*. New York: Reynal & Hitchcock, 1936.

———. *The Good Earth*. New York: Grosset & Dunlap, 1944.

———. *A House Divided*. New York: Pocket Books, 1935.

Burnford, Sheila. *The Incredible Journey*. Boston: Little, Brown, 1961.

Catton, Bruce. *Stillness at Appomattox*. New York: Doubleday, 1953.

Chisholm, Shirley. *Unbought and Unbossed*. Boston: Houghton Mifflin, 1970.

Cleaver, Eldridge. *Soul on Ice*. New York: Dell, 1970.

Coffin, William Sloane, Jr. *Once to Every Man, A Memoir*. New York: Atheneum, 1977.

Corman, Avery. *Kramer vs. Kramer.* New York: Random House, 1977.

Cousins, Norman. *Anatomy of an Illness as Perceived by the Patient.* New York: Norton, 1979.

Cozzens, James Gould. *By Love Possessed.* New York: Harcourt Brace Jovanovich, 1957.

Darwin, Charles. *The Origin of Species.* New York: Dutton, 1928.

Dickens, Charles. *A Christmas Carol.* New York: Dutton, 1972.

———. *David Copperfield.* New York: Macmillan, 1917.

———. *Great Expectations.* New York: Dutton, 1971.

———. *Oliver Twist.* New York: New American Library, 1966.

———. *A Tale of Two Cities.* New York: Macmillan, 1962.

Dickinson, Emily. "A Light Exists in Spring" in *The Pocket Book of Modern Verse,* 3rd ed., edited by Oscar Williams. New York: Pocket Books, 1973.

Didion, Joan. *A Book of Common Prayer.* New York: Simon & Schuster, 1977.

———. *Play It as It Lays.* New York: Farrar, Straus & Giroux, 1970.

———. *Slouching Towards Bethlehem.* New York: Farrar, Straus & Giroux, 1968.

Dillard, Annie. *Pilgrim at Tinker Creek.* New York: Harper's Magazine Press, 1974.

Eastland, Terry, and Bennett, William J. *Counting by Race: Equality from the Founding Fathers to Baake.* New York: Basic Books, 1979.

Evans, Bergen. *Dictionary of Quotations.* New York: Delacorte, 1968.

Eliot, T. S. *The Cocktail Party.* London: Faber & Faber, 1950.

———. *Four Quartets.* New York: Harcourt Brace Jovanovich, 1968.

Faulkner, William. *As I Lay Dying.* New York: Random House, 1964.

———. *Light in August.* New York: Random House, 1967.

———. *The Sound and the Fury.* New York: Random House, 1966.

Frank, Anne. *Anne Frank: The Diary of a Young Girl.* New York: Random House, 1952.

Franklin, Benjamin. *Poor Richard's Almanack*. New York: Grosset & Dunlap, 1964.

Freeman, William Southall. *Robert E. Lee: A Biography*. New York: Charles Scribner's Sons, 1936.

Fromm, Erich. *The Art of Loving*. New York: Bantam, 1963.

Gaines, Ernest J. *The Autobiography of Miss Jane Pittman*. New York: Dial, 1971.

Galsworthy, John. *The Forsyte Saga*. New York: Charles Scribner's Sons, 1933.

Gardner, John W. *Excellence: Can We Be Equal and Excellent Too?* New York: Harper & Row, 1961.

———. *In Common Cause*. New York: Norton, 1974.

———. *Morale*. New York: Norton, 1978.

———. *Self-Renewal: The Individual and the Innovative Society*. New York: Harper & Row, 1964.

Gibson, William. *The Miracle Worker*. New York: Knopf, 1957.

Gittleson, Natalie. *Dominus: A Woman Looks at Men's Lives*. New York: Farrar, Straus & Giroux, 1978.

Godwin, Gail. *Dream Children*. New York: Knopf, 1976.

———. *Glass People*. New York: Dell, 1975.

Greeley, Andrew M. *And Young Men Shall See Visions*. New York: Sheed & Ward, 1964.

———. *Strangers in the House: Catholic Youth in America*. New York: Sheed & Ward, 1961.

Gregory, Dick. *Dick Gregory's Political Primer*. New York: Harper & Row, 1972.

———. *From the Back of the Bus*. New York: Avon, 1962.

———. *Nigger: An Autobiography*. New York: Dutton, 1964.

Gunther, John. *Death Be Not Proud*. New York: Harper & Row, 1949.

Haley, Alex. *Roots*. New York: Doubleday, 1976.

Hemingway, Ernest. *For Whom the Bell Tolls*. New York: Charles Scribner's Sons, 1940.

———. *A Moveable Feast*. New York: Charles Scribner's Sons, 1964.

———. *The Old Man and the Sea*. New York: Charles Scribner's Sons, 1952.

———. *The Sun Also Rises*. New York: Charles Scribner's Sons, 1970.

Hobson, Laura Z. *Gentlemen's Agreement*. New York: Simon & Schuster, 1947.

Hughes, Richard. *A High Wind in Jamaica*. New York: Harper & Row, 1957.

Jenkins, Dan. *Semi-Tough*. New York: Atheneum, 1972.

Keller, Helen. *The Story of My Life*. New York: Doubleday, Page, 1903.

———. *The World I Live In*. New York: Appleton-Century-Crofts, 1938.

Kennedy, John F. *Profiles in Courage*. New York: Harper & Row, 1961.

———. *A Nation of Immigrants*. New York: Anti-Defamation League of B'nai B'rith, 1959.

Kissinger, Henry. *The White House Years*. New York: Little, Brown, 1979.

Klobuchar, Jim, and Tarkenton, Fran. *Tarkenton*. New York: Harper & Row, 1976.

Komarovsky, Mirra. *Dilemmas of Masculinity: A Study of College Youth*. New York: Norton, 1976.

Kozol, Jonathan. *Death at an Early Age*. Boston: Houghton Mifflin, 1967.

Kübler-Ross, Elisabeth. *Questions and Answers on Death and Dying*. New York: Macmillan, 1974.

Lamb, Charles, and Lamb, Mary. *Poetry for Children*. Freeport, N.Y.: Books for Libraries Press, 1970.

———. *Tales from Shakespeare*. New York: Macmillan, 1958.

Langer, Lawrence. *The Holocaust and the Literary Imagination*. New Haven: Yale University Press, 1975.

Lerner, Max. *Actions and Passions: Notes on the Multiple Revolution of Our Time*. New York: Simon & Schuster, 1964.

———. *America and Its Discontents*. New York: Simon & Schuster, n.d.

Lewis, C. S. *The Case for Christianity*. New York: Macmillan, 1950.

Lindbergh, Anne Morrow. *Gift from the Sea*. New York: Pantheon, 1955.

———. *Listen! The Wind.* New York: Harcourt Brace Jovanovich, 1940.

———. *North to the Orient.* New York: Harcourt Brace Jovanovich, 1935.

McGlashan, Charles F. *History of the Donner Party.* San Francisco: T. C. Wohlbruck, 1931.

Mailer, Norman. *The Executioner's Song.* Boston: Little, Brown, 1979.

Manchester, William. *American Caesar: Douglas MacArthur (1880–1964).* Boston: Little, Brown, 1978.

Mead, Margaret. *Coming of Age in Samoa.* New York: Blue Ribbon Books, 1932.

Melville, Herman. *Billy Budd.* Cambridge, Ma.: Harvard University Press, 1948.

Mill, John Stuart. *Essays on Poetry.* Columbia, S.C.: University of South Carolina Press, 1976.

Mitford, Jessica. *The American Way of Death.* New York: Simon & Schuster, 1963.

Morris, Edmund. *The Rise of Theodore Roosevelt.* New York: Coward, McCann, & Geoghegan, 1979.

Newman, Edwin. *Strictly Speaking: Will America Be the Death of English?* Indianapolis: Bobbs-Merrill, 1974.

O'Connor, Flannery. *A Good Man Is Hard to Find.* New York: Harcourt Brace Jovanovich, 1955.

———. *Everything That Rises Must Converge.* New York: Farrar, Straus & Giroux, 1965.

———. *The Habit of Being.* New York: Farrar, Straus & Giroux, 1979.

Orwell, George. *Animal Farm.* New York: Harcourt Brace Jovanovich, 1946.

———. *1984.* New York: Harcourt Brace Jovanovich, 1949.

———. *Shooting an Elephant and Other Essays.* New York: Harcourt Brace Jovanovich, 1950.

Packard, Vance. *The Status Seekers.* New York: David McKay, 1959.

Perelman, S. J. *Acres and Pains.* New York: Simon & Schuster, 1972.

———. *The Most of S. J. Perelman.* New York: Simon & Schuster, 1958.

———. *The Swiss Family Perelman.* New York: Simon & Schuster, 1950.

Plimpton, George. *One for the Record: The Inside Story of Hank Aaron's Chase for the Home-Run Record.* New York: Harper & Row, 1974.

———. *Out of My League.* New York: Harper & Row, 1961.

———. *Paper Lion.* New York: Harper & Row, 1966.

Porter, Eleanor. *Pollyanna.* Boston: Page, 1919.

Porter, Katherine Anne. *Flowering Judas.* New York: Harcourt Brace Jovanovich, 1930.

———. *Ship of Fools.* New York: Harcourt Brace Jovanovich, 1954.

———. *The Collected Works of Katherine Anne Porter.* New York: Harcourt Brace Jovanovich, 1965.

Read, Piers Paul. *Alive: The Story of the Andes Survivors.* Philadelphia: Lippincott, 1974.

Roethke, Theodore. "Elegy for Jane" in *The Pocket Book of Modern Verse,* 3rd ed., edited by Oscar Williams. New York: Pocket Books, 1973.

Rosenberg, Harold. *Discovering the Present: Three Decades in Art, Culture, and Politics.* Chicago: University of Chicago Press, 1973.

Russell, Bertrand. *A History of Western Philosophy.* New York: Simon & Schuster, 1945.

———. *Education and the Social Order.* Winchester, Ma.: Allen & Unwin, 1932.

———. *My Philosophical Development.* New York: Simon & Schuster, 1959.

———. *The Autobiography of Bertrand Russell, Volume I: 1872–1914.* Winchester, Ma.: Allen & Unwin, 1967.

———. *The Autobiography of Bertrand Russell, Volume II: 1914–1944.* Winchester, Ma.: Allen & Unwin, 1968.

———. *The Autobiography of Bertrand Russell, Volume III: 1944—1969.* New York: Simon & Schuster, 1969.

Sanders, Thomas E., and Peek, Walter. *Literature of the American Indian.* Encino, Ca.: Glencoe, 1973.

Schoor, Gene. *The Jim Thorpe Story: America's Greatest Athlete.* New York: Simon & Schuster, 1951.

Shaw, George Bernard. *Androcles and The Lion, Overruled, Pygmalion.* New York: Brentano's, 1916.

Sheehan, George. *Running and Being*. New York: Simon & Schuster, 1978.

Shulman, Max. *Barefoot Boy with Cheek*. New York: Doubleday, 1943.

———. *Rally Round the Flag, Boys*. New York: Doubleday, 1957.

Smythe, Daniel. *Robert Frost Speaks*. New York: Twayne Publishers, 1964.

Sontag, Susan. *Against Interpretation and Other Essays*. New York: Farrar, Straus & Giroux, 1966.

———. *On Photography*. New York: Farrar, Straus & Giroux, 1976.

Steinberg, Milton. *Basic Judaism*. New York: Harcourt Brace Jovanovich, 1947.

Strunk, William, and White, E. B. *The Elements of Style,* 2nd Ed. New York: Macmillan, 1979.

Sutton, Horace A. *Confessions of a Grand Hotel*. New York: Holt, Rinehart & Winston, 1951.

———. *Sutton's Places*. New York: Holt, Rinehart & Winston, 1954.

Swift, Jonathan. *Gulliver's Travels*. New York: St. Martin's, 1977.

Thomas, Dylan. *Collected Poems, 1934–1952*. New York: Dutton, 1966.

Thomas, Lewis. *The Lives of a Cell*. New York: Viking, 1974.

———. *The Medusa and the Snail*. New York: Viking, 1979.

Thompson, Lawrence, and Winnick, R. H. *Robert Frost: The Later Years, 1938–1963*. New York: Holt, Rinehart & Winston, 1976.

Thoreau, Henry. *The Variorum Walden*. New York: Twayne Publishers, 1962.

Thurber, James. *Fables for Our Time*. New York: Harper & Row, 1940.

———. *A Thurber Carnival*. New York: Harper & Row, 1945.

Thurber, James, and White, E. B. *Is Sex Necessary?* New York: Dell, 1963.

Toffler, Alvin. *Future Shock*. New York: Random House, 1970.

Toqueville, Alexis de. *Democracy in America*. New York: Doubleday, 1969.

Turgenev, Ivan. *A Sportsman's Notebook*. London: Cresset Press, 1950.

Updike, John. *The Coup*. New York: Knopf, 1979.

———. *Couples*. New York: Knopf, 1968.

———. *Rabbit Redux*. New York: Knopf, 1971.

Whitman, Walt. *Leaves of Grass*. New York: New American Library, 1971.

Will, George F. *The Pursuit of Happiness and Other Sobering Thoughts*. New York: Harper/Colophon, 1979.

Woolf, Virginia. *The Death of the Moth and Other Essays*. New York: Harcourt Brace Jovanovich, 1974.

———. *Mrs. Dalloway*. New York: Harcourt Brace Jovanovich, 1949.

———. *To the Lighthouse*. New York: Harcourt Brace Jovanovich, 1949.